BELIEVING IS SEEING

Joanna Michal Hoyt

WolfSinger Publications ♪ Security, Colorado

To Zachary,

who helped me to delight in mysteries
and to see the world from different angles

For we walk by faith, not by sight.

2 Corinthians 5:7

There are none so blind as those who will not see.

John Heywood

A time is coming when men will go mad, and when they see someone who is not mad, they will attack him, saying, "You are mad; you are not like us."

St. Antony the Great

Just because you're paranoid doesn't mean they're not after you.

Joseph Heller

Earth's crammed with heaven,
And every common bush afire with God,
But only he who sees takes off his shoes…

Elizabeth Barrett Browning

If therefore the light that is within thee is darkness, how great is that darkness!

Matthew 6:23

But at the last, what do we know?

Arthur Machen

TABLE OF CONTENTS

STAIRS TO THE SKY

A Fragmentary Retrospective
with a few personal notes

This story was originally published in Holdfast Magazine's summer 2017 anthology.

A.

This is the first sequence from the stairway's history that we've been able to retrieve. The people surrounding the structure stare at it with evident bewilderment, suggesting this may be their first glimpse of it. The place from which the stairway rises is probably not unfamiliar to the onlookers; the market stalls scattered across the field appear weathered. Most of the stalls are unattended. Those few proprietors who have stayed lean across their counters, staring at the stone steps that spiral upward, turning clockwise almost as far as the eye can see, ending at a dizzy height.

How high is it? Someone is pacing out the length of the shadow that extends westward from the market across the plain. The sun is low. The measurer's shadow is at least twice as long as he is tall. Will he calculate the ratio of his shadow to his own height and reduce his tower-height estimate accordingly? Impossible to tell, since this first sequence is without sound.

Most people are looking at the tower itself. Wondering, perhaps, not *How many feet high is it?* but, *How many steps would I have to climb to reach the top?* or, *Where did it come from?* or, *Is there anything on top?*

An old woman begins to climb, followed by a young man. They ascend slowly, right hands against the central stone column into which the narrow end of each wedged step melts with no visible joint. It must have occurred to them that there is no wall or railing on the outside and the fall would be very long.

The old woman reaches the top, where the stair ends in a semicircle of smooth stone. She turns, gazing southward over the wind-tossed grass and the scattered houses, northward to the hills, westward to the dimly glimpsed mountains, eastward across the flatland toward the far gleam of sea. Then she looks into what appears to be empty sky. Her eyes focus on something close by, something we can't see. She takes one more step upward and ahead, over the edge, setting her foot down firmly on thin air, and then she is gone.

She is gone. Not fallen—at least, we do not see her falling, and afterward there is no bone-crazed huddle at the tower's foot. The young man, who had reached out to steady her, lets his arm fall. Looks where she looked. Begins the long climb down.

1.

The docent couldn't or wouldn't explain how these "sequences" were obtained. I've read about Dr Weltanschauung's "psychorefractive image/sound recovery," about the "sequences" she takes at historic or symbolic sites where she believes some kind of localized retrievable memory-record of events exists, but they don't explain how it works. The docent said this exhibit was designed to display records of historical or anthropological interest, and technical methodology was in the domain of another department. I suppose that means she doesn't know.

Monica insisted on replaying the last minute of the first sequence three times, checking whether there was anything under the old woman's feet as she vanished, or any sign the sequence had been tampered with. I suppose now they could engineer it to look perfectly natural. Some people say this entire exhibit is a fake—or, more charitably, a work of art inspired by the strangeness of that stairway.

B.

The market stalls are gone. The stairs rise solitary from the grassland, casting a shortened shadow eastward. One figure stands atop the high platform, huddled under a thick hooded cloak. The watcher's face swings from the broad expanse of wind-bent grass to the sky with its hurrying clouds, then downward and eastward, seaward...

The far line of sea bunches, swells. A small patch of silver lifts like a banner, flaps against the dark clouds on the horizon. Then the whole line of water rises smoothly, surges closer. The watcher clasps hands to mouth, scrambles down with desperate caution, runs southward toward the houses, falls, rises, runs again.

For a while the grassland round the tower is empty. Then people begin to pass. First a few riders, then many runners and walkers, carrying bundles or children toward the northern hills. As the sun sinks to the western horizon a smaller company comes on foot, stumbling, limping. They must have decided—wisely—that they can't make it to the hills. They drag themselves up the stairs. They have almost reached the top when the gold-gleaming water glides over the grass, smooth except where its surface is disturbed by planks, branches, bodies of sheep and men. It rises past the eighteenth stair, and there it remains, churning and sucking, through the evening and the slow hours of the night, while the refugees shiver on the stairs. In the first grey light of morning the water begins to recede.

C.

Later again. There is a small open area around the tower's foot; beyond that is a sprawl of stone buildings with arched doorways. The people gathered in the open space wear bright-hued fringed clothing. There's sound now, excited murmurs, solemn tones of people holding forth, and, away eastward, a sound of singing. As the singing grows louder the crowd-noises fade and the song, modulating steadily higher and higher, would be intelligible to anyone who knew the language.

The singing comes from a small group walking in single file, dressed in plain white clothing, fringeless. They have little in common besides their attire: there are youths, elders, women, men. Some stride confidently; some shuffle; one limps. The leader, the limping man, stands still in front of the first stair. The singing stops. The crowd falls silent. Then, as he begins to climb, as the other white-robed ones follow him, saving their breath for the ascent, the crowd takes up their song, starting at a low pitch, rising.

The short file winds upward. The watchers raise their arms toward them, lift the song higher. Their faces are intent. One or two tip their heads from side to side and bite their lips as though struggling toward a decision.

In the back of the crowd an expressionless woman stands watching the leader, not singing. The boy on her shoulders weeps.

The leader reaches the high platform and, like the woman in our first glimpse, looks around. He raises a hand, perhaps to the weeping boy, who waves frantically. Then he steps up into the air and is gone. One after another they follow him.

The next to last turns and steps up like all the rest, strides into empty space, and falls like a stone. Someone tries to run to her. Others grasp the runner's arms.

She lands head-foremost, is dead at once. The crowd still sings. Some keep their eyes on her while others watch the last climber vanish into the sky. Then they all gather round her. Someone has a stretcher; such things must have happened before. They sing as they bear her away.

2.

After the woman landed, when we saw her close up again, her head was so badly damaged she had no expression. But Monica made the docent show her fall again. For a second while the woman fell her face was turned toward us, and she was smiling.

Peter said that proves she was an actor, the whole thing never happened. But what if it's real? What if she did fall, and did smile?

D.

Later again. The stone buildings near the stairway look old and neglected. Away eastward higher buildings rise. The crowd at the base of the stairs is silent. All the people are dressed darkly and plainly. They are gathered round the stairs again, but at a greater distance. Guards—armed men, at any rate, looking variously impressive and uneasy—stand in a ring around the stairs, facing outward, though it is not clear any of the onlookers would wish to approach the stairs more closely if permitted.

The party which draws all eyes approaches from the west, along the tower's shadow. Four armed guards, and between them a tall young man, unarmed, dressed as darkly and as plainly as the crowd. The young man's eyes move from the tower to the crowd and back again.

One of the armed men stands forward, speaks briefly. His inflection is formal, although his words are unintelligible. The crowd does not move or speak. The young man nods to them before his guards herd him onto the bottom stair. Only one guard follows as he begins to climb.

They mount, the guard always four stairs behind, until the young man stumbles—no, casts himself down, bracing his knee in the tread of the stair above, jabbing at the guard's groin with his other foot. The guard falls over the edge and crumples on the ground. Thrashes. They weren't so far up, maybe twice the guard's height, and he fell legs down. He's trying to sit up. Two of his fellows bend over him while the other hurries after the dark-cloaked young man, who is still climbing. Whatever he intended, it wasn't escape.

The relief guard is still several turns from the stair's head when the young man reaches the top and lifts his foot gingerly, seems to feel for something. His toe curls down over the edge of the platform. He frowns. Looks up. Shrugs. Takes one great stride over the edge and vanishes into the bright air. Some of the watchers shift their eyes downward as soon as he steps out; they look back up when it becomes clear he has not fallen.

As the crowd disperses silently, a few of them thrust their arms up in a half-fierce, half-furtive gesture toward the sky.

E.

A sickle moon in the grey night. Even in this half-light the buildings on the plain around the stairway's base are unmistakably long abandoned, crumbling. The wind blows through the ruins, whistles in the empty window arches, moans around the pillar. The wind makes the long grasses bow, shakes the rough stems of knapweed and thistles.

Something else moves in the waste. Someone, rather. A figure muffled in a long coat crouches behind sagging walls, scuttles across open spaces, moves in stops and sudden darts toward the tower. Only a hundred yards away. Only a hundred feet away. Only three paces…

Another figure, armed, springs out from behind the tower, seizes the furtive one's arm. Whispers unintelligibly, but someone has worked out a translation, for a subtitle appears:

"Bloody fool. Go back. I won't report you. This time."

The other does not answer. Stands still and silent until released. Raises one arm toward the tower-top. Turns, strides away against the wind.

3.

"Is it guarded now?" I asked.
The docent shook her head. "Who has money for that?"

F.

Much later. The noise from the city to the east suggests motorized traffic. The distant buildings are blurred with smoke and heat-haze. A small group of people are busy near the stairway. The old stone structures that once surrounded it are almost entirely flattened. Four people hunt for stones in the tangled grass, make notes, call back and forth. Four more stand in the shadow of the stairway, looking up. One gestures upward. They all talk at once, and we can understand them.

"—ritual purposes, probably, or perhaps an observatory—"

"—a stunning view, I suppose, when the air was clearer—"

"—certainly an odd style of stonework, and not the local stone either—"

"Do you suppose it's safe?" This last question comes out in a pocket of silence.

"Safe?"

"To climb. It doesn't look like the strongest design..." The speaker sounds embarrassed: by his timidity? or by the fact his initial question had another, less answerable meaning?

"It's held up all this time."

"But no one's been up it in—"

"—dog's years."

"Your precise grasp of scientific terminology never fails to awe me."

The next-to-last speaker grins and starts to climb, counting the stairs as he goes. At the top he examines the flat platform, turns to take in the view, makes notes, climbs back down. "Six hundred steps," he says. "Quite uniform. Nothing at the top. No inscription, no picture, not even a sighting line."

The sound fades out. The party moves away to examine the fallen buildings.

4.

That's right. That's how my great-uncle told it. He liked repeating the bit about dog's years.

If they made this up—if they did it with actors—they could make things fit like that.

G.

Daylight. The people walking across the mown grass from the car park at the edge of our viewing frame wear contemporary clothing. Four women, three men, carrying folding easels, picnic-baskets, thermoses, backpacks, binoculars.

"You took your sweet time getting started. See, we've lost the best of the light already."

"Don't whinge so. You're the one who kept us up last night, trying to get the best of the moonlight."

They disperse. One settles on the west, or sunward, side, sets up her easel, unpacks a paintbox. Another sits with his back to the stone of the wall, pulls a notebook from his backpack, starts to write. The rest climb up the stairs to varying heights, sit down and start to write or draw. Most stop well below the halfway mark. The whinger ascends, panting, to the very top before unpacking her sketchpad. She sits cross-legged, her back to the sun and her face to the far-off sea, looks out for a while, opens a box of coloured pencils and begins to draw. She works intently for a long time, bending so low over the page her picture is hidden. Then she stretches, sets the pad down and fossicks in her backpack.

"Oy! Selene!" the painter at the bottom shouts. The artist at the top looks down.

"What now?"

"What are you doing with your sketch pad?"

"I just set it down."

"On the air?"

"On the stone! I didn't drop it, I set it down…I felt it…" Her voice rises a bit as she pats the stone behind her, turns around, and realizes the sketchbook isn't there. She sighs. "I must have bumped it."

"Where is it, then?"

"You must have seen where it fell."

"It didn't fall," the painter says. "It disappeared."

"Of course it didn't." Selene frowns. "I can't see the ground right around the tower from here…"

The painter circles the staircase, finding nothing, and calls to the others in the party. No one has seen Selene's sketchbook. It's nowhere. It's gone.

5.

Moonlight again. I stand at the smooth platform at the top of the stairs, the place I have imagined since I heard Great-uncle Mark's stories, the place I have dreamed about since I saw Weltanschauung's sequences. I didn't dare come here till today. I'm not sure what I was afraid of finding, or not finding.

Nor am I sure what I have found. The stone is cold. The wind is cold. The stars are streaming fire. In the hour since I finished the climb I've twice thought I saw the next step gleaming in the air. In between times it seems clear there's nothing there.

I've felt the air where they stepped out, and I can't feel anything. I put my book bag on the empty space where Selene's sketchbook was. It fell. Just as well; it has my non-suicide note inside, in case this night never appears in the mirror of memory. I still have my notebook to record any last thing I may see…

They won't need to find this or my note if I act sensibly and come back down.

But twice I saw the starlight catch on something just beyond the edge…
There, there it is. I'm going.

HUMANITY

This story was originally published in Mythic Magazine *in December 2016.*

The old man sat bolt upright, biting his lips and waiting for his trial to begin. He had always hated speaking publicly as a civilian; he didn't know what to do with his eyes and hands; and now the stakes were terribly high.

He didn't expect to save his own life. He had fought with the resistance at the end, had held his own for a long time against greater numbers and better weapons, and he'd pay for that. But if he could command any respect or sympathy, if he could intercede for his friend and co-defendant, the doctor, who had never fought…

Above the bench where his judges would sit were carved the words posted in every public building in every world of the diaspora, the final words of the Great Pledge they all repeated daily: "TO PRESERVE AGAINST ALL MENACE FROM WITHOUT, ALL DISSENSION FROM WITHIN, OUR COMMON AND PRECIOUS HUMANITY." That was what he and the doctor and all the Pure had been trying to do.

His advocate, a harsh young man appointed by the court, had dismissed this argument. "Stop posturing. Let them see you're old, frightened, *human*. For humanity's sake don't quote your omnipestilent Commander." The old man hoped his judges would prove more understanding.

The judges filed in. Thick-skinned, small-eyed, squat men and women shaped by generations of Ipiu's harsh atmosphere and fierce insects. None of them were beautiful like his people, who had been shaped by Arraj's kinder climate before the earthquakes and eruptions forced them to take refuge on Ipiu two generations back.

He joined in the reciting of the Pledge. Like his judges he spoke in the clipped Unic of the Interworld Consortium. He might have solaced himself with the rolling cadences of Arraji, but he needed to remind his judges they were all humans united against the common enemy.

An evidentiary declaimed the list of accusations.

Breach of the Code of Humanity—well, the Code was always interpreted by the party in power.

Land seizure—how could they claim that? The Ipiu had

acceded to the Arraji's request for a new homeland as the earthquakes devastated Arraj, and the Arraji had never tried to take anything beyond Andek, the barren and *esur*-infested continent allotted to them.

"Murder; gross inhumanity; cruelty to noncombatants, to children…"

The old man rose. He knew what to do with eyes and hands and voice.

"You must not slander us so! My people have never killed or mistreated children or other noncombatants. Only your soldiers—and a few medics, I suppose—invaded our adopted homeland. None of your children came there. If they had come we would not have harmed them. We never attacked your medics…some may have been accidental casualties of our self-defense…"

Judges, advocates, evidentiaries, reporters, stared at him in apparent bewilderment. Perhaps they were mistaken, not lying. What had they heard?

"We have never neglected our duty toward children and unfortunates. I chaired the Arraji Children's Aid Board before you destroyed their headquarters and confiscated their funds. I contributed more than my share to the Interworld Relief collections; you have paralyzed or destroyed our databanks, but if the lines of communication ever open again to the Interworld Consortium their records will bear me out." He took a deep breath, remembered his priorities. "But I am only an ordinary man, doing as all the Pure did. As, no doubt, Your Honors do. My co-defendant is a more striking case. He has devoted himself to medical research for the good of humanity. He has always been a noncombatant. He has a wife and a small son who are now deprived of his assistance, presence and comfort. Is this not cruelty to children?"

"Are you mad?" the old man's advocate hissed.

"No. Are they?"

An evidentiary rose to speak.

"With the Court's permission, we will begin by itemizing the evidence against the defendant who has just interrupted the Court's proceedings."

"Objection," the advocate said.

"No objection," the old man said.

The evidentiary held up a small, black-bound book.

"Do you recognize this?"

"Yes."

"What is it?"

"My personal duty log from my time as a sanitary coordinator."

"You entered this information yourself? You can vouch for its correctness?"

"Yes."

"I will now show the Court an entry from this book. You may inform us if it has been changed in any way."

The old man nodded. The blank wall at the end of the court lit up, showed an enlarged image of a notebook page covered with his cramped Arraji next to a typed Unic translation.

"Ejeget, 6/17. Standard sanitary operation. Pestilentiaries thermoconverted: 137 mature male, 245 mature female, 44 juvenile male, 56 juvenile female. Energy profit: 46 amplissae."

"Is this entry correct?"

"It is." So many days, so many sites, how could he remember? But it was plausible, and there was nothing there that could be used against him.

"You still deny killing children?"

"Of course I do!"

"Would you tell the Court what you did in the process of this 'sanitary operation'?"

"My unit and I were sent to Ejeget by my superiors. Upon arrival we found the *esurin* verified and isolated in a warehouse at the edge of the town. That location was too close to human habitations for thermoconversion—exudates might have compromised air quality. My men removed the *esurin* to a quarry which was abandoned, stripped of useful material, and well downwind from the town."

"Go on."

"The *esurin* were marched into the quarry. One rank of my sanitaries stood at the lip of the quarry, prepared to shoot any who offered interference. The rest set up the thermoconversion booth, moved the *esurin* through in groups of ten, and interred solid byproducts. Then the booth and battery were removed and we set out for the next town on our list. We encountered no children."

He stopped, thinking.

"No, I had forgotten. There was a young girl, the daughter of a woman who after the daughter's birth had been seduced by an *esur* in our collection group. That girl ran after us, shouting. Two of my sanitaries returned her to her mother. She struggled violently, so her wrists may have been bruised, but there was no cruelty."

"No cruelty, either, to the children who died in your thermo-conversion unit?"

"I tell you, there were no children! To thermoconvert humans would be a clear violation of the Code of Humanity. We would never—I would never—have condoned such a thing."

"Then how would you describe the—juveniles—you killed?"

"They were not children. Not humans! All of them were *esurin*. This was manifestly obvious in most cases. A few were more...well-disguised...those who had interbred with humans, to our shame and to the danger of humanity—but the selection specialists were highly trained and conscientious. All those collected for disposal were *esurin*."

"You have used the Arraji word *esurin* several times. Can you not find an appropriate word in Unic?"

The old man frowned. Linguistics had never been his strong point.

"*Esurin* is one of the true names of the Destroyers, the Children of the Lie. They are not human, though they may appear so to the uninformed. There is no exact translation in your language. Your translators have rendered it as 'pestilentiary", which is close, but..." He turned toward the doctor, who was better at such things.

The doctor caught his glance, rose, and explained.

"'Pestilentiary' is often employed as a figurative term of abuse. Even in the literal sense your pestilentiary is most usually a victim of circumstances, someone who is infected through no fault of his own and who infects others unwillingly. '*Esur*' is always used literally. An *esur* is by nature diseased, and he deliberately spreads disease to humans. His goal is the destruction of humanity."

"This is how you define all non-Arraji?"

The old man shook his head. "No! You Ipi are humans like us."

"And on what grounds do you claim this is not true of the Verekei?" The evidentiary gave the *esurin* their false-name.

The answer was too obvious to speak. The old man felt his knees buckle.

"Adjournment requested. My client is unfit." His advocate's voice was flat.

"Adjournment granted."

In the hallway the doctor came up beside the old man and looked at him with concern before his guards hurried him away. The concern, the old man knew, was not about their impending sentence or the success of the Lie but about his unsteady gait and ragged breathing.

Finally alone, the old man tried to pull his thoughts together. How could he make them see? He could remember pieces of the speeches of the Commander of the Pure, but he could not recall the words, the tones, that had woven the pieces together into a clear and damning whole.

There was history. The *esurin*, who were resettled on Andek along with the Arraji, claimed asylum on the grounds their population on Verek was being decimated by a fatal and highly infectious respiratory disease caused by an organism native to the planet. They complied with quarantine procedures before entering Andek. But they had lived four generations on Verek before the disease was identified. If it had been genuine and planet-specific, it should have struck the first settlers. At first some of the Arraji had suspected the disease was a fabrication, a way of claiming sympathy from Interworld Relief and acquiring land on a planet more centrally located than Verek. (Some of the *esurin* had the gall to draw parallels with the exodus of the Arraji, but that was a different matter; the earthquakes and eruptions that rendered Arraj uninhabitable were verifiable; those who said they resulted from Arraji fuel-extraction operations were politically motivated liars...) When the first generation of refugee *esurin* lived and died in apparent good health on Andek these suspicions seemed to be confirmed. Afterward, when the gut-wasting sickness struck the Arraji and some of the *esurin* also pretended to be stricken, the Commander recognized the truth of the situation. The *esurin* were creators of diseases, which gave them excuses to move into closer proximity to humankind and weapons with which to destroy them.

There was anatomy. The *esurin* might claim their large eyes with bloated pupils and shrunken whites, their translucent skin under which the veins showed blue, resulted from living underground to avoid the sickness on Verek's surface, but after the Commander's artists' work was publicized, who could fail to see these were clear marks of the alien nature of the *esurin*?

There were the loathsome crimes of the *esurin* the Commander's investigative units had uncovered. Not content to wait for their sickness to destroy true humanity on Andek, the *esurin* had stolen human children and killed them. The *esurin* had denied the crimes and alleged a lack of evidence, but the investigators were Arraji of clean descent and good reputations who would not have lied.

The old man repeated the arguments until they were fixed in his mind. He would explain in the morning...

~ * ~

In his dream he was out of prison at last. He walked in sunlight on a high ridge, looking down onto a forest. The breeze sent shivers of silver and shadow through the leaves. Why had he never stopped to see how beautiful the world was?

He couldn't stop. The men with the guns hurried him along, hurried the others along in the line behind him. He went down into the shade of the trees, to the edge of the old quarry. Something down there was throbbing loudly. He didn't want to know what it was.

A harsh voice told him to keep going down. The stairs were steep, he wasn't sure of his balance, but he had to go down or they'd shoot him, he'd fall into the people below him, they'd fall. He went down. Saw the thermoconverter. Kept going. What else could he do?

The thermoconverter's door opened. The charging chamber was empty. He was in front. If he didn't walk in they would drag him as if he was an animal or a *thing*, not a human. He went in, set his back to the wall, turned to see who was with him. Just before the terrible light and the pain began he recognized the doctor.

~ * ~

He woke, sweating and shaking, dressed with unsteady hands, returned to the courtroom. Entry after entry was read out of his book. The evidentiaries refused to call the *esurin* by their proper name or to admit their inhumanity. When he tried to explain they interrupted him. His advocate did not intervene. At the lunch recess the old man called his advocate for a conference.

The advocate stared at him, looking belligerent even for an Ipi. The old man stared back.

"Why do you not object when the evidentiaries refuse to allow me to explain the basic premise of..."

"You have already done yourself enough harm. Your so-called explanations would make things worse if that were still possible. Your chances…"

"I understand that I will almost certainly be executed. I am merely attempting to clear my people and my cause of the slanders which have been advanced against us. And also, if it is possible, to save the life of my co-defendant—an obvious noncombatant—my friend—the doctor." He did not say, "Who is young enough to be my grandson, dear enough to me to be the son I never had."

"I am not here to salvage your delusions. I'm charged with saving your life, if that is possible. You haven't made that any easier." The advocate half-smiled. "Or maybe you have. Let me change your plea. Let me argue that you're mentally unfit. It may even be true."

"No! I do not want to live because of a lie. For myself I want justice or nothing. For the doctor…"

"Justice!" The advocate rose as he spoke. The old man half expected a blow. His guards had hit him before. He didn't cringe.

The advocate dropped back into his seat. "Don't ask for what you deserve."

"May I ask for a chance to speak?"

"Not at the evidentiary stage. They've almost finished questioning you anyhow. They'll be starting on your—*friend*—this afternoon. But defendants may make a final statement before sentencing. If you want the slightest chance of living you'll let me make it for you."

"No."

They watched one another in silence until a guard came to take them back to the courtroom.

~ * ~

When his turn came the doctor explained he had researched possible cures for the gutwasting plague, which had spread among the Arraji to such an extent the eradication of the *esurin* alone did not guarantee control. To that end he had requisitioned juvenile *esurin* for experimentation, since the worst devastation of the plague had occurred among Arraji children. The doctor's account was carefully brought down to a level which his hearers could understand.

His advocate interrupted his explanation of the similarities and differences between *esurin* and humans to remind the court that the children (as the advocate called them) whom he requisitioned would surely otherwise have been thermoconverted.

"That may be," the evidentiary said. "As some of his victims did not die, we have summoned one of them to appear in court during tomorrow's session." The advocate's hands clenched. The court adjourned.

The old man looked for the doctor as he was led away, but the guards kept them separate. He walked grimly upright to his cell. He slept and he dreamed:

He was in the field headquarters of the Southeastern Sanitary Campaign along with the doctor. This was at the beginning of the end; there were rumors of an Ipi invasion along the northeastern seacoast, but these had not been confirmed, and the old man had not yet begun training his sanitaries as soldiers. The coordinators discussed the rumors, still only half afraid. The old man, listening, envied them, pitied them, and then forgot them. There, across the room, looking out the window, was the doctor. He didn't know he was marked for death. The old man didn't plan to tell him. He only wanted to sit beside his friend once more, to talk about music, mountains, mathematics, all the lovely things that endured. He started across the room.

One of his colleagues asked where he was going. He turned to answer, but the words froze on his lips. Her voice was his colleague's voice, her uniform and her hair were right, but her veins showed blue under her skin, her eyes bulged obscenely—*esur!*

He recoiled, trying to see who else had seen, who might help him. All through the room eyes turned toward him, horrible, distorted eyes. She had infected them all with something far worse than the gutwaste. She had turned them into *esurin*. He had to warn the doctor, to get him away before he also was destroyed.

If he took another step he would be able to see himself reflected in the window. If he spoke the doctor would turn toward him. He didn't want to see the doctor's face, or his own.

~ * ~

He woke up cold and rigid. He sat up on his cot and tried unsuccessfully to put together some words in the doctor's defense.

He dragged himself into court for the testimony of the juvenile *esur*. The ushers treated the juvenile with the gentleness due to a human child, stood close enough to it to be contaminated. It took its place between the old man and the judges, facing the judges. It looked, from behind, very human, very young. The old man swallowed hard and silently recited the Revelation of the Commander of the Pure which he and his sanitaries had repeated daily along with the Great Pledge:

The esurin *are Children of the Lie. They practice to deceive. Their aim is the destruction of all human life. The torch that was kindled on the Mother-Earth, the spark that gave light to the worlds, they would extinguish. We must not fear them. We must not believe them. We must not pity them. When they are destroyed the wasting diseases will leave us. Fear, cruelty and shame will leave us. We shall be fully human again. We shall have peace. But until we are free of them there will be no peace. Therefore let us devote our time, our resources, our courage and our strength to the work of Purification. Let us never falter in our resolve to preserve against this worst of menaces our common and precious humanity.*

The old man remembered the first time he had heard those words, listening to the transmitter beside his brother, who had turned gray-haired and silent after his child died of the gutwaste, and his cousin, who had been gray-faced and voluble since the *esurin's* excessive-resource-consumption complaints to the Interworld Consortium closed the mine where he worked. He remembered the hope in those words. His cousin nodding. His brother's head lifting.

The young *esur* spoke in halting Unic. "I saw that doctor when I was in the…the bad place. They had away taken my mother and my father. I was alone with strangers except my cousin. I asked where were my parents and they didn't answer." He stopped, his lips quivering. "My…my aunt says they're dead. A bad way dead." He gulped and resumed in a higher voice. "They took us to a hospital, but before I had only to go to hospitals when I was sick, and I wasn't then sick, only scared. They made us line up. My cousin went into the room front of me. I heard him yell. Then they took me in. That doctor was there, in a suit that covered him all over. He weighed me and measured and asked my age, and then gave me a shot. It hurt much, but I did not yell. Then they sent me into a room with beds and no windows. My cousin was there and I sat with him and I told him shots were not to be afraid of and he told me my favorite story about the astronauts. We went to sleep."

He paused, looked down, continued, "I woke up because my

cousin was screaming. When I touched him he was too hot. There were other ones screaming too, or crying, and one shaking so all her bed rattled. So I knew they were sick. My mother said always to watch for sickness and tell her and she'd call a doctor. I couldn't tell her, but I'd seen the doctor. So I banged on the door and I yelled and I said now there are sick people here and you need to help and he didn't come, and so I thought maybe it was night and he was gone home, but I looked and found a camera in the ceiling and I stood right under it and said the same thing and then I thought he would come and I went back to my cousin and I said someone would help, and he said no, and I thought he was crazy from the fever, so I told him about the astronauts while I waited for the doctor to come, but he did not come."

The old man sat with his head in his hands, remembering his nephew tossing in the fever, screaming, then growing silent. Remembering his brother, smiling at the boy, telling him he would feel better soon; weeping, singing a lullaby; stone-faced, staring at the boy's body.

The young *esur*'s story went on. The housekeepers shoving trays of food in, slamming the door, not listening to the boy's—the *esur*'s—pleas. The orderlies coming in their protective suits, taking temperatures, drawing blood, giving nothing. Telling the boy, when he kept asking why, that they were the control group. The fevers, the screaming, the vomiting, the stench. Many deaths, including the cousin's. Then, finally, the three children who had not sickened and died being taken away for more tests under the doctor's supervision. Kept in another room for a week, monitored daily, having blood drawn, screaming at night from dreams not sickness...

"Are you alright? Can you hear me?" the advocate asked quietly. The old man realized his head was down between his knees. He couldn't straighten up. He couldn't answer.

"You're ill. I'll call the guard to take you back to your cell."

The old man rose, lurched, grasped at the guard's arm. The guard recoiled. The old man fell. Someone lifted him, bundled him into a wheelchair, rolled him away. He kept his eyes down, not wanting to see the disgust on the guard's face again, not wanting to look at the doctor and feel a similar spasm of disgust crossing his own face.

~ * ~

That night he dreamed. He ordered a file of *esurin* into the thermoconversion chamber; one looked back at him with his brother's haunted face. He ordered that an example be made of an *esur* who had attempted to interfere with a collection, and found himself staring at the doctor's mangled body. He didn't notice at first when his victims stopped changing, remained clearly marked as Verekei. When he did notice, his sick horror did not abate.

~ * ~

He called his advocate in.

"Have you decided to let me make your final statement for you?'

"No…that doesn't matter. I needed to tell you…" The old man groped for adequate words.

"You've already told me your *friend* deserves to live. I'm not defending him. His advocate is doing what little can be done."

"No, not that. I had to tell you…I know now…I did not know before, but I know now, that the…Verekei…were human." He had said it. He had broken the First Law of the Pure. The voices in his memory screamed at him: *Traitor! Corrupter! Hater of true humankind!* Newer voices, too sure for screaming, called him worse and truer names.

"So you've decided it's safer to admit that after all? And you think this…revelation…will impress the judges? It's too late."

"No! It isn't calculation, I…I did not know and now I do. Too late to save them."

"You never knew?"

"No! We were told…we were all told…" So they had been. Even before the Commander's rise to power. He remembered the taunts when he failed a test, the scoldings when he was cross with his younger brother. *Don't be such a verek!*

"What do you want now?"

"To confess. To apologize."

"This is not your time to speak in court."

"Must I go back and listen while I cannot speak?"

"No. Your part of the evidence is concluded. Let me know if you change your mind about your statement."

The old man nodded. The advocate left.

~ * ~

The next day was bad. The old man swung between cold horror at what he had done and furtive self-pity for his ignorance. First his statement sounded groveling, then cold, then merely stupid. The night was worse.

Back in court the next day, he listened while the doctor's advocate spoke unhopefully of the duty of victorious nations to be merciful. He stood when his time came to speak.

"I can say nothing in my own defense. My actions were indefensible. I have told this court what I believed, that the...Verekei were not human, that our campaign against them was waged on behalf of humanity. I know now I was horribly wrong. I did not know then, but that does not excuse what I did to my...fellow humans. Nothing can do that. I am guilty of murder, indeed, and of defamation as well. I apologize to those Verekei who survived." He swallowed. "I submit myself to judgment. Whatever sentence I receive, it can be no worse than my actions have deserved. But I ask you to have mercy on my co-defendant, who shared my ignorance, and whose actions, however misguided, sprang from his love for humanity."

He looked at the judges, who stared coldly at him. He looked at the doctor, who did not seem to see his friend at all.

The sentence was death by thermoconversion. Publicly broadcast. In three days.

His advocate walked into his cell unannounced.

"It's over, then. Unless you wish to make an appeal."

"I do not. You are not sorry."

"Should I be?"

"Not for me."

"For humanity?"

"You loathe me. Why did you agree to defend me?"

"You never saw, did you? You stood there explaining the self-evident inhumanity of the Verekei, and you never saw what I was."

"You?"

"My paternal grandfather was Verek. He came to Iberra for a scientific conference and met my Ipi grandmother, stayed there to raise his children, left his son there to marry another Ipi, went back to Andek himself as an old man. I have my mother's features. I was in law school on Iberra when we got word my grandfather was dead. Accused by your Commander of atrocities he never committed and sentenced to death in a sham trial, with no advocate. Then you were taken. No one wanted to defend you. I couldn't bear to have it said you were killed unjustly like my grandfather."

The advocate left abruptly. The old man looked after him, shook his head, activated the viewscreen in his cell; anything to take his mind from memory and regret…

His own image was all over the newsfeeds, together with images of the doctor and the Verek child. Some of the images were photos. Some were 'artistic renderings' which caricatured the slenderness of the Arraji, made him and the doctor look more like insects than men, and gave them expressions that were anything but human.

Ipi commentators and decision-makers, speaking in solemn and elevated tones, discussed the ramifications of the case:

The trial had set a clear precedent for sentencing others complicit in Purification. Mass executions would be more energy-efficient, since so much power was required to activate the thermo-conversion unit.

The serum which the doctor had developed showed some promise against the gutwaste. It would be given to the surviving Verekei and, preventively, to the Ipi presently on Andek, and to other Ipi if they chose to settle there to relieve the overcrowding which had begun to trouble Iberra. It would not be given to the Arraji. Why should they be allowed to profit from torturing children?

The ideology of Purification had spread throughout Arraji society, tainting even those who had not taken an active part in the sanitary campaign. Clearly that ideology posed a fundamental threat to humanity. In view of that threat, might it not be necessary for humanity's sake to eliminate the threat prophylactically?

The old man deactivated the viewscreen and stared into the dark. When he could find words he sent a message to his lawyer: *Have your people decided that we all are* esurin? *Have you been infected by the madness that possessed us? Where will it end? Can none of us help ourselves?* The lawyer did not answer.

He tried to write to the doctor, could not; he didn't know whether he was writing to his friend or to a true *esur*.

A fragment of memory came back to him. The doctor, very early in the sanitary campaign, midway through his struggle against the gutwaste, sitting exhausted at the old man's kitchen table, talking, not meeting his friend's eyes. "Humanity. Did you know that in the source-language, on Old Earth, the word meant two things? They used it for the species, as we do, but it had another definition. It also meant kindness."

"They used the species-name for kindness? On Old Earth, where they killed each other over pigmentation and metaphysics?"

The doctor stared at his friend, stalked out the door. He did not turn when the old man called to him. The next day when they met the doctor apologized, saying he had been distraught after the death of three more patients.

The old man sat up straight on his prison cot, pulled out the paper tablet they had given him, wrote a halting message to the doctor recalling that night. He gave it to the guard to deliver. It was returned, unopened, by the same guard, who said that after hearing the old man's pre-sentencing statement the doctor had refused to receive messages. Since then he had not spoken.

~ * ~

The last morning came. The old man greeted it with relief. The only thing he had left to hope was that Ipiu would be a dead planet before its links to the Interworld Consortium were restored, before the plague he had helped to spread could reach beyond Ipiu. He walked out quietly between his guards.

The doctor walked ahead of him, half carried and half dragged by guards. They reached a flight of stairs. The doctor's feet dragged, caught. He lurched forward. The guard on his left let go of him. The other guard swung round and took the doctor's weight before his head could hit the stairs.

The old man saw the brief convulsion of pity on the guard's face and the hard look that came down over it. He stared, remembering:

He and the doctor sat in the park on a sunny spring morning two months after his nephew died despite the doctor's efforts to save him, two weeks after the first speech of the Commander of the Pure. They did not discuss death or politics. The doctor talked about a new fugue he had heard, whistled a piece of the theme. The old man nodded, listened, smiled; started when the shouting began.

A Verek man ran past them. A crowd of Arraji pursued him,

shouting. Someone threw a stone. Then another. The Verek raised his arms to shield his head, stumbled, fell. The crowd fell on him.

The old man sat staring, cursing himself for a coward and an *esur* because he did not run to the lone man's aid, cursing himself for a traitor for pitying one of the *esurin* who had caused his nephew's agonizing death. The doctor rose abruptly and set off toward a quieter part of the park. The old man went after him, telling himself *It's all right, what could I have done, it didn't matter anyway, he isn't one of us.* He swallowed the Commander's next speech like medicine to cool the fever of self-accusation. In time he taught himself to believe. But he had chosen. He had known.

"Can I speak to my advocate?"

"Too late."

"Not a legal appeal. Just… Can I speak at the end?"

"You'll have a few minutes while the thermoconverter warms up."

They were outside, in a hard-floored courtyard. One thermo-converter, humming as it began the activation sequence. Two con-demned men, four guards, seven judges, one cameraman, and ano-ther man. The old man's advocate.

"Your grandfather died alone?"

"Surrounded by men who hated him."

"I am sorry." The old man tried to meet his advocate's eyes, turned away, looked into the camera. "I have something to say. I… In court I said one thing that was true: the Verekei were human, and I and mine murdered them. I said something, also, that was false. That I was deceived. That I had been an innocent pestilentiary. And when I saw your people were beginning to see mine as *esurin,* to prepare to destroy us before we destroyed humanity, I thought you were innocent pestilentiaries as well, that you could not help your-selves. But this was false." He swallowed hard.

"I knew the Verekei were human. And then there were the shortages, and the plague, and the communications breakdowns, and I was afraid. My nephew died of plague, and I grieved. I did not know how to save the people I loved, and I was ashamed—I reproached myself with the name I thought was most shameful—I called myself a Verek. Then I heard the Commander blaming all our griefs and shames on the Verekei, and I wanted it to be true. I told myself the Verekei were not human. I did things that made me unworthy to lay claim to humanity. It... It is a word that meant kindness, once." He glanced at the doctor's blank face. "I chose to kill, to lie. I did not have to. Many of my people did not choose what I chose. It is not a plague, a fault in our race. It is not a plague in yours. It is a choice you make. You must not make it. Please do not do what I have done. Do not make yourselves into what I have become. We are all human, after all...the kindness, the cruelty, the cowardice, the courage...it is for all of us to choose, it is all human ...Please choose better..."

The words were still wrong. He looked at his advocate, who appeared almost as blank as the doctor.

"Time's up. Machine's ready." The guard turned him away from the advocate and the camera, pushed him—not too hard— toward the open door of the thermoconversion chamber. The old man turned back toward the doctor hanging limply between his guards.

"Come on, my friend," the old man said. And, to the guards, "Let me take him." He forced himself not to recoil from the doctor as the guard had recoiled from him. He pulled the doctor's arm over his shoulders, leaned into the doctor's weight, moved forward with him. Eight careful steps. One last look back.

Just before the door closed, just before the terrible light and the pain began, the old man saw his advocate's face streaked with tears.

AT THE CAVE-MOUTH

This story originally appeared in Flash Fiction Online in June 2020

Welcome to my lair, dragon-slayer.

No, I'm not mocking you. Nor bewitching you, whatever the King said. If I were doing that, it wouldn't occur to you to wonder if I was doing it.

Listen before you throw that spear, or you'll live long to regret it.

Yes, live. I'd be hard pressed to kill you. I can't breathe fire. I have teeth and claws, reasonably sharp, but you've got the better reach with your sword, even if your spear-cast misses, which it shouldn't now you're between me and those golden statues of armed people fleeing. Besides, I have arthritis like my mother; lunging at you would *hurt*. I'm ready to leave this life, this body, this loneliness—even at spearpoint, if you won't choose the better way out.

So you don't believe I can't breathe fire. You saw the burnt wreckage of your lover's house.

You didn't see how the fire started, did you? No. You saw what was left: bones, cinders, melted metal—iron only, no trace of the gold. Who but a dragon would do such things? Who do you think? How do you suppose the King keeps his guardsmen loyal, his capital resplendent, and his critics silent?

True, the heroes who seek the dragon's lair never return. You think that means I kill them? Look again at those statues.

You think *I* turned them to gold? I can no more cast a spell than I can breathe fire. The spell of this place binds me, but I didn't shape it.

Yes, I know things you think I shouldn't. I know the guardsman told you he and his comrades had seen the dragon fly overhead, but by the time they came to the place where the dragon had alighted—to what had been your friend's house—it was too late. Look at me. Do you see wings? He said the guardsmen in their troops could try to fight the dragon off when it attacked human habitations, but that only a single champion could break through the spell and come to the dragon's lair, didn't he? Yes, you remember. And I know how he looked, too: the mole on his left cheek, the chipped top front tooth.

Maybe my mother's Sight came to me like her arthritis. More likely the Sight comes with the dragon-spell. Every curse must have an escape clause, or else it burns a hole in the world and sucks the curse-caster in first of all. Here's the escape in the dragon-spell: I know the truth, and I can tell you. But the curse will still bite us both unless you believe me.

You're starting to believe. You fear that means my spell's gnawing your mind like a worm in wool. Oh, our King's clever. I'll likely be dead if you find me convincing and dead if you don't.

Yes, I know the usual form of the proverb. Choose wrong, and you'll be damned as I am now.

You can still choose to really be the hero, the savior, you wanted to be. You can lay down your weapons and take me by the claw—the left; the right pains me so I might hurt you in spite of myself if you shift it. Look me in the eye—either eye will do. Say, "I set you free." Then I'll have my old shape again, and we can go down and tell the truth…

Yes, my old shape. Don't you understand yet? I hardly needed the Sight to know what the guardsman told you. It's the same thing they told me before I climbed this mountain with my mother's name bitter as ash in my mouth.

I was away when my house burned. My baby brother, my twelve-year-old sister, vanished. My mother, who had the Sight and a tongue that spared no man, was left behind for me to find, though her wedding bands were gone. I came seeking vengeance. You see what happened. I can't undo it now. You can.

Still not sure you can trust me? They weren't sure either, those golden statues, back when they had life and motion. They tried to leave without choosing. Here they stay.

No, those aren't your only choices. I see your hands tightening on the spear-haft. Yes, you can still do that. I can't stop you. I won't even blame you overmuch for choosing what I chose.

CRACKED REFLECTIONS

This story was originally published in Enigmatic Mirror Press's anthology "Mysterion: Rediscovering the Mysteries of the Christian Faith" in 2016. A novel with the same title as this story, describing Kass's experiences during the 1912 textile strikes, was published by Propertius Press in 2021.

January 1919

Kassandra Leonhart hurries carefully down the slushy street in the shadow of the tenements, muttering to herself, oblivious to the stares of passers-by. She hugs herself against the cold of a Massachusetts winter and the cold of the dream that clung to her as she woke. Wind, bone-chill, police whistles splintering the air, a hard grip on her shoulder, a man's face frowning down at her, further away a woman's face twisted with—grief? anger? something raw and desperate—and behind them all the beast-man laughing, extending his clawed hands. The nightmare images slosh in her mind. Icy water sloshes in her boots.

Kass has learned not to speak of the nightmares. She hasn't told her father that her boots leak, either. She's seventeen, old enough to know when to be quiet, and she saw the worry on her father's face when her ten-year-old sister Minnie complained of pinched toes. Before the war, when wages were still rising and prices weren't rising so fast, Herr Leonhart could afford new shoes for his children every year. Things are different now. Kass is glad, just this once, not to be the one he worries about.

Herr Schramm, the diner's owner, wishes her *Guten Morgen.* "The new dishwashers are here," he says. "Herr Baum knew their uncle and asked me to find work for them."

"If they are *Pastor* Baum's friends I will be glad to meet them." Kass still considers Herr Baum her pastor, though the elders—including Herr Schramm—voted him out; though he's in prison, eight months into his ten-year sedition sentence.

Herr Schramm opens the scullery door, says, "Kass, these are the new girls; girls, this is Kass Leonhart, she'll show you what to do."

"Hello and welcome," she says. "Just call me Kass. Who are you?" The new girls stand close together. Both are shorter than Kass.

The fair one's round face is incongruous on her thin body. The dark one's face and figure are all angles. Surely Kass has seen her somewhere before. But where?

"I am Galya," the fair one says, glancing nervously at Kass.

"I am Kseniya." The dark girl throws her name out like a challenge. Seemingly even the new workers know Kass is *geisteskrank*—soul-sick, insane—and they're wary. Kass tries and fails to appreciate Herr Schramm's continuing to employ her instead of resenting his warning the new girls about her. She asks the new girls if they want to go into the kitchen and collect the cart of dirty dishes or stay where they are and fill the sinks. They stare and don't answer.

Kass shrugs and heads into the kitchen. She knows she's not the only one who gets stared at. At church, people look askance at Stefan Beiler, who came back from the war with a nervous tic and haunted eyes. Any loud noise can make him throw himself on the ground, stand up again pale and shaking. Pastor Bower says he's a hero like all the young men who enlisted, but Pastor Bower doesn't look directly at him. Pastor Bower doesn't praise Christoph Geist, who has just come back from the military prison where he was sent for being a conscientious objector. Christoph was a high-spirited boy, but now he barely speaks and he cringes if anyone moves suddenly near him. Herr Pastor Baum gave Christoph a hero's send-off—which he did not do for Stefan, and Stefan's parents haven't forgiven that—but God only knows what happened to Christoph in prison, and now Christoph's come home to people who are ashamed of him. There is so much shame.

Kass grabs the handle of the cart, trying not to flinch at the feel of spilled grease under her fingers. *It doesn't matter*, she tells herself. *You're taking it away with other dirty things, you'll clean them all.*

"Hand me that stack of clean plates, Kass," the cook, Frau Albrecht, says. Kass frowns at her dirty hands, reaches for the faucet handle. "Hurry up!" Kass grabs the plates with her cleaner hand, shoves them at Frau Albrecht, turns away, trying to shake her mind free of the fear of germs and the suspicion Frau Albrecht is frightening her on purpose.

When Kass comes back to the scullery, both sinks are full of hot soapy water. Kseniya and Galya mutter to each other, fall silent as Kass comes in, look warily at her. She sets the tray of dinnerware next to one sink, says curtly, "Start there, both of you," and starts scrubbing pots in the other sink. She should be used to this by now. She remembers when the muttering began.

February 1917

Kass is fifteen, finally done with school and able to wait tables full-time at Herr Schramm's diner. She's glad to be earning her share, and she doesn't miss school. After the war started in Europe, stories about German atrocities appeared in the newspapers, and then sometimes in civics class, and then in the taunts of the students who speak English at home. "Lies," Kass's father said. "Germans don't behave like that." "Who knows?" Pastor Baum said. "When men are trained to kill, who can know that they will not behave like that? Likely the English soldiers are no better." "Don't argue at school," her father told her. She didn't. She's good at not saying things. She's mostly learned to hide her nightmares and her daytime fears so her father won't know she's crazy like her grandmother. He guesses, he worries, but he doesn't know. She hopes no one else guesses.

No one says "Hun" at Herr Schramm's diner. Kass is tired at the end of each workday, but proud too, and she knows how lucky she is. The girls from her class who went to work in the textile mills make less than she does, and the overseers in the mill speak rudely to them and sometimes grab them, and too many of them are killed or injured trying to keep up with their machines. Kass knows this because her father works in the woolen mill. He's a skilled weaver, his pay is acceptable, and he's never been hurt, but he swore his daughters would never be mill hands. He's kept that promise, thanks to Herr Schramm, who is part of his church and his chess club.

This cold morning, Kass comes to work clutching the locket which holds a dried four-leaf clover, trying to clear her head of nightmares, reminding herself of how lucky she is. It takes her a while to notice there are more empty seats than usual. Their German and Quebecois customers come as always when their factory shifts end, but the Flahertys, the Doyles, the Brennans, the O'Malleys, don't come. Neither do weary-eyed Seamus Halloran and his father. She always keeps an eye out for them. Often old Mr Halloran—not so old, really—talks to people who aren't there. Sometimes he recoils, runs away from the table, and hits Seamus when Seamus tries to stop him. Afterward he weeps, apologizes, and sits quietly, head bowed, while Seamus finishes eating. Kass always takes time to speak to the Hallorans. She mentions their absence to the cook, Frau Albrecht.

"Yes, they're not coming, *die patriotischen Idioten*," Frau Albrecht says. "Seamus came in yesterday saying America will get into the war, and people already know the Irish aren't friends to England, so Irishmen here can't be seen eating at a German restaurant if they want to keep their work at the gunpowder factory. *Idioten*. Here they got clean healthy food. Those Irish, how clean do you think their kitchens are?"

Jutta, the other server on Kass's shift, agrees it will serve those Irishmen right if they take sick and lose their jobs and—

"Old Mr Halloran's already sick," Kass says. "They don't need more bad luck."

"*Geisteskrank*," Jutta agrees. "We don't need that kind here, spreading their sicknesses."

Kass opens her mouth to say that sickness in the mind doesn't spread like that. Shuts her mouth. How can she be sure? Where do her nightmares come from? Where does the fear go when it leaves her? *Darum geht aus ihrer Mitte hinaus und sondert euch ab, und hört auf, das Unreine anzurühren; Come out from among them and be separate, and touch not the unclean things*, Kass's grandmother's voice says in the back of her mind. It's one of the verses Großmutter says over and over on her bad days. She says it in response to ideas more often than to dirt. And now her dirty idea, her fear of dirt, is smeared onto Kass's mind, and who knows where it will spread next?

"Hurry up, Kass, go take their orders," Frau Albrecht says. Kass goes—noticing Jutta stays to gossip unrebuked.

It occurs to Kass that she would not be sorry if Jutta took sick. Not a fatal sickness, *natürlich*, just something disgusting and painful.

The thought shames her. Scares her. Behind her eyes the beast-man smiles, approving her malice. The beast-man's face has grown familiar in the years following the magic show. The fear that comes with him has been familiar as long as she can remember.

Kass clutches her clover locket, praying. She will not spread malice. She will not spread germs. She takes great care not to brush against Jutta as she takes the next order, not to breathe on the food.

That night, Kass dreams that she watches herself waiting on tables. The Kass who watches sees particles falling from the hands and the headscarf of the Kass who carries plates and does not see. The diners do not see. They eat, talk, laugh, then bend double, vomiting, gasping, choking.

The next day Kass keeps washing her hands. "Enough already! How dirty can you have gotten in five minutes?" Frau Albrecht asks.

The day after that Jutta is out sick. Kass has to hurry. It's hot inside. She pats her headscarf to make sure her hair isn't coming out. Her scarf is wet; she has sweat on her hands, she has to wash them again—

"Enough!" Frau Albrecht says. "Take these plates!"

Kass grabs them, hurries off. Sets two of them down. Realizes as she hustles toward the last customer that a drop of sweat has rolled off her face and landed—where? Maybe on the plate. There might be microbes in it. She drops the plate.

She has to clean it up, wash her hands again, wait while Frau Albrecht fills another plate, run with it, knowing she has dried her hands on her skirt, which must have gotten dirty while she was kneeling to pick up the mess she'd made…

At the end of the shift Frau Albrecht takes her aside.

"What's wrong with you?"

"I was trying to be clean," Kass says. "I was…afraid of the germs." She feels cold sweat breaking out on her forehead, hears her voice shaking. Frau Albrecht narrows her eyes, turns away.

The day after that Jutta is back, muttering with Frau Albrecht about something which they stop discussing whenever Kass enters the kitchen.

January 1919

Kass hears the new girls muttering to each other, splashing loudly to cover the sound of their conversation. Shame roils in Kass's stomach. She struggles to look steadily at the shame until she can pull free of it. *Die Warheit wird euch frei machen, the truth shall set you free*, she mutters in her head over and over, clutching her clover locket, looking for the crack in the air, for the image in the invisible mirror.

The shame loosens enough so Kass realizes it's not all hers. Someone else, someone nearby, is also angry and ashamed. Kass looks at the new girls. Galya blushes, turns away.

Kass goes over to her and Kseniya. "What's wrong? Have I offended you?"

Galya keeps her head down. "Please?" she says softly.

"Please what?" Kass feels shame swirling around her, and also a dogged courage like her own.

Kseniya turns to face Kass. "We are still learn English."

"Is that all? I'm sorry. I thought… Can you not understand me, or is it just that you're not sure how to answer?"

Kseniya turns to Galya, says something quick and full of consonants. Galya shushes her.

"She doesn't have to be quiet," Kass tells Galya. "We can talk here. No problem."

"No problem talk Russian? I think no," Kseniya says. Galya whispers. Kseniya raises her eyebrows. "Galya says is no good saying, you will not understand."

"I understand," Kass says. "I remember when we were warned not to speak German outside our neighbourhood." Kseniya looks surprised, but not lost—she understands.

July 1916

Dieter Leonhart is taking his *Kinder* to a magic show in the fine part of town. Minnie bounces and laughs while her father reminds her to keep quiet or speak English on this outing. Kass clasps her locket that holds a dried four-leaf clover. She's kept it with her day and night for the last month, hoping it will ward off madness. She got the idea first from Frau Geist, Christoph's mother, who tells *Märchen* to the children. They've heard some over and over, like Dornröschen's hundred-year sleep, but last month Kass heard the tale of the girl and the sorcerer for the first time. The girl saw through the sorcerer's tricks because she was holding a four-leaf clover, "and so was proof against all malice and deceit." Kass listened and wondered. Just two days later she heard old Mr Flaherty at the diner, after a few steins of beer, weeping a little and telling the table at large that he'd carried a four-leaf clover with him from the old country "just the way Mother Eve did when she left Paradise, for a reminder of that blessed land, and a protection in the hard wide world."

Kass wants that protection. She's taking the locket to the show to see if it really works. Her nightmares haven't stopped, but she hopes the clover charm may keep her clear-eyed and sane by day.

They ride past houses that grow taller, brighter, cleaner, and then they are at the theatre itself.

"*Haben wir Stehplätze?*" Minnie asks, pointing to the weary-eyed people standing against the back wall.

"Here come the Huns," someone mutters.

"No, we don't have to stand," Papa says in careful English. "We paid for seats."

"Where do they get their money from?" another English voice asks from the back. Papa looks back, worried, but just then the overhead lights go out and a bright light comes on over the empty stage with its intricately patterned floor. Then the light is obscured by a billow of smoke.

When the smoke clears, a man in a fine suit stands onstage, smiling at his audience. Kass watches, wide-eyed, while he floats a silver orb above his palm, snaps his fingers and brings a shower of coins out of the air, reaches behind his ear and pulls out a rainbow-colored scarf which rises wavering from his hand like the flame of a torch and then floats away into the darkness offstage. She's forgotten to look for tricks. She's seeing magic.

Someone in front is less absorbed. Someone mutters. The magician smiles.

"Perhaps such trifling pastimes do not interest you," he says. "Well, then…"

He spreads his arms and strokes the air with the index finger of his left hand. All the lights go out. Kass is too old to be afraid of the dark. *Trotzdem*, she is afraid.

One light comes on toward the back of the stage. An old man sits under it in a wooden chair, reading a book as big as a pulpit Bible. There is no one between him and the audience. The magician is gone.

There is no smoke, but suddenly someone appears in the middle of the dim stage, glowing like snow at night. He wears a suit like the magician's, but his eyes are dark all over like the eyes of a beast and his face is salt-white.

The old man on the stage stares at the beast-man, who turns and advances on him like a tightrope walker, one foot placed straight in front of the other. His arms lift and spread. Each finger is tipped by a claw. The old man lurches to his feet, throws the book—which falls on the other side of the beast-man, so it must have gone right through him—and dodges behind the chair. The beast-man kicks the chair, which falls, and strikes at the old man, who claps his hand to his cheek, then lowers it to reveal a line of bright blood. Somebody in the audience screams.

The beast-man strokes the air with the index finger of his left hand. A host of darkly shining shapes gather around him, slowly solidifying. This is worse even than Kass's nightmares. She can't wake up from this.

Thinking that, she thinks of what she's thought of every morning in the last month when she's awakened from nightmare. Her clover. *Proof against all malice and deceit. Protection sent from the Blessed Land.*

As she thinks the words she sees the glowing crack in the empty air onstage. But it isn't empty air. She's seen the same thing when the light of the streetcar comes through the scratched glass of her window.

There's a mirror running diagonally across the stage, obliquely facing both the audience and the heavily curtained wing. Now that Kass knows what to look for she can see the thin frame that holds the mirror, its base concealed among the crisscrossing lines of the stage floor. She can see that the beast-man is a reflection from the wing moving across the mirror's surface. He's not really on the stage behind the mirror where the old man cringes. The old man kicked the chair over, daubed red paint on his own cheek. It's all right.

Kass means to think this silently to herself, is startled to realize she's shouted it in German. Someone tells her—in English—to shut up. Someone says "Krauts". Kass doesn't care. The clover charm works. She is safe.

May 1919

It's Sunday afternoon. The factories and the diner are closed —Massachusetts keeps the Lord's Day, *Gott sei Dank*—and Kass walks to the Common to meet Kseniya and Galya. Trees shine with new leaves, and now that so many Germans are back from fighting for America, Kass can sing "*Lachend, lachend, lachend, kommt der Sommer über das Feld*" without anyone yelling *Kraut* or *Hun*.

She stops singing when she sees her friends. Kseniya's face is grim. "What's wrong?" Kass asks.

"You have taught me to read English," Kseniya says. "Now look what I read!" She holds out a newspaper.

Galya looks around. "Not here! Some place with people not so many."

Kass leads them away from the garden and the fountain to a solitary bench. Kseniya unrolls the paper. The bold headline screams "REDS AIM AT AMERICA!" The subheads elaborate: "Price Riots Driven by Foreign Agitators," "Reds Riot in May Day Parade," "Russian Reign of Terror—It Could Happen Here!"

Kass knows about the price riots. They haven't happened in her city yet, but the news has been full of them. Once the unions would have struck for higher wages to meet the rising prices, but now most of the union leaders are serving sentences for sedition. Kass doesn't know who leads the people who shout in the streets, block store entrances, smash windows and take things they can't afford to buy. She's not inclined to blame them. She is inclined to blame whoever has been circulating fliers threatening bombs and bloodshed in the name of justice for the poor. If those fliers really exist—if the papers haven't invented them—how is she supposed to know?

She scans the story about immigrant workers who held a Red Flag parade in Boston on May Day. Bystanders charged them and tried to make them stop. They fought. Too many people were hurt. The Red Flag marchers (and none of their attackers) are in jail for rioting—rightly, the paper says, as they were trying to undermine the peace and freedom so dearly bought in the war, to replace liberty and justice with Bolshevism, mob rule, murder and rapine.

"You see?" Kseniya asks. "They call us killers, stealers—"

"It's not talking about you," Kass says. "Not all Russians, only Communists."

"Galya is not Communist," Kseniya snaps. "But today they call her on the street Bolshie, and one woman—" Kseniya spits in the dirt. "On Galya! Because only she is Russian."

Kass sighs. "I am sorry. I believe you. I remember."

Kseniya cocks her head, waits for the story.

"In nineteen-seventeen, when America has just gone to war, I am too afraid of many things." Kass shuts her eyes for a moment, remembering her frantic hand-washing, remembering Frau Albrecht and Jutta talking behind her back. "I am sick with fear, but I am trying not to show I am afraid. Trying not to seem crazy. I think, if Herr Schramm knows I am crazy I will lose my job, and we need the money, and who will hire a German girl? But I am crazy, seeing germs everywhere, thinking I will make people sick. One day I am walking to work. There is mud everywhere. I have my hands folded in my sleeves so nothing dirty will splash them. I am almost there, and then these older boys come and ask me 'What's wrong with your hands? Won't you wave to us?'" Kass makes her voice hard, mocking, like theirs. "They say maybe I have stolen something, or maybe there is blood on my hands. I tell them to leave me alone— I say it in German, and they say yes, I am a Hun, there is blood on my hands. They shout for me to show my hands. I do, and they throw things. Mud, and…well, we were by one of the alleys, there was sewage."

She falls silent, remembering.

April 1917

Kass stares at the filth on the front of her dress. She can't go to the diner like this. She reaches to wipe it away, freezes. Germs are so small. She might just push them right down through the fabric, to rest against her body, to multiply, to—the dream images ooze in her mind. She can't stand the feel, or the smell, of her dress against her. She tears at it. The boys draw closer.

"Stripping, yet!"

"Now she's shown us her hands, why not everything else?'

They laugh like her nightmares, close in like glittering shadows.

"Leave her alone!" The deep voice cuts through her nightmare. The other voices stop. "For shame! What have you done to this young lady?"

It's Herr Schramm, and she's standing in front of him in a torn dress, filthy…

"Nothing. She's crazy. We never touched her."

He turns her away from the boys, tongue-lashes them until they slink off, waits for her to explain. Waits a long time.

"What's wrong?" a quiet voice asks. She turns her head only. It's Pastor Baum.

"There were boys pestering Kass."

"I'll take her home." Herr Pastor slips his coat around her shoulders. His house is nearby, and one of Frau Baum's dresses almost fits Kass. When she is clean and decent she goes back to the study, makes herself face Pastor Baum.

"Are you all right? What did they do to you?'

She could say they grabbed her, tore her clothes. That might happen to any girl, *geisteskrank* or not.

But it didn't happen to her. She clutches the clover locket, tells him the truth. "And now Herr Schramm will fire me."

"Herr Schramm will still have work for you. Perhaps not waiting tables."

"The choir—"

"You will still sing in the choir. If anyone tries to discourage you, I will speak to them."

"Those boys—"

"Herr Schramm has warned them to leave you alone." He looks out the window. "But take the streetcar from now on."

"But it costs—"

"Less than losing your job; and it's safer than walking." He doesn't say, he doesn't have to say, "Who knows whether the police will protect a German girl?"

"I don't want to go to a doctor who will make me take opium like my grandmother. It doesn't stop her being *geisteskrank,* and it changes her…"

"Your father won't make you take opium. Not if there's anything else you can hold onto." He looks at her, questioning.

Her clover hasn't kept her safe for the last two miserable months. Herr Pastor Baum has spoken before of holding to the Word. What good has that done Großmutter, who can recite verses about filth and curses and unforgivable sin until her words trip over each other and her eyes are wild?

There are other words in the Word, of course. *Perfect love drives out all fear.* Lovely, but all too plainly Kass doesn't love like that. *You shall know the truth, and the truth shall set you free.* The clover hasn't kept her safe. Maybe if she stopped trying to be safe she could learn to be free.

May 1919

Kass tells as much of the end of that story as she thinks her friends will understand. Kseniya stamps her foot.

"They print such lies, these papers, but still people read them! Our papers tell what is true, that it is the rich ones who make trouble, who take everything and leave us only prison. But these papers we cannot mail, we must give at night, hand into hand, or drop in the streets."

Galya hisses something at Kseniya, who snaps back at her, then tells Kass. "Galya says be careful, but I say, too late. It is true, I am Communist."

"But you're not making bombs?" Kass sounds more doubtful than she meant to. Kseniya's face hardens. Kass goes rigid. She may have lost her friend's trust. She has certainly recognized a piece of the nightmare that still hangs over her every morning. The icy wind blows. The police whistles scream. The man frowns. The beast-man advances. Tears run down the woman's fixed and furious face—and the woman is Kseniya.

Kass shakes her head to clear it. "I'm sorry! Kseniya, listen, I don't think you're evil because you're a Communist. I…I know that when people, good people, are afraid, they can do terrible things." She clasps her clover locket and looks hard into Kseniya's eyes, remembering, willing Kseniya to remember.

"You have seen this," Kseniya says.

"Yes."

Galya adds something in Russian. Kass can almost see what she remembers—she and Kseniya have also seen the terrible things frightened people do. Kass can't see what they saw, but she can see it left Galya more afraid, and Kseniya angrier, than Kass has ever had to be.

"Communists do not do such things," Kseniya says. Galya hisses and shakes her head. "They do not," Kseniya repeats, strenuously enough that Kass realizes she isn't sure. "These stories in the papers, they are lies." Then, as an afterthought, "And Galya is not Communist. Only I. Will you tell the police? Will they believe?"

"I will not tell them anything about you," Kass says. "They arrested Pastor Baum. He wasn't a Communist, but he wanted things made right, he protested, and now he is in prison for ten years. I don't want more arrests."

"I do not believe your Church, me," Kseniya muses, "but my uncle said this Baum is a good man, brave. Your pastor now is good and brave too?'

"No!" Kass blurts. "You wouldn't like him," she amends. "And you shouldn't tell him you are a Communist. You shouldn't tell anyone that."

"In English, you only," Kseniya says, smiling.

June 1919

It's Sunday morning, and Kass walks to church with her father and Minnie, listening to the agitated conversations around her. The newspapers have been busy all week with the bomb blasts at the homes or offices of politicians—one legislator, even, here in Massachusetts! Anarchist fliers were left near the bombsites. One of the bombers and a night watchman are dead; all the politicians are still alive. The newspapers say a Red uprising is sure to follow, that there will be arson and murder everywhere.

"At least we have a good sound pastor now," Herr Beiler says. Kass lifts her head to glare at him, finds she is glaring instead at his son Stefan. Stefan's shell shock isn't wearing off; his eyes look bruised and the muscle in his cheek twitches. Kass smiles apologetically, murmurs *"Guten Morgen."* Stefan nods. Then his brother Georg comes between them. Georg came home from the war whole in body and mind, and he joined the newly formed American Legion. Pastor Bower has praised the Legion's resolution "to foster and perpetuate a one hundred per cent Americanism," as well as their call on Congress "to pass a bill immediately deporting every one of those Bolsheviks." Kass turns away from Georg, ignores his greeting, enters the church already fuming.

Pastor Bower reads from Romans 13: "Everyone must submit himself to the governing authorities, for there is no authority except that which God has established... He who rebels against the authority is rebelling against what God has instituted, and those who do so will bring judgment on themselves." He explains that it is their American and Christian duty to be vigilant against Bolsheviks and anarchists, to report suspicious words or actions to the American Legion, or to the police, or to him.

Kass glowers at him, turns to look at the people around her. Many are nodding. Many of them used to nod when Pastor Baum gave a very different message. How can they bear the change?

Kass remembers the months after war was declared, after the Sedition Act banned speech against the war effort. Pastor Baum kept preaching on texts like "Love your enemies" and "Thou shalt not kill." The church elders warned him. He didn't stop. Men from the newly formed American Protective League "advised" him to buy Liberty Bonds to support the war, raise an American flag, change the sign from "*Emanuel-Kirche, erste evangelisch-lutherische Kirche in Guerdon*" to "Emmanuel Lutheran Church" or "First Lutheran Church of Guerdon," and preach in English. The elders advised him to go along with all those requests except the last. They didn't want to lose German. Some of the elders spoke little English, and anyway Bach composed to German texts, and what would church be without Bach? Pastor Baum disregarded all the recommendations. Kass admired him. Herr and Frau Geist were grateful he supported their Christoph's refusal to serve in the army. Herr and Frau Beiler were furious with him when he would not pray for the success of the army their sons had joined—though he did pray for their safety. Jim Knowles of the League began coming to church with the Beilers, listening attentively and making notes during the sermon.

So it went for weeks and months, while the English papers reported on German-American spies and German atrocities, while the German-American papers reported on the beating, tarring and feathering of Germans-Americans by the League and their allies, while death telegrams came to many neighbours and crippled or blank-eyed young men came home to a few, while Kass's nightmares showed a mob of men with axes marching on the church. And then…

April 1918

Kass walks to church behind her father and Herr Schramm. They keep their voices low, but Kass knows what they're talking about. The news of Frank Prager's lynching came on Thursday. The papers agree on the facts. He was an Austrian immigrant, a Socialist, anti-war, loud-mouthed and irritable. His neighbours accused him of disloyalty, stripped him, beat him, wrapped him in an American flag, hanged him. Loyal citizens dealing with a traitor, some English papers say. Overzealous men who should just have had him arrested, others say. Irresponsible hotheads, a few say. Who will be next? the German papers ask.

Herr Beiler sits in a back pew, glowering, muttering to Mr. Knowles. On Good Friday, when Pastor Baum preached on "He who draws the sword shall perish by the sword," Herr Beiler walked out in the middle of the service. A week ago, on Easter Sunday, he left just before the benediction.

Today the choir sings Bach's setting of *"Ach, lieben Christen, seid getrost, wie tut ihr so verzagen?"* — "Ah, dear Christians, be comforted; what makes you so disheartened? Since the Lord sends affliction upon us…" Kass sings out of her fear, hears the same fear in the voices of her neighbours.

Pastor Baum reads from John's account of Christ's appearing to Peter after the Resurrection. The question and the charge: "Do you love me? … Feed my sheep." And the warning of Peter's coming martyrdom: "When you were younger you dressed yourself and went where you wanted, but when you are old you will stretch out your hands and someone else will dress you and lead you where you do not want to go."

He speaks of Prager as a good man, a worker for justice and against war. He reminds his congregation that, while Socialists may not be spoken of as good men in the newspapers, they helped to lead the 1912 strikes that won all the city's factory workers— German, English and all the rest—wages that would feed and clothe and house their families. And as for the war…

Pastor Baum looks directly at the Beilers and Mr Knowles as he denounces the war even more openly than he has done before. Mr Knowles and the Beilers leave together before the benediction. When Pastor Baum spreads his arms to give the blessing, Kass thinks she sees his left index finger scratching the air, summoning the darkness.

Kass's father and Minnie go to walk on the Common after church. Kass goes home alone, stares blindly out the window. The beast-man stalks behind her eyes, carrying an axe and an American flag.

It's an illusion, she tells herself. It's only a reflection. She puts her hand to her locket.

Reflections are of real things, she answers herself. They may not be where they seem to be, but they are real somewhere. We see through a glass darkly, but we do see. It's not just her mind that is disturbed. Somewhere outside another fear calls to her own.

She leaves the house, waits until she can feel that other fear pushing at her like a cold wind, walks into it.

The men gathered around Herr Schramm on the sidewalk don't notice Kass.

"But the Geists have bought bonds already."

"*Trotzdem*, the League men and some others are at the Geist house. Most of the men there have gotten telegrams. They say young Geist is safe in the lock-up while their son…"

"We must do something."

"Pastor Baum's there already. Lucky the Geists live so close to the church. He came with his vestments on and the Book in his hand, and he was preaching when I left. At least he'll distract them."

Kass bolts toward the Geist house, but she doesn't have to run quite so far. As she passes the *Kirche*, light from the church windows, light from the streetlamps, show her the church sign chopped apart, the axe lying next to it, the circle of men on the church lawn. She can't see faces in that light, but she knows Pastor Baum's voice. He's speaking German now, talking to himself or God. "*Er hat auf Gott vertraut; er befreie ihn nun, wenn er will.*" "He trusts in God; let God rescue him now if he wants him." All the other voices speak English.

"Stop blathering and speak like a man," one of them says. "You've had plenty to say about Christianity. What kind of Christian supports the murdering bastards who killed my son?"

"—and those children in Belgium—"

"—and crucified the Canadian soldier—"

"—and poisoned the bandages we're sending our boys—"

There is a glowing crack in the night. Kass can see what the angry men see in the mirror. The figure from the war posters, red-handed, bloated, evil-eyed—another sort of beast-man—looms over them, over their sons. The beast-man's image shimmers in front of Pastor Baum. The League men can't tell them apart.

She turns, sees the crack in the air shifting, sees what Pastor Baum sees. Not one beast-man but a herd of them, circling him, carrying a rope. He is steeling himself to bear whatever they do, not to beg, to control his bowels and his tongue.

She clasps her clover locket, looks again at the men. They have no rope. They have hacked the sign but not the church windows. They put the axe down. For a mob, they could be much worse. *Trotzdem*, they are getting angrier, they may become worse.

"Nothing to say?" one of them says. "I'm not sure he deserves that robe he's wearing." Why do they laugh at that? Why does Pastor Baum hang his head?

He takes a step back and the light of the window falls on him. He's wrapped in a flag, his arms pinned to his sides, his legs bare to the knee.

Kass launches herself into the circle, musters her best English. "Are you all as crazy as I am?"

Silence. She has surprised them. That's a start. Now if she can shift the mirror in front of their eyes… "I'm the crazy Kraut girl, the mad *Mädchen,* the one who sees germs everywhere. I see germs, you see German spies. But I swear you're crazier than I am. I only tore my own clothes, I never did that to anyone else!"

She looks again at the men who have gathered, focuses on Seamus Halloran's face. "Where's your father?" she asks him. "Not crazy enough for the rest of you?" Seamus looks down. "Tell him hello from me," Kass says. "Tell him I'm glad we're insane in a different way from the rest of the world. He never hit anyone without being sorry afterward. You'll be sorry afterward, too. Why not stop now?"

"Get out of this." That's the man who's done most of the talking. One of the fathers of dead sons. He grabs Kass's shoulder. She flinches.

Seamus catches his arm. "Leave her be! You can see she's not right in the head."

"Get her out, then, and let us deal with him."

Pastor Baum hisses: *geh,* go, keep yourself safe! He's ashamed, she realizes—not only by what these men have done, might do, but by the fact that, while the sane and respectable members of his congregation have left him, this crazy girl, this public embarrassment, has come to try to save him. She hadn't known he saw her like that. She can't think of that now. She has to shift the mirror.

She can't hold the mirror up. It crashes down on her, breaks around her. Its cold sharp fragments scrape her skin, her soul, like claws.

That's only another nightmare image, she tells herself. Nothing really happened.

She doesn't believe herself. There is only fear in her mind. Her fear, his fear, their fear, she doesn't know. Perfect fear drives out all love, and all knowledge as well. She is falling. Someone is taking Pastor Baum away—they'll kill him—

Seamus bends over her. "It's all right," he says. Then he stands. "Officer, sure I'm not doing anything to the girl. She fell, she...had a fit."

"We all did," Kass says. "He didn't hurt me."

"Kass?" Herr Schramm kneels where Seamus was. "Come away. Come home. Your father will be looking for you."

"But Pastor Baum—"

"I called the police. They've arrested him. He'll be safe now, and he won't bring us into any more danger." Herr Schramm helps Kass up.

Seamus mutters, "Look, I had to join. You know what they're saying about the Irish."

"You'd better go with your friends," the officer says to Seamus, "if you don't want to explain things to me, which I'd just as soon you didn't." Seamus goes.

There is no pastor at church next week. There is an American flag above the sign, which says "Emmanuel Lutheran Church". Herr Baum is in jail, no longer their pastor. The choir sings Bach. Kass sings with them. Frau Geist hugs her, calls her brave. Frau Beiler and many other women avoid her eyes, mutter to each other.

The week after that they have a pastor again. Reverend Henry Bower was born Heinrich Bauer, but he conducts the service in English and prays for God's blessing on their nation's righteous cause, and the choir sings "My Country 'Tis Of Thee". Kass doesn't sing with them.

June 1919

Kass still sits in the pews, not the choir loft. She turns away from Pastor Bower. Christoph Geist huddles with his head in his hands. Stefan Beiler's head is bowed and a tremor runs through his body. Georg Beiler sits erect and confident beside his father.

Kass feels the cold wind from her nightmare blowing in her bones, sees behind her eyes the beast-man, the weeping woman who is Kseniya, the frowning man…that's it. The frowning man has Georg's face.

January 20, 1920

It's Tuesday afternoon, the end of the shift. Kass hesitates before stepping out into the cold. Not that the restaurant is so very warm; the fall was unusually cold and dark, the winter has been the same, and with the coal miners striking the heat has been turned down everywhere. Kseniya's boarding-house is colder than Kass's apartment, much colder than Herr Schramm's restaurant; she and Galya come to work with newspapers stuffed under their coats, put off leaving as long as possible. But tonight Kseniya hurries out. "I have the meeting," she says. Kass doesn't ask about the meeting. Not that she'd tell Pastor Bower anything if she did know. Though if he'd believe her she'd tell him something provably false. Better yet, she'd tell someone else *he* was a secret Red agitator. Let *him* get dragged off by the police and spend ten years in prison.

Shame sours her stomach. Behind her eyes the beast-man smiles. Behind him something else moves. Someone else's fear and spite echo her own. She puts her hand to her clover locket, looks for the crack in the air.

Someone else is thinking gleefully of an enemy who should be in prison. There's another place where their thoughts touch hers …Kseniya. The meeting. Her nightmare. In her mind she hears the police whistles again, sees Kseniya weeping.

Kass hurries ahead, catches at Kseniya's arm. "Wait!"

"I have not much time; the meeting soon begins."

"Don't go. Someone—some enemy—will break in. Don't go tonight."

Kseniya folds her arms. "How do you know?"

"Something I heard. I can't explain now. Don't go!"

Kseniya looks Kass hard in the eyes. Nods. "So. Always there was danger and there now is more. I believe you. The others also must be told."

"I'll tell them. Tell me where to go and what to say—something short."

Kseniya whispers, hurries home while Kass hurries the other way, bent against the bitter wind.

The part of the city where Kseniya has sent Kass was German once, then Irish and Quebecois, now Russian; always the newest, the poorest people live there. The houses are decrepit, the street narrow and foul-smelling. Kass finds the number, knocks at the door, whispers the password, adds *"Ya Kseniyi podruga. Ubiraytes' otsyuda! Vas politsiya ishchet!"*

A man's voice behind the door pours out an incomprehensible torrent of Russian. She shakes her head, wishing she knew how to say she doesn't understand. *"Nyet. Ubiraytes' otsyuda!"*

The door opens. The man behind it is thin, bearded, threadbare—he'd pass for a cartoon Bolshevik except he clutches a notebook, not a bomb. He asks something else in Russian. She repeats that they have to go now, that the police are coming; fishes out her locket, dumps clover into his hand, says *"Die Warheit wird euch frei machen."* This man doesn't know the language, he might not recognize the verse anyway, but he stares into her eyes and it seems he recognizes the truth of what she's saying. She doesn't know if that's enough to keep him free.

He blinks, leads her to a back door. Shouts up the back stairs. Holds the door open. She goes. Others follow her. She turns the way most of them don't turn. She hears a police whistle. A crash. Voices, all English. Someone grabs her shoulder.

"Where are you off to in such a hurry?"

"Ich gehe nach Hause."

"This one's foreign," the man calls.

"German, not Russian. Let her go," another man's voice answers.

"There are German Bolshies."

The other speaker comes over, frowns down at her. It's Georg Beiler. Kass locks her knees to keep herself from falling as her nightmare eddies around her.

"Not her," Georg says. "I know her from church."

"What's she doing here, then?'

"I...don't know," she says. "I...heard something, I was afraid, I got lost. I want to go...home." She makes her English slow and accented. There may be safety in being a slow, stupid, sick girl.

"Ach, let her go, David," Georg says. "She's... Her nerves. It runs in the family. Anyway, she was born here, and we're not looking for citizens tonight."

"Go home, then," David tells her. Another police whistle sounds nearby.

"I'll take her back," Georg says. "By streetcar. I can vouch for her since I have a Legion badge."

David shrugs, lets them go. Kass prepares to avoid Georg's questions, is grateful when he doesn't ask them.

Her stop, finally. Georg gets off with her.

"*Danke*," she says.

"*Danke*," he answers softly.

"For what?'

He turns his head away. She can't see what he remembers, but she feels the shame of it, the gratitude that, this time, he has not…

"I wish you had been home when they came for Pastor Baum," Kass says.

"Ah yes." Georg's voice hardens. "Our sainted Herr Pastor, who preached that if Stefan and I died it would be God's punishment for our joining the army instead of keeping our hands clean like him and Christoph Geist. I suppose he thinks Stefan's being punished now."

"Oh no, surely…" Kass begins, but she is not quite sure, and before she can straighten her thoughts out Georg is gone.

January 25, 1920

Kass hurries to church early. She has told her father she needs some quiet time there to pray. That's not exactly a lie.

On Thursday and Friday the newspapers lauded the Palmer Raids for apprehending thousands of Bolsheviks across the country and preventing murder, arson and rapine. On Saturday the local police and the Legion marched their prisoners down the main street to the train station to stand trial in another city. Kass and Kseniya stood on the sidewalk, shaking with anger and cold, while the man who had let Kass in limped past with one arm in a sling and the other handcuffed to Galya, who looked uninjured but dirty and afraid. She didn't meet their eyes. Galya! Kseniya learned about her arrest late Tuesday night and told Kass all about it on Wednesday. Galya stopped to buy food on the way home, was still walking when the Legionnaires began banging on doors. She heard them speaking English to someone who spoke only Russian in return, so she ran up to them and started to translate.

"And they thought that made her Communist?"

"She was Russian. She was not citizen. For what else did they want? You maybe can talk them sweet, they let you go, such a good American citizen."

Kass hung her head.

Kseniya sighed. "Not your fault. You warned me. I warned not Galya. I saw not the need."

~ * ~

No one is in the sanctuary when Kass enters. She hurries along the pews, setting a four-leaf clover at either end of each. She has just enough for that. She's spent plenty of summer Sunday afternoons hunting through the clover on the Common, picking and pressing any four-leaf stems she finds, partly as a talisman, partly because it's better than looking around and wondering who will be willing to walk or talk with her. She had another piece to put in her locket after warning Kseniya's friends; she's brought all the rest to church today. If anyone comes in and asks her why, she plans to repeat what Frau Geist told her when she noticed what Kass was collecting: "Ah yes, four-leaf clover, the living sign of the Cross." But she doesn't have to tell anyone. By the time the organist arrives, Kass is sitting demurely at the end of her pew, praying.

Pastor Bower reads the Old Testament warnings to the Israelites against aliens and their detestable foreign practices. He describes the threat to decent home life and godliness posed by Bolsheviks and anarchists. He points out the dirtiness and cringing demeanour of the prisoners they saw yesterday.

Kass clutches her locket and rises. "Whose fault is that?" she asks in German. Heads turn toward her, people make shushing noises. She doesn't shush. She slips out of the pew, out of her father's reach. "Galya, my friend who worked with me, was one of the prisoners. She never looked like that when we worked together. How can she be clean if they don't let her wash? How can she not be afraid if they hurt her friends, if they won't let her go? Why is the wrong one always ashamed? Pastor Baum was ashamed when they stripped him, and they laughed, but they were the ones who should have been ashamed. I was ashamed when they threw filth at me and called me crazy, but who should have been ashamed? During the war, when they all threw filth on us, should we have been ashamed? I say we should be ashamed now, if we throw filth on other people!'"

The words are not right. She has to make them see...

She sees the crack in the air again, feels her own urgency echoed in another mind. Pastor Bower also is trying to make his people see, trying to protect them from the Reds and from those members of the Legion who still hold the war against them. He has laboured so hard to build a small safe place for his people, to act in a way that will reassure the world. *Narrow is the gate.* Everywhere outside the beast-men prowl *the outer darkness, where there is weeping and gnashing of teeth.* There is no room inside for Galya, for Kseriya, for Pastor Baum...or, perhaps, for Kass. But Kass already knows there is no safety anywhere.

"We want to be safe, we all want to be safe," she says. "I wanted this when my hands were cracked from washing, when I tore my clothes because they were soiled. The men who came for Pastor Baum were afraid, they wanted to be safe, they wanted their sons to be safe. Now you want to be safe, and you only make more sickness, more danger. If you could see..." She gropes for words and, like her grandmother, grasps at the Word to say what she can't: "*Wenn du, ja du, an diesem Tag die Dinge erkannt hättest, die mit Frieden zu tun haben—doch nun...*" "O that at this time thou hadst known—yes, even thou—the things which are for thy peace! But now..."

The organ launches into a thunderous anthem. No one can hear her. Her father takes her arm, pleads with her to come home, to lie down. "No," she protests. "It's not my sickness talking now, it's knowledge of sickness, that's different."

But she doesn't have the words to give the knowledge to anyone else. She turns away, lets her father guide her toward the door.

Steps follow her. She turns back to see who's come out with her. Minnie, of course. The Geists. And Georg.

"What you said was true," he says, low and gruff, opening his hand to show the four-leaf clover.

ARE YOU THERE?

This story is being published for the first time in this book.

When Serla was a child she lived in a small village in the edge of the wild hill-country, and she loved the One as she loved her mother Lia and the light of the sun. On Dancing Days when she leaped and whirled with her neighbors on the village green, on Remembrance Nights when she stood silent beside them on the dark hilltop clutching a beeswax taper in her cold hands, she felt a warmth about her heart and heard a sound behind her like the beating of great wings. She never turned to look. She never needed to. Even on the Crying Days, when her neighbors stood up and pleaded with the heavens for what they needed, or lay facedown and whispered their pleas for the One to hear and heal, the warmth and the wings were there, and she knew that what was needed would be given.

She still believed that when she turned sixteen in the summer of the drought. The sun beat down from a sky of molten blue. The grain grew sparse and short, and then stopped growing altogether. The pastures burned brown and the goats cried.

On Midsummer's Day the first well ran dry. A month later the only well that still yielded water (though it came slow and muddy) belonged to Serla's neighbor Luca. Luca kept that to water the healing herbs in her garden—a reservation her neighbors resented. Still, they didn't complain too much, as Luca carried water from the spring in the valley to neighbors too old or sick to fetch their own. When the fevers began, when sufferers turned hot and parched as the land, people were grateful for Luca's medicines and most of them stopped muttering.

Serla didn't get the fever and she didn't mutter. She wasn't afraid of the drought. It was a trial, she thought, like the old ones in the holy stories. If they didn't complain, if they prayed, if they trusted, the rains would come in time—or, if they did not come, the One would open the heavens and pour grain down on them. She prayed early and late, to make up for her neighbors' complaining, and sometimes as she prayed she heard the wings behind her and she smiled.

But it was neither rain nor grain that poured from heaven in the middle of the night five weeks past midsummer. Serla woke to a roaring so vast and continuous she did not recognize it as thunder. Lia seized her daughter's shoulder, thrust her toward the door, and shouted at her to hurry straight to the cave by the spring. Serla stumbled across the threshold of her house into a hard pulsing radiance blinding as utter darkness.

Her feet still knew the way. She ran, closing her eyes against the lightning-flashes. When she felt the warmth at her back and heard a roaring that wasn't the sound of thunder, Serla thought the One had come in a blaze of glory. For once in her life she turned to look.

The blaze came from the thatched roof of a house. Someone was screaming inside, calling for the One to save her. Serla stood staring.

Lia pushed her away and shouted at her. She had never handled her daughter so roughly before. Serla ran, more from her mother's anger than from the blaze. When she stopped and looked back again the blaze had spread, and it was a neighbor, not her mother, who pushed her ahead.

Serla was among the fortunate ones who reached the shelter of the caves. She willed herself to sing prayers with the others, but the warmth about her heart had become a painful heat that dried her mouth. She couldn't make a sound. She stared at the faces around her, trying not to believe that her mother was not there. Finally she shook herself like a dog coming out of water, crawled through the tunnel to the open air and ran up the hill.

Someone—Serla never looked over her shoulder to see who —caught her arms and held her. She heard that person's breathing at her back, a ragged human sound that she could not mistake for wings. She struggled briefly, then stood still, staring back uphill at the flames until at last the rain fell straight and hard, quenching the light and turning the ashes to hot grey mud.

Serla found her mother the next morning. Alive, still alive— "Praise be to the One," said Luca, who had pulled her out of the burning rubble and dragged her into the little shelter afforded by a leaning stone wall. Lia couldn't say anything. The fire had turned her face to a red blistered mask, had taken her voice.

Serla also kept silent for a whole moon-change while the survivors replanted the ashfields that had once been grainfields, while they ate scanty meals once a day, while a little expedition set off on the week's journey to the next village, carrying what valuables they had left, and returned with what might possibly be enough food to keep everyone alive on short rations until the next harvest, while Lia's breathing grew harsher.

When Lia died, Serla left the village in the middle of the night and climbed into the wild hill-country, following the directions in an old tale Lia used to tell about the spring where faithful seekers might see true visions from the One. Serla didn't know if she believed that. She'd believed all the tales of the One, once. But she found the path at noon on the first day and kept walking up and up, the bones of the hills growing rougher under her feet, the stars growing closer.

The hut of the hermit who kept the spring was where the stories said it was, in a hollow just below the treeline, shadowy in the dawn. The hermit, a middle-aged woman with a strong blunt-featured face, gave Serla bread and berries and told her how to find the spring.

Serla climbed up out of the trees. The sun shone on her shoulders. Inside her was a coldness the sun couldn't touch.

The spring lay open to the sky, cupped in a rough granite bowl. One place on the lip of that bowl had been worn smooth by the knees of pilgrims. Serla knelt there, closed her eyes, thought desperately, *Are you there?*

She knelt there for a long time with her eyes tight shut, while the stones grew warm with sunlight, while the wind keened at her back. She had not understood how much she feared the answer. She opened her eyes when she was sure that the fear was worse than any answer could be.

The surface of the spring was smooth, untroubled by the wind. It reflected a glory of light, and amidst the glory a face. A girl's face, copper-colored, sharp-featured, with fierce eyes and trembling lips. After a moment Serla knew the face for hers.

"There's nothing here to see," she said aloud in a flat dead voice.

The glory in the mirrored sky began to fade, but for a moment the reflected figure's eyes shone with a lovely and terrible light. Then they were dark and troubled again. Serla looked deep into them and read another answer there.

Her neighbors that night, screaming for the One to save them …She had heard them and hurried away, trapped in her own terror. She had not tried to pull anyone free from the burning houses. She had passed them by. The One had passed them by. She had…she had…

All those Crying Days she had joined her voice to the chorus of petition, thinking no more was needed. But if this reflection told the truth, if she was the One…

She rose abruptly and descended back into the trees, not stopping at the hermit's house.

It had taken her two days to reach the spring of vision, going by the straightest road. It took her four days to come back to the house that had been hers, but she came with hazelnuts bundled into her shawl and her underskirt. She found Luca in the dooryard, praying for her safe return, and she smiled a little at how easy it was to grant the first petition she had heard after understanding who she was meant to be.

When Luca had left off hugging Serla and scolding her for leaving without a word to anyone, Serla explained that there were more nuts in the hazel copse about a day's journey away, and blackberries in the glade to the south cleared by an old burning, and trout resting in a pool a way upstream…Before sundown Luca's nephew Hento went with two other men to catch the trout, and Luca's niece Aniela went with some other women after berries and nuts, praising the One. Luca couldn't go herself—she had too many sick to tend. Serla couldn't go either. Whether she was the One or no, she sorely needed sleep. But in the days that followed she went often with the foraging parties, and sometimes she made expeditions of her own.

She was always in the village on the Crying Days. She did not join the petitioners' chorus, but she listened hard. She learned to read the faces of the petitioners, to lie down near those who looked most desperate and hear the secret words they sobbed into the earth. Often she could do nothing but weep for them. "Let my child live!" they cried, and "Forgive me!"

Sometimes she could help. After Arsha with her haunted eyes whispered into the ground about her nightmares, Serla crouched outside the wattle-and-daub wall of Arsha's cottage in the first grey light and sang sleep-songs in a voice just above a whisper. That morning Arsha had a new light in her eyes. On the next Crying Day Luca whispered, "I am too tred to go on..." Serla hadn't Luca's comforting way with the sick, couldn't take her place there. But she began to scout for healing herbs, which she left on Luca's doorstep in the middle of the night. "A gift from the One," she heard Luca telling one of her sick, "and a mercy for you and for me." That was the first time after the fire that Serla smiled. Later, alone in the woods, she wept.

Twelve years passed. The rains came again in their season, and the villagers' faces grew round again, the skin no longer pulled tight over their bones. Serla was still sharp-faced with fatigue and loneliness and the burden of their needs. But she walked straight and tall, and she took some satisfaction in learning to be a better providence.

Then the plague came. Luca didn't recognize it in her patient until the first sore broke, filling the house with its putrid smell and its contagion. Luca shut the doors of her house to keep the sickness in, shouted at Serla through the door, telling her to keep clear. But she also told Serla to spread the word that other plague victims could come to Luca's house and she'd tend them as well as she could.

Serla gave the message once she had control of her face and voice. Some people said Luca was a holy woman, a gift from the One. Others made the sign against evil and asked the One to shield them from ever needing to shelter in a plague-house. Aniela wept. Serla thought approvingly, *She loves her aunt,* and desperately, *whom I can't save*...But then Aniela protested, "In three weeks' time she could be clean of the plague if she doesn't take more people in, and my baby's coming in six weeks, and she promised she'd help me!"

"Other people will need her more," Serla said, biting her tongue too late and hoping her words wouldn't make it true.

"But they're not her kin," Aniela wailed. Serla walked away.

Every day after that Serla brought vegetables from her own garden, apples from Aniela's orchard, eggs from Hento's chickens, and grain from the village field to Luca's door. She pumped water from Luca's well into pails and kettles which she left under the window. She brought willow bark from the trees by the stream to ease pain and swelling. Garlic to fight infection and roses to soothe sores grew in Luca's garden, and in others, where Serla begged or traded for all the householders would spare. Soon there was no garlic to be had for love or money—though at the far end of the village Beta had a fine crop of garlic which she swore she'd keep for her healthy family, to keep the plague from catching hold of them. Serla explained this to Luca, standing a foot from the wall and speaking loudly. "Don't fret," Luca said from inside. "I'll have what I need. In the worst of the drought year, when I hadn't the strength to tend my patients and gather medicines, the One left me what I needed."

Serla winced at the pleasure she'd taken in hearing Luca call her gift a miracle. What a child she had been. What a foolish, self-satisfied child. She hardly noticed Luca's last discouraged words: "I doubt the garlic will help the ones who are sick enough to come here, anyway."

That night Serla lingered outside Luca's house and listened to the sick ones moaning in fever-dreams or in waking pain. She would have wept had her eyes not been dry stones. In the gray hour before dawn she stole barefoot to Beta's garden, found the garlic plants by their scent, and began to pull them.

By the time she heard the dog snarling it was too late to run. She pulled the carrying pole out from her panniers of garlic and lashed it across the dog's muzzle. The dog yelped and fled. Serla bent to pick up her half-full pannier, heard feet running up behind her. *The dog again,* she thought, *a vicious brute working for a selfish woman.* She struck out with the full force of her anger and her fear.

The sun slipped over the horizon, and the light brightened around them, showing Beta lying on her side, a bloody wound behind her ear. Serla gasped, bent over her. Beta still breathed, heavily, strangely. Serla remembered her mother breathing like that after the fire. The dog whined, and a voice called from the house. Serla rose and fled.

~ * ~

The woods was full of birdsong and the smell of berries. Serla's mind was full of shadows. She had heard the stories of the wrath and righteous judgment of the One. She trusted her own judgment not at all.

I should turn back, she told herself. *Someone must carry water from the spring, someone must bring food for the sick...*

And I can do neither if I'm killed for killing Beta, she thought. But that was an excuse. The truth, which rose in her mind as slowly and painfully as the blisters rose on her bare feet, was that she had run out of care for her neighbors and out of trust for herself.

She passed the hermit's house by without stopping. She wanted to meet no one.

She didn't get what she wanted. The hermit, a blunt-faced aging woman with piercing eyes, met her not far from the spring. An older, frailer woman clung to the hermit's arm for support.

"She's seen what she needed to see," the hermit said. "It's your turn now."

Serla stumbled across the rough rock to the spring, thinking of the moaning from the plague-house, thinking of Beta's breathing. She closed her eyes, knelt over the spring. She kept her eyes closed for a long time, fearing to look into the water and see a monster's face.

Hearing sounds behind, her she bit her lip and opened her eyes. She saw a deep blue sky brushed with wisps of white cloud, a bird passing over high and fast, and two human faces. Her own face was still human, not monstrous, though it was slack with exhaustion and thin with long fretting, her skin stretched tight over her bones. Her neighbors had looked like that in the drought year. They did not look like that now. (Those who had the plague, of course, looked worse…) The hermit's face was broad and quiet. Her eyes looked straight into the reflection of Serla's eyes. The reflecting pool held all their images framed in one great eye. All one.

Serla took the hermit's arm to pull herself up, for her knees were locked and her muscles stiff. She followed the hermit home to her cottage, slept long and deeply on a pile of fern in the corner. Late the next morning she set off for home with a large bundle of garlic in the pack on her back.

~ * ~

Serla came down to the village by way of the burial ground, saw two men digging.

"Is Beta dead?"

"Not that I've heard," the taller man said. He was Avro, Luca's cousin, and father to the second child who'd died in the plague. "But the plague's taken six more. And Aniela's baby was born dead."

Serla bit her lip, looked down. She'd never told Luca what Aniela had said. But if Luca had been there, would it really have made a difference?

"Aniela's not dying," Avro offered by way of reassurance. "And what's this you've brought? Garlic? Luca'll be glad of that, but I doubt it'll save anyone. It's not garlic we need now, but a miracle."

"I doubt there'll be any miracle but what we make," Serla said. "But how has Luca kept? Did no one bring water and…"

"Be easy, you're not the only one with strong arms and a heart. We left that to you while you seemed set on doing everything yourself, but when you went away…"

Serla sat down abruptly and cried. Avro patted her shoulder and went back to digging. In a little while Serla stood and carried her bundle down the hill.

~ * ~

The next moon-change was hot and miserable. The clearing filled with graves, and there were more plague-houses. Beta's was one of those. When the garlic was gone Serla scavenged for witch-hazel, and when that was gone there was nothing to do but ease the dying, though indeed the dying didn't go very much faster once the medicine was gone. It was a bitter time, but there was also a sweetness in it for Serla that she was almost ashamed to acknowledge, for she bore the bitterness with her neighbors instead of trying to bear it for them.

Then the wind veered to the north, the weather broke, and the plague burned itself out. Two moon-changes after Serla's return from the spring Luca opened her door and walked out to meet her neighbors. Her face was scarred and thin, her eyes hollow, but she lived. She went to Serla first and held her tight. Serla relaxed into her embrace, let herself be held up instead of doing the holding up. When she finally let go she saw Aniela, who had hurried toward her favorite aunt, looking at them with strange eyes.

The years wheeled by, the plague-scars on the faces of survivors faded, and the burial ground burgeoned with wildflowers. Serla still went to the Crying Days, still listened to her neighbors' needs, but she danced with them as well, and the tightness left her face and her heart. As Luca grew slower and weaker she taught Serla all she knew of healing, of tincturing and poulticing and bonesetting, and of the steadiness that eased either life or death for the sufferer. In the evenings they sat together in Luca's flower garden and watched the sun go down. They didn't talk much of their own lives; Luca's kindness and her interest were all poured into her work, and that meant Serla didn't have to pass on the questions that pained her, or conceal them either. Sometimes Luca sang in the evening, love-songs, planting-songs, brewing-songs, and chants to the One. Serla did not sing.

But when Serla stood in a circle with her neighbors around Luca's grave, when they sang the song giving back her body to the earth and her breath to the wind and her soul to the One, Serla sang too, and for her comfort reminded herself of how the pool had held together all the things that had seemed separate. *She is still part of the One,* Serla told herself. *We are all one.*

She held that thought to her heart, trying to warm herself, as she walked back by Luca's house. Walked by, and then stopped, for Hento and Aniela stood in Luca's garden arguing.

"It's mine!" Aniela said with a sweeping gesture that took in the house and garden. "My mother was older than your father."

"But the son inherits before the daughter, so my father..."

"But Aunt Luca always loved me better than you. I was like another daughter to her. She said so. I was always at her house. You remember. Everyone remembers. She loved me."

"When you were a child, sure," Hento said. "But you've been cold enough to her since the plague year, when you never helped her..."

"Well, how should I have? I was half dead after losing the child —and I wouldn't have lost him if she'd come to me, if she'd—" Aniela stopped abruptly, swallowed hard.

"If she'd loved you like a daughter," Hento finished.

"I took care of her in the plague year," Serla said, the warmth about her heart kindled to a blaze. "Then and ever after. And she taught me all she knew."

"And you think you should get her house as well as her teaching? That everything's yours?"

"I already have a house," Serla pointed out. "As you do. But the garden...I know what to do with the plants there..."

"So do I," Hento and Aniela said at once. "And, more to the point, the well's in the garden," Hento added.

So it was: Luca's well, that had lasted the longest in the drought year. Even in a good year the water there was uncommonly sweet, and some said the water made as much difference as the herbs in Luca's draughts…

"Surely there's water enough in the well for anyone who wants it," Serla said. "We've had rain enough this season."

"Oh yes, this season," Aniela said. "And next year if there's drought and you've already staked your claim it will be too late."

Serla grabbed Aniela's shoulder. She was too angry to speak.

"Plan to half kill her, the way you did Beta?" Hento inquired blandly.

Serla froze. Let go of Aniela. Walked away, thinking, *I am not one with them, I am not vile and grasping like that,* and *It wasn't really my fault about Beta, and anyway she got better…*

The council of elders heard the dispute between Hento and Aniela—Serla made no claim, and made sure she was away from the village on the hearing day—and gave house, garden and well to Aniela.

Two weeks later Aniela's son heard something scrabbling at the back wall in the night. He went out and found no one there, but in the dawn light he saw a crow's foot tied up with a bundle of black locust leaves—an ill-wish if ever there was one.

The morning after that Hento's dog was found with its throat cut.

The night after that Serla's dreams were evil. She tried songs, chants, and the soothing herbs that grew in her own garden. But the lavender bush was at Luca's house—no, Aniela's house.

Lavender, lavender. If only she could smell it, she could sleep peacefully. She was sure of that. Almost sure. She pulled her cloak around her and stole barefoot through the dark toward Luca's house, approaching from the back, from the woods.

She smelled smoke not lavender, came out from under the trees at a run, and collided with Hento. His clothes smelled of smoke and his breathing came quick and ragged. Behind him she heard a woman scream. Half mazed with dreams as she was, Serla almost believed it was her mother. "Murderer!" she hissed at Hento. She threw herself at him, knocked him down. Had her hands round his throat when she heard the woman screaming closer at hand, screaming what she had screamed: "Murderer!" Screaming at Serla.

Serla recoiled as though her hands were burning, fled into the woods.

"Where do you think you're going?" Aniela shouted after her.

"To the hermit," Serla answered, fearing that if she didn't answer Aniela would follow, and she was too tired to think of a lie. "To the spring."

~ * ~

Her bare feet were bloody again when she came to the treeline. The hermit, a frail old woman with quiet eyes, came to the door, reached out to take Serla's hand. Serla pulled away. People were separate, not one. and when they touched each other they shattered like rotten ice. Serla was done with touching. "I know the way," she said.

Serla limped to the spring. She didn't close her eyes. The spring had shown her nothing but lies, she told herself, but she could imagine few lies that would be worse than the truth. Silently cursing herself for a fool, she lowered herself to her knees and whispered aloud, "Are you there?"

The sky in the reflecting pool was sea-green at the edges, deep blue at the top, and across that dark cap stars were strewn like dandelion seeds. The shadow of Serla's head was hardly noticeable in all that beauty.

She sat watching all night while the sea-green faded to blue-black and the stars thickened, while the grey dawn-light sapped the stars, while the grey turned to a flood of molten gold.

In the depths of the pool something that was not a reflection stirred and glowed. Serla's eyes shone with an answering brightness. There was something in there after all. Something beyond. Something so beautiful…She felt a warmth about her heart, and behind her she heard a noise of wings.

~ * ~

The next morning Aniela and Hento knocked on the hermit's door. They fidgeted and looked at their feet.

"We're looking for our neighbor, Serla. She has a sharp face and a birthmark on her cheek. She said she was coming this way, and we need to tell her…"

"That nobody takes her for a murderer now," Hento said.

"It was a misunderstanding," Aniela said. "Hento and I were

arguing and he knocked the candle over, and it caught in the straw in the corner, and then in the thatch of the roof, and we both ran, but he ran faster, and she must have thought…and I saw her and I thought…anyway, she's all right, we're all right." She looked up at the woman in the doorway. Swallowed hard. "Serla?" she said. "I'm sorry, I thought you were the hermit."

"I am. The old woman said she had something to say to the people back in her village, but she didn't want to leave the spring untended."

"When she comes back, will you come home?"

"Home?" Serla said. "That's here, or nowhere, I think. I know so little, but I know that much." She smiled at them, the sudden bright smile she'd had as a child. "Do you want to look in the spring before you go?"

THE WAY OUT

This story was originally published in Forge *magazine in 2013.*

Mum and Dad are arguing again downstairs. They think I'm asleep. I can't sleep. I wriggle down under the blankets and put my pillow over my head and hug the doll Mum made me, but I can still hear. I won't call for them. I don't want them to come into my room with their downstairs nighttime voices.

There are other sounds downstairs. They aren't very loud, I can just barely hear them, but they're nasty. I can imagine the things that make those sounds—slimy shapeless blobs dragging themselves around. But those are downstairs things. They won't come upstairs. They won't. That noise wasn't from my door, it was from downstairs, all the way down, it just sounded funny because of this pillow over my head…

I uncover my head, cup my hands together and hold them up so my soul can come back from listening at the door and land in them. I can't see it in the dark, but I know what it must look like. Not a big white bird like the Holy Spirit in my Bible with the pictures. A sparrow, dusty brown and small but old enough to fly.

I put my hands over my ear, let the bird fly into my head, away from the dark and the sound of their voices, toward the safe places I made in my mind. I fly in and in until I can feel the wind thrumming under my wings and see the green slope of the place with the horses.

Here come the horses down over the hill, black and brown and gray and golden, long tails streaming behind them. I can smell their sweat as they run under me. When I used to come here as a girl I sat on their backs to ride them. It was hard getting up, but once I was up I never fell off, even when we went like the wind through long grass swishing against my legs. Now I don't have to climb, I just flutter down and grip the lead mare's tossing black mane with my bird feet. I don't weigh anything. I don't slow her down as she gallops away.

But the clean sweat-smell is changing, turning sour, and there are little jerks in the rhythm of her feet. She's turning, they're all turning, galloping back up the hill, and now she's in back. The river has turned brown and thick and oozy and started to swell up out of its banks, up and up and up. It did that when I came here as a girl the night after Aunt Louise died. I almost drowned that night, woke up choking. That's why I stay a bird now. I let go of the horse's mane, fly up and up, higher than the water, higher than the hill. The blue sky is graying, roughening, falling like a roof...

There. There's always a crack, a place I can fly out through if I see it in time. This time it was trying to trick me; it looked almost like a bar of cloud, but it isn't thick cement gray like the other clouds. I can see through it to another place where the flood can't come.

~ * ~

Golden grainfields all around, and the castle ahead. I fly over the moat and past the guard-house and nobody challenges me. When I was a girl they let me in. I was brave with them. I had a horse and a sword and sharp eyes to spot danger coming. But the night after the day I stepped on Jessamyn's turtle and it died—that was an accident, really it was, I was running and I didn't see it—I tried to go back to the castle but I wasn't brave. I was just me, and I didn't know how to help, and I didn't know what to do when they looked at me. So now I come as a bird, so they don't notice me except if I warn them that I've seen enemies coming. I keep my human voice for that. I always warn them in time, and the draw-bridge comes up, and the portcullis goes down, and we are safe. This time I didn't see enemies, and the drawbridge is down, and in the hall the bard is singing about the bird that warned the watch-men, and the Queen and her ladies are listening, and out in the garden the servants are laughing.

But the laughing is getting thinner, higher, it isn't right. I fly down from the back of the Queen's chair shouting "Danger! Danger!" Only this time I can't find my human voice, just a bird's voice, jay-shrill. A lady hits at me with her fan. Her fingers are turning into claws—they are claws. And her eyes... Sometimes the enemies had eyes like that. I fly up above her head, flap in circles, try to make them look at her and see the danger.

They look. They look with terrible eyes like hers, eyes that try to suck me down into a dark place with no air. I fly up toward the high window that always stands open to let the sea-wind in. The shutters are closing over it. I pump my wings until they hurt, and I squeeze through the crack between the window-frame and the shutter just in time, into another place, the place where they're dancing.

~ * ~

They're all here: Lindy, who moved away, and Jessamyn, who got run over by a car, and Uncle John, who can't dance in the day because of his polio, and Uncle George, who doesn't talk to people in our family any more, and Aunt Louise and Great-Grammie Julia who both died last summer...all dancing, together, higher and higher and faster and faster, never getting tired, dancing on the grass in the sun, dancing under the bright new leaves on the beech trees. Now they're starting the petronilla, everyone spinning one place over. Uncle John is next to Jessamyn, laughing.

Uncle John spins left just as Jessamyn spins right, and they hit each other, they fall down, and Grammie trips over them, and she falls. Everybody falls, and when they get back up they don't dance. They squinch their eyes up and say *What did I expect, after what you did last time?* and *Just get out of my sight.*

The music sort of shakes and stops, and I can hear the sound the slimy shapeless blobs make, coming closer and closer.

I look up. High in the sky floats another cloud that's not a cloud. I could get out through it to another place, and from that place into another...

I look down. The blobs are getting closer. Behind them grass and trees crumple into slime, into nothing. The people on the grass don't notice the blobs yet. They can't get up into the sky, they can't get away. I can't leave them. The blobs aren't coming after them. They're coming after me.

I fly down, down, closer and closer to the growing pulsing blobs. They don't have any eyes, but they see me. I don't like them seeing me. I keep flying toward them.

Now I can see pictures flashing in their slimy sides. Jessamyn crying about her turtle when it died. Me crying too so people would know it wasn't my fault. Leola crying about Jessamyn when she died. The people at Aunt Louise's funeral, looking at each other, muttering, thinking whose fault it was. Mum looking the way she looks when someone disappoints her, her lips tight together, not saying anything.

The last picture is me alone in the dark, scrunched up on my bed with my eyes shut and my hands over my ear.

I fly into the picture. The dark fills my eyes and my beak like slime. But I keep pumping my wings, and the dark pulls back a little, and I let my soul spread out to fill up my human body. Behind my eyes I can still see the pictures the blobs carried. But I can see the other true pictures too. Me flying kites with Jessamyn, the kites pulling and twirling in the wind, both of us laughing. Mum and Aunt Louise singing "My Anchor Holds" in harmony. Me picking raspberries with Mum, getting the whole patch picked just before the thunderstorm hits. Mum teaching me to swim, holding onto me in the water, telling me over and over I can put my face down and pick my feet up, I won't sink, I won't drown. Me not drowning, diving down into the swirls of light and dark in the water, coming up laughing.

I open my eyes and uncover my ears. They're still arguing downstairs. Outside the window the crescent moon shines and the peeping frogs sing. I hum along with them. I hum "My Anchor Holds."

WHEN THE BRIGHT BIRDS COME

This story is being published for the first time in this book

Dilys:

Twilight at the burial ground. Murmurs, prayers of relief, as the dead are set like seeds in their furrows. *Only seven killed today, and all men. The fighting's far from our walls, praise the Lady's mercy, praise her.* Said loud and bright by the Lady's faithful fearless ones. Muttered quick and shamed by us cowards guiltily grateful for one more day above the earth. Said very loud by the fearfully faithful trying to drown out any mourners or doubters who might anger the Lady and cause her to abandon us. (What do they think would happen if she did that? The village burned again, the women scavenging rags enough to cover the bruises, the bleeding, the... No, not that. The last time that happened they said the Lady was with us still. No, they fear something worse. They think she'd take the birds away. Could she take the birds away? What would happen if she did? I mustn't think like that, or she might take them away.)

The furrows filled, tamped down, the good words said. The crowd sighing soft and longing. They're coming, the mercies, the birds. Feathered with starlight and shadow, their long bills open wide, their sleek throats swelled with song.

The aching harmonies wash over me. I can never remember the notes when the birds are gone, any more than I can remember the look of the birds, though I can't forget the beauty of either. But now, now!

The people shift like leaves under wind, shimmer like water under light. Dancing, then stilled by the trance the birds bring. The birds that wake the dead and lull the living to sleep... (How is it that I'm still awake, watching my neighbors in their trance? Has the Lady rejected me, or have I...?)

Now I can see what my neighbors see. Silver shoots rise from the new-sown ground. The dead, their faces fairer and their eyes clearer than they ever were in life, lift their hands toward us, blessing us. Graceful as dancers they are, graceful as birds, even Rhys who moved in jerks because of his stiff old bones (and he never smiled like that, and would have called anyone that did a dafty… *That's not Rhys. I shouldn't think such things. But that's never Rhys.*) As the good words we said at the dead-planting promised, they bow, they turn away from us toward something beautiful that we can't see, they lift their swords and run toward that unseen beauty, swifter than leaping stags. So fair. So brave. (*But that was never Rhys.*)

The music echoes, eddies as it fades. O beautiful…

Slowly the people stir from trance. It lingers longest on the kin of the new-sown dead (of poor Goronwy, who was too simple to fight, or so they said until there weren't enough hale men left for the levy; of Rhys, who was not Rhys when he rose; of Cadoc, and who's to feed his five children? But see how bright the children's eyes are now…) and on the new-called young who will take their places in the fighting tomorrow. (Arvel—Lady's mercy, he's only twelve, but he heard the call and he can't be stopped, it would be a sin against the Lady, so the deadspeakers tell us. Davydd—once at noonday, far away from the birdsong, he told me he hated the war, said he wouldn't go. See how he smiles now. Something is wrong. Something is terribly wrong.)

Mari:

Awake. I'm awake now. It was only a dream. A dream. I can breathe. There are no explosions. No choking smoke. No poison in the air. I can rest. I don't have to run. They are not coming. Not now—not that I know. Maybe not now.

But the screaming is still going on.

That blank-eyed woman who came in yesterday is screaming. Dreaming too, surely. I should wake her. Comfort her.

I'd have to touch her first. What if her nightmare seizes me?

Only a lunatic would think such a thing. Nightmares aren't contagious.

We're all insane. How can we not be? When was the last week without killing, the last season without hunger, the last day when we had heart to sing, the last night of untroubled sleep?

I remember my mother singing to me when I was small. Surely I do. Surely it wasn't a dream. She died so long ago, and there was so little time…

The woman's still screaming. I should go to her.

No need. Her man's there, waking her, soothing her.

She's stopped screaming, started crooning her son's name. Well, he's dead, right enough, if what her sister said is true; she can't wake from that. Can't forget how he died. Can't… She's pushing her man away. He sighs, goes back to his place, muttering in the dark: "They will pay."

They will, and we will, until there's nothing left. We are all mad with grief, pain, exhaustion, and there is no healing. What can we do but attack each other?

My mother told me a story once—unless that was a dream too. A tale of the birds of Rhiannon who raised the dead and soothed the living to sleep with the beauty of their songs. That's what we need. Sleep, music, beauty. But they don't exist.

Dilys:

Seven days ago when the new recruits went out early in the morning, the twilight serenity vanished like the twilight music, I caught Davydd's arm and asked him if he truly willed to go. He looked at me with stark fear, and then he looked away. Arvel, on his other side, still smiled as though he heard an echo of the birdsong.

Tonight they are laying Arvel in the ground. Beside me Davydd leans hard on his crutch, taking harsh laboring breaths through his broken mouth, stinking with fear-sweat. He does not speak the good words over Arvel, over all the others. Neither do I. He has excuse—his words blur and stumble, he might say them wrong, and what would follow? And I: my mouth holds its right shape, but if I open it now the words that come out will scald.

They're here, the birds. The aching harmonies weave around me again. But I can still hear Davydd's harsh breathing. He can't hear that, or any mortal sound, after the hurt to his head. He stares at our lips, turns away in frustration. Thanks be to the Lady, he can read, at least; when I scrawl in the dirt he stares, nods, answers as best he can.

Seems he can't hear the birds either. I was halfway into trance when he stumbled and caught my shoulder. With his hands on me I heard his breathing louder than the music, and I looked at him, and I'm still looking. The ruin of his face is hard to read, but I see no bliss there. And when Arvel rises, smiling, and blesses us, the eyes of the tranced ones follow him, but Davydd's good eye is still fixed on the ground.

He's trying to say something. His voice is low, but if I keep my eyes and mind fixed on his face I can make out the words through the music. "Come away," he says.

I want to, I do, but I can't tear all the way free of the music, can't follow him, except with my eyes, as he lurches down the hill alone. The tranced ones around me don't even do that much. Is it that they can't see him, or that they don't allow themselves to look? The music pulls at me like the suck of ebbtide around a wader's legs, but I keep my eyes on him.

In the grey morning Davydd and I return to the burial ground, where no one will interrupt us; our people don't care to be left with our dead when the music is gone.

Davydd is still hard to understand. Slowly the words take shape through the blurring fog of sounds. "Why didn't they rise?"

"Who?" I write.

He points to the newest furrow, where Arvel lay.

"They did," I write. "I saw."

"No," he says. "I watched. No rise."

I wonder if his good eye is not so good after all. "Can you see me now?"

He points to the words I have been tracing in the dirt. Of course, the more fool I. He can see. But…

"Did you see the birds come?"

He nods.

"Did you hear them?"

He shakes his head. Tears leak from his eye, start down his cheek, flow crooked along the lines of his scars.

Mari:

Awake. I'm awake now. It was only a dream. They're not here, the beautiful birds with their long wings and narrow tails, with their music.

They are not here—but they were not only lovelier but also somehow more real than anything I've ever known. They must exist somewhere, sometime. There is nothing in my memory, in my mind, that could have conjured anything so beautiful unless it truly existed somewhere outside me.

Surely, if they are somewhere, I can find them. We have such need.

Yes, and when has our need brought us medicine or food or safety or comfort?

But in a world that has such birds…

There are words my mother said to me in secret before she died. She told me they wouldn't keep me safe—we all know nothing can do that. Words, nonetheless, passed down from mother to daughter, that she said I should know, though she couldn't tell me what the good was of that or anything. She said when I knew that I'd know the use of the words.

I have heard goodness now. I will go after it.

Dilys:

Davydd's breathing is harsher than ever as we labor up the hill together, well behind the others. No one will reproach me for lagging. We don't love our ugly wounded living as we love our beautiful, blessed dead, but still it's a Lady-favored act to care for them. So they say.

Time was when I came back from the dead-planting and dreamed of the bright birds. I do not dream of them now. I dream of Davydd as he was, then as he is, and of how he might have come by his wounds. (He will not tell me. After the way he looked at me when I asked, I will never ask again.) From those dreams I wake stiff, cold with sweat, and choking. I dream, also, of a young woman whom I have never met. Her clothes are strange, but her face is marked with a pain I think I understand. She stares at me, urgent, demanding, and I see her mouth shaping words, but there is no sound, and I can no more read lips than Davydd can.

It was those dreams, maybe, that made me think of making myself more like Davydd when the birds return. After I'm sure no one else will see us, I reach into the pouch at my neck, pull out the two small wads of waxed wool, make sure Davydd sees me put them in my ears.

We stand apart, at the back. I can still hear the murmur of the deadspeaker's invocation, of the people echoing the good words, but it is faint, far from me, and I do not speak along with my people. When the birds come, I press the plugs down further into my ears, warding off the music.

I see the birds dancing in the air, beautiful as flames leaping, as water flashing in the sun, as Davydd dancing when he had both legs. I look back at him, hunched and grim-faced, then down at my people, what is left of us: swaying, smiling, staring at empty air. At empty air above the graves from which no one rises. The crowd bows their heads for the blessing, but there is no one there to bless them. They do not see that. They reach out their hands as I did after my father's spirit rose and went over the hill. But only the birds are there, dancing, departing.

Davydd and I look at each other while the others are still rising out of trance. The grass is solid here, and the only stick nearby is the one he leans on. I point to the sky where the birds have gone, extend my left arm, curl the fingers of my left hand toward me, hold my right hand by my chin with my right elbow pulled back, make a quick plucking motion toward myself. I do not know whether the sound he makes is meant for a laugh or a sob, but I think he has understood me.

Mari:

It was only a dream. The birds aren't really dead. The woman with the bow was only in my mind. The song isn't really lost.

Why should that be less real than the birds existing?

She shot them with a bow. Why not a gun?

Her clothes were strange, too. Like something out of an illustration in a storybook about long-past times. I had books like that once, before...

Maybe the birds, the music, have been gone for centuries. Well, why else would the world be as it is? Maybe she shot them long ago and they are lost forever.

But just at the end, as the last bird fell, lumpy and songless and dead, she looked at me. She saw me. Something I didn't understand moved across her face.

She saw me. I reached her. Can I reach her again? Can I change what she—did? will do? must not do?

Dilys:

I'm awake at last. Time to forget her importuning face, look at the sunrise, remember what I must do at sunset...

That isn't sunrise light. The color's right, but it's falling the wrong way.

Sunset already. How could I have slept by day, with what I have to do? Not that I've slept well of nights; even when I don't dream of Davydd, or of the dead unrisen, the woman in my dreams pleads, weeps, demands something of me—I don't know what, since I still can't hear her. She—

She is here. Standing in my doorway, her face gone bloodless. Am I still asleep? I must be. Her mouth opens again to plead silently.

But I can hear her words now. I still can't understand. Her speech is strange as her clothes.

She's not one of our enemies. They speak our language too. Who is she? When I ask, she stares, shakes her head. Motions with her hands, thumbs linked together, fingers spread to either side, flapping gently.

I understand that much. The birds...

The birds. The dead-planting is beginning, surely. I told Davydd to stay home—I can run if they come after me, he can't— and the others will think I waited to help him. I must go.

I shake my head, take up the bow—Davydd's, it was, back when he had two good arms to use it—and hurry to the door. She follows me, gabbling in her foreign tongue. Puts her hand on my arm. I pull away. Only after I pull free do I realize what I have heard. Just while she touched me, her words came clear: "...beg you, we need..." Now she's gabbling again.

I wheel back, seize her wrist. "What did you say?" I ask. At least, start to ask. Her knee takes me in the gut, cuts off my question and my wind.

When I uncurl she is holding my bow behind her back with her right hand, but she is staring at me with as much wonder as fear, and she reaches her left hand out toward me, stops just short of touching.

She has the bow, and she fights well, and she's bigger than I am, and her strange tight-fitting clothes will be harder for me to grab than my smock will be for her. Best talk to her, if I can. Perhaps I can.

I reach out, touch her extended hand lightly. "You can understand me now?"

"Yes. Look, I'm sorry I hit you." There is a blurring echo around her words. The sounds are still wrong, but while she touches me I know what the words mean. "I was...I..." She clamps her lips together. Trying not to be sick, I think, and I think I understand why.

"You have been grabbed before. It was terrible."

She nods. Gulps. "The men… After… While the fires were still burning, while…" She shakes her head.

"There is war where you come from, too?"

"That's why we need the birds. To sing to us, to ease… So we can heal. So we can sleep. So we can end the war. We need the birds alive. You can't kill them. Why were you going to kill them?"

I wonder if the magic that lets us hear each other's words has somehow distorted their meaning. "I need to shoot them so we can end the war."

We stare at each other. Try to explain. The war—that doesn't need explaining. Nor does the grim hopelessness I saw in Davydd's eyes as he marched out in the morning and as he stood marred and deaf by my side under the song, and that she sees, seemingly, day and night without relief. But I cannot make her understand, though I tell her as best I can, about the deadspeakers, the good words, the rising, the way the birdsong seduces us back into the fight again and again.

"Come see for yourself," I say at last.

She eyes me, eyes the door, and tightens her grip on the bow.

"I won't shoot them tonight," I promise. "There'll be another time for that. Come!" She nods. Flinches when I step past her, wheels with the bow still behind her—but I'm only reaching for the waxed wool. She tosses the bow back into the corner once I am out the door, sets a hand on my shoulder as she follows me up the hill to the dead-sowing ground.

Mari:

The birds will be safe for this night, at least. I look about me as we climb. The—cottages? huts? are flimsy enough, raw and new-looking, and the few old stone buildings have char marks. But once we climb the hill…oh, it's green, so green, so alive, the sort of blessed country those birds should live in. And she steps out quick and confident as a woman who's never had to fear land mines.

So this is the burying ground. Green grass, small saplings, hacked or charred stumps of older trees, and then a section of raw earth. A crowd of people in the same antique clothes the bird-hunter wears. A few men, dressed more elaborately but still very oddly, stand by fresh piles of earth saying—I am not touching them, so I can't understand what they are saying. Something about glory and ladies, if this strange woman's story is honest as the fear in her. She's listening grimly now, darting her eyes from them to me. Then she looks to the sky, mutters a curse, stuffs little round gobs into her ears.

Then the birds are coming. The arch of their wings, of their throats; the patterns they cut on the silver sky—

And the music, the music! Of course my mother sang to me when I was a child. It wasn't this song; she couldn't have sung this song with her lungs bad from the gas; she couldn't have sung it even if she'd spent all her life breathing pure air; but it was a faint echo of this. This!

I can see it now. Not the strange business of ghosts and swords this woman talked about. I can see these silver birds sifting through the ruins we still live in, almost the way the snow came once and hid all the ugliness. But these birds are brighter than snow, and their song holds all the wonder in the world, and our hearts are healed—

She's shaking me by the shoulders, grating through the song: "So they lull us, and we send more out to kill and die! We smile as stupidly as you do. But they only sing at twilight, and there's all the bitter day to harm and be harmed in."

Maybe. Maybe we need more than comfort.

What did my mother tell me of the birds? Think, think, if I can think through their beauty that burns in my brain...

They wake the dead and soothe the living to sleep.

Wake the dead. But when they come with me, they mustn't wake our dead to bless the war; that's what this woman is hissing at me about. What then?

Wake the dead. Our dead. The blasted bodies made whole again, but still marked with blood and fear. Sorrowful but bearable, at least while the music lasts. Their dead, too, also bloodied and pained but whole. And behind them, all the ones who love them, who mourn them. All the harm we have suffered, all the harm we have done, all the goodness lost...

Yes, that's it. The music swells with love and grief, and we walk toward each other, we and our enemies that were, our arms extended, our empty hands softly open. We will touch each other, hear each other's grief. We will mourn for each other, with each other. We will lie down and sleep in peace.

Dilys:

I should have known better than to bring her here. She's tranced, she's trapped.

Mari:

The birds have seen me now, are flying toward me. They will come with me. We will all be free.

WHATSOEVER YE SHALL ASK

This story was first published in Mysterion *in September 2019.*

Where Two or Three Are Gathered:
August 12, 1179:
The Anchorhold, near Altney Village

Edytha crouched in the corner of Royse's cell, the clean linens she should have left there before the service still bundled in her arms. She swallowed hard, tried not to cough, not even to breathe too loudly, lest the sound should carry through the thin walls into the chapel where Royse, Ibb, Stace, and the priests were gathered to make God do their will.

No, that wasn't how a woman of faith should think of what was supposed to happen in there. Although Edytha didn't think she wanted the kind of faith that had elevated and imprisoned the three girls.

She'd chosen to wait and listen in the cell of Royse, who had been the witch-girl, because it felt at once safer and less confining than the others, though the cells and their windows were all equally small, and each cell opened only into the chapel, and Edytha was not permitted to be in any of them while the miracle happened. Scrupulous Ibb, who had been the killer, might protest at finding Edytha in her clean bare cell. Kindly Stace, who had been the child saint, would say nothing to get Edytha into trouble, but in her cell, there was nowhere to escape from the bruised eyes of the crucified Christ. Royse wasn't going to give her fellow conspirator away, and in her cell, with its collection of feathers and evergreen twigs, Edytha could have breathed freely if not for her fear of making a noise.

She wondered if the presence of a doubter, even on the other side of the wall, would hinder the girls' prayers, prevent God's granting them.

She wondered, too, if that was what she wanted.

In the Beginning:
November 1178:
Altney Village

Father Tancred, alone in the rectory, was trying to pray instead of fretting over the latest ugly gossip when he heard the first knock on the door. His mind dropped the effort of prayer eagerly, but his knees were less willing to change position. By the time he had unlocked them and started for the door, the knocking had become a desperate pounding, and he'd had time to think of several parishioners who might urgently need him.

He had not thought of Ibb. She fell at his feet like a shot sparrow when he opened the door, Ibb who for all her thirteen years had carried herself straight and proud. She wasn't tall, but her presence filled a room; she wasn't pretty—though that might change in a few more years, especially if by some miracle she got enough to eat—but people looked at her twice. They were drawn, Tancred thought, by her self-possession. Though she might have assumed they were staring at the daughter of the tosspot woman and the man killed for poaching. That might have explained the stiffness in her spine.

But here at his door her back was bent. She knelt, her thick nut-brown hair tangled around her face, her dry sobs blurring and scattering her words.

"Breathe, child," he said. "What do you need?"

Ibb breathed. She stayed on her knees, but her spine straightened, and her eyes rose to meet his. "Sanctuary."

"Who's after you? How close are they? Can we reach the church before they reach you?" Tancred did not protest that Ibb could not have committed a crime requiring sanctuary. He suspected there was very little Ibb could not have done.

"They'll not follow me yet, I think." Ibb's voice had leveled, but it sounded dead. "And I couldn't go to the church. Couldn't be alone with God. I'm dangerous enough out here. I don't want anyone else to die."

"Anyone else?"

"I killed Otto," she said. "Or God did, but I asked God to, so the sin is mine."

Tancred laid a hand on her forehead. She didn't feel feverish, and she wasn't in the habit of lying. "What are you saying, child?"

"They were taunting Daft Joan again."

Tancred winced. Daft Joan was one of the poor unfortunates who should be under God's protection, but her muttered blessings, her shouted imprecations, and the fact she might at any time decide to take off her clothes for the angels made her an object of derision more often than charity. While her parents lived, they had kept her too closely confined to embarrass her neighbors more than once a fortnight. Now...

"Geoff told her the angels were watching," Ibb said. "And when she started to take her clothes off, Geoff told her she was beautiful. And when I told her not to listen to them, Otto grabbed me and covered my mouth. And when she was all naked they laughed at her and called her foul names, and Otto let go of me so he could throw things at her, and when I grabbed his arm he just laughed at me and pushed me away, and I fell, and I couldn't stop him, so I said, 'May God strike you dead.'" Ibb extended her left arm suddenly.

Tancred was glad she had not pointed at him. "And?"

"And God did."

"Child..."

"God moved through me, and Otto fell down, and when I ran to him and tried to pick him up, he didn't move. Geoff yelled for him not to be a fool, and he just kept lying there. So then Geoff tried to pick him up, and he just hung there in Geoff's arms."

"Geoff didn't harm you?" Tancred looked again at Ibb's muddy face and tangled hair. He didn't see blood.

Ibb laughed, a short hard bark like an old soldier's. "He didn't dare. He knows it should have been him dead instead of Otto. Or maybe both of them dead, but Geoff mostly, because he started it."

"Did you...?"

"I didn't kill Geoff. He should have been dead, but I...I didn't want to kill him. And I wish I hadn't killed Otto, mostly, but..."

"Daughter, be reasonable." It was not what Tancred would have said to most other parishioners needing comfort, but he knew Ibb. She would rather be reasoned with than comforted. "If you truly had the power you think you have, then surely you could have prayed him alive again."

"Any wight can kill," Ibb said reasonably, "and only Jesus

makes men live again. And I wasn't main sure I wanted Otto alive. I had time to think, and I thought maybe he was better being dead and not making life a misery to Joan or anyone else who was any way afflicted. I didn't have time before—I was so angry, and just for that moment I willed him dead and I didn't doubt at all."

"Are you so sure he is dead?" Tancred asked. "Perhaps he swooned. It might do him a bit of good, at that."

"I am sure," Ibb said. "I didn't say: may God make you swoon, I said: may God strike you dead, and God did."

"All right. But let me go and make certain."

"I told you, it is certain! You taught us all about praying and not doubting! You taught us how our Lord Jesus cursed the fig tree! You taught us about how anyone with faith the size of a mustard seed could make mountains fall into the sea! You read it to us from Holy Writ! Why don't you believe me?"

Tancred bit off several unhelpful answers.

Ibb bored into him with her eyes. "Don't leave me!"

"Of course. You need to be somewhere safe if…if Otto is dead, and if Otto's family and friends come after you…"

"Joan needs to be safe that way," Ibb said, pulled out of her own nightmare for a moment. "If they blame her, if they're afraid of me and blame her instead… Yes, go make sure she's safe. I don't think they'd try to hurt me. I don't think they'd dare. But when Joan's safe, come back, and take me somewhere safe where I can't kill anyone else."

Where Two or Three Are Gathered: August 12, 1179. The Anchorhold

While the Latin words of the Mass slipped over her head, lovely and incomprehensible as birdsong, Edytha went back in her mind over the conversation she'd overheard the day before back at the manor house where she'd gone to fetch more linen. Two of the voices had been the same ones she heard now: Father Amaury, rector of all the churches in Lord Estienne's gift, who was leading the Mass; and Father Tancred, Father Amaury's vicar in Altney Village, who was murmuring the responses. The third man she'd listened in on, Lord Estienne, had not come to the chapel—his own chapel built with his own monies for the holy women, as he had reminded the priests—for the praying.

Lord Estienne's absence was partly due to the urgent entreaties of Father Tancred. Father Tancred might be the lowest-ranking person in the room, but he was the one who had first brought the killer Ibb under the protection of the lord and the Lord, and he had been sent when the other miracle-working children were reported. Sent, Edytha thought, because he was slightly less afraid of them than either his rector or his lord were.

That fear was most of what had kept Lord Estienne away from the praying. It was all very well to have three miracle-workers praying for what he wanted, but if they did not want to see him, as Father Tancred had assured him they did not; and if the one who had killed once already would not approve of some of his requests, as even Father Amaury had agreed she would not if they were presented honestly; and if he insisted on appearing before them in a holy place to make his demands—who could be sure they would not strike him dead by the hand of God?

The Mass was ending, the words of blessing and dismissal spoken. But there was no dismissal yet. It was time for the prayer God could not deny.

Father Amaury still spoke in Latin, but there was a different tension in his voice, and he waited for Father Tancred to put the words into English. For the holy women, the miracle-workers, were not learned in Latin.

At first Edytha had thought this strange. Could they not pray to learn that and more besides? She had wondered, and had asked, despite the rule forbidding light talk between the holy women and their lay servant.

"Why would I want to know Latin?" Royse had asked, laughing her fey laugh and returning Edytha's attention to her request for more feathers.

Ibb, austere as ever, had kept the rule of silence, shaking her head.

"We must not pray for ourselves," Stace had explained earnestly when Edytha dropped the question into her explanation of her nephew's broken leg and her hope—not for an obvious miracle cure, no, that wouldn't do at all, but for the leg to set clean and the flesh not to fester. "We must not. Saint James said, 'You ask and you do not receive, because you ask wrongly, to spend it on your passions.'"

"If you can't get the wrong thing by asking for it," Edytha asked, "why worry? Why not just ask for everything, and know you'll get what's right and won't get the rest?"

"What if asking wrongly once means you are never to receive again?"

Edytha considered that. If the power to receive in prayer came from perfect faith, and if the person with perfect faith failed to receive and began to doubt, would that break the spell? No, of course it was a blessing of the Holy Ghost, not a spell—but in any case, was it so easily broken?

That was what Edytha thought. Who could say what Stace thought behind that dark still face, those wide-set eyes?

In the Beginning:
January 1179.
Bainford Village

"Why did you do that? Have you forgotten everything I ever told you? How stupid can you be?" Stace's mother Aldith demanded furiously.

"I remembered you told me not to show off in front of the lord's folk," Stace answered. She had folded her hands in front of her almost demurely, but now they were clenched tightly together, straining. "I wasn't showing off! It wasn't vanity! The bailiff was hurt, I tell you! Bad hurt! The horse fell on him! I was making him better, that's all!"

"Oh, that's all, is it? And when they cry you for a witch, and me too, like as not, for I had the raising of you, is that still what you'll say?"

Stace didn't answer. Her face had gone bloodless under its summer bronze. Her lips moved. No sound came out, but Aldith thought she traced the words, "A witch?"

Aldith opened her mouth, closed it again. She hadn't spoken her fear to her daughter before. Hadn't wanted to frighten the girl, put burdens on her too great for a child of eleven to bear. Hadn't wanted, either, to rob her of that radiant certainty that pulled the power down to heal. And that, Aldith thought, had been selfish on her part. She had wanted to keep the protection Stace's prayers had brought to her and her breech-born babe—that was the first time she'd understood the miracles of which her eager, earnest younger daughter was capable—and to the bloody flux that had nearly killed Eda, Stace's older sister. Aldith had meant to keep them all safe. What had she done to them?

Three days later, when Lord Estienne's horsemen came, with their full-fed faces and their furred cloaks and their swords, Stace stared with wide surprise, having forgotten her fear. Aldith, who had forgotten nothing, sent Stace out behind the byre with instructions, if she heard her mother cry out, to run through the dyer's yard and into the fallow field and on into the forest. Aldith closed the cottage door behind her and planted herself in front of it as though the one she wished to save were still inside. When a skinny old priest—not their own Father Amaury—slid from the saddle of an undistinguished cob and walked to meet her a few paces from his armed escort, Aldith was not in the least reassured. When he introduced himself as Father Tancred, the rector of the village of Altney just over the hill, and asked her—in very good English, not Norman-French—for the child who prayed, she answered, wooden-faced, that they were all good Christian praying folk.

"You know what I mean," Father Tancred insisted.

"How do you know what I know?" Aldith's hands were on her hips, her voice rising, so she didn't hear the footsteps behind her. The first thing she heard and understood was Stace's voice.

"You can't hurt my mother," Stace said. For a moment Aldith was proud of the self-control that let her daughter breathe defiance in such a calm voice, even as she wished she could silence the child. Then, with a cold shudder, she realized Stace had not intended defiance, but only a statement of fact. The horsemen seemed to understand that as well. They shifted uneasily, and one made the sign of the cross.

Father Tancred stood his ground. "We haven't come to hurt anyone," he said, slow and quiet. "Child, you have a gift. You've used it for the good, haven't you?"

"For sick people, mostly," Stace said. "Or people who other people hurt." That was closer to defiance; Stace was looking from her mother to the horsemen.

"How many?"

"I'm not supposed to boast."

"It's not boasting," Father Tancred said. "Our Lord commanded his followers not to hide their lights under bushels. How many?"

"Eleven," Stace said. "It should have been more, but I didn't know I could, at first."

"Eleven," Father Tancred said gravely. "You have done great things for your village. But there are many more who need your gift. Come with me, and you can help them all."

Aldith looked at her daughter's face, saw the conflict there. Seemingly Father Tancred saw it too. "Are you afraid to leave your home?"

"Afraid of helping all those people," Stace said in a small, choked voice. "Every time…it hurts."

Father Tancred looked at her with sympathy, spoke gently. "I think that with time and training, and the company of a very faithful sister in prayer, the pain may become less."

"A sister?" Aldith asked. "Our Eda's promised already, and anyway she doesn't have—"

"There is another young woman with a gift like yours, from Altney Village, who is already under Lord Estienne's protection," Father Tancred said, still speaking to Stace as though she were the only one who mattered. "She would be glad of some company."

That was all it took to win Stace. Aldith, carrying a double burden of doubt as usual, insisted on going to see the place where her daughter would be kept. Father Tancred argued in French, which Aldith didn't understand, with the horsemen, but his nod toward Stace and the fear in their faces made the main thrust of his argument clear.

So Aldith rode unhappily before an unhappy man-at-arms, and Aldith saw the neat stone chapel and the whitewashed timber enclosure on the east side where they said the sister in prayer lived, and saw the newly erected enclosure on the west side that would be Stace's and the garden where the girls could walk and work together when the lay servant or a priest were free to watch them. It wasn't what Aldith wanted for her daughter, but it was what she could get, and anyway it was better than having Stace hanged for a witch. As Aldith had expected, her muddled, muddied angry prayers did not stir God to change their minds and let Stace come home. Perhaps they would not have done so even if Aldith had been sure she could keep Stace safe there.

Where Two or Three Are Gathered:
August 12, 1179:
The Anchorhold

Father Amaury spoke the petition in Latin. Father Tancred repeated it in English. The girls repeated it and added the fixed words at the end. Did they wonder, as Edytha did, whether the priests refrained from making their own words into full prayers lest any doubts of theirs should impair the girls' radiant certainty?

"That God may comfort the sick in all Lord Estienne's lands, both in body and in spirit."

"That God may comfort the sick in all Lord Estienne's lands, both in body and in spirit, we ask of our Lord through His dear Son, Jesus Christ. Amen."

That prayer, Stace had told her, was the same every week. Clearly it was Stace's favorite prayer. She had wanted to add, *And heal them all*, but Father Tancred had managed to persuade her that people were meant to be mortal, and that there were gentle sicknesses that took the aged. In the months since the girls were enclosed, people in Edytha's village had still died from sickness, but not, mostly, in agonizing pain or delirious terror, and that was a mercy, as far as it went. Edytha secretly brought particular requests for healing to Stace, who prayed about them despite the fact this was forbidden. The ban did not seem to impede the efficacy of the prayers, and Stace, good girl that she was, had apparently remembered to pray that the healings should be gradual and unspectacular enough so word of her trespass would not get back to the priests or Lord Estienne—or out to anyone else who might be more of a danger to the girls and to the men who protected, or guided, or used them.

"That Lord Estienne may be blessed with good health of mind and body."

The lord was young enough that Stace would not yet see any conflict between this petition and Father Tancred's explanation for why universal prayers of healing were not allowed. Edytha expected another set of smooth responses. But instead she heard Royse beginning to cough, a terrible racking sound that went on and on. Edytha began to fear Royse had prayed herself into a true sickness.

For a time, there was no sound but the terrible coughing. Then Father Amaury said something Latin that included the word *Satanas*. Edytha hoped the priest was just banishing Satan in a general sort of way, not accusing him of working through anyone in particular.

Father Tancred said urgently, "Pray for your sister!"

"You did tell us that we must not pray for ourselves," Ibb said.

"You may pray for each other!" Father Tancred insisted, then translated the exchange to Father Amaury, who said something else in French. "In this case, you may pray for each other," Father Tancred amended.

Stace's voice, soft and urgent, took up a prayer. Ibb said, "Just what may we pray?"

"That she may be well," Father Tancred said, in English then (Edytha thought) in French. This time he didn't translate Father Amaury's reply.

"That Royse may be well, *et fiat volunta tua*," Ibb said in a low and resounding voice. Even Edytha knew that much Latin, though she wasn't sure why anyone had to ask God to let God's will be done. Surely God could do that much unprompted.

Royse kept coughing.

"Get her out of the chapel and let her lie down," Father Tancred said. Edytha cursed herself for a fool. They'd find her, they'd…

"Stace," Royse said through her coughs. "Stace, take me."

In the Beginning:
March 1179.
Altney Village

"Behave yourself, Royse!" Amice said again, trying not to snarl. Amice always felt bad afterward if she snarled at her little sister or slapped her. Royse was so golden and smiling, so surprised by any chastisement. But Royse was ten, old enough to know something about how a woman should comport herself, and Amice, who hadn't Royse's golden ways, would get the rough side of her mother's tongue and her mother's hand if Royse got herself into trouble again. Most of all if Royse got herself into trouble in some way that was impossible to properly explain. It was bad enough when she turned up overhead in the elm tree, higher than the boldest, tallest, lightest boys could climb. It was worse when the bailiff's horse began to bow and dance in front of Royse. Oh, Royse was always happy to explain— "I just told God what I wanted, and it happened" —but the explanation was as bad as anything Royse might do to require it.

"I am behaving!" Royse laughed.

"No, you're not! You're supposed to be planting the peas, not dancing around as if you were four years old."

"They're already planted." Royse took another twirling leap into the air.

"Don't lie, Royse. I've been making holes for the seeds since we came out, and all you've done is—"

"Look in the holes and see."

Amice glowered at her sister and stepped back to the last row of holes she'd poked. Only they weren't there.

"You filled them in? When?"

"I told God, and God put the peas in and covered them up," Royse said. "So I had time to dance."

"Those peas had better be in there," Amice began uncomfortably. "And don't talk about God in front of everybody!"

"I'll show you!" Royse sang. She opened her arms wide, looked up, and moved her lips soundlessly, still dancing.

Amice lowered her eyes from her sister's face, stared at the ground. Green tendrils rose up through the soil, swaying a little in time with Royse's dancing feet. Then stems and leaves. The pea vines were growing in rows before her, as though a month could pass in the space of three breaths. And the plants were dancing, and the dance…

"Make it stop!" Amice screamed. She regretted the scream as soon as it was out of her. Heads turned toward her, and other people began to cry out, to hurry closer. "Royse, it's not safe, they'll see! You know what they'll think!"

Royse laughed aloud, then whispered something, and a thick wall of fog swirled between the other villagers and the pea vines which had begun to set blossoms.

"Make it stop! You can't do that! It's—" Amice didn't even want to say the word *witchcraft*. "It's bad!"

"No." The voice spoke firmly behind Amice. "It is a gift of God, but it must be rightly trained and rightly used."

Amice whipped around. Father Tancred was looking at Royse with troubled eyes. "Father…" she said awkwardly.

"You came." Royse half-said, half-sang to him. "You came to take me where there are people like me and where nobody will yell stop, stop!"

"I did." He looked at least as frightened as Amice felt. "But you can't leave the plants like this; it will make talk."

Royse nodded serenely. "They're almost done."

Indeed, the peas were heavy with fat pods. As Amice and Father Tancred stared, the plants turned brown and sere. A few pods plucked themselves from the plants and split, dropping their seed at Amice's feet. The rest of the plants shriveled, faded to dust, and vanished along with the blanketing fog.

"They're gone, and I can go," Royse said, laughing.

"You're leaving?" Amice said bleakly. "What will I tell Mother?"

Royse didn't answer. She took the old priest's hand and they walked away. Amice stared after them. She didn't look around to see her neighbors back at their tasks, or look down to resume her own, until her sister and the priest were long gone from her sight.

Where Two or Three Are Gathered:
August 12, 1179:
The Anchorhold

Stace, obedient as ever, supported Royse back into her cell, knelt worriedly over her. It was only when Royse gave over coughing and smiled her most conspiratorial smile that Stace looked up and saw Edytha. She opened her mouth, then closed it again soundlessly.

"I'm better now," Royse whispered. "But I can't go back to the chapel and pray now. I can't."

Stace nodded, rose, and walked back into the chapel.

"Perhaps we should wait, and pray for God to reveal His will to us before we pray for anything else," Stace said. Her voice was mild as ever.

"Indeed we should," Ibb answered, low and rough. Stace had been suggesting, but Ibb was pronouncing. There was an awkward silence that swelled and grew. This was perhaps the first time any of the ones who were bound either by vow or by enclosure had stopped to think who truly held authority.

"Very well," Father Tancred said at length. "Father Amaury and I will speak and pray about this outside. Do you wait patiently." He paused, listening to Father Amaury, and said, "Wait patiently for the Lord's will to be revealed, and do not pray lightly."

Royse, invisible to all but Edytha, grinned broadly.

Stace said nothing.

Ibb's voice came low as a sob. "Father, have you forgotten why I came here? Do you think I would do anything lightly?"

"The sick girl shouldn't be alone," Father Tancred said after another awkward pause.

"I'll look after her," Stace said.

"I'll send for the lay servant," Father Tancred said. "There should be someone who is free to go out and call for help if she takes a turn for the worse."

"Edytha planned to be here after prayers in any case," Stace said carefully. It was not exactly a lie.

"She already brought the linens..."

"Sometimes there is need for something more, for one of us," Stace said with equal care, glancing briefly at Ibb and then looking down with her most demure expression. Edytha grinned this time. Let the priests think Stace was delicately alluding to Ibb's monthly courses, which naturally neither one of them would want to discuss. Ibb hadn't actually started them yet, but she was old enough.

"Well, so be it," Father Tancred said. "We'll return soon to see if...if all is well."

Edytha heard the priests leaving by the door to the open world, the door the girls never passed through. Then she heard Ibb walking quickly and evenly back into her cell. Ibb would be able to hear something even of a whispered conversation from there, but she was no tattletale.

Stace didn't come back into Royse's cell. Instead she followed Ibb.

"Come see Royse with me," she said. "I think she needs you."

"The rules are—"

"I think it will do more harm if you keep them," Stace said firmly.

Ibb settled herself just outside the doorway of Royse's cell. She raised her eyebrows when she saw Edytha but said nothing.

"What's wrong?" Stace asked Royse.

"I don't know yet," Royse said. "But Edytha told me to do something to stop the prayers before saying Amen when they prayed for...what? Something about the truth was what she said they'd say. I didn't remember the right words, so I started to cough early."

"You trust her more than the priests?" Stace asked.

"I wanted to see what would happen." Royse smiled.

"The prayer was that the truth might be revealed to all men when Lord Estienne held his hallmote," Edytha said.

"And why should we want the truth concealed?" Ibb asked from the doorway.

Edytha licked her lips and tried to steady her breath.

Ibb's face changed, watching her. "The truth about what?"

"About offenses against the vert and the venison, though they weren't going to say that out loud at the prayers," Edytha said.

Royse looked puzzled. "What?"

"Stealing from the lord's forest," Ibb explained. She had cause to know about that. "It's Lord Estienne's forest, not the king's, so he judges, but the punishments are the same as if it was the king's. What did they steal? What would happen to them?"

Edytha noted gratefully Ibb did not ask who 'they' were. Then remembered Ibb didn't have to ask her, she could just ask God.

"All last winter people stole wood, but it was so cold nobody tried very hard to find out who took it, not even Heriger Woodward. But now they've found a fresh-killed deer." And failed to find two others, Edytha did not say. "And they say the lord was too lenient, so the law is held in contempt, and now anyone who took anything from the forest must pay for it."

"And they would pay..."

"For the wood, they'd be amerced money, but I tell you half the village stole wood last winter, and most have no money to spare. But for the deer..."

"They'd be hanged," Ibb said.

"But why?" Stace asked. "Why did they kill the deer? We prayed for a good harvest."

"Well and good for them that have their own land," Ibb said harshly. Her father had not.

"Why didn't they tell us to pray for no one to be hungry?" Stace persisted. "Why didn't we think to pray it ourselves?"

"How would the prayer have been answered?" Ibb shot back. "The dead don't hunger; that would have been the easiest answer."

"Well then, for God to put food into every home."

Edytha knew the answer to that. "If that happened, the word would spread far and wide. And if the Pope knew what you can do, or the King…"

Stace caught her breath, nodded. "I see. They'd take us away to Rome, or anyway to one of the King's castles, and who would be left to pray for our villages?"

"They'd make us pray to kill their enemies," Ibb said, staring blindly.

"Maybe they'd just be scared of us and kill us," Royse said. "If they could. If God let them."

A very uncomfortable silence was broken by the opening of the outside door. Ibb rose, turned and made a wide gesture with her arms, largely blocking the door into the cell. Stace stood in front of Edytha. Royse prayed quietly but clearly, "Dear God, don't let them see Edytha in my cell, or hear her, and don't let them be mad at her for anything we say, in Jesus' name, Amen."

Father Tancred came in alone, his face drawn with worry.

"Royse will be all right now," Stace said, edging out the door and into the chapel.

"We are not all right," Ibb said, setting her hands on her hips. "I told you I wanted to be where I could not kill again. I said that for cause. I meant it. No more killing. Not poachers. Not anyone."

"Who told you…?" Father Tancred began. Then he bit his lip.

"We were to pray that the truth would prevail, yes?" Ibb was relentless. "Well, now we know the truth. I thought, once, that you would tell me the truth, but God has other ways to tell me, since you will not. Since you lied to me. You!"

Edytha bit her lips. She'd been thinking of Ibb as a miracle-worker, not as a maid of fourteen who had trusted this man like a father. *Christ aid,* she prayed silently, bleakly, without confidence. *Don't let her kill him.*

"I have not lied to you," Father Tancred said in a rather small voice.

"You would have deceived me into getting a man hanged."

"Would you rather let an innocent man be hanged for an offense he never committed?"

"Would Lord Estienne hang someone who was not proven to be guilty? Knowing God would requite him?"

"He believes God will show him the truth," Father Tancred said, growing quieter and steadier as Ibb's voice rose. "He trusts God. He trusts you. Well, and he trusted me to tell you what to pray, knowing that otherwise he would proceed against the likeliest man."

There was an ugly little silence. Then, "Christ God," Ibb said, and Edytha could not tell whether it was oath or prayer. Father Tancred flinched.

Stace turned away from them both, knelt facing the altar, raised her hands before her. "Christ God," she echoed, "I need to know what will happen because of what we pray. And because of what people think we are praying. This isn't praying for me, it's so we can help people and not hurt them. So let it be, Amen."

Edytha braced herself, waiting for a wind, a flame, an earthquake, a trumpet blast. There was nothing. Nothing. And then a very small sound like a sob.

Stace stood up. Her face... It was not right for a young girl's face to look that way. She looked worse even than Michael Stotte that time he came back from the raid into Wales murmuring about dead children whose voices were never out of his ears, whose faces were never out of his eyes, who wouldn't let him sleep.

Stace turned her back to Edytha and the altar, turned to face Father Tancred, who groaned, took a step toward her, and then stopped, arms hanging limp at his sides.

Ibb half-turned, looked Stace in the face.

"So, it's like that," she said. She turned back to Father Tancred. "I asked you to let me do no more harm," she said. Her voice was low and broken. "I shouldn't have trusted you."

"He did the best he knew," Stace said. "Any way you choose..."

Ibb nodded. "Well. If I live, then I will do harm." She raised her arms. "God," she began, "in your dear Son's name—"

"No!" Stace caught at her arms. "No! If you ask God to strike you dead, that does harm too. Think! They'll blame him, they'll blame us, the fear will spread. And I won't be able to pray you back. I won't be able to stop it. I know too much, now, to be able to pray like that. Ibb, don't!"

The two girls stood staring at each other. Edytha stared at them, too afraid to pray for anything. She heard Royse whisper behind her. Then she heard the sound of wings.

A small brown bird flew over Edytha's shoulder, out the cell door, close by where Ibb and Stace stood as though they were wrestling or embracing, and out the other door, into the open world. Stace, Ibb and the priest followed its flight with their eyes.

Royse walked past Edytha, stood beside her sisters in prayer. "God showed us," she said. "Let's go."

Ibb pulled her left arm away from Stace, took Royse's hand. Stace looked her in the face, nodded, and turned to face the door, still lightly holding Ibb's right hand.

Ibb gave Father Tancred a long look. "Do not follow us," she told him.

He nodded, and Edytha ached for the plain human pain in his face.

The girls were still holding hands as they walked together out the door into the world. Edytha rose and called after them, but Royse's prayer had been granted. No one heard Edytha.

Father Tancred knelt slowly, stiffly, facing the door the girls had passed through, not the altar. He raised his hands and spoke in English.

"Help them," he said. "Protect them. Please. I couldn't, but you…"

He made a small sound as though he'd had the wind knocked out of him. His hands dropped to his sides. At last he said, hollow-voiced and still in English, "Lord, I believe. Help thou my unbelief."

COME AGAIN

This story was first published by Metapsychosis *in September 2018.*

The visitor scrapes the dirt off his broken-down shoes, steps into the gleaming entrance hall, returns the usher's smile. Unlike the usher, he keep his lips shut—understandably, if his teeth differ from the usher's as much as his clothes do.

The usher gestures him into the sanctuary. He stops just inside the door, staring at the banks of seats, the spotlighted stage, the screens filled with the rapt faces of singers whose music, prodigiously amplified, pulses in his head, flutters in his empty stomach. "I will bring praise; no weapon formed against me shall remain…" People in the congregation sing and sway. The visitor remembers men standing and swaying to the chant of prayer in another time and place; the words were different, but the movement was much the same.

Another greeter smiles in his face, gestures him to a seat in the back row. For a while he looks down at his hands. Then he takes a deep breath and looks around him again.

The music has stopped. The screens show the preacher's face. The preacher's eyes shine like his teeth; his arms sweep out in a wide gesture of welcome. "Have you believed the lies of this world?" the preacher asks. "Have you let the Enemy establish a beachhead in your mind? Have you let him tell you that you're no good, that you're poor, that you're sick, that you've done terrible things? Have you let Satan tell you Jesus doesn't want you? Well, let me tell you the truth. Jesus wants you. Jesus came for you."

The congregation leans into the promise. The visitor remembers another crowd leaning in as though it were midwinter and the words were fire, their eyes full of the hunger which bites as deep as the hunger for bread. Leaning toward him.

"Maybe you're thinking, 'That's easy for him to say. He's a minister of the Word, he's a righteous man, he's got a nice house, a good life—how does he know what my life is like? How does he know Jesus wants me?'" The congregation waits eagerly for the answer.

"I know," the preacher assures them. "I know, because I wasn't always the man you see before you now. If you knew the way I grew up… Brothers and sisters, believe me, whatever you've been through, it's no worse than that."

The visitor rubs his right thumb over the scar on his left hand, focuses on the preacher's words to keep the memories at bay.

"I've known poverty. I've known sin. Drinking, porn…you name it, I tried it. I was lost, friends, I was lost in the darkness. I was destroying my health, I was bankrupt, but worse than that: my soul was dark and hollow, and I was a stranger to God."

The congregation listens as though this is the first time they have heard his account of how the preacher hit bottom, fell to his knees and asked Jesus into his heart. The visitor studies the preacher's face as though trying to remember something.

"And he came to me. He came to me, and He filled my life, He filled it with blessings, just the way he promised in his precious Word. Do you know what it says there? It says that God has plans to prosper you and not to harm you. Plans to prosper you. Friends, that word is for you, for every blessing you need in your life. If you open your life to the power of God, if you surrender to His precious will, He will shower you with blessings. When you let God into your heart, then the blessings come until your cup overflows, until you think you can't take any more blessing—and still they come! When you let God arise, he scatters every enemy. No more sickness, no more poverty, no more sadness, no more pain. When you let God arise, then health comes, then joy comes, then prosperity comes. The path of the righteous gets brighter and brighter. God will give you the victory. God will give you the victory in everything."

The congregation laughs, claps, shouts out loud. The visitor in the back row clutches his left side with his right hand. The wound there is old, should be healed, but sometimes the memories bring the pain back. Drops of sweat fall from his forehead to the carpet.

"Are you ready?" the preacher calls. "Are you ready to say yes to the blessing? Are you ready to say yes to God, to put your life in his hands and let him fill your cup with every good thing? Then stand with me and tell our Heavenly Father…"

The congregation rises like a wave. The visitor rocks back and forth like a piece of flotsam battered by the tide. Words tumble from his mouth in fragments: *Father…this cup…your will…your hands…*

The visitor edges toward the nearest aisle; the people he has to pass by let him through, wrinkling their noses as he passes. His stomach growls, and as the preacher's voice rises in prayer he makes his way to the exit, head bowed.

He stands on the steps for a few minutes, watching two sparrows chasing each other through the branches of the hawthorn tree by the door. Slowly he lifts his hands. One of the sparrows perches on his crooked finger, turns a bright eye on him, flies away singing.

Later he sits at a long gray table, one in a crowd of shabbily dressed people eating macaroni and hot dogs from paper plates inside the Good Shepherd Soup Kitchen. He looks around at his fellow diners. No one looks back at him. Some bend over their food. Others look toward the TV screen on the wall.

"I thank God for finally sending us a President who truly values and protects Christians," the man on the screen says. His compelling blue eyes stare directly at his listeners. "Our Lord Jesus Christ told us the world would hate us because we bear His name. We see that every day, don't we? Look at the violent Islamists massacring Christians for their faith. Look at the terrorists who hate America, who hate us just because we're free, we're Christian, we're blessed by God…"

"Amen!" says one of the diners. The visitor looks at her snaggled teeth and hair, the cross pinned to her sweatshirt, the hunger in her eyes.

He looks back at the screen as the interviewer asks about the church people who criticize the President for turning away refugees. "That simply isn't a Bible issue," the interviewee says. "A country has laws, a country has the duty to protect its own. That means not letting in people who want to kill us."

The visitor no longer sees the speaker on the screen. The memories are on him again. Earlier memories, this time. His mother's hand over his mouth as they creep out of the village in the dead of night, and again every time a patrol might be passing near them. The heat beating down, the hurt in his dry throat and empty gut, the long, long journey through the desert. And when they arrive…His father—at least, the man he always called father—asking directions, first in the language of the country they fled from, then, awkwardly, brokenly, in the language of the new land.

People not answering. People laughing, a hard-edged laughter. People answering—he didn't know their language then, but he understood *You are not wanted*. That is one of the first messages any child learns to understand, especially a child of refugees.

He was a small boy then; many people would say he was too young to remember. Nevertheless he remembers. He also remembers what anyone would say he should not, what he was not there to see, what they fled, what happened just after they escaped the village. The soldiers shouting; the women wailing; the children screaming briefly, then silenced; the soft thuds of bodies dropped in the dust; the silence among the living that followed the soldiers' departure, broken occasionally by a curse, a prayer, a sob, then settling again like dust over the hopeless and the dead...

"Hey, what's wrong with him?" a voice asks. "What's he staring at?" He pulls himself out of the memories far enough to see the faces of his fellow diners turned toward him, far enough to see the fear that stirs behind the faces. Some of them are looking at his dark troubled eyes. Some are looking at his brown skin, long beard and hooked nose. "Hey, where are you from, anyway?" the first speaker asks. He doesn't answer. "Has anyone heard him say anything?"

"Yeah, I was behind him in line. He said he was hungry. Said he didn't want a hot dog. Wouldn't say why. He had a funny accent."

"Don't you eat pork?"

"Where are you from?"

"I was a stranger..." he begins; bites the rest off.

"What kind of accent is that? What kind of stranger are you? What're you here for, anyway?"

"This place is to feed Americans."

That look in their eyes. He remembers that look. He pushes himself back from the table, walks away, leaving his food uneaten. They don't follow him. Their voices do, and their fear. The servers don't look at him; they are still busy scooping food onto plates for newer arrivals.

Most of the diners don't look either; they keep their eyes down, their bodies curled around their own treasures and wounds. A woman with a beaky face and a tangle of grey hair fumbles in her jacket pocket until the pocket tears out. Coins ring and roll. Scraps of paper covered in spiky writing flutter in several directions; her attempts to grab them make eddies in the air that only push them further away.

He kneels beside her, catching the papers as they fall. A girl with dark makeup around her eyes and a dark bruise on her jaw crouches on the woman's other side, raking coins together. The woman screams, a high tearing sound. "No!" she cries. "Those are mine!"

"I know," he says. She darts a glance at him. Looks away. Looks back, steadying her eyes on his; takes a deep breath; doesn't start screaming again.

"Oh," she says. "Oh. I'm sorry." And to the well-dressed man hurrying over from the server's line, "No, it's all right. He's helping. They're both helping. I didn't know."

The girl bundles the coins back into the woman's remaining pocket. The visitor holds the papers up to the woman in his cupped hands. She reaches down to take them. Leaves her hands in his while her breath comes deeper and slower. He feels something stirring inside him, something that comes from beyond him.

"You'll be all right," he says to her, knowing it for the truth.

She nods. "Will you be?"

He has no answer. He releases her hands gently, goes out the back door. Pauses to pick up a sheet of paper from the table by the door: The Daily Word, it says across the top. The woman at the table smiles encouragingly at him as he carries it out into the light.

The man from the television screen looks into his eyes from the paper. He reads the curly script under the photo: Hebrews 13:17. "Submit to your leaders and those in authority."

"Listen, all of you, black or white or any other color. There's no reason for you to be afraid of the police," the message begins. The reader remembers other words like that: Have no fear of those who can kill the body... The words trail shadows, remembered fears. He shakes his head to clear it, looks back at the words on the page. "There's a simple way to keep safe: OBEY. Follow God's guidance. Submit to your leaders and those in authority. If a policeman tells you to do something, you do it. If they say freeze, you freeze. If they say lie down, you lie down. Obey. Don't argue, whether or not you think they're right—OBEY, as God commanded you. Remember Romans 13, the opening verses: Everyone must submit himself to the governing authorities, for there is no authority except what God has established… He who rebels against the authority is rebelling against what God has instituted, and those who do so will not escape judgment… Authorities hold no terror for those who do right, but for those who do wrong."

The reader crumples the paper in his hand. He's not seeing the printed words now, he's seeing the images from his childhood: the bodies nailed to posts along the roadside as a warning from the authorities, a sign to strike terror into the hearts of would-be rebels.

He shakes his head. That was another country and another time, he tells himself. In this land, in this time, when the authorities kill they may leave the bodies lying in the road for hours, but they don't stick them up beside the road for days. Well, they hardly need to, now that the images of the bodies can pass from screen to screen in an instant, so everyone sees and remembers what they can do to you if…

The memories catch him, drag him forward. He is a man, not a boy, back in that other country. He is a man, but the guards treat him like a beast; they have taken his clothes away, they have blindfolded him, they are hitting him again and again. They are authorities. They say he has rebelled. This is the beginning of the judgment.

He clutches at his side again. Sits curled around the wound and also around that presence like a fire in his bones.

A shadow falls across him and he flinches. The woman standing over him flinches too, drops something on the ground in front of him—on purpose, he thinks it's on purpose—and backs away. He looks at her: the fish with the name JESUS on her sweatshirt front, the shirt's frayed neck, the kindness and the fear in her face. She turns and hurries down the street.

He picks up the thing she dropped, examines it. There's a portrait of a bewigged man over the words ONE DOLLAR. He flips it over. There's an eagle, a bunch of arrows, the emblems the armies of the occupiers used in his other country. But the inscription says IN GOD WE TRUST. He looks back and forth between the pictures and the words. To whom does this belong? Who does she think he is, that she has rendered it to him?

The back of the Daily Word sheet is printed with the addresses of local churches that support the soup kitchen. The church he went to earlier is there. So is another church on the same street as the soup kitchen—a church with an afternoon service.

He walks to that church. Music spills from an open door. He waits in the foyer until the music stops; goes in quietly and takes a seat in the back as people sit back down and the preacher stands to speak.

By the time he has quieted his memories she is well launched into her message. She wears white robes and gold earrings; she speaks eagerly and warmly.

"Don't let anyone lay a burden on you," she says. "Those problems you think you have? God has already taken them away. They're not yours any more. All good things are yours through the power of Jesus." She makes a sudden gesture of throwing down. "There is no burden for those who believe!" she says. "Jesus took it all on himself. Jesus took all the evil on himself, so all the good was left for us. Jesus was wounded so we could be healed! Jesus took on our poverty so we could have God's rich abundance! Jesus became a curse so we could have the blessing! Jesus died so we could live!"

It is only in his mind, the visitor knows—or in their minds; the distinction is not absolute—that the people of the congregation answer *Yes. Yes, the blessing is for us. Let the foreigners stay in their bloody hungry countries: the richness of this land is for us. Let the rebellious die in the streets: the protection is for us. Let the people who didn't get the blessing go hungry; we will want for nothing. Let Jesus suffer and die. We are the living, we are the prosperous, we will inherit the earth.*

The visitor unclenches his fist, tears his gaze away from the preacher, looks above her to the crimson curtain and the empty cross that hangs in front of it, waiting. He flinches, looks back down, shutting his teeth against the phantom pain.

But it's not just his own pain that moves through him now. It's the pain of the people around him, the strain under their smiles. Their desperation. Their certainty the curse remains, that if they ever set aside their armor of insistent faith in being blessed, if they ever relax their conviction that they deserve more than the rest, it might lay hold of them. He remembers that fear as well from the other country and the other time.

He knew words for that. *Woe to you rich... Give to the poor, and then come, follow me... Woe to you when all speak well of you... Take up your cross and follow me... My kingdom is not of this world... Have no fear of those who kill the body... Be not afraid... Perfect love drives out all fear... Love your neighbor... Love your enemy... I was a stranger and you welcomed me... Enter into the joy of your Lord...*

These people in the church with him today have heard all those words over and over; they can't really hear them anymore. He remembers other words: *If they do not listen to Moses and the Prophets, they will not be convinced even if someone rises from the dead.*

And yet, and yet...

He rises. The wound in his side is still throbbing, but the wind is blowing through him now, the light is shining. As their faces turn toward him, he opens his mouth to speak again.

OUT OF DUST

This story was originally published in Oren Litwin's anthology
"The Wand That Rocks The Cradle" *in 2019.*

Translations from the journal of Cristina Fuentes:

April 7, 1954

My name is Cristina Guadalupe Fuentes Espinosa. I am ten years old. In this book I will write the story of my adventures with my papi in El Norte, where we are going tomorrow. We don't have money for me to go to school here, and in El Norte they will not let me go to school even if we have money. But Papi says that is no reason to be ignorant. So I will not be ignorant. I read every day in the Bible, and now I will write every day in this book, and in El Norte...in the *United States*...I will learn English too. Papi says I have to keep learning, and I do what he says.

But when he said to stay here with my Aunt Lancha while he went North, I said no. I told him he is all the family I have now and I am all the family he has and we have to stay together.

"All the family we have in this world," he said.

"This is the world where I live," I said. "Anyway Aunt Lancha doesn't like me."

He said she did like me, only it was hard for her having so many children to take care of and not enough money.

I said I was old enough to take care of myself if I went with him, and in El Norte there would be enough money.

"It's not safe, where I'm going," he said. "You know I don't want to go."

I know that. I know he wants to stay here with me but he has to go. He is very good at fixing things but so are a lot of the other men who can't find work, and he is very good at making beautiful things from clay, things that are a little bit alive, but nobody pays money for things like that, and we can't eat them. In El Norte there is work and money for everyone. There is more money for the people who had enough money here to pay the officials so they could go to El Norte and stay inside the law, but there is some money there even for people who have no money here. I knew that was why my papi had to go there. I knew, too, that I had to go with him. "It's not safe anywhere," I said. And my papi agreed to take me with him.

Soon I have to stop writing and finish packing the bag I will carry across the river and the desert. But there is not very much to pack, just clothes and tortillas and the Bible and this book and the family bowl Papi made with all the hands around the rim. Anyway Papi is happy to see me writing.

April 15

We are here on a big farm in El Norte. We found an easy place to cross the river, and a short place to cross the desert, and I was hungry and tired but we came to a town where Papi bought food and found people who spoke Spanish. Those people told us which way to go to find work, and Papi found this place before we were all the way out of money.

It is a good thing Papi brought me with him, because I can help. Not in the fields: Pedro is doing fieldwork and he's just thirteen, but Papi says I shouldn't do that. But I can take care of Doña Lupe and Doña Marcela's babies, and I can boil the beans for the workers to eat at lunch and at supper, and I can bring good water to them while they're in the field. There's a water pump not far from the edge of the big melon field, but if you drink that water straight from the pump you get sick-sick-sick. Doña Dolores drank some that way last month.

Doña Dolores doesn't have children who are still alive. She is a little bit crazy. My papi says not to stare at her when she talks funny, or when she stares at me. She has cracks, my papi says, but God has breathed into them.

Anyway, the water is safe if you boil it, so I do that. We have two great big pots, too big for me to carry, and four little pots I can carry even when they're full, and one wagon. I pump water into all the little pots and put them in my wagon and pull them back to the bunkhouse and boil them, and then I put a big pot in the wagon and pour all the boiled water into it, and then I pull that pot out to the field and call for someone to lift it off the wagon; then I take the mostly-empty pot they've been drinking from back and I do everything again. Sometimes my papi comes to take the water pot out of my wagon, sometimes somebody else. When Don Fermin or Doña Lupe come they smile at me and call me Senorita Fuertes the fountain girl. When Doña Dolores comes she looks at me with her hungry face and doesn't say anything. And then they go away and I go back to singing to the babies or to reading or to writing in this book.

I have more books to read now because of my cousins. Doña Concepcion is my mother's second cousin, but I call her Aunt Chon because it is easier. Aunt Chon and Uncle Miguel came to El Norte with their parents long long ago. They have a casita of their own on the edge of Mr. Martin's farm a mile up the road. They stay there all year, even in winter, to take care of his animals, and their son David goes to school with other Mexican kids who stay all the time in El Norte. So instead of sleeping in the bunkhouse with my papi and the other workers, I go with David every evening and eat supper with my cousins and sleep on a pallet by my aunt's bed, the way I used to sleep near my mami when I was little and she was alive. And I get to borrow books David takes home from school.

I won't have time to read much today because I have done so much writing. That is okay.

May 1

There is not much to write about today. The things that change from one day to another day are small. Yesterday my papi and the others picked rocks up out of the field and threw them into a big wagon. Everybody was tired and sore and even Don Fermin did not smile at me. Today they are planting, so they will just be sore from bending and not quite so tired. Yesterday they were in the north field. Today they are in the east field, which is a longer way to pull the water wagon. Tonight maybe it will rain, and they are hurrying to plant before the rain comes. I am not hurrying. I am waiting for the water to boil and trying to write so I will not be ignorant.

Today at the lunch break I told Papi I didn't know what to write, and he told me to think of three beautiful things every day and write about them. I will do that.

When Doña Marcela walked back out to the field after eating she sang one of the songs about La Guadalupana that my mami used to sing. Her voice is very beautiful.

Last night the moon was so small it was almost gone, and there were no rain clouds, and the sky was full of stars all low and close like fireflies.

That is two things. My papi didn't say to write only beautiful things that happened today. So I will write now about the family bowl that Papi made, because that is the most beautiful thing.

Papa made it after my little brother Santiago—Chago—cut his leg playing in the river and got infected and died. I was seven then, still a child, and I stopped singing and stopped eating and stopped talking. My papi sat down by me and told me Chago and my mami and all the dead people are still with us, even though we can't see them, and after we die we will see them again. I said it would be better just to be dead right away and see them. He cried, and he went away, and I was afraid I would not see him again either. But after work—that was in the three months when he had work on the road crew, before the weather turned bad and they sent him away—he came back and told me to come with him, and I went.

He took me to the raw bank where they had just cut the new roadbed, and I helped him get good clay dirt out of the bank and put it in a big glass jar. After he'd soaked it with water I helped him squish the wet mud and break up all the clumps. While we squished he talked about Chago, about how he went straight from scooting on his stomach to walking without ever learning to crawl, about the time when he carried the king snake home and Mami thought it was a coral snake and was very very afraid, about the time he found the dove's nest and brought it back to see if we could hatch the eggs. Then Papi told me to sleep while the mud soaked up water. In the morning he went to work. While he was gone I did what he'd told me to do. I saw the line that separated the clay water from the rocks and other kinds of dirt in the bottom of the jar. I poured off the clay water into a new jar, dumped out the rest. I did that over and over, and while I worked I sang every song I could remember my mami singing.

After the cleaned clay had dried, hung up in one of Chago's shirts, Papi took it out and started to shape it. Sometimes he told stories about when he and my mami were young. Sometimes I told what I remembered about Chago and my abuelita and all the other ones who are dead. And while we talked his hands shaped little figures in the clay, and shaped another piece of that same clay into a round bowl.

The bowl is painted black like a night sky with no stars, and the people pressed all around the outside of it are the reddish color of the clay. There are spaces between their bodies, spaces full of shadows, but at the top their hands are clasped together. Their faces look alive. One of the people has my face, and one has Papi's, and there are other people who look like Mami and Chago and Abuelita. In between us are five other people with faces that don't look quite like anyone I know—and I swear their faces change every time I look at them. Papi says those five are for all our people on the other side, the ones whose faces we don't remember.

Sometimes I think the people are holding on tight to each other so the wind out of those dark empty places doesn't blow them apart. Sometimes I think they are dancing.

The bowl stays under Papi's bed in the bunkhouse. The bunkhouse is crowded and ugly and smells like sweating people and mold, but people have their home things in it—Lupe's icon of La Guadalupana, and Don Fermin's guitar, and Papi's bowl that holds us all together. Sometimes while I wait for the water to boil I sit and I hold the clay hands of the people on the bowl. Sometimes when I touch my mami's hand I can hear her singing. Sometimes when I touch Chago's hand I can hear him laughing. And sometimes when I touch the hands of the other people, the ones with the changing faces I feel something, I understand something…I don't have words for that. I have words for everything else, Spanish words and now some English ones, but I don't have words for that.

There. That is a lot of writing. Now the little pots are boiling and it is time for me to pour them.

June 10

Now Papi and the rest of the workers are weeding all day every day. The melons will not be ready to pick for two more months, Don Fermin says. He also says harvesting will be hotter, harder work than weeding. But when I am hot and tired pulling the water wagon I think about eating a whole watermelon and spitting seeds the way I used to do with Chago.

I think about fruit a lot now. That's because on Mr. Martin's farm the plums are ripe, and the plum smell comes in the window of the room where Aunt Chon and I sleep. Sometimes the smell is almost too much because the air is so heavy with heat. And I go to sleep wanting plums and I wake up wanting plums. But if Aunt Chon and Uncle Miguel want plums they have to buy them; if the crew boss sees them eating plums or taking them away they could lose their job and their casita too. Still, Aunt Chon says tomorrow morning, Saturday, when Mexicans are allowed to shop where the Anglos are, she will buy me a plum.

It is very different from home. Aunt Lancha had two pear trees in her back yard, and when the pears were ripe enough so we could smell them we could eat all the pears we wanted and it did not cost anything.

Fruit is the easiest thing I miss. I miss the way the sky looked and the ground smelled back home. I miss Aunt Lancha even though she didn't like me. I miss fiestas in town.

But I don't miss worrying about money. Here we always have enough to eat, and on Sunday special things like spicy sausages or plums, and still my papi is saving money to take home this winter. He keeps half of the saving money in his shoe. I keep the other half in this book because that is what he said to do. I have almost stopped worrying but my papi has not.

Uncle Miguel is worrying too. He bought a newspaper yesterday and talked about it with Aunt Chon last night when David and I were all supposed to be asleep. I was hot and thinking about plums, and I heard him talking about the President. First I didn't listen much. Complaining about the President is just what grown-ups do, in Mexico or here. But then he read a piece out of the newspaper—the English paper—and I listened hard because that helps me learn English and not be ignorant. Some of the words were too hard for me to understand, but I heard some words I knew from David's books or from other newspapers. *Criminals. Invasion. Stealing jobs. Invasion* again.

Invasion… I knew I had seen that in David's history book. That is when soldiers attack. That is a very bad thing. Like when my abuelita's abuelita was a girl and the norteamericanos *invaded* Mexico and took a big piece of it away to be part of their country, and they burned the house where my abuelita's abuelita lived, and she screamed at night after that, and later she had a boy with blond hair and blue eyes who had the same last names as her because she wasn't married—not then, but she was married later, when she had my abuelita's mama. It was bad, too, when my papi was a boy and the soldiers burned their house down, but that was the civil war not an invasion, which means it was all our people fighting, which means it is not quite as bad, maybe, I don't know.

I got up and pulled my serape around me and ran out into the kitchen where Aunt Chon and Uncle Miguel were. "Where is the *invasion*?" I said. "How close are they? Can I get to my papi before we have to run?"

"You're supposed to be sleeping, not eavesdropping," my uncle Miguel said.

"But if there are soldiers coming…"

My aunt sighed. "Come with me," she said, and she walked me out through the dewy grass toward the plum trees. And she explained.

It wasn't soldiers coming. It was us. Mexicans. The paper writers said people like my papi were invaders coming to steal jobs from the real Americans, and maybe to steal other things

"My papi does not steal," I told her. "I do not steal." I meant to say it strong and angry, but I cried instead.

These are my three beautiful things from last night:

The smell of the plums.

The noise the crickets made all around us.

Aunt Chon holding me like her very own and only daughter until I had finished crying.

June 18

I am too tired for a long write, but these are four beautiful things from today:

Tomasito chasing butterflies on the edge of the squash field. He is four and he has a big laugh like his mama Doña Lupe and he doesn't seem to mind that he never catches the butterflies.

Doña Marcela's twins José and Rosita curled up together all sweaty and asleep and smiling and not pushing each other for a while

The star that fell down the sky while I walked to Aunt Chon's house.

My papi giving me an extra kiss before I went, and sitting with me for a few minutes with the family bowl between us, not saying anything, remembering. He looked sad. I hope that was just from remembering.

June 19

I am writing because my papi told me to and because when Aunt Chon comes to check on me if she sees me writing she does not fuss around and try to cheer me up. I am not cheered up and I do not want to have to act like I am cheered up when my papi is gone.

She wants to make sure I do not run away after my papi. I am old enough to know I cannot run fast enough to catch up with the truck they took him away on, even if I knew the right way to go. Anyway Doña Dolores says Papi told me to stay with Aunt Chon and Uncle Miguel, and even though she is crazy I think that part is true.

This is what happened:

I left Aunt Chon's house at six-thirty this morning. We walked down the road with the light still new around us, and I sang a morning song my mami used to sing. But before we got down to the fields we heard trucks coming up the road, and David told me to get down in the ditch right away. He said it in a voice like my papi uses when there's no time to ask questions. I didn't ask questions. I hid, and he hid with me, and we heard the trucks going by. Even when they were gone he didn't stand up for what felt like a very long time, and when I asked why we had been hiding he didn't answer.

We got up and started walking again. The hem of my skirt was all wet and sticking to my legs and I kept pulling on it. And then Doña Dolores came running up the road toward us, and she didn't look a little crazy any more. She looked very very crazy, like all the cracks in her were getting wider and wider and maybe it wasn't just God breathing through them. She waved her hands at us like she was scaring chickens and said go back, go back, go back. And I said where's my papi, and she said he was gone where I couldn't go, which is what Jesus said to the disciples when he knew he was going to be dead.

I thought she said that just because she was crazy. I ran toward her, ducked when she grabbed at me, ran past her. There was nobody in the melon field. Nobody in the squash field. No pot under the pump. The wagon was tipped up on its side. I ran to the bunkhouse. There was nobody there. The blankets were gone from the beds, and the boxes and bags with clothes in them were gone, and Don Fermin's guitar, and La Guadalupana. There were gouges in the wall that hadn't been there before, and one window was broken. My papi's bowl was gone too.

I thought Aunt Chon and Uncle Miguel had lied to me. There had been a real invasion after all.

I looked for the bowl. I kept thinking if I could find it I could find my papi. But all I found was a shoe with the heel ripped out— a shoe that had been Don Fermin's—and a dirty diaper that must have been José's or Rosita's, and a crumble of clay-colored dust on the floor.

David and Doña Dolores found me sitting on the floor with those clay crumbs in my hand. I wasn't crying. My eyes felt hot and hard and dead.

Doña Dolores held out a wadded-up bandanna, and I thought it was for me to cry in, and I shook my head. Then she unwadded the bandanna and pulled out what was inside. A piece of the bowl. The piece had me in it except for my left arm, and one of the people-who-went-before, whole, and another left arm that I knew had been my papi's because he was on the right side of the before person who was on the right side of me. I held onto his clay hand while Doña Dolores told us what had happened.

The men with guns came at sunrise, when Doña Marcela was nursing the twins and everyone else was pulling their shoes on to head out to the fields. The trucks came loud, loud, and pulled up all around the house, and somebody shouted in English, which most people didn't understand, and then they said it again in bad Spanish: come out in ones with your hands up, don't make any jokes (she thinks that wasn't the word they meant) or we'll shoot.

Don Fermin was the first one out that door, going very slowly and holding his hands over his head and not saying anything because he didn't know what they might think was a joke, and the people inside waited to see if the men would shoot him anyway, but they didn't, so another man went after him, and the gun men didn't shoot him either, but they shouted for everyone else to come on out, hurry up. My papi didn't come right out, he was putting things into his bag, and then he took out the bowl and looked at it like he didn't know what to do with it, and then two of the gun men came in and grabbed him. They dropped the bowl on the floor and it broke. They stuffed most of the pieces into his bag, but they missed the piece that went under the bed. Doña Dolores saw that before they made her come out too.

By the time Doña Dolores went our people were standing with their hands held up behind their heads, and the men with guns were feeling them all over to make sure they didn't have guns or knives or anything—they took away Don Pedro's whittling knife and my papi's pocketknife and everybody's razors. They were going to feel Doña Dolores too, but when they went to touch her she was afraid and she screamed and fell down. That was for real, but when they backed away she did more screaming and rolling around and acting crazy so they'd stay away. They didn't touch her, though one man kept a gun pointed at her. And then they made all the people pile into the backs of their trucks, shoved in tight like steers going to market; but when they tried to make Doña Dolores go she acted crazy again and they left her.

My papi told Doña Dolores to give me the piece of our bowl that was left, and to tell me to stay with my aunt and uncle. He said it in very fast Spanish and she thought the gun men didn't understand. Then they put things like cages over the backs of the trucks where the people were and they drove away. Doña Dolores couldn't ask where they were going because she had to keep acting crazy. Don Fermin did ask. She said they didn't answer. Maybe she said this so I wouldn't go after him. She wouldn't even point which way they went. David made me stop shouting at her to show me, and he walked me back to his house.

Aunt Chon went back to look for Doña Dolores and see if she needed help, but Doña Dolores was gone, I don't know where. I hope she is safe. But if it was a choice between her and my papi, I would want him to be the safe one.

June 20

There are stories in the newspaper today about *wetbacks* getting arrested. Aunt Chon explained that means us, because of crossing the river—though I was not wet when I crossed, because

I sat high up on my papi's shoulders. One story says the President had to send out the gun men to push back the *engulfing tide* of illegal aliens. I am learning a lot of English and I do not want to. I do not want anything about this country any more. I just want to be safe away from it with my papi. But I can't do that.

The other story talked about *aliens* being kept in big dirt yards near the cities that have bus and train stations. One is almost an hour west of us even for people in trucks, and the other is about that far east, and the papers didn't say which people went where. It said some of the men that were arrested acted like animals and threw rocks at the newspaper people. If I had a rock I would throw it at the men with the guns instead. Only then maybe they would shoot people, so maybe I would not.

My papi, I think, would not throw rocks at anyone. But they should not keep him out in the dirt like that. They should not make him go back to Aunt Lancha's house without me, and without his pay for the week (they were supposed to pay him on the day when they took him away instead).

And what if somebody else throws rocks and my papi gets shot?

Aunt Chon says to pray instead of worrying. Padre Vincentio said the same thing during the Mass, and again after to me when Aunt Chon took me to see him. But Padre Vincentio's father is not standing in the dirt somewhere with gun men around him so it is easy for him not to worry. Padre Vincentio has a telephone, so he called some places and tried to ask about my papi, but they said they didn't have a list of names, and they wouldn't take a message, and anyway we didn't know what would be a safe message to leave.

Aunt Chon hugged me and I pushed her away. She gave me a plum and I tried to eat it but I cried and choked instead. She tried to talk to me but I ran to my alone place under the juniper and I held onto my papi's clay hand, and when I came back I started writing right away so she would leave me alone.

June 21

I am not going to tell Aunt Chon what I saw, because she would maybe think I am getting crazy like Doña Dolores. But I think what I saw was real and not crazy. I do not want it to be real.

but I think it is.

Yesterday when everybody else was gone to work or to school and I had swept the floor and washed the dishes and put the beans on to soak I sat down and held my papi's clay hand again and I tried to pray. I am not good at praying. But I could feel my papi's hand getting warmer, and then I felt like I fell into a hole in the ground, like the time I was eight and fell in the cistern where the boards on top were rotten and I thought I would die there but instead my papi found me. Only this time when I fell through I found him.

I must have been hanging in the air like an angel—no, not really like an angel; angels talk to people and tell them not to be afraid and give them good news and keep them safe, and I did not have any good news and I was afraid and I shouted for my papi but he could not hear me at all. I could hear him, though, and see him.

He was still in one of those cage trucks, in a long line of cage trucks bumping down a dusty road. There was dirt on his face and his hands and his clothes. There wasn't dirt in his hair because he didn't have any hair. His head was all bald and sunburned. One of the newspapers said they were shaving people's heads so they couldn't come back to El Norte without being recognized. My papi looked older and uglier and sadder being bald like that. His head drooped down and his shoulders drooped down and he held something in his hands. I looked all around the truck and all I could see was tan sand with bits of dead grass growing on it like fur on a mangy animal. Somebody in the truck was cursing, and somebody was praying the rosary out loud, and my papi wasn't saying anything at all. I thought it was maybe a rosary he had in his hands, but when I looked closer I saw it was a piece of the bowl. He was holding my clay hand.

Then the truck stopped. My papi put the piece with my clay hand in his pocket, and he kept his hand on it there. Three of the gun men got out. They unlocked the cage and unlatched the back of the truck and said to jump down.

"Here?" said the man who'd been swearing. "But we left Mexicali more than an hour ago, and out here…"

"You won't be back over the river in a hurry, will you?" one of the gun men said.

One of the other gun men reached up to help a woman get down out of the truck, and he looked like he wanted to cry, though maybe that was just from being hot and dirty. "What about water?" the woman asked him. He gave her a big bottle and then he walked away looking even sadder and climbed into the front of the truck. A man asked the other gun men for water, but they didn't give him any. Another man tried to climb back into the truck, but they hit him and he stopped.

When my papi and all the people with him had gotten down out of the trucks, the gun men got back in the trucks and drove away. The dust shone in the sun like stars falling. I could just see and hear, not feel or smell, but I knew how hot it must be from the shine in the air and the way the people breathed. They stood there, looking all around for shade, but there wasn't any, and for water, but there wasn't any.

Someone said it would take too long to get back to Mexicali, and someone else said it would take longer to get anywhere else, and my papi didn't say anything, but he took José on his shoulders, with his extra shirt spread out over José's head to keep the sun from beating on it. That way Doña Marcela just had Rosita to carry, and she tied her in a sling in front of her. Then they all started walking back up the road. I wanted to be there with him and have José back in El Norte with people who would try to talk to him and feed him plums. I would not sit on my papi and make him tired. I would walk beside him. I would help him.

They walked and walked for a long time, and they went slower and slower. Rosita started to cry, and instead of singing to Rosita or taking her in her arms Doña Marcela put her hands over her own ears.

I remembered something then. I opened my eyes, so I could see the casita as well as the desert, but I kept my hand tight on my papi's clay hand, and even with my eyes open I could still see the desert light. I found my Bible and looked in the very first book for the part where they send Hagar and her baby out in the desert without enough food or water or anywhere safe to go. There was sort of a light around the words, the way that sometimes there's sort of a light around the clay things my papi makes. I can't put life into things with my hands the way he can, but sometimes I can with my voice. So I read the words out loud. I read this:

"When the water in the skin was gone, she put the boy under one of the bushes. Then she went off and sat down about a bowshot away, for she thought, 'I cannot watch the boy die.' And as she sat there, she began to sob."

I was starting to sob then too, but it was not time for sobbing, it was time for reading. I read the good part too: "Then God opened her eyes and she saw a well of water. So she went and filled the skin with water and gave the boy a drink."

I shut my eyes and saw the desert again, and Doña Marcela with her hands over her ears. I waited for clouds to come over the sky, or for someone to see green trees in the distance and know there was water, or for a truck full of kind people with water jugs to come down the road. I said the good words again and again, but none of those things happened. The people kept walking, and the baby kept crying, and the sun kept getting higher in the sky, and the clay hand in my hand felt dry as dust and I thought it was going to crumble apart.

After a long time, with me saying the words dry-mouthed and gasping, and them gasping and not talking, the land started to twist around them: a big slope of sand went up on the left of the road, a big slope of sand went down on the right. The sun was coming from the right, so there wasn't any shade for them. My papi's eyes looked wrong, like he wasn't really seeing the things in front of him. *Do something!* I said to God again. But all that happened was that my papi stumbled. Someone took José off his shoulders. He straightened up and took a few more steps, but then he stumbled again and fell on the edge of the road. He flailed out with his arms to catch himself, and I saw the bowl shard in his right hand fly up and away, and then down, down into the sand that sloped away. And then I couldn't see anything at all. I had fallen back through the hole and my papi was gone.

July 1

Every day I cry. Every night I want to dream about my papi and I do not. Instead I dream about water that disappears when I try to touch my hand or my lips to it.

Every day I read something in the Bible or in David's books and I write something in this book because that is what my papi told me to do. When I can't think of anything beautiful I write that I can't think of anything beautiful.

Every morning Aunt Chon makes me get up, and makes me eat, and because I have eaten and because I have to do something with the day I work a little in the house although she would not make me do that.

Every morning and every night I put my hand on my papi's clay hand, but I do not feel any warmth. I do not see anything. I do not keep it in my pocket any more because it was flaking into dust there. Now I keep it by my pallet but it is flaking into dust there too.

Translation of a letter from Angel Felipe Fuentes Ortiz to Cristina Guadalupe Fuentes Espinosa, care of Concepcion Soledad Navarro Reyes

July 15, 1954

To my dear daughter:

This is to tell you that I am all right. Your Aunt Lancha gave me the message that Padre Vincentio called in to the town hall here saying you were safe at your aunt and uncle's house, thanks be to God. But she didn't have a number to call the priest back, so I am writing you this letter instead. Write back to the town hall, not to your aunt's house—by the time the letter gets here it may not be your aunt's house any more; I am looking for work, so is she, but I do not know if we can pay the rent next month. Write, but stay where you are. I am sorry, but there is not money to buy you a ticket, and there is not money to keep you here. You know your cousins Raul and Felipe were working in El Norte and sending money home to your aunt Lancha. Well, Felipe came back with his head shaved, and Raul has not come home at all. Felipe was lucky: the train he was on left people right in Nogales, so he could call from the church there and tell his mami he was all right. Raul...We hope Raul is all right.

I did not want to tell you anything about the danger there is for people who are sent back, but Lancha tells me the papers have stories about the people who died from being left in the desert in the heat, so you will already know and be worried. Don't worry. Raul wrote his mother a letter the day those people died in the desert, so we know he wasn't on those buses. And I am safe, I am all right. They put us in the desert too, but not so far in, and we found water. How we found it is a strange story, but I think you will believe me when I tell it, Cris.

I hope you still have the piece of the bowl I gave Doña Dolores to give to you. I kept the other pieces, and I held your clay hand and asked God to keep you safe. I was still holding that when they put us out in the desert and we started walking back. But I fell, and it flew out of my hand and off the road in a place where the slope dropped off steeply. I felt as though I was losing you again, and I ran after the piece, and then my feet slid and the sand slid under me and I went down, down, and I didn't know if I was strong enough to climb back up. When I stopped sliding I kept my eyes closed for a little while because I was afraid to look up and see how far I would have to climb. But they were shouting to me from the road, and I had to sit up and open my eyes. And I saw an opening in front of me, going back into the sand bank. Just a little opening, one I could go through on my hands and knees. But it was dark inside that opening, and I thought how cool it would be, and I crawled in. And just a little way inside the rock lifted above me and I could stand. It was cool there, blessedly cool, and I smelled water.

Cris, you have the gift for words, you could say better than I can how I felt when I heard the water. But you know from the Bible, *At the scent of water he shall revive.* And I did.

I called, and the others came, and we drank, and we rested in the heat of the day, and then we started walking again, and before we could get badly sick from the cave water we came into the city, hot and filthy and sick and tired and very, very glad to be alive. But I was not as glad as the others, because I did not know what had happened to you, or even to the little piece of you I had left in clay.

Well, that was foolishness. You are safe. I love you, Cris. I will tell you how much I love you when I see you again. I do not know when or how, but I will see you again.

~ * ~

Operation Wetback really did happen in 1954. The US Border Patrol rounded up close to one million undocumented immigrants from farms and factories across the country, shaved their heads and shipped them deep into Mexico. 88 people died after being left in the desert on a blistering hot day. Many more survived, but some of them were separated from their families and didn't get word from their relatives for many years. I made the Fuentes family luckier.

IN MY FATHER'S HOUSE

This story was originally published in Vox et Liber's anthology
Graveyard Visits *in fall 2020*

The setting sun smeared a bloody glow across the clouds as I climbed out of my rental car in the driveway of my childhood home and shut the driver's door. I glared at the sky. "Bad things are no likelier to happen under a sky like that," I said in my best brave rational voice, "than under the maidenliest stars in the firmament." I didn't altogether convince myself.

There was a car parked in front of me, a blue Toyota, which was what Dad had said he drove; it was cleaner on the outside than my rental car, but not quite as immaculate as Dad used to keep his publicly visible possessions. The garden between the drive and the house was overgrown with weeds. He'd kept the hedge trimmed very neatly. That was all you could see from the road; the driveway curved enough so passing drivers couldn't see the garden, and I had the impression no one ever came to visit him. This meant I didn't know how long he'd been missing, or if he was missing at all.

I'd called Dad once a month ever since we left, so he wouldn't forget he had a daughter. He never called, never asked me anything, never seemed to remember anything about my life, but he answered politely when I asked what he'd been doing. The substance of the answers didn't change much until he retired, when, instead of talking about people at the office, he started talking about people at the church and the gym. All of them, in his telling, liked him very much. I didn't know how seriously to take that; I had learned as a child that the substance of Dad's remarks was determined by their desired effect rather than by the facts to which they appeared to refer. But when I called him several times every day for two weeks in a row and he never answered, I knew where to make inquiries.

The gym said he hadn't been in for about four weeks, though before that he'd come in daily for months. He'd also missed four Sundays at the church. I thought about calling the police but decided not to. Dad wasn't seventy yet. He hadn't had a heart attack or a stroke (that he'd admitted to me). He was (by his own account) the poster boy of the gym's Silver Section. He had every right to take a trip without notifying his estranged family, or his pastor, or the gym staff. But something still felt wrong enough so that, come Saturday, I rented a cheap car and drove nine hours to his house.

The windows reflected the sunset redly and I had the distinct impression the house was glaring balefully at me. "You're supposed to be just neurotic, not paranoid," I told myself. This, I recalled, was negative self-talk. "It's all right," I added more kindly. "All you have to do is walk up to the door and knock…"

Then I heard the dog howling.

I don't care for dogs at the best of times, not since the neighbor's German shepherd bit me when I was three—or, perhaps, since I first registered that Dad, who consistently forgot my birthday, consistently commented on the anniversary of the day when he got his puppy Blackie.

I think I might have been spooked even without my dog phobia; this howl was eldritch and alarmingly close. I grabbed the handle of the driver's door. It was locked. I fumbled in my pocket for the key. It wasn't there. I looked in through the driver's window. The key lay on the seat.

The howl sounded again, closer.

I pounded on the front door of the house. Nobody answered. I jiggled the doorknob. It didn't turn. Something growled close behind me.

The window into the mudroom was half open. I pulled the screen out and stuffed myself in through the bottom half of the sash. My fall was broken by a cardboard box full of boots under the window.

"Dad?" I called. I didn't want to get mistaken for a burglar and shot. "Dad, it's Gillian. I just came to check on you. Are you OK?"

No answer. No echo. The thick air swallowed my voice.

I counted my breaths, willed myself not to panic, sidled along the wall to the door, flicked the light on, and recoiled.

Someone stood, still and silent, just on the other side of the doorway.

For a moment I thought I must be having my first-ever actual hallucination. A huge black dog, upright and immobile on its hind paws, stared me in the face.

No, not a dog. A statue of a dog. Of something like a dog. More or less. More.

The head was a dog's, jet-black, with a long muzzle, upswept ears, and disconcertingly human eyes. The body was human, with the chest of a bodybuilder above a gold loincloth. The hand that held a long golden object was human too. I couldn't tell if it held a staff, spear, or scepter.

I'd seen a picture like that in National Geographic. *Anubis.* I almost said it out loud, but then I stopped myself. I know perfectly well what magical thinking is and why it doesn't work. I knew saying a statue's name couldn't cause it to come to life. Still…I turned away, took three deep calming breaths, and walked to the living room door.

The window in that door was covered with a picture of another almost-dog. This one also stood upright and had a long narrow muzzle and human eyes, but it was wearing full body armor, somewhat bloodied, and raising a bloody sword in its left hand. Its right hand held an enormous cross upraised in a way that struck me as more menacing than benedictory. There was a golden circle behind the dog's head, and under its feet there were words etched in pseudo-antique capital letters: ST. CHRISTOPHER, PROTECT US.

As I turned the doorknob I thought, *'But Dad's a Methodist…'*

The knob turned. The door swung open about forty-five degrees, then stopped.

"Dad?" I called again. "It's Gillian. Dad, are you okay?"

No answer. No echo.

I stepped inside. The room was completely dark. It shouldn't have been. There were two big south-facing windows in the wall to my right—at least, there had been—and there was no way I could have lingered in the mudroom long enough for the black night to descend. Anyway the clouds hadn't covered that much of the sky, and the moon was waxing and near the full.

I groped behind me for the light switch. It worked.

The floor was piled waist-deep with boxes, magazines, newspapers, other papers, books, vinyl records, CDs: the sort of stuff with which the walk-in closet in Dad's room used to be jammed, but seemingly he'd run out of closet space. Right ahead of me there was an open path to the foot of the stairs. To my right another path ran to the middle of the south wall, somewhere in between the windows, I supposed. I had to suppose because I couldn't see it. There was a curtain or vinyl screen or something pulled down behind the windows. It was heavily, opaquely black except for an equally opaque white stripe down the middle.

In front of the white stripe stood another Anubis statue. In the black square to Anubis' right was a gold-framed picture of a black spaniel pup with curly hair, adoring eyes, and a shoe in its mouth. The pup was gazing with disgusting devotion at a golden-haired boy turned away from the viewer. In the black square to Anubis' left was a picture of a pale-skinned man on a black horse with a sword in each hand. A corpse lay under the horse. An angel hovered above the swordsman, holding its arms out in what looked more like a gesture of blessing than an attempt to stop the carnage. Behind the swordsman stood two men with dogs' heads and blood-streaked white muzzles, holding long spears and baring sharp teeth in unpleasant enthusiasm.

A shriek started building up somewhere north of my dia-phragm. I managed to let the shriek out at a lower pitch and at an almost reasonable volume. My shriek changed into one word: "Dad?"

No answer. No echo.

He had every right to not be home.

His car was in the driveway.

Maybe he'd bought a new one.

Maybe a friend had come to pick him up.

From this house? I didn't think so.

Maybe he'd gone for a walk.

He always hated walking. Though he talked fondly about how he used to go for walks with Blackie.

I made myself go closer to the statue and the pictures. Yes, there was a cleared path to the door that led into the dining room and kitchen.

The dust on the piles around me must have been a quarter-inch deep, but Anubis was completely dust-free.

So? Maybe Dad dusted selectively.

Something obtruded into my brave self-talk. A smell. A stench.

'Oh, Christ,' I thought, somewhere between praying and swear-ing. 'He's dead, he's rotting, and nobody knew. What kind of a daughter am I? Oh, Christ...' The smell grew stronger as I approached the door into the dining room and kitchen. All I wanted was to get away.

'Denial doesn't help,' I told myself. 'What you can see, you can deal with.' I hadn't been convinced of that when I started CBT. I had thought I'd become convinced, but…

I made myself walk through the door. The smell sucked me in like quicksand. I pulled the neck of my turtleneck up over my mouth and nose before looking around for the source.

He wasn't sitting in one of the dining chairs, or in the wooden rocker where I used to watch birds by the east window. Not on the bar stool by the counter. Not slumped across the counter or the table. Not on the part of the floor that I could see. I edged up to the counter and steeled myself to look over.

Dad wasn't on the floor there, either. The oven door was shut. A full-grown man couldn't fit inside that anyway. The fridge door, though, was slightly open. I swallowed bile, imagining him leaning in to get something and having—a stroke? A heart attack?

There weren't feet sticking out the door.

But the smell came from there.

'Well, no wonder,' I thought after I had forced myself to yank the door wide open. There was something soggy and brown in a produce bag in the crisper drawer, and a package of meat on the fridge shelf, apparently quite rotten.

I slammed the door shut, muting the very worst of the smell. As I did that I noticed what was on the fridge door—I mean, besides the mildew spots. He hadn't thrown out the bright alphabet-letter fridge magnets I used to play with when I was little. He'd arranged them into three lines of words, two words on each line. On the top: THIS IS followed by a long letterless space. On the next line: SEE RUN, the two words spaced widely apart. On the bottom line, RUN RUN, spaced equally wide, but not quite lined up under the words above them.

I don't know how long I stood there staring at the door before it occurred to me the message was, if you counted the mildew-spots after and between the words, a Dick-and-Jane rebus. The words thumped dully in my brain in time with the pulsing ache that was building in the middle of my skull. SEE RUN RUN RUN. I didn't.

'No more running' was one of the things I'd said to myself over and over while I was trying to unpick my compulsions. I'd seen enough to suggest something was seriously wrong with Dad, and I'd find it hard to live with myself if I went home without trying to find him. I couldn't get up the nerve to search the yard in the dark with the Hound of the Baskervilles loose, but I could at least go upstairs and look in the half-bath and the bedrooms.

I retreated from the kitchen and marched myself—that is how it felt, as if I stood behind myself, forcing myself along with a cold sharp object prodding the small of my back—past the pictures and the Anubis statue. I kept my eyes fixed on the stripe of carpet in front of me, along the cleared pathways through the living room and to the foot of the stairs.

The stairs were clear of everything but dust. All the doors opening onto the hallway at the head of the stair were half-open.

The bathroom at the head of the stair was empty.

The door on the right led to the smaller bedroom that had once been my refuge from the world. My bedroom light didn't go on. '*It's all right*,' I told myself. '*The bulb's burned out*.' I felt in my pocket, pulled out my LED light, and flashed it around the room.

At first, I thought the hulking shape in the corner was another giant dog statue. I clenched my teeth and shone the light in its eyes as if it was still alive and capable of being blinded. Then I realized that it was Boreas, my grey rocking horse, sitting just where he used to sit when I was four. There was a clear inch of dust on the floor, and on Boreas too. Dad must have gotten him back out of the walk-in storage closet behind his and Mum's room quite some time ago.

The rest of my room also seemed to have gone back in time. I'd taken my favorite books when I left, but there should still have been abandoned volumes of Macdonald, Saint-Exupery, and Euripides. Instead, only a few chunky board books sat on the shelves. My little rocking chair sat on the floor facing Boreas, and my stuffed bear Arthur, with his lopsided smile and his left ear half chewed off, sat in the chair.

I remembered sitting in that chair with Arthur in my lap, Dad sitting in front of me, making polite conversation with Arthur while we waited for the plastic tea kettle to boil in the patch of sunlight on the floor.

If Dad had been in that room in the past month he'd have left tracks in the dust. Nevertheless, I made myself look under the bed and in the little closet, mostly to put off going into Dad's room. Finally, I patted the worst of the dust off Arthur and stuffed him under my left arm as I marched myself up to Dad's door.

The door swung wide without a sound. The light worked.

Dad wasn't on the bed. As the bed had little built-in storage compartments underneath, he couldn't be under it either. He wasn't lying on the floor between the bed and dresser, or in the clear space of rug at the end of the bed and in front of the door of the walk-in closet. For one stomach-turning moment, I thought he was slumped immobile in the armchair at the foot of the bed, but then I saw that it was a pile of full black plastic garment bags with hangers sticking out the top. Dad's suits, I supposed, back from the cleaner.

I poked through the pile just in case. Suits, indeed. I turned my back on the chair and shoved open the door of the walk-in closet.

Most of the opening was filled with a rack on which other plastic-sheeted suits hung. I approached that gingerly, feeling for the in-closet light.

It came on, more or less. It hummed, a thin unpleasant sound, while flickering constantly, aggravating my headache. I looked around the rack into the closet.

The boxes of papers and books Dad used to keep there had been removed—likely dumped into the piles downstairs. The heavy old Morris chair that had been Dad's father's, carved elaborately enough to be a throne, sat facing the closet's back corner.

Dad sat in the chair, staring away from me. He'd let his hair grow long and shaggy, but it was black as the suit he wore. Dyed, then; he'd been more than half grey the last time I saw him. He sat entirely still, not moving in response to the light or to the strangled noise I made. At his feet, on a dog bed on the floor, sitting up on its haunches with its head pressed against his knees, was a bony grey-haired dog, immobile as Dad, also wearing a suit.

'*You're cracking up,*' I told myself, and then, more soothingly, '*The dog on the floor is just another statue.*' But the way it pressed against Dad's leg—if that was a hard statue, it would hurt.

I tried to speak to him again, but no sound came out. I stepped toward the back wall of the closet and turned so I could look him in the face.

For a moment I stared dumbly, my brain whimpering. Then I realized what I was seeing.

The figure in the chair must have been a statue, or a doll, or something of the sort. Another dog-headed man. This one had long silky black hair, big soulful eyes, and long sharp bone-white teeth.

The figure crouching on the blanket was Dad. His hair was greyer and shaggier than I remembered. His slenderness had become emaciation. His arms went straight down to the floor, elbows locked straight—he sat in the most doglike posture a human body could manage. He didn't turn to look at me.

I couldn't speak. It took me a while to convince myself that knowing he was dead wouldn't be any worse than standing there thinking he must be dead. It took me even longer to persuade myself the thing on the chair wouldn't sink its teeth into the back of my neck if I stooped over Dad.

I reached out and touched the back of Dad's neck, expecting to find it stiff and cold.

His neck felt cooler than my hand, but not corpse-cold. I slid my hand round to the front to feel for a pulse. It was there, but terribly slow. I reached my left hand up (careful to not drop Arthur) and felt my pulse for comparison. It beat about four times to Dad's one. Though it was likely going rather faster than the ideal.

The light went out. The light from the bedroom beyond cast a pale grey illumination into the other half of the closet, but Dad and the dog and I were fully shadowed. I wouldn't be able to see if the thing in the chair moved, or if Dad looked at me.

I could feel the hard lump of my LED light in my right pocket. I knew I could fish that out and turn it on if I just took my hand off Dad's neck.

I also knew, as surely as I knew that two and two made four, or that God was real—or as I had once thought I knew I had to go and check for the seventeenth time in a given evening to see if I had really shut the oven off so as not to kill myself and my fellow tenants with a gas explosion—that if I took my hand away I wouldn't be able to reach Dad again.

A fragment of poetry floated through my mind, a bit of the Euripides I had started reading to impress Dad with my maturity and precocity. That I had kept reading because it was beautiful and haunting, and also because some of those plays featured families significantly more messed up than my own.

> To win thee forth from Hades I had gone
> into the depths; not Hell's grim hound nor he

who plies his oars upon the tide of death
had hindered me from bearing back thy life
unto the light again…

The "had," I remembered, was not past perfect but conditional, meaning *I would have gone if…* If what?

I kept my right hand at Dad's pulse and set my left hand on Dad's shoulder, Arthur squashed between my arm and Dad's. The dark spun around me, and I felt myself falling. When the light gathered again I was not wholly surprised to find myself somewhere else.

It didn't look like Hades. The living room in which I stood was warmly illuminated by several floor lamps. Layers of heavy curtains covered the windows. The slender boy—Dad; I knew him from photo albums from his childhood—sat on the plush red carpet in a pool of lamplight, his head bent and his back half turned to me, intent on the black spaniel puppy which lay on its back in front of him wriggling in subservient delight. The dog made adoring little squeals that varied in pitch and timbre so they might almost have been speech, though not in any language I knew. Once they sounded almost like a woman crying out in ecstatic surrender; once like a baby babbling happily; then again they were wholly canine. The boy scratched the dog's chest, and the dog thrummed with joy, and the world was good.

I didn't want to speak to the boy, to intrude. Dad had never seemed so delighted, so at ease, since I'd known him.

I also did want to speak to the boy, for precisely the same reason. Dad's happiness shut me out more thoroughly than his unhappiness had ever done.

For a while, I was too busy wrangling my mind to notice the sounds from outside the room. But then, through the muffled window, I heard the howling that had driven me into my father's house.

I tiptoed towards the window. The puppy glanced at me, but the boy kneaded her chest harder so she turned her attention back to him.

Yes, that was definitely howling out there. Not one animal but a whole hunting pack. Like the puppy inside, they had a disquietingly rich vocal range. Sometimes I could have sworn I heard human voices, now menacing, now reproachful. Once I thought I caught an echo of Dad's father's voice in one of his long rants about the disappointments of his life, amongst whom he included his descendants. Once an echo of my mother's voice, tense and weary, coming up from downstairs when I was supposed to be asleep. Once of my own. But before I could be certain of any of those resemblances the noise became merely howling again. Through all its changes it kept getting louder.

The boy crooned to the dog. To cover up the sounds from outside?

There were other sounds. Footsteps on the other side of the room's closed door, coming up the stairs. A deep voice called out...I couldn't tell if that voice was canine or human. If it was human, I couldn't make out its words, but the contempt and the command in its tone were unmistakable.

The boy's hand froze on the puppy's chest. Then he sighed. "You know what you have to do," he said, and while his face was still a boy's face, his voice was an old man's.

"What do I have to do?" I said. "I don't know."

He didn't answer me. He didn't look at me.

The dog stood facing the door. Then it began to grow and change. Its silky hair turned short and bristly; its muzzle elongated and showed sharp teeth in a snarl; its feet developed prodigious claws. When it was the size of a pony its form stabilized and it looked over its shoulder at the boy, slavering.

The boy shook as though he'd just been hauled out of deep cold water, but he managed to point at the door. "Go!" he said, and his voice was a child's again, a child's in the night alone. "Go get them!"

The door slammed open as the dog hurled itself at it. There was a terrible clash and a snarl, and then the door slammed shut. The clamor of fighting dogs slowly receded down the stairs.

The boy cupped his hands, crooned, stared at the shadow cupped in his palms. Then it was something more than a shadow: it was a tiny black puppy...

As surely as I had known that if I let go of Dad I'd lose him, I knew the dog he'd just launched down the stairs would join the hunting pack howling under the windows. And the lead hound, or the huntsman, or whoever it was, would climb the stairs again and again...

"It won't work," I said. "It won't last. That way's no good. Let me help you."

He flinched a little, hunched his shoulders, stared harder into his hands.

I stood right over him. "Dad," I said. I'd meant to sound kind. I sounded furious. "Dad, it's Gillian. Your daughter. Your real daughter, not some imaginary cur!" The last sound trailed into a growl.

The boy shouted and pulled his hands apart. The tiny pup transformed itself with alarming speed, paling, elongating, rearing up on its hind legs, until I was facing a dog-headed soldier like the ones in the picture in the living room—snow-white, blank-eyed, long-clawed, clutching a long black spear.

I gulped and backed to the wall. No good; the room was tiny.

My hand, groping behind me, felt a doorknob. It turned. I shoved the door open, glanced over my shoulder.

There was my childhood bedroom, the carpet bright green as my imaginary meadow. In the back corner, Boreas waited to take me away to the safe bright lands. By the door stood Arthur, no mere teddy but a full-grown bear more than capable of defending me even from the dog-man in front of me. If I could just dodge behind Arthur, I'd be safe.

I felt the sweet flood of relief I used to feel when I first gave in to compulsion, before the sick feeling and the sense of futility set in.

I thought what I had doggedly trained myself to think when I felt that way. *'That won't help. That's a trap. Don't run from fear. Face it.'*

I made myself step back toward the toothy monster that glared at me. I said, "You're a very ugly mutt, but you're not real," in a voice considerably less brave than my words. I stared at the monster hard enough to memorize it, and then I dropped my eyes to the boy cringing against the wall. I walked right past the monster. I felt its hot breath on my neck. I even saw its spear jab at my gut, evaporating as it touched me. I knelt by the boy.

"I shouldn't have snarled at you," I said. "I'm sorry. Look at me, please."

He shot me a terrified glance as if I was still snarling at him. I saw myself for a moment in his eyes—at least, I saw a figure wearing my rust-colored sweater, but its head was a dog's head, growling.

"No," I said. "No, that's not me. Keep looking. I came here to help you." I kept on like that, the same way I talked to my goat when she was in hard labor, my level voice and the fact of my nearness mattering more than the words. Gradually his head lifted and he looked at me again, starting to smile.

I saw myself in his eyes. My hair was black and silky, topped with a pink bow, and my ears were soft and long.

"No," I said again. "That's not me either. I don't adore you. I don't want to hurt you. I want you to be alive, do you hear me? I want you to wake up. I want you to live!"

I reached out and took his hands, tried to hold them and his eyes as firmly as I could.

The dark lurched around us again. My knees hurt. I was back in the closet. Arthur, dusty again, lay at my feet. The buzzy light bulb had flickered back on. Dad and I were clutching each other's forearms as if we might be about to jump off a high place, or to embrace, or to wrestle. His face was turned toward me, and awareness—together with his usual anxious disappointed look— came into his eyes.

"Gillian?" he said.

TELL IT SLANT

This story was originally published by Crossed Genres *in 2015.*

Take it easy, sir. I'm not resisting arrest. I'm unarmed. I'm not stupid enough to try anything with all these guardsmen glaring at me. Anyway, I'm not the one you want. I'm not Alija. Surely you can see that; I'm old enough to be her mother...

Someone told you I was the storyteller? I wish I was. I'm just *a* storyteller. It was Alija who stirred things up with her stories that reminded people of the old uprising your lot don't want us to mention in case people should take it into their heads to try it again.

Yes, they do seem to be trying it again. Don't blame me. This isn't my story.

No, I'm not squealing on Alija. She's dead. Not arrested, just shot. Didn't you know? Maybe they didn't realize who they were shooting. Or maybe they didn't tell you...do you ever wonder about that?

Sorry, I wasn't insulting you, just thinking out loud. For all I know you're their right-hand man. No need to shove me.

Look, why don't we finish this conversation here, outside? I can tell you more that way. Who's going to interfere? Everyone else left when you arrived. Anyway, if you took me off to the dungeons I wouldn't say anything useful.

No, that's not defiance. Alija would have called on the memory of...the people we aren't to mention...and refused to tell you anything. Me, I'm just explaining. Apart from the stories that get around about your lock-ups—and yes, I know how stories can get exaggerated—I can't stand being shut away from air and light. I'd lose whatever reason I still have. I'd be no use to anybody. Could be I never was. I'm not Alija; I'm not Avall come again...

Sorry, sorry! But you've heard his name before, and now I'm not talking to a crowd that could get the wrong ideas. You know how they say Avall started the last uprising with his stories. I'm just trying to tell you I don't have it in me to be the Avall of this age.

What do I have it in me to be? Well, I could be a bit like Nadi, maybe.

Never heard of Nadi? Ah well, your great-grandchildren

won't have heard of me. After they took Avall away, made him into a story, Nadi was still loose, being too unimportant to arrest. He was a storyteller too, but of another breed. Avall was all light and fire. They say when he told the old tale of the Bright Rising against the Ilid kings, the people who listened to him could see Sirin's ship burning on the sea, feel the cold air in the mountain passes where the fugitives went to live free, hear the brave servant-girl's dying cry in the royal courtyard and the hoarse singing of the servants and peasants and workmen who laid their tools down and kept vigil about the castle after she died…

All right, all right, I know I'm not supposed to tell that story either. I'm just trying to explain about Avall. The thing is, people remembered his stories and started to think how close their times were to the Ilid days, so next time a few people disappeared together, and no one had seen the guardsmen come, everyone thought of the mountains, and next time someone was found dead everyone thought of the servant-girl.

Now Nadi, he didn't tell stories like that. Didn't want to be arrested, maybe. Didn't want to creak out on a one-stringed fiddle what Avall had done with a full orchestra, more likely. Do you know what that's like? To have someone reach into the back of your mind and the strings of your guts and speak the things you know and want and fear that you don't even admit to yourself, and then to have that person taken away to be a hero, and yourself left standing there with your brain and your guts unstrung, and then to have someone ask you for a story?

No, I guess you don't know. I do, and Nadi did. So Nadi told little stories. Glow-worms. Hot-water bottles to keep your feet warm of a winter's night. He'd tell about the tricks a young girl played on her older sister who was a palace servant, how she resented her and loved her. He'd have you laughing a little, wincing a little, as the girl went through the palace by night to spy on her sister, thinking she was meeting a lover; and then you'd hear heavy feet run by and see the young girl in the shadows, watching the moonlight on the courtyard and hearing her sister's dying cry. About the time the guardsmen on duty realized he'd come out to the ending of one of Avall's stories, Nadi would be gone, vanished into the crowd.

Next day he'd appear in another square, telling about the jealousies of a pair of sheep in a poor man's farm on the coast, putting in jokes I won't repeat in front of your upstanding men; and just as the ewe was laughing at the ram with his horns stuck through the hole in the fence, she'd smell smoke and turn her head, and there would be a ship out on the sea, burning to the waterline; and the guards would perk their ears up, and Nadi would be gone.

Folk remembered the stories, remembered what he didn't say more than what he said, and it kept something alive in them. Aval's memory, yes, and something more. You know how that story ended.

No, I haven't made a very good case for my own harmlessness, have I? Well, I wouldn't be in a hurry to act on that if I were you. There are people behind you. They won't like it if you hurt me. Since they can't save Alija, I'm the next best thing.

That's right. Put your sword up. Turn around.

No, your eyes aren't playing tricks on you. The prison gate is open, and there's a new flag flying.

Don't blame me. This isn't my story. My job was just to remind those people of something, and to distract you while they worked the main story out behind your back.

They don't need me now. They've gotten to the end of the chapter. Maybe they think it's the happy ending of the story, the same as they thought after the Bright Rising, the same as they thought in Nadi's day. I know better than that, but I don't know what happens next. Alija might have been able to guess. She might have been able to shape it into something better worth telling. I wish we had her here to try.

THE USUAL PRICE

This story was first published in
Flame Tree Publishing's Heroic Fantasy *anthology in 2016*

I see him clearly in the scrying-glass: another hero, a frightened young man trying to keep his seat on a nervous horse, just starting to climb the slope before my castle. In another hundred yards he'll be directly under the guard-tower, which will crush him if I tell it to throw itself down.

The first time this happened I thought I had no choice. I'd spent two weeks ordering the walls to ward the first would-be champion off, two wretched weeks in which I kept starting to doze and jerking back to wakefulness as the castle pushed him away. I couldn't take it any longer. Since I couldn't dream at night, I found myself slipping into waking dreams of the bad time I thought I'd left behind forever…that I had to leave behind. So I opened the gate for the bright-eyed young man, and while he was still laughing with joy I made the stones beneath his feet open and swallow him, close again and crush him. It was quick, at least—I thought I owed him that. By the tenth time I was past caring, though I did take care to finish each one out in the open for the sake of the witnesses.

There are always witnesses, grooms or serving-maids in the castle peering from windows, waiting for a chance to slip out by the postern gate and bear the news. At first I thought they would say it was hopeless to come against the Castle of the Golden Sun, that kings' younger sons and brave foundlings should save their energy for better quests and forget the king's daughter who languished here, bound by enchantment. I hoped, I mostly hoped, that was what they would say. But this young man is the twenty-fourth to come as a rescuer during my reign, just as I was the twenty-fourth during the old enchanter's time.

This hero doesn't look much like me, though. I was taller, and I didn't breathe through my mouth like that. It makes him look like an idiot. I wasn't as strong as my eldest brother, or as handsome as my second one—and they took care I should remember that—but I looked well enough, and I learned to carry myself so no one would call me a coward. I never showed how frightened I was. Not when my brothers knocked me down. Not when I rode out into the world seeking a valiant quest—no doubt my brothers thought I was running away from them, but it wasn't so—and got myself more than half killed by the first highwaymen I met. Not even when I first approached the old enchanter's castle.

When I saw that windowless bulk looming above me, when I wanted to run, I reminded myself of the hidden folk who must be watching me, taking courage from the lift of my chin and the light in my eyes. When the portcullis lifted silently to let me in and crashed down behind me I reminded myself of the princess, helpless, beautiful, afraid, waiting for me. When the door opened into the shadowy keep and that smell that I half-remembered from a nightmare eddied out to greet me I imagined how the princess and the people would scorn me if I heeded my heart and turned to flee.

When I met the princess I didn't know what to think. The villagers made songs of her beauty, but here she was, clearly royal— she had the ring and diadem to show it, and the hardness behind her eyes that comes from never being able to let your guard down, to be clumsy, tired, hot, dirty, human—and old enough to be my mother, and ugly. Her skin was blotched, her eyes sunken, her face and body all angry angles. She looked me in the eye like a swordsman measuring his opponent and said, "Set me free."

"From this—from how he's made you look—is there an enchantment on you?"

"No enchantment, only time, and what he's made me, and what I've made myself. You can't help with that. Set me free from this place. I can't go alone. Nor can you, not now. Get out, and take me with you. It's my only chance, and yours."

"Like this?" I asked again, staring at her. She nodded. Hero that I was, I couldn't refuse her, but I couldn't make myself go out into the light with her either, before those watching eyes.

She grimaced, turned half away from me, and held a hand mirror up so I could see her face reflected in it. Only it wasn't her face; it was the lovely, gentle, young face of the princess I'd imagined. I couldn't help myself. I set my lips to the cold glass that held the image of her forehead.

"All right," the harridan rasped. "Have it your way." I kept my eyes on the mirror-maiden, and she told me in her sweet voice what

I had to do: go through the secret door into the inner courtyard, slay the wild bull there, catch the fire-bird that rose from its body, pull the burning golden egg from the bird, cool the egg in the well until it cracked, take out the crystal ball from its brittle shell, enter the throne room and hold the ball before the old enchanter's eyes.

I did it all, and when I stood before him, singed and sore and dripping blood from a gash in my arm and another on my forehead, his ice-grim face cracked into what might have been a smile.

"You've won, boy," he said. "The castle is yours. It will do and be whatever you tell it to, so long as you stay within the walls. May you have joy of it! Just give me that ball."

I feared treachery, and I wouldn't have given it to him, but he seized my hand in an iron grip, squeezed until my bones hurt, and pried the ball from my numbed fingers. He stared into it, and I think he was surprised to see his own death's-head grin reflected there— there were no mirrors in the castle. He let my hand go just before flames erupted from the ball and swallowed him.

~ * ~

He'd told me the truth. Castle and courtyard, drawbridge and walls, were all in my power. I spoke the word, and the dank walls turned warm and golden, pierced by great arched windows. I formed the wish, and the bloodstained stones outside the windows became a garden brimming with flowers. I rolled the clouds away and brought great shafts of golden light in through the windows. I thought there was nothing left to remind the lady of the place that had been her prison. Unless I myself... My face and body were stiff and clumsy with fatigue and tamped-down fear. There was an ugly little thought scuttling around the back corners of my mind, whispering that the old enchanter might have given me power over the place but set a curse on me, made me in his likeness, crabbed and hideous.

I firmed my lips and wished a mirror in the wall, and I almost shouted with relief. It was my own face I saw reflected there, but my jawline was firmer than it had been, my eyes were brighter, and I looked as though I'd never heard of fear. Even my oldest brother might have feared me. Even my mother would have had to call me handsomest among her sons. But it wasn't my mother I wished for.

I saw her in the mirror first, my princess, lovely and young as she'd been in the harridan's mirror, coming to meet me. I was almost afraid to turn and look, but the real woman who fell at my feet murmuring gratitude and love matched her reflection—soft-bodied, tender-eyed, beautiful as the day.

~ * ~

Fool that I was, I was happy, and I tried, I tried so hard. I knew it was in my power to keep my love from ever growing old again so long as she stayed within the castle walls, but I didn't know if I could keep that hag's cold disappointment out of my love's beautiful eyes. I couldn't bear to see her look so at me.

At first I thought I'd made her happy with my gifts of flowers and jewels and music, with my praises and caresses. She smiled, she laughed, she sang, she danced, she told me the things I longed to hear, the things I would have been ashamed to ask anyone to say. I think it took years—though within my walls it was always summer—for me to realize she always, only, spoke the words I formed in my secret wishes. I tried wishing for her, and then telling her, to tell me of her love in her own words, in words I had never thought of. She looked at me, miserable, trying to please, not able to. I couldn't bear to look at her. I gave her more gifts. Finally I gave her a daughter. Still she gave me only cloying, copy-cat devotion. I left her to her own devices then, turned my attention to my subjects.

I wished to be a well-loved king. I couldn't extend the endless summer outside my walls, but within the walls I called into being grain and fruit and meat, more than could ever have grown there by nature, and I sent it out to my people. They took it with thanks, and I thought they were pleased.

I might have kept thinking so if it hadn't been for my daughter. I didn't really know what a girl-child should be, so except for making her beautiful (I knew that mattered), I let her go her own way. Her mother didn't seem surprised when that way took her outside the castle walls. I spent all day searching, and I couldn't find the girl. Finally I wished myself a scrying-glass in which I could see where she had gone.

I saw her in a peasant's hut, a close dim place with goats and people all crowded into one room for warmth, for it was winter there. The peasants hunched over a meal of oat-porridge and roots. My daughter, huddled under a coarse cloak, ate gingerly and spoke eagerly. I willed to hear her words, and I did.

"Is this all you have?' she asked them. "What about the food from the castle?"

They made the sign against the Evil Eye.

"Enchanter's food?" The father snorted. "Where do you come from, girl, that you don't know not to eat that? It's not for the likes of us. There's no sun in it, and no rain, and no soil, just his will. Maybe it would make us fat and smooth like you. Maybe it would turn it into poison in our bellies."

"Worse." That was an old woman speaking, maybe the grand-mother. "You are what you eat, you should know that, girl. If we ate that we'd be his people, and no help for it, no choice left."

I sent the guards to bring my daughter in. I never went outside the walls myself, fearing that my power would leave me when I left the gate, that I'd come home to find myself weak and growing old, to find my wife already old and scornful. So I stayed and fretted until the girl rode in between two guardsmen. At first she wouldn't speak to me of what she'd done. When I commanded her to speak she told me exactly what I wished to hear, that it was a girl's whim, an idle fancy, and she'd never do it again. I knew she said that only because I willed her to. It was worse than almost anything she could have said of her own will.

I let her go to her own rooms unrebuked, but I ordered the outer gates not to let her pass through, commanded the walls not to let her climb them. I woke at night, feeling them pushing her back again, again, again. That was the first time I slipped into dreams by day. They sat on the marble sills of my arched windows and stared at me—my brothers with their mocking eyes, my mother measuring me and finding me wanting, my father, old and sick, grinning his thin-lipped grin and saying *You'll come to this soon enough, boy, wait and see.* My commands didn't banish the ghosts. My daughter finally gave up on trying to get out. I slept again, and if I dreamed by night I forgot it in the morning.

~ * ~

Later in the changeless summer I watched my daughter plant a piece of garden with oats and peas, seed she'd brought with her from beyond the walls. I let her do that. I even brought rain-clouds to water the plants so they'd grow for her. I offered her seeds of fine flowers and rare herbs, but she wouldn't take them.

I remembered the faces of the folk she'd stayed with. When the old woman came to pay the tax on her family's land—a token fee to show their loyalty, for I needed nothing from my people, meant to deprive them of nothing—I asked her why she had lied to my daughter.

"I haven't," she told me. "You wish I had." She didn't wait to be dismissed. She turned and walked away. I didn't have time to think. As she went out the entrance hall I had a stone statue fall from its niche in the wall onto her head.

I was sorry for her, seeing her limp and broken, and I wished her alive again. Nothing changed; she just lay there. I was angry and afraid. I had the stone floor swallow her and wipe itself clean. It did that readily enough.

I thought that no one saw, and I was ready to swear she'd been taken by bandits as she traveled to the castle. But word got out somehow, as it always does. Nobody ever asked me about her. After her death the people came to pay their taxes warily, reluctantly, and one tried to stab me as he rose from his knees, and after he died a party of his friends tried shooting fire-arrows over the walls. I extinguished them, re-grew my scorched gardens—and my daughter's plants as well—and set warding spells on the walls outside as well as in.

My daughter came to me, called me a murderer, said she couldn't bear to live with me any longer, tried to order me to let her go. I sent her away from me, but not from the castle. I feared what the people might do to her if they learned she was mine.

My wife sent a servant and asked me to come to her. I went. I didn't know what to hope from her. She was lovely as ever, but her eyes were bitter and I hadn't the heart to change them. She held up the mirror that had shown me her fair young face long ago. Now it showed me the hard woman she had seemed to be then, only far older and grimmer. She began to turn it further, to show me my face. I knew I still showed young and handsome in the mirrors in hall and throne room. I didn't want to see what I might look like in her mirror. I threw it onto the floor. I heard the glass shatter.

I didn't kill her, I swear I didn't. She died on her own soon after that, maybe from anger or grief, maybe from old age my wishing had hidden but not undone. It was after her death the first champion came, and I dealt with him.

~ * ~

And I could deal with this one, too, this wary-eyed young fool making his way on foot up to my gates. There are a thousand things that I could do to him before he reaches my daughter's chambers, a thousand quick and not too painful ways to cure him of heroism once and for all.

Then I would have to live another day, another endless round of days, waiting for the next challenger. I cannot bear the thought.

My daughter's hand comes down heavily on my shoulder. I've stopped shutting her away from me since her mother died, and I haven't given her sweet words to speak, either. I am lonely for another voice that does not speak my own thoughts, even if it curses me. I've kept her young, though. If my will or my skill fails and some young man comes to her I won't have him disappointed.

"What will you do to this one?" Her voice is flat and hard as her eyes. She stares at me and her brows rise. "You're not going to kill him, then? Shall I go to my room and adorn myself and think up some rigmarole of a quest to put him through while you set your affairs in order?"

"What do you mean?"

"Shall I trap him here? Shall I do to him what my mother did to you? What you made her do to you, since you wouldn't set her free?"

"When did she tell you that? She never told me..."

"How could she? With you, when you were thinking of her, she had to think and say and do what you wanted. But sometimes you forgot her, and then she came to me and told me what was true. The way she tried to tell you at the end, after you'd tried to forget her."

"That isn't all that's true," I say thickly. "I was a hero once. I was."

She doesn't answer. Still, it's true. I was. Perhaps I am. Perhaps I am.

"Have it your way," I say. I check the scrying-glass again. "He's almost to the gate. Go out to him. The gate will open for you. Get away with him, as fast and as far as you can." She stares at me. "If you want to," I add. "Do you not want to? You'd be older, I don't know how much older."

"I'll be sixty-eight."

"How do you know?"

"My mother counted my birthdays when I was still a child. After I left and you brought me back I counted the days. I told myself *Now it is winter*, though I couldn't even look out to the winter lands any more, and *Now I am old*. But of course I want to go out. With you."

I start to argue, check myself. "Go ahead," I tell her. "He won't trust me, but he'll listen to you. Warn him away. I'll follow you, I swear."

I see her go. I see her warn him. I form the wish and a great voice echoes from every wall, ordering my servants and my guards to flee through the postern gate, which springs open before them. I follow my girl, as I swore I would.

The shadow of the gate falls over me. The last of my people have fled. I look down the slope to catch a last glimpse of my daughter and her hero before I bring the lintel down on my head, but they're already out of sight. They're safe. The enchantment will be broken once and for all, and my life the payment. The hero's way. Just one more look, and then I—

Someone grabs me around the waist, yanks me through the gateway. Someone shoves me onto a horse's back. I can't stop him—it is him, it's a man's thick hairy arm across my chest, a man's sweat I smell—because I'm outside, my wishes are worth nothing now, and I have no strength to fight. My lungs labor with each breath.

"I forgot," says a voice at my ear. "Of course, you're even older than I am."

A woman with shapely bones and a froth of silver-gray hair is staring at me in dismay. A beautiful woman, though I'd not have thought it possible for anyone so old to be so beautiful; her skin is almost translucent, and her eyes, her eyes...

I had thought she was a stranger, but surely I know those eyes, dark and bright in their deep sockets. But they never shone so before.

"Don't you know me, Father?" she asks.

"Don't I?" I echo. She is no more a stranger to me than my own body is. I stare from the paper-thin skin on my hands to the ancient ruin moldering on the hilltop behind its crumbling wall.

"That's done with. Can you stay up on the horse? We'll take it slow." Her voice and the bewildered voice of her young champion drift around me. I ride slowly down the street that I rode up so long ago. The world blurs.

Someone helps me down off the horse. Another cracked voice joins the conversation. A leathery hand takes my elbow, steers me to a bench.

The bench sits against a cottage wall, facing out into a weedy garden sweet with the scent of lavender and mint. Goats bleat somewhere down the hill. Another elderly stranger with familiar eyes stoops over me.

"Are you all right now?" he asks. Am I? How can I be? I look for my daughter.

"It's all right, Father," she says. "I stayed at his house before, when I ran away, when he was a boy and I was a girl. He says we can stay. His wife died, so he needs help with his holding, and I can help him."

It isn't all right. I can't stay here. His grandmother...

"Do you know who I am?" I don't recognize my own voice, thin and wheezy as it has become. The old man answers me.

"My friend's father. She said you went to the castle as a rescuer, but it trapped you because you weren't pure in heart, but now you've been disenchanted. She said you were very brave."

Well, then. After all this time I am a hero in the eyes of at least one of my people. I can have what I wanted, at the usual price: a lie.

I chose that once before. Look where it got me.

"No, I wasn't brave," I tell him. "I wanted people to think I was. Let me tell you what really happened, and then you can choose whether or not to shelter me."

Perhaps it's not too late for me to be a hero after all.

BONE STORIES

This story was originally published in On Spec *in fall 2020*

The Librarian-Porter wakes abruptly, feeling the charge in the air, like a thunderstorm brewing in the cold rainy night. She hears someone banging on the Library's front door, shoves on rubber boots and a bathrobe. The knocking has stopped by the time she reaches the hallway. She pulls the door open, squints into the fog, runs toward the receding sound of lurching steps.

The sound shifts to muffled swearing, which she follows to the visitor who thrashes in the brambles, trying to extricate his raincoat from the thorns without shredding it further. His breath smells of alcohol.

"Come out of the rain," she says, taking his elbow.

"Was a path," he says. "W'n I came in. Saw that. Thought, why not, nothing else works, this won' either but can' make worse. Thought wasn' real. Thass what they say: not real, none of it."

"Speak so I can understand you," she says. "You're not that drunk, or you wouldn't have gotten this far on foot. Yes, they say the Library isn't real; I suppose some people feel safer that way. People still find it when they need it. You found us. Why leave?"

"I came to the door. It was locked," he says more clearly. "I knocked. Nobody answered. So I knew this was real, and that meant it couldn't help."

She tugs his raincoat free and takes his arm.

"The path's still here," he says, wondering.

"Of course."

"So you didn't make the brush grow to stop me leaving?"

She doesn't answer.

"Who are you?"

"Porter," she says. That's all he needs to know. "You?"

"James."

She sits him down in the dim kitchen, yanks the bellpull for the Librarian-Scribe's room, and puts the kettle on. "So you have a story that has to come out of you," she says. "Well, give Scribe a few minutes to wake up."

"No," James says. "No, there's nothing inside me. There's

never been anything. That's why I had to come here. Nothing. I kept trying. School. Work. Parties. Marches. Meditation. Girls. Guys. Drugs. Just—Just nothing, you know? None of it mattered. None of it was real. But the stories say this place is full of the kind of books that can burn your eyes out. Drive you crazy. I thought, anyway, I'll feel something."

"You will," she says. "You'll get a new story before you leave. Can't leave without one. But the one you're carrying has to come out first. Can't just stuff another one in there and let you tear yourself apart between them."

"I told you, there's nothing."

"There's something big enough to block everything else out."

"I have *not*," James says, "been molested, traumatized…"

"I didn't say you had. Here's Scribe. Go along."

He blanches at the apparition in the doorway: a short upright figure, face invisible under a cowl, hands invisible in long sleeves, body invisible under a long loose robe. "What the hell do you… Can't you take that off?"

"You've seen plenty of people with their clothes off," says Scribe's level voice. A woman's voice, not young. "That didn't help you. Come."

"You were eavesdropping," James complains. "Anyway, I didn't mean—I just meant, do you need that Ghost of Christmas Yet to Come look?"

Scribe obligingly extends one stubby brown finger from the end of her left sleeve and points silently back through the doorway she just exited. James blanches. Laughs uncertainly. Follows her.

Porter watches Scribe's door close behind them. Then she clears away the tea things, sets her cot up in the entrance hall so James can't get out again without stepping over her, turns over once and falls deeply asleep.

~ * ~

Porter wakes, exhausted, to hear the Librarian-Lector clumping around the kitchen.

"Did our guest go to you for a new story yet?" she asks, accepting a plate of pancakes.

"Tried," Lector says in the slight colorless voice he uses when he doesn't mean to bring anything into being. "I read him the first pages of twenty-four different stories."

And?"

"They stayed flat. Nothing took. Might not have taken even if he'd been listening as if he meant it instead of making eyes at the books in the restricted section." He smiles at Porter's look. "I've made sure that section's sealed itself. And when he's ready I have a few more stories to try on him. I think one of them might work, if he could stop worrying about missing a better one." He looks down, and this time his wry smile is directed at himself. "Maybe not. I should know."

"So that's why James tried to get out the back way," Porter says, nodding. "Not running away from his new story. Running because he's afraid there's no story for him."

"He tried...?"

She nods. In her dreams she kept the garden walls rearranging themselves into labyrinthine patterns he couldn't escape. She woke up more tired than when she went to sleep.

~ * ~

She is alone in the kitchen when James comes in the back door with twigs in his hair and resentment in his eyes. "You didn't tell me this place was a prison!"

"It isn't. You came of your own free will."

"But you won't let me out."

"Not without a story."

"I've lived without—" He shuts his mouth.

"No. You thought you were living without a story. That was bad enough. "

"The one I had," James says, sounding about six years old, "was pathetic."

"And that's out. Now you need another. Nature abhors a vacuum."

"You're saying I'm unnatural right now?"

"I'm saying you can't go back out into the world like this. You've heard things about the stories here. Some of the Library's stories are terrible, yes. But they're all true."

"How do you know?"

"Was the story you told Scribe true?"

He winces. "I meant it to be, but...no, it wasn't all true, not the way I told it. But the story your Scribe wrote, that was true."

Porter notes the grudging wonder in his tone. Nods.

"So fiction's dangerous?" James asks.

"Life is dangerous. Death is dangerous. Fiction is dangerous. Facts are dangerous. Lies are evil."

"And?"

"Some lies are so big they only fit inside someone who's empty. Someone who's had the story in their bones scraped out and not replaced."

"Someone who's been here and left early?"

"That would be one way, if we let anyone do that. There are others."

"What...?"

"Someone else is coming. We don't have long... How do you think hate starts? It takes people who are empty. Who've had their meaning, the universe inside their breath and their bones, ripped out. Can't you think of any ways the world outside these walls can do that?"

"You're saying if shit happens to people they can't help turning into neo-Nazis or something?"

"No!"

He recoils from the fury in Porter's voice as though she had physically struck him. "What?"

"No! Some of them find something even bigger and more dangerous to take in, but it goes down hard, I can tell you that."

"More dangerous than hate?"

"I don't think you know anything about love," Porter tells him. "Go!"

"You said..."

"Not out the front door. Back to the reading room, or the garden. Just give me some space."

He goes back toward the reading room. Porter hurries to the front door.

This time it opens on an expanse of flat sand broken by occasional boulders. The shadow of one boulder flickers. Porter walks slowly toward the flicker, saying, "You can come out. I know where you are, and I don't have a weapon, and I don't want to hurt you. Nobody else can see you now. Come in."

The woman uncurls from behind the rock, eyes Porter warily.

"You do not say," she observes, "that I am perfectly safe here."

"Nobody has ever been perfectly safe anywhere."

"You are not a fool," the woman says as though this is cause for wonder. "Maybe you can help."

"Maybe we can. Come in."

The woman sits straight-backed, facing the door, her eyes scanning the room as Porter makes tea.

"I am Isra," she says. "You?"

"I am Porter, now. I left my name behind when I chose to stay here."

"Is that what I have to do?" Isra's voice is as level as her gaze. "Leave my name? What else? My memories?"

"Most people take their names away with them again. I was…different. But didn't you come here to be free of your memories?"

"I do not know," Isra says. Pauses. "I do not trust you, but I do not trust myself either, and I cannot go on as I am. Well. Yes, I need to be free from the memories. I need not to scream in front of the children—not when I sleep, not when an airplane flies overhead, not when a car backfires. Already they are afraid enough without me screaming."

"But…?"

"But I need not to forget. When they wake up screaming, I must remember why. Also I must not forget how to look for danger. Other people, people who think they are helping, they tell me now we are in a safe place, there is no danger here, we do not need to worry. Pfft. Once I thought there was no danger where we came from." She looks over Porter's shoulder into something terrible that only she can see. Looks down when Porter nudges the aromatic tea closer under her nose. "There is danger everywhere, I know this now. I must see when danger is coming toward my children." She sighs. "I must know, without the knowing making me mad. Keeping me mad. Is this possible?"

"Yes," Porter says. "Your memories can be healed here, but you won't lose them. Scribe always makes two copies of the books. One will stay here, in the reading room. The other will go with you. You will remember it as you would remember a story you have read often. A well-told story that has touched your heart and your mind."

Isra's eyes soften. "I loved to read stories, once," she said. "In stories you could see people's hearts. You could know why they did what they did. And you did not have to save them."

"Go this way, when you are ready," Porter tells her. Isra nods. Takes three deep breaths. Rises. "I am ready now," she says, going.

Porter sits alone at the table, weeping into her cold tea.

Later she sees Isra pass into the reading room holding two books whose covers are a swirl of red and gold: one book to keep, one to leave for someone else. For the first time in more years than she wishes to reckon over, Porter thinks of looking between the covers; Porter wants to know a story more than she wants to get away from it. She is not altogether happy about this change. She is not foolish enough to believe unhappiness changes anything. She will ponder all this sometime when she is not so tired…

James leaves the reading room carrying one red and gold book, one silver and green book. Stops by the table.

"Can I go now?"

"What do you think?"

He considers.

"Before, I wanted to get out, but I couldn't. Now, I think I can, but…"

"Why don't you want to?"

"It's a scary world out there."

"You didn't find it so before?"

He runs his thumb along the red and gold book's spine. "You have to care enough to be afraid, I guess."

"And now you do."

He looks up. Smiles. Sighs.

"I do. All right, I'm ready to go. Maybe to make something better."

The Porter accompanies him to the end of the hall, opens the door for him, watches him set off down the path into the sunlit woods.

~ * ~

Early in the afternoon Porter means to take a catnap. Instead she falls heavily asleep. Wakes to find Isra standing over her, saying, "All right, it was only a dream."

Porter blinks up at her. "Was I…"

"Screaming. So this place cannot heal?"

"I haven't dreamed about my old life since I came here." Porter frowns. "Hadn't. Seemingly I'm changing… You should be all right once you find your story. Don't worry. Thank you for waking me. Go on back to the reading room, or the garden."

"So you can be alone." Isra nods.

"Alone with the one who is coming."

Isra listens, hears nothing; looks out the window in the door, sees no one; nods and leaves.

The footsteps approaching the front door echo strangely. The door opens into a cement corridor, long and windowless, lined with locked steel doors. The smell, the sounds, would be horrible even if they came from animals, but Porter can hear human words mixed in with the sounds.

The woman in the uniform walks slow and straight-backed down the corridor toward Porter. Her uniform is clean; her posture is good; her young face is unmarked; her eyes are bowls of broken glass.

She stops a couple of paces from Porter. Stands at attention. Turns her head just a little to look over Porter's shoulder.

The corridor behind Porter is stone-floored, green-walled, open to the kitchen at the far end.

"This is the place. The Library." The uniformed woman's tone is flat; it takes Porter a moment to register that she is asking a question.

"Yes."

"I don't have a pass, or a password."

"You don't need either. But give me that." Porter motions to the holstered gun at the woman's side.

The woman unclips the holster from her belt, hands it over.

"You could shoot me," she says. "I don't care. Better shut the door first, or someone will hear you, and this isn't a place you want to get caught in."

"I can't be caught there," Porter says. "That hall's only in your mind—at least," she adds, seeing the flicker in the woman's eyes, "you're only in it in your mind now. Shooting you wouldn't do any good." That sounds harsher than Porter had intended. "Come in," she adds, trying to soften her voice.

"What good would that do, if this Library is all in my mind?" The uniformed woman considers. "It's a new sort of hallucination."

She shrugs. "An improvement over the others." She compresses her lips. "So far."

"The Library is real, and you will really be in it when you cross the threshold."

The woman, who did not look afraid when she handed the gun over, cringes visibly as the door shuts behind her.

"You are…."

"Porter. I'm not here to punish you. I think you've been doing that yourself. You are?"

"Langholme."

Porter opens her mouth to direct Langholme to Scribe's door. Sees Scribe in the doorway, left arm out, palm outward. The gesture seems obvious enough: *Don't let her come in here.* But Scribe is bound to take anyone who has a story needing to come out, which this woman plainly does. Time, though—Porter can give Scribe that. *Ten minutes*, she mouths. Scribe drops her arms to her sides, steps back into the shadows as Porter leads the uniformed woman into the kitchen.

"Have a seat," Porter says. "Have something to drink."

"No. I tried drinking. It didn't help. It made them quieter for a little while, then it made them louder and I couldn't, I couldn't…"

"Cocoa? Tea?"

"If you have poison for me I will drink it," the woman quotes. Laughs mirthlessly at Porter's surprised look. "I was in the college production of *Lear*. I was Cordelia. I remembered some of the lines—not just my lines. I didn't remember the lesson, though, obviously. Not till it was too late." She sucks her breath in. "Well, in the play he doesn't really make the warning clear enough. Cornwall dies right after blinding old Gloucester. He doesn't have to hear Gloucester screaming in his mind, all night, every night, for years and years."

This is not my job, Porter thinks desperately, pulling herself back in her seat, as far away from Langholme as she can get. "But you still hear…?"

"I still hear them. The screaming ones, I mean. And the… The noise someone makes, trying to breathe when… And I can't hear the other ones any more."

"Which ones?"

"The ones telling me we're doing what we have to do to

protect our people, our country, everything that's good and right. That I have to… They told me I had to. I believed them. They gave the orders. I just obeyed them. It's their fault, isn't it?"

"Oh yes," Scribe says from the door in a raw voice Porter has not heard before. "You're innocent. Let someone else get punished. Let someone else suffer for you. Like last time."

Langholme lowers her face into her hands.

"That's right," Porter says automatically, "cry, you'll feel better."

"She can't," Scribe says, at the same time Langholme says, "I can't. Can't cry. Can't sleep." She looks up.

Langholme and Scribe stare at each other. For the first since her arrival at the Library many years ago, Scribe wears a plain dress, short-sleeved and unhooded. Porter and Langholme can see her right hand—two fingers missing, the other three twisted. Can see the jagged line of her nose, broken in two places. Can see her missing teeth and the scar on her neck. Can see her eyes…her eyes…her eyes…

"Come," Scribe says. Langholme rises slowly. Scribe adds, to Porter, "You come too."

"But…"

"You'd better write for both of us."

~ * ~

One copy of the story Langholme told is still in the Library. One copy is wherever in the world Soli is—the one who used to be called Scribe. The same is true of the story Soli told.

Before Soli left, and after Isra took her new story and went on her way, they all sat together in the kitchen: Lector, hoarse-voiced and hollow-eyed; Soli, her eyes far and quiet; the new Scribe, who used to be Porter; and the new Porter, who used to be Langholme.

"Is this how you were chosen?" the new Porter asked the new Scribe. "I would have thought the Librarians needed wisdom, or magic."

"The magic's in the place," Lector said.

"The wisdom's in anyone," Soli said.

"We stay here because we couldn't leave," the new Scribe said. "Couldn't release our stories, or couldn't find new ones."

"And you think I can stay here and do no harm, after what I've done." The new Porter sounded hopeful as much as fearful.

"I think you'll do no more harm, now you know what you've done," the new Scribe said; but the new Porter's eyes still turned toward Soli.

Soli answered in Spanish. Until then they had all spoken in the language of the Library, the heart-language which is the same wherever you come from. But the outside world was taking hold of Soli again.

She half-smiled at them, translated.

"And they shall look upon me, the one they have pierced; and they shall mourn as for an only child…"

The new Porter nodded. They touched hands, let go.

"Stay," Lector said to the new Porter. "Stay, and keep the door, until you're ready to go back out into the world, or to come further in."

For a moment they sat still together, beyond words.

BOUND

This story was first published in After Dinner Conversation *in June 2020*

I came fully awake as I sat up and cracked my head on the thwart of my upturned canoe. The pain cleared my head. I felt under my bedroll for my knife, hoping I hadn't made enough noise to attract the attention of whatever—whoever?—had waked me. I didn't hear footsteps. I was just starting to drift back down into sleep when I heard the voice speaking from the high ridge above the brushy bit of riverbank where I had camped, meaning to get a good night's sleep before venturing into Sheneshe. The speaker must have been just about directly above me.

"This is the third night, and the second asking," the voice said. A man's voice, elderly, melodious, and exhausted. "If I knew anything more to say to change your mind, I would say it."

"And it would not change my mind. My answer is no." The answering voice was younger, harsher.

A sigh. "Then all I can do is sit with you until dawn."

"Until three nights ago, I might have thought that was kind of you."

"Arlin," the old man said, "the Law was given in kindness, but that kindness was meant for the people, not the Keepers—or the breakers either."

I could hear the capital in the old man's voice as he said 'the Law.' I heard something else too, something I couldn't put a name to, something that set my teeth on edge. Though perhaps that was only the fear that came from the rumors I had heard…

Gossips in the towns downriver had told me no woman in her right mind would paddle on upstream past Sennipol to Sheneshe. When I observed I could paddle as well as most men, they sighed and said no sane man would go that way either. When I inquired whether there were rapids, they explained the problem was not in the river, but in Sheneshe itself—that its folk were unchancy.

"Unchancy how?" I asked. "Lawless? Cruel?" Some stared blankly at me or shrugged, plainly parroting something they'd heard and never thought to question. Others looked hard at me and then held their hands up before their chests, fingers splayed—the curse-warding sign. Some made it vaguely toward the north, toward Sheneshe. Some made it toward me. Maybe the shadow of what I'd left behind, the reason for my flight, was in my eyes. Maybe they thought the cursed place drew accursed travelers to itself. They might have been right, at that.

In Sennipol, the last town downriver from Sheneshe, there was a great deal of curse-warding and a bit of muttering and spitting; I left the inn with all discreet haste. One man, a thin stopping fellow with ragged clothes and haunted eyes, followed me back to my boat and tried to give me an answer.

"They're not lawless in Sheneshe," he said, spitting aside. "Their Law interferes in far too many things, if the tales are true. But they killed their god long ago, and the curse is still on them."

"The folk downriver in Marvi kill their god every autumn, and mourn for him every winter, and he comes back every spring and blesses them," I said.

He spat again. "Southland lunatics," he said. "But the folk up northaway... I've heard of no blessing there."

I remembered that warning as I listened to the young man's voice in the dark, answering the mention of the Law with words I couldn't make out and fury I couldn't help hearing. I was several paces away from my boat before I understood I was going to the voices. I didn't stop. I've learned to move quietly, and the young man's voice covered the noises I couldn't help making as I climbed.

I was maybe ten paces from the young man when he stopped speaking and I stopped moving. The circle of light from the old man's lantern stopped five paces from me. It showed me the old man's face, heavy with grief. It didn't reach to the young man. I stood there for a long time, watching the old man watching the young man, watching first hint of grey smudging the eastern horizon. When the old man looked up and said, "The third night, and the third asking," and the young man answered "No," the lantern-light flashed from the knife in the old man's hand.

I was between him and the young man before I had time to recall this wasn't my affair. I was also between him and the lantern-light, and the dawn light wasn't much help yet; I think he saw a bulky black silhouette against the glow, not a rawboned middle-aged woman trying to hold her own knife steady.

"You can't do that," I said.

"You do not understand," he answered, lowering his knife hand.

"No, I don't," I admitted. "I thought you meant to use that on him." I jerked a thumb back over my shoulder at the young man. "Was I wrong?"

The heavy silence answered well enough.

"I can't let you do that," I said.

"I had no choice. I gave him his choice, and he chose," the old man said.

"Had, not have?" I asked.

He didn't answer that either. We stood looking at each other while the light came up in the sky. Then he sheathed his knife and sat down. I stepped back so I could see both men. The young one was sitting very straight against a beech-bole—tied to it, not cruelly tight, but enough to keep him in place. His hands were tied in front of him.

"Who did you say had a choice here?" I asked the old man. "He's bound and you're not."

"I am bound by the Law, and he has broken the bond."

"You carry out your Law in secret, in the middle of the night?" I asked.

"His Law is all secrets and lies," the young man said. "I would have told them the truth."

"I keep them safe," the old man said.

"Keep who safe? Safe from what?" I asked.

"The god," both men said together in the same heavy tone.

"So he's after you for sacrilege?" I asked the young man, wishing I'd stayed out of it. I thought I'd learned not to meddle in religion in foreign parts. For one thing, meddling was an easy way to get yourself killed; for another, it was an easy way to hurt people in ways you'd never imagine ahead of time. But I couldn't just go off and leave the young man to get murdered, or sacrificed, or whatever it was. I'd seen too much to let me leave, and I hadn't seen enough to know what I should do instead of leaving.

"Not sacrilege," the young man said. "It isn't the god he's protecting."

I waited for one of them to explain. I kept waiting.

Another voice finally broke the silence, a woman's voice on

the far side of the ridge, calling, "Lord Keeper?" By then the sun had come up, restoring the color of the old man's long blue robe and the smell of the late blackberries tangled in the long grass.

"Go back!" the old man called.

"Only if you want murder done," I shouted before I could remind myself about the evils of meddling.

"Who's there?" she called.

They didn't answer, so I did. "An old man with a knife, and a young man tied up—I guess one of them's your Lord Keeper—and me, a stranger."

"Athele, it's me, it's Arlin," the young man called in his rough tired voice.

Athele, who looked near my age, came over the ridge and stopped to stare at us. She looked first at Arlin, but it was to the old man she spoke after a long uncomfortable pause.

"Lord Keeper, you said Arlin had run off," Athele said slowly. "Said you were going to find him. What happened? And who is she?"

The two men I'd interrupted answered together again: "The god's messenger." They both sounded afraid.

"I don't think so," I said. "I don't know your god." They ignored this.

Arlin looked at the Keeper. "Too late now for your way," he said.

"Too late," the Lord Keeper agreed. He nodded to me. "Loose him, then. We'll go back together."

I cut Arlin's ropes and he stepped forward, staggered. *The third night...* I thought. *No wonder he's stiff.* I reached out an arm to steady him; when the old man reached for him I came round between them again.

"I will not hurt him," the Keeper said. "Not now. Take this." He loosened the sheathed knife from his belt, gave it to me, took Arlin's arm over his shoulders and started to help the younger man along. "Go back, then," he told Athele, "and gather them all in front of the Place. If the story must be told, let it be told only once."

Arlin's legs limbered soon so he could walk at a decent pace and bear his own weight, though neither he nor the Keeper seemed eager to let each other go. We hurried through woods, then through pastureland loud with sheep and calves, then over the last hill into the village. The white stone houses were small and sturdy. I heard and saw no people. Right through the village we went, out the other side, through fields of oats and pease, then back into wild country. At the top of another hill we came to a tall hedge of roses with a few late blossoms, white and scentless, still clinging to their thorns. Inside was a turfed courtyard surrounding a round wall of white stone too tall to see over and too smooth to climb. The door in that wall was locked. Six or seven score people milled around the courtyard, buzzing like a hive of bees that's almost made up its mind to swarm. When they saw us most of them raised their left hands to their foreheads as they looked at the Lord Keeper; I took it for a gesture of respect, though not one I'd seen before. A few of them made the curse-warding sign.

"Lord Keeper," they said uneasily.

"It is yet to be seen whether I am still your Keeper," he answered.

They didn't seem to find this much clearer than I did. "Are you stepping aside for Arlin, then, Lord?" one man asked.

"He will never be Keeper," the old man said.

"He speaks truth in that, for once," Arlin said. "The secret has been kept too long. It is time you knew the truth. It is time the gates opened and you saw..."

"Wait." The Keeper spoke so softly that even Arlin quieted to hear him. "Wait. You want them set free, Arlin, and then you want to make their choice for them?"

"It is the god I would set free."

"Ill words," someone said, and "What does he mean?" said another.

"I'll tell you..." Arlin began.

"Do you want him to tell you?" the Keeper interrupted. "Or will you keep the Law and your own protection?"

"And let your Lord Keeper sneak off in the middle of the night and kill people," I added.

They seemed to notice me for the first time when I spoke.

"Who are you?" a woman asked. "Did he threaten you?"

"He didn't threaten me," I said, "but seemingly he would have killed your Arlin here." Arlin shook his sleeves back, let them see the rope marks on his wrists.

"He wouldn't! He didn't!" several voices cried. "You never

did, Lord Keeper?"

"I did," the Keeper said.

"Why?" The question spread quickly through the crowd.

The Keeper turned his palms upward, nodded. "You have won," he said. "I will tell the story, Arlin."

The people sat, and Arlin sat too, facing the Keeper. I sat where I could get between them again if I had to—not that either of them appeared to notice. Arlin's eyes were fixed on the Keeper, smoldering with anger—though there was something else there too; something I took for an affection that had grown so far into him he didn't know how to get rid of it all at once. The Keeper looked into the empty air as though he could see the things he spoke of happening there. I can't rightly remember the words he used, but I won't soon forget the gist of the tale.

It began, he said, when the grandfathers of their grandfathers were still babes in the womb. (From him, that sounded less like a tale-teller's flourish than an actual accounting of how much time had passed.) The women in whose wombs they rested, and their men, lived then in Sennipol, a town down the river which had been locked in its fears and its petty rivalries for generations: rich and poor feared and resented each other, families brooded over slights from generations past, but they all agreed it was far better to live in Sennipol than in any of the backward or decadent towns downriver, or in the wild hill-country upstream which was said to be demon-haunted. (I bit back a snort of laughter, remembering Sennipol and wondering how the good folk of the inn would take to that description.)

But one of the Sennipoli, an old woman named Myriona, was haunted by a dream of better things: of a sweet country where the air was fresh, not stinking as in the alleys of Sennipol; a place where men and women worked and sang and were glad together in the light of the face of the god. Oh yes, she dreamed of the god too. It was his voice that urged her to come up the river to the hill-country and live free, and to take with her any brave souls who were willing to come. Myriona obeyed, and got away from Sennipol before anyone actually got round to disposing of her as a witch; a fair number of other people who were weary of the course of their lives followed her.

There was no obvious sign of a curse on the hill-country. The streams were sweet and clear, the soil deep enough to work, the game plentiful. And there was one spring-fed pool whose waters seemed little short of miraculous; drinking them cured Myriona's lameness, and Alden's sleeplessness and fear, and the children's summer sickness. Above that spring there was a great outcropping of shining stone which Myriona worked into the shape of the face of the god she had seen in her dreams, the one who had led them there.

In the first year rain and sun came in season and all things grew and prospered. At the first-year festival when the people danced around the spring and gave thanks for the god's gifts, some looked into the water and saw the reflection of the carved figure's calm face smiled more broadly than it had when Myriona first carved it, and the reflected eyes followed the dancers as they leapt and spun.

The next year also passed in peace and plenty, and the year after that wasn't bad, though there were more pests eating the crops and a few lambs born wrong, to their loss and their mothers'—no more than might have been expected back in their old life, but it didn't quite seem to fit with the blessed new life. A few murmurs started then about who might have been less than properly grateful for their blessings, but nothing much came of it.

In the twelfth year there was drought. The vegetables were scanty, the grain headed too early, the goats took sick and their milk came out dark and foul-smelling. The pool fed by the spring shrank in the drought. Some said the healing water shouldn't be wasted on sick goats; others said it was sin not to use it and trusted all they needed would be given.

One night Myriona woke from a nightmare to see flames rising from the thatched roof of her neighbor Ansa's goat-shed. She knew Ansa had taken blessed water for her goats. She knew, too, their neighbor Evrena had called it a sacrilege and a waste. She ran out and found Evrena standing with her hands on her hips and laughing at the flames.

"What have you done?" Myriona hissed. Evrena whirled to run. Myriona caught her arm. They struggled silently until the flames leaped from Ansa's byre to Ansa's house on one side and Evrena's hen-coop on the other. Then they stared at each other and ran opposite ways down the street, shouting for help in fighting the flames. Too late.

Half the village burned that night. All might have been lost if the rains had not come at last, torrential, drenching, pounding the standing grain into the ground. The villagers huddled together in the unburned houses. Some blessed the god, and some cursed him, and many cursed the human fire-starter. Myriona, afraid they might think her guilty of that, told them how she'd waked to find Evrena by the stall. Evrena didn't deny it. Her face was stiff with fear even before word came that Ansa's oldest daughter Tereu, a girl of sixteen, was dead.

Tereu had taken a dream-draught, hoping for word from the god about why the rain did not come; she did not hear the flames, or the shouting. When the blaze kindled in the roof Ansa picked the baby up, and her husband Goran took their sickly four-year old; when they would have gone back in to pull Tereu out the roof fell in, blazing.

When the rain rolled away Myriona climbed stiffly up the hill to the spring and stopped, staring at the god's stone face. The face was scarred and blistered, the mouth twisted with pain. She feared her eyes or her mind were playing her false, and she stooped to drink from the spring, hoping it still had grace to clear her mind. She didn't drink after all. She stared instead into a reflection that was not a reflection. In the still water she saw the flaming roof collapsing on Tereu. Then she saw Evrena's face, streaked with blood. When Myriona looked up, blood ran down the face of the god-stone.

Myriona fled, but as she passed into the trees she heard foot-steps blundering up the path toward her. Goran stumbled up the hill, wild-eyed and haggard.

"What are you looking for?' Myriona asked.

"The one who killed my daughter is dead," Goran said. "Surely I did right in that. The curse-bringer is dead, and now the god must take the curse away."

"The god!" Myriona cried. "See what you have done to the god!" She took Goran's arm and pushed him up the path ahead of her, out of the trees, face to face with the god-stone. Goran stared awhile, then turned back to her with the vacant stare of an idiot and fled back the way he had come.

Myriona looked again and saw the god-stone was as blank-eyed as Goran had become, though the stone face reflected in the spring was a mask of grief. She stumbled back down the slippery stones of the path and told her neighbors what she had seen.

"What are we to do?" they asked her.

"Nothing else to grieve the god," she said.

"What would not grieve the god?"

She opened her mouth, closed it. "I do not know," she said at last, low and troubled.

"Why did you bring us here, if you didn't know?" Ansa asked. Myriona couldn't answer that either, except to urge them to await the god's will.

Some of them hoped grief had turned Myriona's mind, and they went to the spring and the god-stone. They returned with grim faces. None said what they had seen, but one man, Marn, the son of a Sennipoli alderman who had left after a bitter quarrel with his father, said plainly the thing there by the spring meant them no good; that rather than waiting its will they should take thought to protect themselves from the god and from each other.

"You mean go back to Sennipol?"

"What do you think they'd do to a cursed and empty-handed lot of fugitives?" asked Marn. "No, I mean learn another way of living here."

They talked and wept and argued for a night and a day. At the end of that time most of them agreed they had had enough of women's visions and women's quarrels, and they chose Marn to lead them. They slept that night, or tried to, and in the morning they set to work quarrying stone. Half of the stone they used to build homes that would not burn, and the other half to build a wall to shut away the god-stone and the spring. Myriona spoke against this, but the power had gone from her and she was overruled; still, at her bidding they left a door in the wall round the spring, though they locked the door, and gave the key to Marn.

On the night when the wall was finished the same dream came to Marn and to Myriona and to every man, woman and child in Sheneshe. They were locked inside that wall with the god-stone, which labored for breath in its new enclosure, a terrible hoarse rasping that grated on their lungs and their souls.

"He can't be shut away from us all," Myriona said. "Someone must see him. Let me."

"It is not your burden now," Marn told her kindly. "I will go to him every day."

Marn went in to the god at sundown. That night none of Marn's people dreamed. The next morning Marn came out, bent like an old man and gray faced. Before he went back to the god that night Marn told them the laws and their penalties, and the people agreed to be bound. They swore that none of them would seek to pass the gate, and they would never speak to one another, or to their children yet to be born, of the god or the spring or the founding of Sheneshe; none of them but only the Keeper, and he only, in his old age or illness, to the Keeper who was to take the burden from him.

Myriona was the only one who would not swear. When she did not wake in the morning, but lay cold and silent in her bed, people looked at each other, but they kept their oath and said nothing to each other of how she might have died.

Ever since then the spring and the god-stone had been shut away. The Keeper went before the god every day, and there were no more god-dreams. There were droughts and sicknesses, but none of the people had called on the god or blamed each other for offending him—first because they were afraid, then because they were forbidden, then because they knew no god on whom to call. There had been lawbreaking, and the lawbreakers had made restitution or done penance or been put to death, and lawlessness did not spread. At first travelers were turned away by the Keepers, lest they should encourage the Sheneshi to think of gods; in time travelers lost the habit of coming. And every Keeper chose his heir, a brave, wise, sober and responsible man to protect the people after him.

"But I chose poorly," the Lord Keeper said. "You know how brave and fair-minded Arlin is, and how quickly he learned the Law. But when it was time...when I told him the story, so he would know what to expect when I died and he had to take up the burden..."

"Then I knew we had done wrong," Arlin said, his voice softer and older than it had been. "And I slipped in after you when you went to the god, and I saw his pain at being caged; and I knew it was time to open the gate to all the people."

"It may be so," Athele said. "Last night I dreamed..." She did not finish. "And I woke, and I sought the Lord Keeper in my trouble, and he was gone; so I went to the place where the trouble began in my dream, and I found the Lord Keeper there, and Arlin, and this woman."

"And I dreamed," a boy in the crowd said.

"And I...And I..." The words echoed through the crowd. I thought, also, that I heard an echo from within the wall.

"Open the door," Arlin said. There was power in his words, and the crowd echoed them. I kept my mouth shut and edged back toward the door we'd come in through. I moved slowly, not wanting to draw attention—their attention, or that of whatever waited within the wall. I hadn't got to the door yet when the Lord Keeper bowed his head, took a key from the folds of his cloak and gave it to Arlin.

I got to the hedge door just as Arlin reached the door in the stones. I hesitated a moment to see what would happen. I saw the light flash from the door at his touch, and I saw the wall fall away—not crushing the people, not like that; it fell into the air and was gone. I saw faces, too. Maybe not the faces the rest of them saw. My mother, when I left for the last time—not that I told her it was that, but she knew, and knew why. That man in Armol three years ago—he jumped me, mind, it wasn't my fault, unless you call it fault that I was soberer and quicker-handed, but I'd always hated the look of him dead, and it was worse now. Verina, before I left home—I still don't want to talk about her. And then—

Oh, then there was the look I used to think I caught echoes of in my mother's face, or in the face of that man I was fool enough to think might love me, or in the sunrise on those days that are like the first morning of the world. The look I had always longed to see and to believe in.

And then there was the fire. White fire, dancing, and the people under it—in it—dancing too, and singing. I swear they were singing, not screaming. Were they burning? I don't know; I didn't stay to find out. They weren't my people. That wasn't my god. I fled through the rose hedge and slammed the door behind me. The flames didn't follow me. The music did.

I might almost think the whole thing had been a dream if I didn't have that music in my mind. It's like nothing I've heard up or down the River, and it never leaves me. No, I can't sing it for you. And I have the Lord Keeper's knife, too. See those funny designs on the handle? I don't rightly know what they mean, but the blade's sharp. It's a very good knife.

HARROWING

This story appeared in Newtown Presbyterian's online exhibit
"Moved by the Spirit" in August 2021

Alma assumed Sibyl was joking, so she forced a laugh; new in town and new at church, Alma couldn't snub someone at coffee hour. Then she saw the outrage on Sibyl's face.

"Sorry. You really mean——?"

"Don't worry about hurting my feelings. It's just that we're concerned about you. Grace saw you hanging around there. Of course you wouldn't go in," (her tone implied that was just what Alma would do), "but people who choose to spend time in that area…"

"What's really down there?"

"I just told you," Sibyl said.

"I thought you called them stairs to Hell."

"I did."

Alma backed away. Was Sibyl crazy?

"It's true," David said.

"That's the name of a nightclub?" Alma asked. "Or an occult bookstore?"

"No, it's Hell—the real thing," David assured her.

"You think the Gates of Hell are in that vacant lot?"

"*A* Gate of Hell," Sibyl said. "Maybe every town has one. We know where ours is, and we stay away from it."

"How do you know?"

"Everybody knows," Gloria said, leaning over Sibyl's shoulder.

"So people end up in Hell because they wander down the stairs?" Alma tried not to sound as incredulous as she felt. "Otherwise they'd all go to Heaven?"

"I'm sure," Sibyl said, "that nine times out of ten the appropriate authorities—angels, fallen angels, whoever—*take* people there at the…the usual time. For cause. But you do hear about things…"

"Kids daring each other," David said.

"Drunks," Sibyl added.

"Not drunks—they'd break their necks before they reached

the bottom," Gloria contradicted. "The stairs are so steep."

"You've seen them?" Alma asked.

There was a nasty little silence.

After coffee hour Alma walked back to the vacant lot and leaned into the open-fronted shed. Stepping inside, she looked down the stairs to where the green indoor-outdoor carpeting faded into shadow. Then she turned away.

Early next morning Alma was back, with a cross pinned to her blouse and a flashlight, a penknife, and pepper spray ready in her jeans pocket. She tacked a note to the shed: ALMA FOSTER WENT IN TO EXPLORE AT 5:30 AM ON SEPTEMBER 2.

She had given up on writing an explanation. "Because I need to know…" "Because if you're pulling my leg I'm tired of it…" "Because if angels or demons are hauling people into Hell against their will I'll organize a strike against God…" "Because if there are people trapped down there maybe I could help them get out…" They all sounded juvenile, though she meant them all.

~ * ~

The staircase was very long. The irregular pulsations of the fluorescent lights overhead gave Alma a headache after a while. By the time she thought of counting the stairs, she had been descending so long that it seemed pointless.

The stairs ended on a cement landing before a neat exterior door which was windowless and institutional green like the stairs. There was no inscription on the lintel.

Alma tried the knob. It wasn't locked.

She cracked the door open.

No sulfurous fumes. No tormented wails. Just a low buzz of conversation.

Opening the door a couple of inches, Alma peered in at a strip of green carpet and a white wall.

She opened the door wide and stepped across the threshold. No alarm bell sounded. One of the well-dressed people inside noticed her—a blond man with an insipid face. His gaze met hers, slid away, then dragged itself back before he returned to his conversation. Something flashed through his eyes as he looked at her. Not agony, she thought, or rage, or lust. Fear? Maybe. Or hope?

Alma drew the door to, but not quite shut, behind her as she stepped into the room.

"Shut the door, can't you?" The woman's cultured voice was thin and shrill. "Don't let that air in—you know what it can do."

"What can it do?" Alma asked.

The woman's face tightened. "Just close it!"

Alma shut the door, panicked, and tested the knob. It turned freely. She took a step toward the woman. "I was just out there, and the air seemed to be fine," Alma said. "What bothers you about it?"

"I wasn't complaining." The woman's eyes darted around the room.

"Nobody thought you were," another woman said in tones of exaggerated patience, motioning the first woman away from Alma and the door.

If this was a well-disguised Hell, Alma thought, and people were kept there by the irrational fear of something on the stairs, she could explain and save them all. But first she had to understand.

She walked further into the room. The carpet indoors was the same dead green as the stairs outdoors. The walls were off-white with a hint of green—though the green was just slightly wrong. So were the people. Women in slacks and fitted tops or in little dresses, men in suits and ties, all with decorous little smiles—what felt wrong about them?

She drifted closer to a pair of women.

"They didn't do a bad job redecorating the restaurant."

"I suppose Management has to accommodate the other Groups too…they wouldn't appreciate anything really tasteful."

"Is the new decor tasteless?"

"You haven't seen it? Weren't you at breakfast?'

"There didn't seem to be much point." The speaker tittered nervously. "I mean, I was so busy."

"Of course." Was the sweetness of the answering voice exaggerated?

The titterer blanched, murmured "Oh dear, I shall be late…" and hurried away, stumbling in her high heels. *Like the White Rabbit,* Alma thought. *But what did the other woman say to upset her?*

Alma realized she was staring at the other woman just as the other woman caught her eye. Alma looked away from the woman's face to her necklace. The pearls resembled pupilless eyes which, nevertheless, saw her. Alma mentally christened the woman Pearl—

it fit the smooth pallor of her face, the sparkle of her teeth.

"What are you doing here?" Pearl asked. "Which Group are you in? You're not one of us, are you?"

"I'm new here."

"Nobody's sorted you? Put you with..." she eyed Alma's thrift-store jeans and blouse, Alma's brown arms—"*your* people?"

"No. Should somebody have met me at the door?"

"I'm sure they've done just what they should have," Pearl said, looking away. "Make yourself at home." The invitation didn't sit well in Alma's stomach.

Alma sidled toward another pair: a nondescript woman dressed for the office, a man with a smart black suit and gold-rimmed glasses.

"Sorry I missed the committee meeting, Gladys," Goldman said. "Another appointment."

"Of course, we all know you're terribly busy."

"But your notes are as clear and succinct as Mr. Stone said."

"He...he mentions me?'

A secretary in love with her boss, Alma thought. But would infatuation make Gladys' hand hover at her throat like that?

"All the time," Goldman said.

"He...he's very kind," Gladys gasped, turning to look out a nearby window.

A window? So far underground? Alma hurried toward it.

It was a mirror. Alma's reflection looked warily back at her. Behind Alma, Goldman fidgeted with something in his pocket in a way that made Alma feel motion-sick.

No, he wasn't the problem. The unsettling thing was not looking at Goldman's reflection, but looking at his and at her own at the same time. Alma didn't seem to fit with Goldman, or Gladys, or any of them. It wasn't just her clothes. She looked solid, while Gladys, Goldman, and the rest looked like pictures on faded news-print. And Alma was the only one standing still. The others all moved their hands or shifted their weight in quick arrhythmic gestures. Alma's headache intensified.

In the mirror she caught sight of another pair nearby, strained to separate their words from the buzz of talk around them.

"...doesn't seem to belong." The dark-haired man tapped his toes as he spoke. "A sorting mistake?"

"Did you hear what she said to Marguerite?" The fair-haired man pushed back his cuticles. "Asking, 'Should somebody have met me?' as if…"

"That shows she doesn't belong in our Group, doesn't it? She doesn't look like a foreigner—not all the way, though she's a little brown—or talk like one, but if she's one of the layabouts…or one of the eggheads? Some of them don't dress properly. Which of *us* would have asked a thing like that?"

"Oh, she's not one of *us*. But what if Management sent her? If she's with *them*, and we displease her…"

The dark-haired man inhaled sharply. "I…I forgot, I have to be at a meeting."

"You won't mention anything about what I said if you, er, meet her?"

The dark-haired man caught Alma's eyes in the mirror, gulped, and hurried away without answering.

The fair-haired man stared at Alma, his hands moving faster and faster. Other people began to turn toward them. Began to look at Alma with those frightened, frightening eyes, to gesture toward her with unsteady hands.

Alma backed away. There was an interior door in the wall near Gladys. She hurried through it into an empty corridor. It was too tall and narrow for comfort, but at least she had it to herself.

Alma froze, staring. The door at the far end had not opened, but she was no longer alone. The figure before her wasn't washed out like the others. He was bright as a stained-glass window with the sun coming through it, substantial as earth, more real than anything she'd ever seen. There was too much of him to take in. She tried to focus. First the colors came clear: the red-purple of his clothing, the mahogany of his skin. Then the face dimmed enough so she could see it. A wide, kind face, familiar from book covers and newscasts.

"Archbishop Tutu? What are you doing here? You aren't dead, are you? We need you…"

"You are not dead," he pointed out. His voice, like his face, was far more real than hers. "I am. I am not dead, and I am not only the good man you named. You see what you can see and trust."

"You don't belong here."

"No one does. Come away. Come with me."

"But I don't understand yet. I have to understand."

"Do you need to understand this place before you can work or love in the world you left?"

Alma shook her head. Working, loving, those were always possible, but they went on for such a long time, and she got so tired, and they weren't talismans against fear, not like knowing.

"Do you understand me?" he asked.

She looked at him, felt the headache fading.

"No. But I trust you." *Maybe you shouldn't trust someone you met in Hell*, her mind muttered, but she didn't believe it. Not then.

"Then come."

"What about the rest of them? Why aren't you getting them out?"

"I do not force anyone to leave."

"You've been here before?"

"Many times."

"Please, I need to understand. I won't stay here, but I can't leave yet." She remembered the conversation about the restaurant. "After lunch. Let me stay until then, see if I can understand, if I can help. Then I'll come with you." She paused. "I'm sorry. You must be terribly busy. Maybe you can't come back then."

"I can come back."

"Is it dangerous for me to eat here? Is it like eating in the land of the dead?"

"There is no danger from the food."

"But…"

He was gone. Her headache throbbed.

She opened the door at the end of the corridor and entered the restaurant. The carpet (almost the same beige as the walls) was spotless. Framed pictures hung on the walls, but the light glared off the glass over them so Alma couldn't see what they depicted.

About half the blond wood tables were occupied by pairs, trios, or foursomes of well-dressed people. No one ate or drank. No one was alone. Some people glared at a door in the far end through which a few scruffily dressed people hurried, shooed along by a uniformed waiter who hissed, "You know your Group's lunch is over. Move along."

The people here eat in shifts, Alma thought, *and I've arrived in between, so no one's getting served now.*

She listened to the conversation at the nearest table.

"This is the third time they've been late with the shift change."

"You're not complaining about Management, are you?" The speaker smiled unpleasantly. The listener blanched.

"Of course not!" The speaker swallowed hard. "No, I... no! Of course those people don't understand punctuality.... their Group, I mean, not Management, of course. Sorry. Long morning. Let's start over. What do you think of the new photographs?"

"Not bad. The long exposures, the perspectives..."

"Very distinctive."

"Mostly original, though after Crantham's exhibit..."

"Crantham, of course, but isn't that a deliberate homage?"

A waiter glided toward Alma. "Are you waiting for a party?"

"No."

"This way." The waiter beckoned her to an empty table and pulled out a chair. "Are you sure you're in the right Group?"

"I'm new."

"But you're in this rotation?" He gestured to the diners. "Do you know anyone in this Group?"

"There's Gladys, she's a secretary..."

"All right." He passed Alma a menu. "We'll send her to your table when she arrives."

Alma ordered spanakopita, feeling very hungry. The waiter hurried away.

Alma waited.

And waited. Glanced at her watch. Frowned.

Her watch said five-thirty am.

It's no big deal, she told herself. *It doesn't mean anything, It does not, does* not, *mean anything at all... Okay, or if it does, it just means...*

It means nobody will miss me up there, however long I stay here. Nobody will come and save me.

Who would have cared enough to do that anyway?

She shook her head, looked around for a clock. There, on the wall at her right hand. It had cherubs around the frame—vacuous puffy pink-and-gold cherubs, not six-winged cherubim. The light glared off the clock face so she couldn't read it. She got up, went closer, passing one of the photographs on the walls, in which she could see nothing but the fluorescent light's reflection.

"Rather conventional," murmured a voice behind her, "but it's hardly the venue for innovative work."

"You can see it?" Alma asked, turning toward the svelte woman who had spoken. "I can't. It must be the angle."

"Well, as Mr. Stone said…"

"Can I stand where you're standing?" Alma asked. "From here I can't see anything at all."

The woman moved over. Alma took her place. Frowned. "I still can't see."

The woman walked unsteadily away.

Alma looked down at her own feet, realized her toes were tapping. She willed them to stop. They didn't. It was like trying to get her fingers to stop tapping in the DMV waiting room before her dreaded road test: the more she willed herself to stop, to sit still, the more she saw herself twitching, which meant, she knew, she looked crazy, and that thought just made her twitch more….

"Your lunch partner has arrived." The waiter hovered at Alma's shoulder, gesturing back toward the table where Gladys sat bolt upright and twitching. Alma went with him.

"Gladys? I'm Alma."

"I…Yes, I…How…?" Gladys' long nails dug into her handbag.

"I heard someone saying how good your work was," Alma said. "Saying how proud Mr. Stone was of you."

Gladys' right hand came up to her throat, clenched and unclenched.

"You know Mr. Stone?" Gladys asked breathlessly.

"I'm new here. I don't know anybody."

Gladys flicked a glance around the room, leaned forward. "Don't go to work for him!" she whispered.

"I won't," Alma whispered back. "I'm just visiting. What's wrong with him? What does he do? What does he make you do?" Revolting possibilities flickered through Alma's mind.

"I'm not telling you anything!" Gladys gasped. Then she deflated. "But it's already too late, if you're an Inspector…"

"What does he make you do?" Alma asked again.

"I update the mailing list, send out memos…it should be child's play, but it isn't; I'm always doing something wrong—dates mistyped, words misspelled—"

"He complains? Punishes you?"

"No! No, he tells me, he tells everyone how good I am. How conscientious, how capable, how efficient. And they smile and say yes, yes, and I know they're all laughing at me. Waiting until he has enough in my personnel file to get me."

"To get you what?"

"*Expelled*," Gladys mouthed. "Out of this Group. Forever. Out in the dark with... *Them*."

"Who are *They*?" Alma asked aloud. "What would happen to you if you were with them?"

Gladys gulped. Her face went salt-white. Her right hand clenched and unclenched in front of her throat. Her left hand, trembling slightly, reached toward Alma, who recoiled.

Gladys leaned back abruptly as the waiter appeared at her shoulder with a menu.

"When will my spanakopita be ready?" Alma asked. "Are you waiting so we can eat at the same time?"

Gladys and the waiter stared at Alma. She looked around. No one was eating.

There is no danger from the food, the Archbishop had said.

"Do you ever feed anyone here?"

Gladys and the waiter tightened their faces as though Alma had passed gas.

"Do you?" Alma insisted.

The waiter walked away. Gladys rose from her seat. "You're crazy!" she whispered. "If you say what I said, no one will believe you."

Alma hurried after the waiter into a room of countertops and clean dishes. No food in sight. Alma went through a door in the back wall.

A big room. Cabinets, butcher-blocks, pans, mixing bowls, spoons. Knives—Alma avoided the wall to her left where they hung. No food. No movement. "Is anybody here?" she called. No answer.

There was a door in the opposite wall, mostly closed. A sign on it said EMPLOYEES ONLY. Alma edged round the right-hand wall and through the door.

She was in a dim little anteroom with whitish walls and a gray linoleum floor. The whole back wall was made of glass—no, was the glass doors leading a walk-in cooler.

There was food, all right. Heads of lettuce, quarters of lamb, wheels of cheese, pizzas, salmon fillets, lobsters, olives. Alma stepped closer to look. Then froze, feeling a draft on the back of her neck. She'd closed the door behind her, hadn't she? She clasped her hands to stop them twitching, then turned.

A thin man in a spotless white chef's uniform stood in the open doorway, glaring at Alma and sucking his teeth. His face was hard and sharp-featured, skin drawn tight over the bones: a knife of a face. His name tag said Nick.

Alma stared at the name tag, then back at his face. He didn't look powerful or evil enough… Well, names weren't everything. But he looked frightened as much as frightening. Not that that necessarily made him safer. Still, she bit off the apology for entering an employees-only area that had been on the tip of her tongue. If he also took her for an inspector—

"This looks well-stocked," she said neutrally.

"Matches the invoice," Nick said in a tight colorless voice. "My invoice copy's in the cabinet there." He motioned to a file cabinet.

"Your records of what you've served?" she improvised.

Nick stood absolutely immobile except for his darting eyes.

Alma stepped closer to the glass doors. Squinted. There was something wrong with the light, something that cast a grayish-blue bloom over the food…

It wasn't the light. Scum floated over the olives; mold laced the salmon fillets.

"Spoiled," she said, appetite giving way to nausea. "The unit went bad? You're waiting for a replacement part?"

"What in hell are you playing at?" Nick snapped. Then he ducked his head and resumed tonelessly, "Unit's in good order. Best unit made won't keep the food good forever. It's all in the reports…you must have seen the reports…"

"Why don't you try explaining this in your own words?" Alma demanded. "Why didn't you give this to people while it was fresh? Why not clean it out and order new food?"

"I can order, but that doesn't mean it will come."

"You tried ordering, and nothing came?"

"You have copies of everything," he said, tight-lipped. "No back channels. You've seen my personnel file. No inappropriate behavior. No citations." His voice was rising, pleading almost.

Alma tried to think what a real inspector would say next. A real inspector would know what he'd written…

Her doubt must have shown in her face. Nick took a step toward her, his empty hands clenching and unclenching at his sides. The fear hadn't left his face, but it had changed.

"Where's your badge, then?"

"What badge?" Alma's voice shook.

He came a step closer. "You're no inspector. What do you think you're doing in here, then? Didn't you see the sign?"

"I wanted something to eat! Nobody out there's getting anything…"

"Course they're not getting anything. Never have, have they? Why'd they expect that to change now?" His eyes bored into hers. "You been agitating them? Getting them together to attack us?"

"Nobody's getting together to do anything! But why didn't you feed them this stuff while it was good and then order more?"

"Order more. Sure, miss. Sounds easy, doesn't it? But what if they don't send it?"

"Why wouldn't they send it?" Alma's voice was rising.

"Why do they do anything? Don't you go shouting and getting the others worked up—don't you get them expecting food!"

"They don't expect food? They don't starve? Don't they have to eat?"

"Who *has* to do anything, here? But if I started to feed them they'd *expect* it. Expect food from the kitchen staff. Figure they'd get it out of us, one way or another." He ran a finger along his forearm like a knife. "One way or another. And there's more of them than us, and only so much you can do to defend yourself with kitchen knives. And who knows what they've got, what they'd do with it, if they'd decided… I've told Management a thousand times we need better security, but who's listening?" His face had gone pale as Gladys' face, pale as his uniform. He reached an unsteady hand out to Alma. Pleading? Preparing to grab? Alma leaned left. When he moved that way she sprinted to the right around him, out through the door, through the knife room. Only the echo of her own lurching footsteps followed her.

She stopped to catch her breath under the clock in the dining room. The light still glared off its face, she couldn't read it from any angle, but she could hear it ticking, ticking, skip and ticking again, then dragging out and out slow, then jerking ahead…

She hurried away, slowed so as not to bump into the waiter. But he—He was walking in, in time, in the no-time of the clock's ticking. And the diner punching something into his cell phone—his fingers flicked, stuttered in just the same rhythm. Just the…just the same…

Alma tried not…not to see her fingers twitching in that just just-wrong time, bolted into the corridor where she couldn't hear…couldn't hear the clock (if she stopped looking at her hands her feet if she…if she ignored the irrhythm of her breaths, maybe she could forget…could…)

"Please," she gasped. "Please, Archbishop…please, whoever you are…please, come back. Get me out of here."

There was nobody else in the hall. Then there was an old black man in a purple cassock. No radiance. Was that really, was that what the Archbishop's face looked like, wasn't it too long, but hadn't he said anyway he really wasn't, what had he said, did she, did she really remember anything?

"Are you ready to leave?' he asked.

"I…have to," she said, forcing words through the syncopated babbling in her brain. "Can you still get me out?"

"You can get yourself out. I can go with you." He reached out to her. She didn't reach back didn't dare. *You shouldn't trust anyone you meet in Hell…*

"Who…who are you, really?"

"I couldn't tell you anything you'd believe or understand. Come."

"But how do I know it's safe?"

"Nothing is safe. But you can leave."

She was afraid of him more afraid of trying to leave without him most afraid of not leaving at all most totally afraid

"I'll follow you," she said.

He opened the door at the end of the corridor.

The room looked like the high school lobby right before the buses arrived. Girls with brand name T-shirts and hair *it never comes blond like that except out of a bottle but mostly the roots don't show oh who cares but look at their fingernails…* Other girls with layers of makeup on their faces, not much cloth on their bodies *I was never that trashy it wasn't just because I didn't have much to show off it wasn't really it was it wasn't....* Other girls hunched under overlarge sweatshirts, heads drooped. *I never looked that pathetic I never looked really I didn't did I...* And boys, strutting or slouching or curled in on themselves. Words—about members of their own sex (derogatory), about the other sex (speculative), about their parents (disgusted)... *I got out of there ten years ago I got out forever I was done it's done why am I here again what have I done am I done for can I get out why can't I get out*

Alma's eyes caught on a girl who seemed to feel the same way. Looking at her, Alma felt her own mind unfogging a little. The girl wore earbuds and a big shapeless shirt, stood a little apart from the others. Her toes tapped in the same dragging and jerking time as the clock. Her eyes were unfocused and miserable. But when she looked at Alma and the man who might be the Archbishop, Alma saw the hope she'd felt when a stranger from the adult world passed through the high school halls: *There is another world out there, other possibilities.* Alma nodded toward the girl, looked at the door. The girl looked at the door too. Her toes stopped tapping. She took a step toward it... *We can get out, we can, see, it's all right...*

"Move it, wide-ride," a boy said, slapping the earbud girl's buttocks and pushing past her—not to the door; to one of the blonde girls. Earbuds recoiled, hung her head, started tapping her toes again.

Alma's stomach lurched. Her brain chattered *He touched...He touched her...Now she's trapped...Now she can't go...If they touch me...If It's not the food...It's the people...It's when they touch you...It's touch...But nobody...nobody touched me yet, I pulled away from Gladys I dodged Nick I'm safe...safe...safe... But how can I get through them all how can I without them touching me...if they touch me...if they touch*

"We have to go out later," Alma gasped. "When the room's empty."

"It is never empty. Come!"

"When there's a different crowd in there, maybe. Not them! I can't! If they touch me..."

"You can still leave." He reached a hand toward her again. "All will be well."

That's not how the Archbishop talks, Alma thought. *The sentences are too short He's a devil He's a demon I I I...*

She backed up. Reached for the door into the hallway.

Stopped, seeing another girl between herself and the door. Turned her head away. Caught sight of herself in the mirror. Her hands twitched, and she was pale and insubstantial as a picture on faded newsprint.

Maybe I'm damned already.

She looked away from the mirror. Down at the carpet. *I won't look I won't go through them I don't have to know I can try later if I don't try I'll always know I can try I...* The rhythm, the irrhythm, seemed to matter more than the sense of the words. Alma's brain and her stomach seemed to have turned into a timeless clock beating out the nonsense, sending out the pulse that kept...that kept them all in in...

A whimpering noise distracted her. She wasn't making that sound. Earbuds was whimpering, staring at Alma, her eyes glassy with hopelessness. *There is no other world.* Alma didn't know if she was hearing her own thoughts or the girl's. *Nothing is possible.*

Those must be the girl's thoughts. Alma briefly caught her own twitching eyes in the mirror, and read her fear in them: fear that something else *was* possible, something even worse. Something so much worse she couldn't bear to name it to picture it—couldn't bear to know it was there...

"Don't be afraid," the old man said.

"That's impossible," Alma snapped.

"Everything's impossible," Earbuds said.

"No," Alma said. "You can get out of here."

"She can, with you," the old man said. "And you with her. You can help her leave, or you can make it harder. Love drives out fear..."

He's quoting the Bible wrong It says perfect love It says all fear It says... But she'd heard the real Archbishop talk about how people needed each other in order to be fully human. Had he never been to an American high school?...Anyway, Alma couldn't leave Earbuds stuck there—couldn't be part of what stuck her there. *I won't be a demon I won't be a damner. If I'm damned I'm damned. At least I tried...*

Her hands kept twitching. She took a step. Two steps. Someone's shoulder brushed hers. She winced. Kept moving. Passing Earbuds, she reached out her left hand. Their fingers locked. The panic drilled deep, but she took one more step, two, three, the door open ahead of her, the grip on her right hand warm and firm, the one on her left sweaty and cold.

The snick of the door closing behind her. The panic-pulse dying away. The smell, from the stairhead, of cut grass and ripe apples and dog poop. (Smells! There had been none on the other side of the door...) Her right hand empty, and her left hand curled in the hand of the girl who stood beside her, wide-eyed, upright under her shapeless clothes, staring at the warm living light that reached down the stairs to meet them.

THE TERROR BY NIGHT

This story is being published for the first time in this book.

Nobody listens for the Wild Hunt now, Sasha Ehrlich writes, hunched over a yellow legal pad at the battered old table in the apartment kitchen. Her eyesight isn't bad, and her mother has told her repeatedly she shouldn't hunch, but she's living on her own now where her mother can't see, and the fluorescent light is weak and flickering, and the effort of wrestling with words always constricts her body. *Nobody closes the windows and bolts the doors when the Gabriel Hounds course the heavens in full cry. They were only ever geese, the scholars say. Who could hear geese now, over the noise of the cities of the New World, and who would care? As for the Hunt's appearance presaging plague, war, and death—we need no omens when all these things surround us every day. The prudent still stay inside after dark, but not for fear of the Huntsman and the Hounds of Hell. At least, not by those names.*

She frowns down at the page. She's too tired to write well. It's already long past her bedtime, since she has to get up at five to do her paper route before helping to open the store. But the images, nightmares which do not seem to be merely her own, push against the inside of her skull; she feels as though they, not eyestrain and fatigue, are causing her throbbing headache.

The Huntsman doesn't need our awareness, she adds. *The souls of living sleepers rode in his train back when people slept deep. Nowadays noise and light keep our sleep short and shallow, but still our souls escape while we stare, entranced, into the flickering screens showing images of the Enemies, the Strangers, the Others. Our bodies sit behind locked doors, our brains cycle through alpha waves and our souls slip out into the night, screaming, fed on and feeding a frenzy of fear and rage so pure as to be almost innocent.*

Forget the geese. Now the Huntsman's metal birds course the skies and drop their bombs. The victims scream louder than the hunting hounds. Half the souls in the Huntsman's train cry out their victory, and the other half cry out their desperate need for revenge, and he rides their combined fury, laughing, to the next victims.

But the Huntsman has not wholly forsaken his old pastimes. Sometimes he still picks a single prey, gives it room to run, and finds a fellow mortal to set on it.

The mortal hunter could be any of us. Anyone who's learned to fear— and who has a gun (with or without a badge), or a truck, or a tire iron, or just the advantage of size and strength. The undead Huntsman breathes in the human hunter's ear: There! That one! The thief, the terrorist, the mugger, the criminal, the alien. Give them what they deserve. *Then he summons the hounds, and the cry of the hunting pack fills the human hunter's ears.*

Sasha stops. Elie Wiesel, in one of the books her grandfather Ehrlich, who came over to America as a boy, pressed on her with that fierce look in his usually gentle eyes, said a human being's death is a private thing, not to be ogled by strangers. She's always told herself that doesn't apply to imaginary characters in fantasy stories. But now she is writing her way toward something terrible and real. She tears off the sheet, stares at the blank page below.

She is unsurprised, as she often is in dreams, when a window appears in the middle of the page. The glass is smudged. She pushes the sash up—it's surprisingly heavy for such a small thing. Recoils at the sound of dogs baying and something wilder laughing, laughing.

This can't be real, she reminds herself. *You sat up late writing creepy trash, and you fell asleep, and you're having another nightmare.* She has learned the hard way she can't break out of those by sheer force of will.

The window grows as large as the table. Through the open sash she sees the back door of the Good Shepherd Home three blocks from her apartment, which she passes every day on her way to work. A short brown-skinned man steps outside, starts down the buckled brick sidewalk. A CNA, likely, heading home after the four-to-midnight shift. He moves like someone whose back hurts, the way Sasha's mother used to move after eight hours of getting the stronger clients up to go to the bathroom, moving the weaker ones enough to change their sheets so they wouldn't get bedsores, always hurrying. He doesn't seem to hear the hounds. He does notice the police car approaching. He straightens abruptly, steps into the shadows. Did he steal something?

Of course, a cold voice that is not Sasha's says inside Sasha's skull. *He stole every breath he's taken in this country, every step on its streets, every bite of food. He stole across the border, he stole some American's job...*

"Liar!" Sasha says.

Oh, he crossed the desert...

"Fine, but that doesn't make him a thief. I don't believe that. He has a right..."

They believe me, the voice answers.

Sasha looks back through the window. The police car continues without slowing down, and the man emerges from the shadows, hurries down the sidewalk. But another car has seen his emergence. It stops. People get out. Three men—no, four. The leader calls, "Where are you going in such a hurry?"

The man doesn't answer. He begins to back away.

"Why are you hiding from the police?" another adds.

The one in back lifts out something that flashes under the streetlight. Sasha can't quite make it out. The hounds yip eagerly. Sasha still can't see them.

The shift worker turns away from them, breaks into a stumbling run.

The window Sasha sees through follows him. No, follows his pursuers. He dodges into an alley between buildings. They follow. Come out the other side—they're just two streets over from Sasha's apartment now. The pursuers stop, looking up and down the street. The only man in sight under the dark closed windows of the apartment buildings is larger than their quarry, and he stands like someone whose back doesn't hurt.

"Which way did he go?" one of the human hunters calls.

Even in the times when people knew what the Hunt was, they sometimes helped it. *Hold my horse,* the Huntsman might say to them. Or, *Tell me what you saw.* Sometimes they obeyed, and later they saw the Huntsman riding back with the elf-women slung across his horse, unconscious, bound together by their hair. Sometimes the Huntsman left a reward for his helper. A boot full of gold. A haunch of rotten beef. A woman's leg, still wearing a red shoe.

"That way," the man on the sidewalk says, pointing. "What did he do?" The hunters run on without answering, catch sight of the hunted man, who plunges across a street without waiting for the light. They're one block from Sasha's apartment.

A woman walks up the sidewalk toward them, hunched over her phone. She looks up and stares as their footsteps thud toward her. Then she does what prudent peasants do in tales: lies down, covers her eyes and ears. *I am not here. I do not see you. I cannot hear you. Your chase has nothing to do with me.* The hounds part round the prostrate woman like water round a rock. The four men don't look at her, don't step on her. The window moves away before the woman rises, before Sasha can see whether she looks relieved or ashamed.

The hunted man stumbles along, his ankles turning as he hits the humps and hollows of the broken pavement, his breath coming short and hard. He turns onto Sasha's street. He can't keep this up much longer. They'll catch him soon. Sasha doesn't want to see what will happen then. It's too late to call the police, even if she thought the police would help him more than they'd harm him. She turns away from the window. Overhead the fluorescent flickers painfully. She shuts her eyes.

She hears a voice through the magic window: the hunted man —praying, maybe? Not in a language she knows.

If she shuts the window she will not be able to hear him.

That's right, the cold voice says. *Close your eyes, cover your ears, and let me pass.*

Because this is obviously a dream, and because it will be quite as unpleasant to wake up shamed by her own dreamed cowardice as to wake up terrified by her own dreamed death, Sasha scrambles to the door, pausing only to grab her heavy cardigan against the brisk September air.

When the lock snicks shut behind her she realizes three things in rapid succession. First, that the apartment key is still inside (and this is no hour at which to call the landlord). Second, that she is wide awake. Third, that she can still hear the Hunt and its quarry in the street below.

What the hell is she supposed to do now? Her brain freezes on that question as her feet keep stumbling down the stairs. Sometimes in the stories prayer banished the Hunt, or at least kept a bystander safe. She murmurs, "O Lord, heal me, for my bones are shaking with terror." The noise of the Hunt is undiminished. So is her fear. Well, the Hunt stories don't come from Sasha's people. She makes the sign of the cross, which doesn't seem to help either. She steps from the apartment's entryway into the pale gleam of the streetlights.

The hunted man runs by her, gasping, too breathless to pray. Sasha looks away from him, then wishes she hadn't.

The hounds, their eyes the same dried-blood color as the flecks on their sharp muzzles, their almost-white hides tinged with sickly green, their long narrow heads as high as Sasha's waist, are maybe ten yards away. They seem more real to Sasha than the men who run among them, stumbling and gasping like their quarry, but laughing too.

"Stop!" Sasha tries to call commandingly, ends up squeaking. The hounds prick their ears and turn their wild eyes on her. Her stomach seethes. Her pulse hammers. Her throat constricts. She wants desperately to run.

"Never run." Sasha's mother told her that when she was six years old, when a dog came out into the road after them, head and tail low, snarling. Sasha started to bolt. Her mother grabbed her by the arm, held her daughter behind her while she faced the dog and told it in a hard level voice to go home.

Sasha stands her ground, shaking. The dogs stop, stand, stare, pointing and baying. Has she defeated them so easily?

No. They are crying as mortal hounds might if they had treed an animal, and the Huntsman is coming. He is laughing inside her skull. He is also approaching behind the dogs, behind the stumbling men, in a vortex of sick radiance that obscures his form rather than illuminating it.

Sasha remembers her great-aunt Rocheleh, the superstitious one, bending over her during a childhood illness, chanting the fever-demon's long name in ever-shorter form to break its power. If Sasha knew the Huntsman's name… In some tales he's Woden. She whispers, "Woden, Oden, den, en." The sick light curdles, takes form: a great stallion, greenish-white like the hunting hounds, and on its back a rider of giant stature, his one eye blazing gas-flame blue, his left hand flourishing a whip, his right clutching the handle of a long spear. He does not appear to be shrinking.

She's read news stories about Odinist neo-Nazis. If that's who these four louts are, they'd be quite as happy to chase her as to chase the nursing-home worker. She makes herself look back at them. Their hair and eyes seem colorless in the wan light. They turn to look at her, still laughing in time to the baying of the hounds. Their faces are oddly slack.

"No," Sasha whimpers. "Go back!"

"That's what we told him to do," says the least breathless of the four. "Go back where he came from."

"He'd already finished his shift," Sasha says.

"We don't have time for this," another man says. "Go home,

girl, if you know what's good for you."

"Or don't," the first speaker says. "Might be more fun this way."

Fury rises through her fear. "You and your fun!" she spits. "You cowards, you murderers, you…! It's you should go back to the pestholes you came from; it's you should run till your breath fails, and always too slow…"

"An interesting proposition," says the Huntsman. She hears his voice, sickeningly, in stereo—in her mind and also, half a beat behind, with her ears. "Shall I set them to run before the hounds, not with them?"

Sasha can imagine that. Their stupid faces slack with fear instead of eagerness, their breath rasping like that of the man they were chasing—but they're not like him. They deserve it. They worshipped this monster. Let him hunt them. Let him crush them. Let them break, body and mind and soul.

Sasha begins to laugh. She doesn't like the sound of that laughter. She doesn't know how to stop. The hounds' yapping takes on the timing and the cadence of her laughter.

A hand closes on her elbow. She jerks free. The four men are still too far away to touch her, but the hand grasps her arm again. "Do not go with him!" gasps a thickly accented voice.

Sasha blinks, and the world sways around her. The man who had fled is holding her left arm and muttering urgently at her. The Huntsman is on her other side, his proffered hand only a few inches from her right hand, which is half-raised to take it. How did she not see that? She whips her hand back.

"Well then, we'll go on as before." Once again the Huntsman faces her from behind the dogs and men. He no longer resembles Odin, or anyone else in particular.

"I named you wrong," she says aloud. "No wonder you nearly took me." Sasha has only met one person who actually claims to be a devotee of Odin's, and that man's as passionate for justice as anyone in Sasha's family. The Huntsman is not someone else's God. Who is he?

She squints into the glaring unlight. The blurred face flashes through changes faster than she can name them. Witch hunters, slave catchers, pogromchiks, from illustrations in old books, all with dull frantic look of the human hunters. None of them can be the

Huntsman's true face. He should be harder, colder, surer.

The next face that shapes itself in the unlight is proud and self-righteous, pale and stone-hard. Literally. It's carved in stone. A statue. One of the ones they fight over... As she thinks that the Huntsman's face becomes the torchlit face of one of the statue's defenders caught on a newscast, mouth wide open, eyes glassy with fury. She feels again the seethe of fury and disgust that she felt when she almost took the Huntsman's hand.

Now it's a Huntswoman who looks back at her. A woman with terribly familiar features. With Sasha's features, set in an expression of deepest contempt.

No. It's a lie. I don't look like that. That's the expression she remembers on the faces of the children who taunted her at school.

The expression she remembers, also, on the faces of the children taunting Mary Blanche, Sasha's particular nemesis, after Sasha lost all patience and yelled out in the middle of lunch hour what her mother had told her in strict confidence, believing that it would help her to *understand* Mary. She remembers, still, with an odd mix of shame and satisfaction, how Mary's face crumpled, how Mary couldn't think of a lie to tell until her friends had all seen her shame and turned on her. As well they might, little mercy as she'd ever shown to anyone else. And how they turned! The pointing, the laughing, the...

The cry of the hunting pack, given a new quarry, and not for that day only. Set on by Sasha. She knows what she thought the men in the street deserved for running with the Hunt. What does she deserve?

The hounds stop baying and run at her, heads lowered, snarling. She totters, too shamed and confused either to run or stand. She'll fall. They'll be at her throat. She has no right no chance to...

Someone catches her by the arms, holds her up. The man she came out to save. Yes, she did try to help him. There's something in that.

"No," she says to the Hunter. "No. You can use me, if I let you, but I am not you. At least, that isn't all I am. Who are you? Show me your true face."

Sasha's knees solidify. The hounds stand still again, just out of reach. Now the Hunter's face is hidden by a pointed hood and a white mask.

What if its true face is a mask? she thinks. At first the idea seems stupid. But she's read something about that before. In—in one of the books from her grandfather Ehrlich.

In *The Trial of God*. The handsome stranger who speaks in defense of God, proclaiming God's triumphant justice in the face of the brutal rapes and murders that have been carried out in God's name, that God has not prevented; the man who seems so wise, so just, so Godly, until he dons his Purim mask and calls for another pogrom.

Yes, until he puts the mask on they don't know him for…

She laughs as the Huntsman's face solidifies into the horned mask. This isn't the frantic laughter that accompanied the hounds. "I see you, Accuser," she says. "We see you. We're not running from you—or with you, either." She turns to the man who supports her. "Thank you," she says. "I can stand now. And I'm not going with him." She steps back from the man, squeezes and then releases his hands, turns to face the Hunt. She takes three steps forward. The hounds part to let her through. "I see you, Accuser," she repeats. "And I don't believe you. He didn't deserve to be hunted. They… Maybe they don't either. Maybe we all deserve you, taken at our worst, but the worst isn't all. It's never all."

She raises her arms, looks away from the Huntsman, into the sky above the buildings. There are too many lights here, so she can't see the stars she used to watch from her bedroom window when she was a child afraid of the dark, but she remembers the words her mother said over her in the darkness, and she repeats them. "Remove Satan from in front of us and from behind us, and cradle us in the shadow of your wings."

The Hunter's sickly radiance flares up, then vanishes along with the hell-hounds. Sasha and the fugitive face four men who look tired, breathless, and also, now, rather confused.

"Go home," Sasha says in the same tone her mother used on the dog. She slides her cell phone from her pocket, lifts it so it catches the moonlight. "Go home and stop harassing us. I'm filming you. I see you." She bites her lip. "I see you," she repeats in a somewhat gentler voice. "I see what you are now. I don't know what you could be. What you are when you remember who you are. Go home and be better."

The four men blink at her, then turn away, stumbling. The

Huntsman's spell, Sasha supposes, is fading for the moment, and the sky is gray with dawn.

THE FOUR LAST SINGS

This story was originally published in Breaking Rules Publishing's anthology "The Scribe" in January 2021

1. The Rainbow Sign

On the third morning of the apocalypse, Arlie painted "WELCOME" in straggling rainbow capitals on the side of the rabbit shed that faced the road. Well, as close to rainbow as she could get, since she had five colors, some of them clashing, with which to render seven letters. Fretting over the colors, she gave insufficient attention to spacing, so the last "E" was exceedingly straight and narrow. Before she could paint it over and start again, Lucinda came down from the garden and stared at her.

"What's the idea?" Lucinda demanded.

"What it says. Why else did you breed all the rabbits? We can't eat that many ourselves. And the garden expansion you staked out could feed a lot more than two people."

"Those kits won't be at butcher weight for three months, and there won't be anything to eat from the garden for another month and a half."

"What about the stuff in the freezer? We'll need help eating all that before it spoils."

"Unless the electricity comes back on."

"You know what you said this morning when I said it might come back on."

"I know." Lucinda's face settled back into the grim expression it had worn as she confirmed there was still no dial tone and no Internet, as she put new solar-charged batteries in the radio and turned the knob slowly, finding only static. This should probably have been more pleasant to listen to than the reports on the first day of the apocalypse, which all seemed to agree the country was being taken over by terrorists although they couldn't agree on just who was terrorizing whom. But Lucinda had snorted reassuringly all through those reports, criticizing both their grammar and their internal consistency. When the broadcasts cut off at the same time as the Internet, Lucinda's mouth had set hard while the vertical lines bit deep into her forehead. Arlie had improvised a monologue on the benefits of digital detoxification and kept at it until Lucinda's jawline eased a little. It still hadn't eased very much two days later, but sometimes arguing put Lucinda in a better mood. "Probably it won't come back," Lucinda conceded. "And the store's likely out of paint already—"

"—so, since paint must be carefully rationed in the event of an apocalypse, I have likely shortened our collective life expectancy by this careless use."

"Who-all belongs to this collective?"

"The two of us, and anyone else who shows up. You didn't ask how long our life expectancy was before I shortened it."

"Didn't want to know. Neither do you. What's with the colors? You advertising this as a haunt of lesbians?"

"Sure, to haunted lesbians. And to Christians, lesbian or otherwise, it's for the promise God gave Noah about springtime and harvest not failing—"

"—so long as the earth endures," Lucinda finished. "Any bets on how long that'll be?"

Arlie made an ugly little sound halfway between a laugh and a sob.

Lucinda put her arms around Arlie and sang into Arlie's ear in her rich contralto.

"God gave Noah the rainbow sign, don't you see…"

They were pretty nearly of a height, but there was a lot more of Lucinda than of Arlie, and the song vibrated strong in all that space. Arlie felt as well as heard Lucinda singing, "No more water, but the fire next time," and the vibrations comforted her more than the words disturbed her. When Lucinda reached "There's honey in that rock, don't you see," Arlie joined an octave up and rocked her honey as they sang.

After the last note faded, Lucinda said, "You planning to wait till someone answers your invitation, or can we add people to this collective ourselves?"

"Who did you mean to add?"

"Whom, you mean." Lucinda smiled fairly convincingly at Arlie's groan. "Esther."

~ * ~

An hour later, Arlie swore under her breath, put the last goat off the milk stand without letting her finish her grain, and got her bicycle out of the tool shed. Esther still lived on her own four miles up the road; though the road was bumpy and unpaved, it shouldn't have taken Lucinda and the car more than ten minutes each way. Arlie had spent the last thirty minutes unsuccessfully trying not to think of all the things that might be going wrong.

It was almost a relief to let herself think about who—whom —else Lucinda might have encountered and what Arlie could pack in the bike panniers to improve the situation. The double-chocolate cookies could be trade goods or peace offerings. The unusually strong homemade wine from Mike Morris might pass for a peace offering, and might also incapacitate a kidnapper if taken internally, or if applied externally while still in the bottle. Arlie also carried a first-aid kit, pepper spray, matches, and a squirt gun loaded with red-dyed water (an A. A. Milne mystery had given her the idea of shooting someone with that so they would think they were bleeding, and would therefore think she had an actual gun).

As Arlie pedaled up the first hill it occurred to her that the squirt gun itself, unlike the one in Milne's novel, did not look like anything other than a squirt gun. She wobbled to a halt on the shoulder. She hadn't come up with any good gun disguises when she heard a motor approaching from ahead of her, on the other side of the hill.

The car stopped. The passenger window rolled down. "Are you all right?" Esther asked.

The relief hit Arlie a few seconds after the embarrassment. "Fine," Arlie muttered, feeling her face heat up. "And you're all right! We should have come earlier, but..."

"You thought it might be a tempest in a teapot," Esther said, nodding. Esther was eighty-seven, and her hips and knees weren't all they used to be, but her mind remained intact. "And then when you thought it wasn't you didn't know what to do. So you fetched me. Was that wise?"

"It'll be good to have you," Arlie said.

"So long as I can help," Esther answered.

2. Hunker In Your Bunker

There was plenty for Esther to help with. Arlie and Lucinda had potatoes to plant, fences to mend, and new ground to dig over, and it was a relief to have someone else keeping up with the inside work, though Arlie felt bad for Esther, who was sweating by the wood stove as she canned whatever frozen goods were amenable to that process (most of them, according to Esther).

The apocalypse was six days old, the radio was stubbornly silent, the pantry shelves were so full of canned goods that it looked more like fall than spring in there, and Esther was arguing with Lucinda (who had just come in from a long day in the garden) about the merits of canning thawed chopped onions, when a car pulled into the driveway, spitting gravel. Esther seized the shop-vac handle which she'd said could pass for a gun muzzle if it was stuck out the window in the right way. Lucinda froze. Arlie tried to remember where she'd put Mike's wine. Esther, fidgeting with the window, said, "That's Mike's truck."

Arlie was halfway out the door when Lucinda hissed behind her, "But it might not be Mike in it." Arlie shut the door behind her before she'd really had time to process that, and then she thought ducking back into the house would make her look frightened and defenseless. She took two long steps toward the truck.

The passenger door opened. "Get in, quick," Mike said. "Is Lucinda alive?"

"We're all alive. But I can't go driving now; I haven't milked the goats."

"Forget the goats," he said. "We've got to get out of Dodge. You especially."

"Why?" Lucinda asked, sticking her head out the second-story window overlooking the parking lot. Lucinda's hands rested on the windowsill, clutching a heavy paperweight.

"I don't think you need that right now," Arlie said.

Mike, who was headed for a bunker in what he called "an undisclosed location" (which Arlie took to mean his fishing camp), had left town because he saw smoke rising, didn't hear the fire siren, and assumed terrorists had struck. He was prepared to make room for, and share frozen MREs with, Arlie and Lucinda, to whom he thought terrorists would be likely to do something particularly unpleasant on account of their, um, *lifestyle*.

Lucinda's lips tightened in response to that word. Arlie, remembering that Mike had been a good neighbor for twenty-odd years despite turning pink and looking at his boots if the word *lesbian* was mentioned, said she didn't see why terrorists should persecute farmers. "Anyway the garden's just barely in, and won't be bearing for another six weeks, and they'd have to do all the gardening themselves if they shot us."

"Now, your bunker full of ready-to-eat food—" Lucinda began.

Arlie saw Mike's face twitch. "Don't mind Lu," she said. "But you could stay with us."

Mike declined. As the sound of the motor faded, Lucinda came out the door to join Arlie, saying ruefully, "I should have kept my fat flapping mouth shut. No use scaring him."

"He'd already scared himself," Arlie said. "Scared me, too. What do you think's happening in town? We should've checked on more people. And picked things up…"

"We didn't go," Lucinda reminded her, "because I said the townies who didn't have food put up and didn't have wood to heat with would need things more than we did, and you said we might get shot."

"I guess I've always been scared," Arlie admitted.

"So has Mike," Esther said from the doorway, "but I think he likes it. First it was that two thousand computer thing, and then some Mayan prophecy…"

"He's always wanted some excuse to go hunker in his bunker," Arlie agreed.

Lucinda crooned "Won't you hunker in my bunker?" to the tune of "It's So Peaceful In The Country." Arlie laughed.

Half an hour later Arlie and Lucinda circled the living room, Lucinda growling "Can you, can you…" at the bottom of her vocal range while Arlie yipped "do, do the bunker-hunker" in falsetto and Esther played syncopated percussion with a ladle on an assortment of pots.

When Esther broke into a frenetic banging that bore no relation to the rhythms of the vocalists, Arlie wondered if she was having some kind of seizure. She stopped singing and turned to look.

Esther jerked her head toward the kitchen window. Arlie saw a pale oval flattened against the glass. Then it slid out of sight.

Hell, Arlie thought. *Somebody finally saw my sign and came for help, and now they think we're nuts and they're leaving.* She ran outside. Several figures ran ahead of her.

"Hello," she called. "Can we help?" They kept running. "Come back!" Arlie yelled. "We've got food! We're not crazy!"

The hindmost running figure glanced over her shoulder, then ran off again, her long gun bouncing on her back. She hopped into the back of a black SUV, which roared away.

Lucinda's hands came down on Arlie's shoulders. "Are you completely out of your ever-loving mind?"

"I shouldn't have scared them like that, should I?"

"You shouldn't have scared *me* like that," Lucinda snapped. "Seven of them, and four at least with guns. I thought you were afraid of whatever Mike ran from in town."

"Oh," Arlie said weakly. Then, rallying, "If they wanted to hurt us, why did they run?"

"Because the Lord protects fools and children, maybe, but eventually he might get tired of that."

"Or maybe they thought a crazy unarmed girl running after them must have really good backup, and so they figured we were trying to... kidnap them into some sort of cult with horrible orgies? Or maybe they thought we were cannibals."

"Cannibals!" Lucinda huffed. "We've got too much stuff from the freezer to eat already, and we're just about out of canning jars... Why are you looking at me like that?"

3. Shoes For Barefoot Angels

Arlie glanced around to make sure Lucinda was out of sight before allowing herself to stand up between the bean-rows and groan loudly. The black flies were thick, her back felt ready to snap off her hips, and weeding was too monotonous to distract her from worrying.

Esther's nose and eyes oozed and her breathing didn't sound good. After their last decongestant pills and Lucinda's echinacea-elderberry-mallow tea had failed to help appreciably, Arlie had biked to town. The pharmacy windows were broken, and when Arlie picked her way in she'd found the shelves empty. The same was true of the grocery store. She'd started down the road to the clinic, but a pack of dogs had chased her and she'd fled, choosing her route by the steepness of the downhill slope. The dogs had given up before she ran out of downhill, but nobody had called them off or offered Arlie shelter. Most driveways had been carless, though at least half the houses had looked intact. Arlie had started across the lawn toward Jennie Sproule's house, but when a voice that was not Jennie's yelled at her to leave she had complied.

As she weeded she worried about Jennie as well as Esther. Maybe someone was there helping her; maybe Jennie had gone to stay with her kids and a refugee had moved into her house; but maybe Jennie was being held captive and Arlie hadn't even tried to rescue her... Trying not to think about that, she started worrying about whether all these extra plants they'd put in would actually bear a crop; you couldn't count on that any more, as the weather kept getting stranger... She groaned again.

"Shh!" said Lucinda behind her. Arlie turned around, hands on hips. "Well, you try..." she began. Then stopped. Lucinda wasn't there.

Arlie bit her lip. She'd felt all morning that someone was watching her. Apparently the apocalypse was cracking her brain. Maybe the people who'd wrecked the pharmacy and the houses in town, and the people who'd brought the grid down, had succumbed to the same problem a little earlier, probably on account of not having Lucinda in their lives. Maybe the wondering was all that had gone wrong. Maybe that idea was irrational enough to confirm Arlie had serious brain cracks...

A bush near the end of the hedgerow by the bean-field thrashed, stilled. Arlie held her hoe high as she approached it.

"Don't hit us!" a shrill voice said from the bush. "We didn't eat anything!"

"I won't hit you if you don't hit me," Arlie said, "and I'll get you stuff to eat if you don't smash things. Okay? Can you come out so I can see who—whom—I'm talking to?"

Voices in the hedgerow conferred briefly, and two figures emerged. The skinny wary-eyed girl who stood in front was halfway between shoulder-height and waist height to Arlie. The round-faced boy was considerably shorter.

Arlie blinked. "Kids," she said, setting the hoe down. "I'm Arlie. Who are you? Where are your folks?"

"*¿Como?*" the boy asked.

The girl said something in Spanish that Arlie couldn't follow at that speed, then said slowly and carefully in English, "I'm Rosa. We have—we *are* hungry, but we did not take anything."

"Come on down to the house, then, and we'll get you lunch. When was the last time you had something to eat?"

"Yesterday." Rosa spoke rapidly to the little kid. Arlie's Spanish was limited and rusty, but she thought she'd heard "*todos ustedes.*"

"Are there more of you?" Arlie asked.

"I said, we didn't hurt no thing."

"I didn't think you did," Arlie said. "I'm not mad. I want to help."

"The other ones said that," Rosa said. "They told us the bad people would say that too. But they said they weren't bad people…"

"Who are these 'other ones?'"

"You can't make us go back to them," Rosa said, moving between Arlie and the boy.

"I won't make you do anything."

A boy near Rosa's height shouldered his way out of the hedgerow, carrying a very small girl in his arms. He looked squarely at Arlie. "I'm Joel." He said it English-fashion, with a hard J. "We'll help with stuff if you give us food. And do you have medicine we can give Coco?"

"Not much," Arlie said. "What's wrong with Coco?"

"She's sick," Joel said. "She can't breathe right." Coco's breathing sounded a lot like Esther's.

"We have someone else who's sick like that. We've put her in a warm place with steam so she can breathe better. I don't know if it helps, but it's the best we can do. Traveling like this must be hard for the girl…"

"We were cold and hungry too before, and they would not give anything to help Coco," Rosa said. "You can not send us…"

"Of course not," Arlie said.

An hour later six children and three adults sat at the picnic table (Rosa insisted on staying outside), eating lettuce and goat cheese as well as rabbit-asparagus soup slightly burned by the solar cooker Arlie had jury-rigged. All the children except Coco, into whom Rosa spooned soup with great determination and limited success, ate with enthusiasm. None of the healthy five asked for second helpings. None declined when second, or third, helpings were offered.

"That was good," Joel said. "Thanks." And, to Rosa, "Told you they weren't sodomites."

Arlie set her spoon down very carefully, as though it might explode.

"*What?*" Lucinda asked.

"They said if we ran away, if they didn't get us back first, the bad people would get us," Joel said. "The aliens and the cannibals and the sodomites."

"We wanted the aliens to find us," said Martina, the little girl at Joel's elbow. Seven or eight, Arlie guessed her to be, and probably Joel's sister—at least she kept close to his side and she shared his easy English. "They called Mami an alien."

"Shut up!" hissed Joel, and "*¡Cállate!*" snapped Rosa.

"Good God," Arlie said. "They took away your parents? I'm so sorry. Do you know where…"

Lucinda stomped on Arlie's foot. Too late. Martina wasn't the only one crying in the bleak, almost noiseless way of a child who has learned not to assume tears will bring help. Arlie told herself trying to take any one of the criers into her arms was not likely to produce good results. For several reasons.

"Do you know what sodomites are?" Lucinda asked.

Rosa shook her head.

Joel shrugged. "Dunno. Something bad."

"Sodomites," Lucinda said, "are people who lived in a city called Sodom a long, long time ago. They had lots of money, lots of food, but they didn't want to share it. When strangers came to town, the people who'd lived in Sodom their whole lives didn't say 'Welcome.' They didn't feed them. The only person who helped the strangers was an alien who'd moved into town a little while ago. But the people who'd spent their whole lives in Sodom didn't like that alien being kind to strangers. And in the night they banged on his door and told him to send those people outside."

"What were they going to do with them?" Joel asks.

Arlie kicked. Lucinda, who had already moved her leg aside,

said, "Assault them."

"*¿Como?*"

"*Assault* means, among other things, to beat somebody up," Lucinda said. Lucinda disapproved of outright lying, but she was good at cutting corners.

"Did they die?" Joel asked.

"No," Lucinda said. "God sent an angel down and made all the bullies go blind so they couldn't see who was the alien and who was another mean Sodomite. So they fought with each other, and they went away mad, and the strangers didn't get hurt."

"And then what happened?" Martina asked.

Arlie had the impression Lucinda had meant to end the story there. But she'd hesitated too long to make "Nothing" convincing.

"The alien and the strangers went away with the angel," Arlie said, "to a place where nobody would try to hurt them. And Sodom… um… caught fire. It's gone."

"So the only sodomites left now are the nice sodomite aliens," Joel clarified.

Arlie faked a cough.

"People aren't nice just because their parents were, or mean either," Lucinda said.

"Well, you're not mean sodomites, because you fed us," Joel said. "We'll help now. I promise." Rosa nodded.

"You don't have to…" Arlie began.

"If we're going to grow enough food for everyone to eat this year, we'll need help," Lucinda said.

After a long afternoon in which the older kids pitched into the garden along with Arlie while the younger ones played in the back yard and Coco rested beside Esther in the steam tent, the children consented to come inside for supper and to sleep in the living room. Arlie thought she would stay awake all night worrying. Instead she fell heavily asleep.

She woke abruptly in the dark. Surely she'd heard one of the children cry out.

Lucinda caught her arm as she started to slide out of bed. "Hush. Listen."

Arlie did. A rough little voice was singing:

"*A la puerta del cielo venden zapatos para los angelitos que andan descalzos…*"

"Shoes," Arlie whispered. "Rosa's and Marisol's are falling apart..."

"Shh," Lucinda said. "Sleep."

Arlie closed her eyes and let the music lead her back down into quiet.

4. Love

"Come sit by me, Lu," Arlie said, patting the wide seat of the "chariot."

"I'm fine," Lucinda insisted breathlessly enough to disprove her own assertion.

"Sure, you're fine," Arlie said. "Come keep me company."

Lucinda turned, stumbled. Jaime's hand was instantly at her elbow. Lucinda frowned, then smiled her sudden smile.

"All right, Joel," she said. "You're a good kid."

It was one of Lucinda's more understandable mistakes; Jaime looked much as his father had twenty years earlier. Arlie wondered who—whom? —Lucinda considered Jaime's partner Greg to be. She knew better than to ask. Lucinda's knees were better at eighty-eight than Arlie's were at eighty-four, but Lyme disease and old age were making visible gaps in Lucinda's memory and her awareness of when she was. Whether her irritability when those lapses became evident was due to Lyme, age, or just her basic Lucinda-ness was more than Arlie could tell.

Lucinda sat down gingerly on the padded bench of the stump puller which Greg and Joel had transformed into a two-wheel cart in which two strong pullers could transport two elderly people who'd involuntarily lost a fair bit of weight. The pullers were Greg and Jaime. Jaime said the ride was the first part of Arlie and Lucinda's anniversary celebration. Lucinda, once she got over being upset that she'd forgotten the anniversary, had clearly enjoyed the trip. The light was clear and golden in a way that Arlie had once taken for granted in the autumn and was now grateful for whenever it came. The leaves on the surviving deciduous trees flamed scarlet and gold, the bare white branches of the long-dead ash trees stood stark and cool against the flame, and the geese (who had somehow survived everything, including the sicknesses that killed many of the smaller songbirds, the plague of feral cats, and the rapidly improving hunting skills of Lucinda and some of the neighbors) streamed overhead, trumpeting.

"Joel's eyes look better," Lucinda said. "Lost that stray-cat expression. Lucky for him that girl brought them back."

"Rosa's a brave one," Arlie said. That remained true, though it had been almost thirty years since Rosa had joined the bicycle couriers and eventually come back with Joel's mother, Coco's father, and her own aunt. That wasn't altogether a happy homecoming— Rosa's parents were dead, and her aunt didn't want to say how; Coco's father had a grave to visit, not a daughter; and Rosa's stories of the ways other communities had found to survive weren't all good to hear—but it had been a relief to see Joel let himself be a child again.

"Brave," Lucinda sniffed. "That's Mike's kind of talk." Lucinda believed in speaking no ill of the dead, but plainly she was back in the time when Mike was still alive. She'd been glad to see him when he got lonely in his bunker, ran out of freeze-dried meals, came back to see if they were alive, and stayed to eat real food and also to hook up his photovoltaics and work with Arlie on other solar projects. She'd shown her gladness mainly by snapping at him. "Brave," she said again, shaking her head. "You just do what you have to do. We did."

Arlie squeezed her hand and smiled. Lucinda looked down at their joined hands. "How'd we get so old?" she asked. Then, looking back at Arlie's face, she added, "That's not a senile question! I know how we did it: just kept living. But how did we manage that?"

That was a fair question, considering the little ring of graves on the hill behind the garden and the ruin that had once been town. Considering the year when pillars of smoke and fire rose on the horizon, and the year of the influenza, and the year of the July 4 frost that killed most of the garden… Arlie kept thinking about that after Lucinda's mind, or at least her conversation, had wandered to other matters.

The question lingered with her as she ate the dinner Greg and Jaime had made, looking around at the other celebrants. Jaime and Greg lived with Arlie and Lucinda, or perhaps now it was the other way around; so did Esele, who had come back with Rosa from a courier trip six years ago and had grown from a wide-eyed silent child into a rather authoritative young woman. Joel and Rosa had just walked half a mile down the road from their own farm at Esther's old place. Enoch, Mike's youngest grandson, who had spent several years of his childhood on Arlie and Lucinda's farm, had come from his bivouac at the fishing camp.

"Look at our family," Lucinda said to Arlie. "And can they cook! Esther ought to get this frittata recipe."

"It's a good one," Arlie said noncommittally.

Lucinda blinked, then glared. "Why don't you just say Esther's dead and I'm senile? I hate it when you're patient with me!"

Arlie tried not to cry.

"And you hate it when I'm not patient with you," Lucinda said. "I know. Come on, Arlie, don't drip snot in your soup."

Arlie gave a hard short laugh like a sob. "Really, Lucinda!"

"How did we manage to stay married to each other all these years, being this cussed?" Lucinda asked. "And why is it so hard being old?"

"We couldn't help loving each other, I guess," Arlie said, "and I don't guess we'll stop. Won't stop loving each other, or any of the rest either." She waved her arm vaguely in a gesture which could equally have indicated "the rest" meant the family gathered round their table or all the things that might not exactly be love but that somehow got rolled in with it. "Everything's hard," Arlie said, "but we don't stop." Feeling herself still on the edge of tears, she launched into song. "O Love that will not let me go, I rest my weary soul in thee…"

Her voice quavered and missed the high note. Lately she missed her strong clear mezzo voice more than she missed having working knees.

Maddie's voice came in underneath hers, holding the melody. "I give thee back the life I owe…"

Around the table people joined in: Enoch strengthening the melody, Rosa singing a third up, Esele adding a more complicated high harmony, Greg holding a warm bass line, Jaime singing half a step flat as usual, and Lucinda humming the alto part. "That in thine ocean depths its flow may richer, purer, be…"

The music flowed around them, and for a little while under the autumn light Arlie felt herself buoyed up by an ocean of complicated and abiding love.

SWEET TIME

This story was originally published in
Black Hare Press's Lockdown Science Fiction Collection #2 in September 2020

Liberty stepped one more time just inside the airlock door of the bunker where she'd spent the last nineteen years. She was as ready to face the world Outside as she'd ever be. She wore the tick-and-sun-proof suit, the air mask, the gun, the knife, and the heavy framed backpack whose contents she'd triple-checked. Sixty freeze-dried MREs—they tasted just as disgusting as she'd remembered, worse even than the self-sustaining indoor fungus growing kit she'd been living off, but they hadn't spoiled. Water purification tablets. *The Complete Survivalist's Handbook, 23rd Edition.* Matches. Iodine. Bandages. Antibiotics. Painkillers. Cyanide pill.

That was all she had. Anything else she'd have to get from Outside. If anything edible still grew Outside, if anything salvageable hadn't been used up or destroyed, if the terrorists or the gangsters or the looters didn't get her first.

And if they did get her, that wouldn't be as bad as living in the bunker for another everlasting year with no contact with the outside world, hearing no voice but her own.

Liberty punched in her keycode. When the door slid back into the wall, she stepped Outside.

The light broke over her like a wave. She'd forgotten sunlight in all those years under fluorescents. She dropped to her knees and shut her eyes. She didn't cover her ears. If someone was sneaking up on her she had to be able to hear them.

She heard: Wind scraping over stones and rustling in leaves. Birdsong. When had she forgotten to miss birdsong? Mosquito whine. Snaps and rustles that could be assassins or raccoons. She opened her eyes. Closed them again. Squinted in the painful light.

Green all around her. Grass and low brambles close in, trees surrounding the bramble clearing, more than half of them apparently alive.

She rose. Any attacker who'd seen her emerge would surely have moved to grab her already. Any friendly observer would have come out to help her.

Maybe there wasn't anyone left Outside. Maybe they'd all died in storms or pandemics or... Maybe her communiscreen had gone dead, not because of technical failure, but because all the other bunker-dwellers had died. When the main newsfeed died, the rest of her survivalist pod had speculated the official shelters where most of the approved populace had gone had been hacked by bitter people who failed their health and security checks, or had been taken over by terrorists exploiting loopholes in the security screening, or had collapsed due to design errors. Her fellow survivalists hadn't been too concerned. They were still there in their private shelters, the independent, the resourceful ones. They would inherit the earth.

Then the pod's webfeed died. She checked and rechecked her hardware, her software: nothing wrong. She read the plays and novels she'd brought in aloud to herself for hours on end to give the illusion of dialogue. Finally she left.

In the trees a wood thrush called, a liquid glide followed by a lilting laugh. She laughed too, swallowed salt—sweat? tears? —and set off toward the thrush-song, stumbling on the hummocky ground, savouring the stretch and pull in her muscles. She'd walked two miles a day, circling inside the bunker, but that was on flat ground. She'd forgotten some of the muscles in her legs. That was all right. Her lungs weren't all right. They flattened and burned, demanding more oxygen than she could pull through the hazmask. Maybe the filter was clogged—with condensation? Sweat? Deadly particles being filtered out?

She couldn't take it off. If any of the people who failed their screenings and couldn't afford private bunkers had survived Outside they might be using chemical weapons, burning trash, breathing out superbugs. They might...

She needed air. She took inhaled deeply, whipped the mask off. It was clogged with yellow powder. Mustard gas? She sneezed explosively. Pollen, apparently. She gulped in unfiltered air after the sneeze—she couldn't help it—and, after that, what would have been the point of putting the mask back on? She stuffed it into her pack and kept going, eased of the pain in her lungs, distracted by the rasp of unfiltered air on her throat and also by the densely woven scents. Wet greens, rot, roses, fruit, and something rank that she couldn't place. She was just starting to wonder what that was when she heard the first scream.

It was high, hoarse, barely human. What kind of fear—or pain—could make somebody sound like that? It went on for what seemed an impossibly long time, barely paused, began again. It was close by, she judged. Liberty crawled toward it, hoping the dense brush would hide her until she was close. If she ever sounded like that she'd want someone to come rescue her, or at least finish her off.

The sound was very close, and she couldn't see two feet ahead. She crouched beside a tree, slid the gun from its holster, rose as smoothly as she could (not very), keeping her body pressed against the trunk, keeping her gun hand free…

"*Que haces? Son* nuestras *gallinas!*" The furious voice sounded close behind her. Liberty turned, gun first, desperately aware that she was too late, that the shouter—an illegal alien, by the sound of it—had the jump on her.

The child glaring at Liberty might have been eight or ten. She had both fists braced on her hips. Her tight black braids stood out from her head. Her off-white dress was streaked with purple stains—too much blue in the purple for blood, Liberty told herself, hoping it was true.

"What do you want?" Liberty demanded.

"*Ingles?* Put that down, dummy! I'll tell Manruth!"

"Who else is here?" Liberty kept her gun aimed over the girl's head. She couldn't cover a kid with a weapon, but she couldn't be captured by whoever was making somebody scream like that.

"Ranza?" Liberty didn't know what language that was, but the voice was deep and tense. When the young man—or boy, maybe—came crashing out of the woods, Liberty had the gun levelled at his chest. He saw. He froze, staring at her and at the girl. Swallowed hard. Behind Liberty the screaming broke out again.

"Are you Manruth?" Liberty demanded. "What's happening back there?" She gestured with her left (gunless) hand.

"He's Manuel, silly, Manruth's back home," the girl began.

"Let Ranza go," he said on a much higher note. Boy, not man, then, his voice not settled, but he was as big as Liberty.

"Who's getting tortured?" Liberty demanded.

"Nobody's hurt," Ranza said, even as another scream sawed through the air. "You tick-sick?" She stepped toward Liberty, whose gun hand twitched toward her.

"Ranza!" Manuel's voice had come down again. "Go! Tell Manruth there's a new one here; she's fear-sick, maybe tick-sick too. Go!"

Ranza backed up.

"No. Neither of you is going anywhere, getting anyone, until you tell me what's going on here." Liberty's mind sputtered. Why hadn't any of the adults who were terrorizing people come to deal with her?

"Give me that, lady," Manuel said to Liberty, holding his hand out. "It's okay. It's going to be okay. Just put that down. You don't want to hurt anyone. You don't want to get hurt."

"Put it down or I'll punch your head," Ranza added. Manuel hissed something in Spanish, and she subsided. He took a step toward Liberty, hand out. Liberty had seen the pose before, in weird old British flicks where the police didn't have guns: officers advancing on criminals, or lunatics, saying *Give it to me...* Good guys said that. And these were children. Liberty shoved the gun back into the holster, cursing herself for a fool.

"*Vete!*" Manuel said to Ranza, who ran off. "Come on," Manuel told Liberty. "Manruth can help you. But you've got to leave the gun behind."

Liberty drew breath to answer, froze as another scream tore the air behind her. Manuel reached out for her, for her gun arm. She couldn't let him disarm her. She couldn't shoot him. She ducked back around the tree and lunged downhill toward the screaming.

Something grabbed her foot, and she pitched forward. Something hit her head, and darkness swallowed her.

~ * ~

I was dreaming, she thought. *I dreamed I went outside and it was beautiful but there were terrible people. I'm still safe in my bunker, where no one can hurt me, where I'll never hear another human voice.*

"She's coming round," a woman's deep voice said off to her left.

"Good!" said a girl's voice, high and excited. Ranza's voice.

Liberty sat up. Winced. Clutched at her head. Felt at her hip—no holster, no gun. Looked at Ranza, and at the short woman who stood next to Ranza watching Liberty through narrowed eyes.

Behind them Liberty saw a stone wall. She swivelled her head cautiously, looked up at the underside of a thatch roof. Not very secure for a prison…but they had her gun.

"You'll be all right," the woman said, "but you'll have a nasty lump. I'm Luz, Ranza and Manuel's mother."

"What are you going to do with me?"

"Take you to see Manruth. If you can stand…"

"Of course I can stand," Liberty said, doing so and trying to act as if movement didn't hurt her head. Chin up, shoulders back.

Ranza giggled.

"Shoo, Ranza," Luz said. "Tell Manruth we're coming. Tell your brother—"

"I'm here," Manuel said, opening the door for Ranza. Liberty winced at the light, looked at the ground. Luz spoke across her to Manuel.

"You did the dangerous part," she said. "You can bring her in."

Liberty didn't like the sound of that. She realized unhappily she was swaying.

"We can carry you," Manuel said.

"No! I can walk."

Manuel shrugged, took Liberty's arm (supporting her as much as restraining her, she had to admit), stuck the handle of a sunshade into her other hand, and guided her out the door.

Liberty squinted out from her safe patch of shade into the harsh light. She'd been expecting a sort of prison-yard. There was indeed a wall of dressed stone, twice Liberty's height, maybe ten yards to her left—to the south—with cages against it. Liberty forced herself to look at the prisoners.

The cages were full of rabbits.

Between Liberty and the rabbits were rock piles and gigantic kale plants. To Liberty's right, similarly oversized eggplant and tomato bushes sprawled toward another high stone wall. Up ahead was a building with grapevines growing all over it. Misshapen black things, roughly football-sized, crawled around between the plants. Things that moved in a horrible jerky way.

"What is this place?"

"A rain-year garden," Luz said behind her. "Come on, let's get you in where you can sit down and Manruth can have a look at you."

The door of the vine-wrapped house creaked shut behind

Liberty. She made herself look around. The shadows blinded her much as the light had done. She could barely see the faces, let alone read them.

"This is her," Manuel said. "The one Ranza found near the mushroom clearing. Her name's Liberty, and she put her gun down when I said."

"I...I didn't mean to scare the girl," Liberty said. "I was afraid..."

"So I see," said a cello-toned voice. "You tick-sick, or just fear-sick?"

"I don't think I can be tick-sick yet. I've only been out..." she checked her watch... "three hours."

"Out of where? The prisons all went down by the end of the first year."

"Prisons!" Liberty spat. "I never—I got my security clearance. I just thought I'd be safer on my own."

"You're a bunkie?" Luz asked. "You been locked up to keep yourself safe all these years?"

Liberty nodded.

"Are more of you coming?"

"I was alone. There wasn't anyone to come with me. And I couldn't talk to anyone in the other shelters."

"For how long?"

"I've been Inside nineteen years. Without communication, one year."

"*Ay Dios!*" Manuel shook his head. "No wonder you're fear-sick."

"I'm not sick," Liberty insisted. "But I really didn't mean to scare your sister."

"You didn't scare me," Ranza said, banging in through another door, swinging a tin pail. "Have some berries."

Blackberries. The smell took Liberty back to childhood summers spent scrambling through the overgrown pasture with her sister, with Grandma Randall—dead, both of them, these twenty years—eating fruit sun-hot off the vine, scratching their hands and tangling their hair and laughing, laughing, laughing.

"You're not going to boil them first?" Liberty asked.

"They're better this way."

"But the germs! You could die of them."

"What you want to die of?" Ranza asked.

"I don't want to die of anything," Liberty said.

"You got to," Ranza said, frowning. Liberty swallowed hard.

"That's the truth," the cello voice said. Liberty strained her eyes to see into the shadows.

The woman who had spoken had a weathered copper-colored face and deep-set eyes. Her face and arms were terribly thin, skin stretched over bone, but under her loose clothes her long broad-shouldered body was swollen as though with pregnancy. Surely she was too old to be pregnant?

Liberty had more urgent concerns. *You got to die. That's the truth.*

"I didn't hurt anyone," Liberty protested.

"Who says you did?"

"Then why is she saying I've got to die?" The question sounded childish to Liberty.

Evidently Ranza found it so as well. "Cause you were born, *Dummkopf.*"

"Ranza," said a man's voice, reproachfully. Liberty blinked at the speaker: a pink-skinned old man in dark blue long-sleeved shirt and long pants, with a straw hat and a long grey beard. She'd seen people dressed like that before, Outside, long ago. They drove horses and buggies, back before so many of the horses had to be put down.

"You listen to Levi," the thin-faced woman said, "and don't go calling names."

"Sorry, Manruth," Ranza said. "Sorry, Levi. Sorry, Liberty."

Manruth shifted her gaze back to Ranza. "But she gave you one of the true answers."

"I don't understand," Liberty said.

"*Alles Fleisch ist grünes Gras...*" Levi said. Liberty shook her head. She didn't know the language.

"All flesh is grass, and all the goodliness thereof is as the flower of the field," Manruth said. "All right?"

"Yes, okay, in general, but..."

First Liberty thought the young man on her right was singing. Then she realized he was speaking, chanting, but she couldn't make the words out.

"Ibrahim, I think she has only one language," Manruth said.

"That means, 'Ye were without life and He gave you life; then will He cause you to die, and will again bring you to life; and again to Him will ye return,'" Ibrahim said. "But it's better in Arabic."

Arabic! Liberty thought. If he spoke that it was no wonder he hadn't come Inside; they wouldn't have given him security clearance; you couldn't be too careful. And he was talking about killing people because of God.

"Men must endure their going hence, even as their coming hither; ripeness is all," said another woman's voice from the shadows.

"Edgar said that in *King Lear*," Liberty said, eager to show herself civilized. "He was right. But he said it when he was trying to save someone's life, not kill him!"

"You really are fear-sick," Manruth said. "No one here intends to kill you. Get that through your head."

"But she said I had to die, and you agreed."

"We used to point that out in logic classes," said the woman who'd quoted *King Lear*. "People generally didn't accuse us of attempted murder."

"But you hit me over the head! I mean, Manuel did."

"You ran and you caught your feet in the berry bushes and you fell and you hit your head on a tree," Manuel explained.

"Oh," Liberty said in a very small voice. "Oh. Sorry. And you carried me back here where people could take care of me. I... Truly I'm sorry."

"You were fear-sick," he said.

"Have some berries," Ranza repeated. "Get some sweet while it lasts."

"The honeybees in our hives died again last winter," Manruth explained, "though we've still got wild bees enough to pollinate; a few sugar maples came back after the blight, but not enough so we can tap them yet. So now we're counting on fruit for sweetness, and the fruit-time's just begun, and who knows how long it'll last." She turned back to Ranza. "Pass them around; whether or not Liberty wants some, the rest of us do."

"I have food in my pack," Liberty said. "I didn't come to take anything from you."

"What did you come out for?" Manruth asked. "You had food. You seem healthy, except fear-sick. Seems you thought you were safe back in your bunker, and you don't think so out here."

"I had to get out of there. I was alone. I was going crazy.

Maybe had gone."

"You were safe dead," Manruth said. "And you wanted to be alive."

"But you're going on about dying being okay."

"Dying, yes. Going into the Trees of Life. That's different from being safe dead."

Liberty, who was increasingly convinced no one intended to kill her, realized she had been discourteous about these people's superstitions. She inclined her head respectfully. "I'm glad you're so sure. Believing's a comfort, I hear."

"Maybe so," Manruth said. "Some of us have that. My Levi does. I don't, not the way I think you mean it, but I've had my sweet time, and I'm going to the Trees of Life, and that's enough for me. You figure out what's enough for you. I don't think you'll hurt anyone here. Stay with us if you like, or go wherever else you like."

"We'd better talk about that," Luz said.

"We will, then," Manruth answered. "Seeing it was your kids…"

"I… I…" Liberty stammered.

"Yes, you explained, and you haven't got a gun now. You might as well go out and look around, unless there's anything else folks want to ask you."

Luz looked hard at her. "If you've lied to us, if you're going to bring more bunkies back here…"

"For what?" Levi asked. "To steal? What do we have that they would want? She had food, they must have food too."

"They think our food is poison," said the woman who had quoted Shakespeare.

"If they were hungry we would feed them anyway," Ibrahim added.

"Any more questions for Liberty?" Manruth asked. Nobody responded. Ranza handed her the pail of berries. Manruth put her face down over the pail, inhaled deeply, then passed the pail on. Liberty raised her eyebrows.

"No, they're not poisoned," Manruth said. "I'm not doing so well with eating." She gestured toward her swollen stomach, and Liberty felt her own stomach lurch. She'd seen that before, that thinness, that swollenness. Not pregnancy. Cancer.

"Someone had better take our visitor back outside," Manruth

said. "She looks to be feeling sick."

"I'm not scared of her," Ranza said. "I'll go."

"I'll come too," Ibrahim said. Luz reflected a moment, then nodded.

Liberty was almost to the door when she remembered. "But who was screaming out there? And why did you pretend they weren't?"

"Take her back out, Ranza, show her," Luz said, laughing. *Laughing!*

Liberty bit her lip, took a sunshade and followed Ranza back out into the heat and light, Ibrahim close at her side. She felt extremely awkward. "They're nice eggplants," she said tentatively. Not a brilliant conversational opening, but...

"Not bad this year, we just had snow two times and we did fires and they didn't die," Ranza said.

"It doesn't snow in summer, and you can't grow eggplant in winter..."

"Ranza's too young," Ibrahim said. "She doesn't remember when there were months with no snow, and months with no ninety-degree days."

Liberty opened her mouth to answer, stopped. One of the misshapen black things lurched toward her. White spots like mildew covered its deformed body. It twitched, lifting a small blunt-beaked head on a long narrow neck, and gave the scream of a soul in torment. Then it pecked a fat orange grub off a potato vine.

"*What is that?*"

"You don't like guineas?" Ranza asked.

"What is that?" Liberty asked again.

"Guinea fowl," Ibrahim said.

"You don't *know* guineas?" Ranza asked. "They were s'posed to be guard animals, like geese but not so mean, we thought they'd scream to warn us about danger, only they scream all the time, and their eggs are tiny and they hide 'em pretty well. But they do eat ticks so we don't get so much tick-sick. And I'm good at finding eggs."

"I'm sure you are," Liberty said weakly. She shook her head. "Hens! All that screaming was hens."

"Told you already," Ranza said, skipping ahead.

"You see," Ibrahim said, "there's not so much to fear."

"All right, the birds… But Manuel said the prisons went down, so the people in them must be somewhere."

"I am here. So are John, Lynn, Morgan, Ezekiel, Domingo, Concepcion, Raquel and Jin. Domingo started us raising guineas. Lynn and I designed the Trombe wall together. Some of the others who came out with us went on toward the cities. Some of the rest are in the Trees of Life."

"Come on," Ranza hollered. Liberty hurried after her; it was easier than apologizing.

They splashed through the swamp containing the moldy remnants of the dry-year garden at the foot of the ridge— "Rained four inches last week, six the week before," Ranza said, "but there's good catfish here now" —out to an island crowded with curving canes of elderberry, the dark blue umbels bending the frail stems down almost far enough to touch the water. Liberty felt the slight resistance of the berries as they pulled free from their stems, the softness of the overripe ones squashing between her fingers. The heat was still stifling, but at least they were under shade; there were a lot of standing dead trees near the island— "The borers killed the ash trees, and some kind of blight got the sugar maple," Ibrahim explained when she asked—but on the island there were live willows bending and reaching over their heads, making a shade and a sleepy little song in the wind.

Ranza sang, less sleepily, in Spanish. "That's pretty," Liberty said. "What's it about?"

"The trees of life."

"I know one like that," Liberty said. "*There grows a tree in Paradise, and the pilgrims call it the Tree of Life…*"

"Levi says Paradise is what we had before we messed it," Ranza said, "but the Trees of Life are right here now."

"What do you mean?"

"These are where they buried the folks from the first year."

"And you eat…"

"Sure, we eat the elderberries. Only we cook them first so we don't get sick. These we can eat right now." She held up a handful of blackberries from the low canes that crawled around the feet of the elderberries.

"But you said people are buried here."

"Mm-hmm. Elders like rich soil. The new Trees-of-Life are

pear, mostly, but we can't eat off those yet, they're too little."

"But…"

"Take and eat, this is my body," Ranza sang, popping a handful of blackberries into her mouth, and holding another handful out for Liberty, who, much to her own surprise, took and ate.

~ * ~

Two weeks later even Luz had accepted Liberty's presence. By then a cold snap had killed some of the tomatoes and eggplants (the ones nearest the Trombe wall had pulled through), raccoons had gotten into the corn (and Liberty had helped shoot and eat some of them), and Liberty and Ranza had picked pail after pail of blackberries (shredding Liberty's ticksuit and sunsuit in the process, thus freeing her to work in less of a sweatbath), so many Manruth's people couldn't eat them all fresh. Liberty was boiling some down, Manruth lying nearby to breathe the blackberry smell, and Manruth's husband Levi sitting over her, grieving, and also slicing tomatoes to dry.

"It's not a bad life," Liberty said, stirring slowly and carefully. "I see that now. But still, what would you do if a criminal came, or a lunatic? Someone armed and dangerous? Someone who threatened you or your children?"

She blinked in surprise to hear Manruth laughing. Then Levi joined, and then Ibrahim. When Liberty finally got the joke she laughed too, laughed so hard she wept into the pot, getting a little salt in with the sweet.

ABOUT THE AUTHOR

Joanna Michal Hoyt is an autodidact who has spent her adult life in unorthodox religious intentional communities living an alternative to the consumer culture, growing food to share, trying to help neighbors in need, and writing curious stories.

Like some of her characters, she tries to follow God and she struggles with irrational anxieties and obsessions. Her passionate political convictions coexist, sometimes uncomfortably, with her respect for loved ones whose beliefs and ways of seeing are at odds with hers.

Her short speculative stories about those fraught gaps in perception have appeared in publications including *On Spec, Mysterion, Crossed Genres*, and *Daily Science Fiction*. Her historical novel *Cracked Reflections* was published by Propertius Press in 2021.

Read more at: https://joannamichalhoyt.com

More Great Anthologies and story collections from WolfSinger Publications

Never Cheat a Witch – edited by Carol Hightshoe

Magical curses. Arcane revenge. Being transformed into a frog. Things evil witches do to mere mortals who cross their path. But, what if there is more to the story…

Deals made with a witch are magically binding and can bring dire consequences to those who even think about breaking them.

Whether they are seeking revenge for wrongs done to them, helping others or simply trying to live their lives—it is NEVER wise to try and cheat a witch.

Open your spell book and join our authors as they relate tales of witches and mortals. From classic fantasy witches to modern day witches and even the legendary Baba Yaga. Good and Evil as well as every shade of gray in between. And, yes—there is a prince who is turned into a frog.

Bast's Chosen Ones – Dana Bell

Long ago in the land of the flooding Nile and sweeping sands, Bast created warriors called the Chosen Ones. They are her warriors. To them has been given the responsibility of protecting cats, whether on Earth or other worlds. Not always an easy task since often an ancient evil lurks, ready to pounce.

Not all felines walk in the goddess's domain. Some live in the far reaches of space, battling beside their humans or walk in lands long thought legend. Others tell their own version of human stories, walk as envoys of the creator, or appear as ghosts.

These cats walk where others dare not and do not prefer the comfort of cuddly lap warmers. Rather, they wish adventure, in present day, the past, or the far future.

US/THEM – edited by Carol Hightshoe

Fear of the *Other* breeds hatred of the *Other*

They aren't like us—so they must be bad…inferior… dangerous…

Humans are by nature social animals, but we tend to bond with other humans with whom we have something in common: beliefs, experiences, likes and dislikes, etc.

With the expansion of humans across the planet, it seems that, even as our numbers grow, we find ways to whittle our groups into ever narrower, specialized, and exclusive blocks. We target the *Other* for the most minor differences and interpret everything from *THEM* as an insult or an attack.

Within these pages you will witness hatred, intolerance and fanaticism as well as love, understanding and acceptance. Most of all, I, and the authors, hope you discover stories that will cause you to pause and think before condemning someone as being *THEM* and not *US*.

Time Capsules – edited by Carol Hightshoe

Time Capsules—history and mystery—a gift or a message from the past to the future?

Messages that can easily be misunderstood.

What were the reasons for passing along a pair of pink, fuzzy handcuffs?

A glass vial containing a perfect dandelion puff?

A Japanese Katana?

A red and blue scarf?

A wooden spoon?

What magic do these items contain? What stories do they tell?

From the past to the future. Mysteries and meanings abound within these pages, as well as reminders of the things people find precious. What will you find?

Crunchy with Ketchup – edited by Carol Hightshoe

It has been said that one should never meddle in the affairs of dragons—for you are crunchy and taste good with ketchup.

Come enter the dragon's lair.

Take your chances with other would-be heroes and heroines who decide to face off against one of the biggest, baddest predators ever.

Witness a dragon civil war.

Hear the true story of the Battle of New Orleans.

Find out what it's like in the belly of a dragon.

Discover why cats can spell disaster when stealing a dragon's egg.

Meet a group of dragon riders who protect us from nuclear devastation.

Follow legends of modern dragons, only to find something very unexpected.

And more…

Crunchy with Chocolate – edited by Carol Hightshoe

It has been said that one should never meddle in the affairs of dragons—for you are crunchy and taste good with chocolate.

Come enter the dragon's lair and roll the dice. Within these pages you will still meet some of the biggest, baddest predators ever—but if you are lucky, you will also discover some that have a sweeter side.

Meet a dragon with a soft spot for hard luck cases and another who is a hopeless romantic.

Enjoy a musical battle between a dragon and the specter of one of the greatest guitarists to ever play.

Meet a dragon in trouble with other magical creatures because he enjoys hanging out with human children.

Join a mother and daughter and their teams of dragons on a dangerous cross-country race.

Reconnect with an imaginary friend—who is not so imaginary and escape the isolation of the pandemic.

And more…

So enter in BUT tread carefully—remember you are crunchy and taste good with chocolate.

Tales From the Fluffy Bunny – edited by Carol Hightshoe

Welcome to the Fluffy Bunny

We welcome everyone—especially those with a story to tell. Adventurers, mercenaries, guardsmen, merchants, noble and peasant. Whoever. If you have a tale to share, then come in and have a seat.

First drink and a hot meal are on the house.

What's a tale without an audience to appreciate it? So, even if you don't have a tale to share, come in, pull up a seat and enjoy these 17 tales of how a warrior or their weapon earned their name.

Cat Tails: War Zone — edited by Rebecca McFarland Kyle and Dana Bell

Cats have been our companions since long before they graced the temples of Ancient Egypt. In addition to being members of our families, they have also stood with us through difficult times. From keeping pests and vermin away from our food stores to providing a comforting paw when we have been wounded; cats have been our sidekicks and friends in many different battles.

Cat Tails: War Zone contains twenty-five stories from Ancient Egypt to the far-flung future, about some amazing cats who have served as compatriots during war times. But beware, for they can also be tricksters sent to teach lessons.

The real heroes are the volunteers of SHADOW CATS, an Austin, Texas-based rescue that has saved the lives of 9,000-plus cats since 1997. Trappers, veterinarians, nurses, and adoption social workers volunteer to trap, neuter and return ferals, provide care for ill, injured and behaviorally challenged cats, find perfect adoptive parents, educate on proper feline care, and advocate for real change in communities.

Proceeds from this book will continue their efforts.

Visit us at www.wolfsingerpubs.com for more information

When Charli bets everything on a secret, will she find the deck stacked

against her?

Former runaway-turned heiress Charli Monroe is hiding her sordid past and planning a future in Colton, Texas. Attending the local college for a degree in social work, she intends to raise cattle on her newly purchased ranch, which she plans to open as a home for troubled teens. Only a few glitches—the Victorian mansion is crumbling, the barn needs a roof, and her oilman neighbor wants more than friendship. When she meets Dylan Quinn, Charli is willing to take a chance on the town drunk to help her rebuild the rundown ranch.

Dylan has his demons, too. The former Special Forces commander can't get past his ex-wife's betrayal and the botched mission that left him with much more than a bad limp. Certain the greedy oilman next door to Charli wants much more than just her heart, Dylan's even willing to stop drinking in order to protect her.

When things get dangerous and secrets of the past are revealed, is he only looking out for his new employer, or is she the new start he so desperately needs?

Books by Sara Walter Ellwood

Colton Gambers Series
Gambling On A Secret, Book One
Gambling On A Heart, Book Two
Gambling On A Dream, Book Three

Heartstrings

Published by Kensington Publishing Corporation

Gambling On A Secret

Colton Gamblers Series

Sara Walter Ellwood

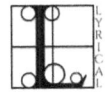

LYRICAL PRESS
Kensington Publishing Corp.
www.kensingtonbooks.com

In Memory of Grandma,
One of the greatest storytellers I've ever known....

Acknowledgements

D'Ann, thank you so much for what you have taught me about the West and ranching. Without your patient guidance, this story wouldn't be what it is.

Martha, thank you for all of your help. You are an awesome critique partner.

Lorraine, thank you so much for your editorial help. Without your suggestions, that "white elephant" would still be in the story.

Finally, thank you to all the service men and women who protect our freedoms that make it possible for me to write and publish such a story. God bless every single one of you.

Foreword

Dear Readers,

Thank you for reading Gambling on a Secret. This is the first book of The Colton Gamblers and will take you to Colton, Texas, a little town about 7o miles south of Dallas. Here the gossip chain is known as the Colton Grapevine and the mayor's wife is the queen at collecting the grapes that grow on it. And there are plenty of backdoor dealings and secrets to go around--and maybe even an occasional murder, too. But don't worry, Colton is full of good, solid folks and enough tough, sexy cowboys and women strong enough to love them to make sure good has a fair chance at always winning...

Love,
Sara

The Colton Gamblers

In 1865, three disillusioned first cousins return from the battlefields of the defeated South to find their home in East Texas a shambles. Determined to make a new start, they head west. In the cowboy town of Dallas, Texas, they decide to pool the few silver dollars they have between them and enter into a poker game. With their gamble, they win over 100,000 acres of good grassland in Central Texas. Over the next century and a half, their descendents build a fortune in cattle and oil, but as time goes by, greed erodes their family bond. These are the stories of the eighth generation gambling on love and bringing back the bond of family...

Chapter 1

"You're twenty minutes late, Mr. Quinn. It wouldn't hurt to show a little punctuality if you wanted a job." Charli Monroe stopped at the gate in the broken picket fence of her newly purchased, broken-down ranch.

The man behind the wheel of the beat up pickup truck peered out the open window. A brown cowboy hat shadowed a face hard enough to be chiseled out of stone. "This old place needs a lot of work. It's been empty for five years."

He spoke with a deep velvet timbre that settled somewhere in her chest and reverberated.

She swallowed and fought the urge to hug herself. He didn't seem too concerned about being late. Was he going to get out of the truck? When he made no move to do so, she wasn't sure if she was relieved or disappointed. He obviously didn't want the job that badly. "Do you know why the place was in probate for so long?"

Dylan Quinn slid the cowboy hat back over his dark hair. A corner of his lips twitched upward. It couldn't be called a smile, but it momentarily softened his mouth. The warmth of the phantom grin never reached his cloudy-day eyes. "Jock Blackwell died without a will, and his sons hate each other and despised their father and this ranch."

That was pretty much what the landlady of the student boarding house where she currently lived had told her. Jock Blackwell had gotten three of his girlfriends pregnant and refused to marry them in a time such behavior was socially unacceptable. Each of his three sons blamed his misfortunes in life on their label of illegitimacy. She knew all about being a bastard. Her dear old dad hadn't stuck around either.

"It was a shame to watch this place go to hell." He looked beyond her at the ramshackle Victorian house. "There was a time when it was one of the best cattle ranches in all of Central Texas."

"You're from around here?" He didn't exactly sound like a born and bred Texan. His accent suggested he was from the Mid-Atlantic area.

He nodded and rubbed over the dark stubble along his angular jaw. "You could say that. My mother grew up on Oak Springs Ranch--your neighbor to the east. I lived there as a teenager. So, are you still looking for a manager, or not?"

Not. But the way he looked at her made the lie stick in her throat. She took a few steps toward the side of the truck.

As she wrapped her arms around herself, a shiver tickled down her spine. She had to be cold, despite the warm early-March sun beating down on her. What else could it be? She wasn't afraid, but something about him put her senses on edge. Was it his rugged handsomeness or the slate gray of his tortured eyes?

"Yes, I am. I'm Charlotte Monroe. I go by Charli. I have to get the place ready for the cattle coming in a few weeks. I'm also buying four horses from Sheriff Zack Cartwright."

Another half-smile tugged on his lips. "You've been busy. Can't get better horses from anywhere else. How many cattle?"

"A hundred Salers calves."

"The French breed?"

Most people had no clue what they were. If her grandfather hadn't been something of a cattle collector, she wouldn't have known them either. "Yes. Do you know about them?"

"I've heard they're good for beef and easy calving." Dylan looked across the gravel driveway. "The barn needs a new roof and the right side looks like it's about ready to collapse. Are all the other buildings in as bad shape?"

Why didn't he want to look for himself? "Unfortunately, yes. The barbed wire fencing also needs fixing. The bunkhouse is worse than the barn." She pointed behind her at the native limestone and clapboard house. "The house needs work, as you can see. At least, the extra stables and storage barn next to it aren't quite as broken down."

"Probably because they're not as old." He looked around again as if confirming her appraisal. "Sounds like you need a carpenter, not a ranch manager."

"I need both. I said as much in the newspaper ad. I'm looking for someone who will help me oversee repairs, hire on hands as needed and make this place a working ranch again."

He regarded her for a long moment and cocked a brow. Damn, was he making fun of her? He looked her up and down. "Wouldn't a woman like you be more comfortable getting manicures and massages in a Dallas spa, not worrying about cattle breeds and barn roofs? It's no secret around town you're the heiress to the Monroe Farm Equipment fortune, and you sold a huge ranch in Oklahoma your grandfather left you. Why on Earth did you buy a dump like this?"

Now he'd pissed her off. She might have more money than she'd ever dreamed of having. She might like to dress in designer clothes, but it was none of this jerk's business which ranch she bought. Or why she wanted it. She had a business plan and a vision for the ranch; what else mattered? "I happen to like this place. It suits me better than the ranch I sold."

"Is that so? Did you bring any equipment with you? A tractor, a planter, hay mower, baler, anything?"

He would bring up one of the stupidest things she'd done. Sighing, she admitted, "I sold the equipment with the ranch when I decided to leave Oklahoma. One more reason I need a manager." Her cheeks burned. "When I sold the ranch after inheriting it, I didn't intend to buy another."

"Why did you buy another ranch?" He slid his gaze back to hers and peered at her as if he could read her every thought--but what had her swallowing hard was the spark of something hot in his eyes.

She tightened her arms in the hug she gave herself—a self-protecting, insecure gesture she'd acquired while she lived with her abusive lover in Las Vegas as a teenage runaway.

"Buying a ranch the size of this one isn't something most folks just wake up and decide to do, Miss Monroe. A ten-thousand-acre spread takes commitment and dedication and is damned hard work."

Yeah, she knew that.

He looked down at her multicolored Manolo Blahnik five-inch heeled slides. The ghost of a smile touched his lips again, but this time little crinkles formed at the corners of his eyes, which held a spark of interest she didn't want.

Damn, he was good-looking. She squelched that notion like the roach she'd killed earlier in the house. Hadn't her life with Ricardo taught her a handsome face meant nothing but trouble?

"I can't imagine you stuffing those pampered and polished feet into rubber boots to muck around in the barn."

Me, either. But she would if she had to.

She drew in a breath and dropped her arms to her sides. "I think we should get back to asking questions about you. When your sister called about my newspaper ad, she said you were exactly what I'm looking for."

He shrugged again in a not-a-care-in-the-world way again. What was this guy's problem? If she weren't running out of time, she would tell him to leave. She couldn't waste this year, which meant she had to get someone hired. And her prospects were limited.

"Can you do the job?"

"Affirmative."

She waited for him to elaborate, but when he didn't, she frowned. "Do you have any references?"

"I expected you to ask. Everything you need to know should be in here."

She moved closer and took the folded sheet of paper he held out the window. After glancing at it, she wasn't surprised it was a resume, but his listed experience had her heart beating a little faster. She looked up at him. "You have a degree in agricultural business from Texas A & M, started up your own ranch and served in the Army?"

He looked off in the distance. "I was in the service for thirteen years, three years in the Corps of Engineers, four in Airborne and the last six in Special Forces." His jaw clenched, making his face the chiseled block of cold stone again. "And I know something about building. When I wasn't deployed, I built the house and barn on my two-hundred acre ranch."

"You don't own the ranch now?"

"No. My ex-wife got it in our divorce settlement. I planned to get out of the Army after my last tour in Afghanistan and raise cattle. But things never happen the way we want them to."

The bitterness of his tone had her stepping away. She shivered again and busied herself with looking at the resume. Whatever his ex-wife had done to him, it wasn't good. "Your reference list is pretty skimpy."

"The first name is my old commander, but I just got word he's shipped out on a secret mission."

Something wasn't adding up. Either he was hiding something or his sister had lied about his experience. "Your sister said you worked on Oak Springs Ranch while in high school, but it's not listed on your resume. Are you related to the owner, Leon Ferguson? You said your mother grew up there."

His eyes narrowed and his lips thinned into a tight line. "Leon is my mother's stepbrother. While my grandfather was still alive and ran the ranch, I worked there until I joined the Army after he died. I chose not to mention it."

But why? She didn't press the matter. She wasn't seriously considering him for the job anyway, was she?

"My landlady said Mr. Ferguson might be willing to contract me the men and equipment I need to get the mesquite cleaned out of my pastures and the fields ready for planting." She shifted her feet. She had no idea what his gripe with the richest man in the county was, and maybe for that reason, she needed his opinion. Dylan Quinn was the first person she'd met who seemed to dislike the tycoon. "I'd like to get some alfalfa and grasses in for hay. It's getting late in the season. Do you think he'd help me out?"

He rubbed his stubble-shadowed jaw. What kind of man went to a job interview and didn't even bother shaving off the scruff? "This might not be any of my business, but since you asked my opinion, let me warn you. The last thing you want to do is to get tangled up with Leon Ferguson. You'll be sorry. He's wanted this land for a long time, and he'll do anything to get it."

"You're right. It isn't any of your business." Why would he think such a thing? After all, someone as rich as Ferguson could have bought the place before she put her bid in. Dylan obviously had a personal problem with Ferguson. Everyone else had nothing but good to say about Leon Ferguson. He was on the board of directors for the college she was attending, the hospital, and had donated a large sum of money to the county schools and other local charities. At least according to her landlady, Aida Mae Pratt.

"Suit yourself. But you did ask for my opinion."

Which had been a big mistake.

She studied the resume again. "Brenda Dailey. Is this person off-limits, too? Or can I speak with her?"

"My ex-wife. I'd appreciate it if you don't involve her. I put her on there because of the ranch."

She looked up at him. "The divorce that bad, huh?"

Dylan shrugged and looked away. He gripped the top of the steering wheel hard enough to whiten his knuckles. "Suppose it's no secret. Our divorce has only been final four months, and she married her baby-daddy the day after it became official. You figure it out."

"Ouch. Okay, I won't call your ex. Nevertheless, I d like to see your house. Your sister mentioned you were a carpenter." She glanced at the address of his former ranch. "Killeen's south of here?"

He nodded. "It's your two hours and tank of gas."

"Thank you for stopping by. Your number's on here. I'll call you."

"Thanks for your time, Miss Monroe. Good luck with this place." He looked around at the buildings and over her before he turned the key in the ignition. The rusted bucket of bolts sputtered and the starter groaned before the engine turned over.

As he pulled away, she looked at the piece of paper in her shaky hand and studied his name at the top.

Damn, she'd hoped he was the one.

She crumpled the paper, and the memory of his weathered eyes, as dull and gray as her ranch buildings, came to her. What ghosts did he see when he closed them?

She opened her palm and stared at the wad of paper. Feeling haunted by the past was something she understood very well.

* * * *

Dylan pulled into the space between the Dumpster and his sister's Taurus and cut the engine. He lifted a half-empty flask of Jim Beam to his lips and swallowed a swig. The bourbon warmed him while he looked out at the back of the small redbrick house.

He lived with Tracy and her son in the shoebox-sized apartment above her beauty salon. Where would he go if Tracy followed through with her threat and tossed his ass out like yesterday's trash? He didn't want a job. He didn't know what he wanted, but everything that mattered had died with his wife's Dear John letter and his men in Kandahar a year ago.

He'd long ago stopped feeling the burn of bourbon he poured down his throat. What had possessed him to show up at this interview and not blow it off like all the others Tracy set up?

An image of Miss Charlotte Monroe popped into his mind as he lowered the bottle from his lips. Damn, what was a woman like her doing owning the Blackwell place? He lifted his flask in a toast. "Whatever your reasons, I'm impressed. Not many people get away with taking something that bastard Ferguson wants out from under his nose."

He'd never hear from Miss Charlotte Monroe again. He turned the flask up again to his lips. Through the Colton Grapevine down at the Longhorn Saloon, he'd heard she was something to see, but they hadn't done her justice.

She'd been one hot number standing there with orange-painted toenails shoved into the craziest sky-high heels he'd ever seen. With the way the brown miniskirt showed off legs going on forever and the fantastic view of her full breasts the tight blue-green sweater gave him, she should have been on a magazine cover, not standing in knee-high weeds.

She was a freaking college kid. What the hell was she doing owning a ranch? She wanted to raise beef? He snorted and took another pull on the flask. Hell, she was more likely to end up making pets out of the calves, and whine when she broke a fingernail.

Shaking his head to dispel all thought of the aquamarine-eyed redhead, he leaned back against the worn leather seat.

Was he really this much of a coward to face his baby sister? He'd faced Taliban, Al-Qaeda and Iraqi insurgents. What happened to the guy who'd killed a drug lord with his bare hands in the jungles of South America?

He cursed under his breath, drained the flask dry and prayed Tracy would be too busy to notice him sneaking in the back door of the salon. He needed another drink.

When he opened the back door, a whiff of perm solution and hair dye burned his eyes, and the whiskey in his belly churned. Holding his breath against the stink and the urge to puke, he attempted to sneak by Tracy's office door to the stairs.

"How'd it go?" his sister called out.

Damn his fucked-up luck.

He stopped, drew in a deep breath, and wished he hadn't when his gut spasmed. He peeked around the doorframe into the small office. As usual, everything in the room was organized and neatly arranged. He shrugged and mumbled, "Don't know. Okay, I guess. Her hands are full with that dump."

Tracy pulled off her reading glasses and looked up at him. "So, what's she like?"

Prickly as a cactus. Why was Charli Monroe getting under his skin? She seemed insecure in the way she'd hugged herself and kept her distance. Although she'd tried hard not to show her fear of him, he'd seen a similar reaction before in the abused young women he and his team had liberated in a mountainous camp in Afghanistan.

He shoved those observations to the back of his mind as he raked his fingers through his hair. "Charlotte Monroe is young. The place cost a small fortune, so she obviously has more money than brains. No one in their right mind would have paid the asking price."

Tracy leaned back in her office chair. "I heard today she'd only lived with her grandfather for the last couple of years before he died. Supposedly, she was in Las Vegas before moving to Oklahoma." She shook her head. "Can't imagine that, though. Mrs. Cartwright says she's only twenty-four, but I guess living in Vegas would explain her expensive city-slicker duds."

"Who cares?" He sure as hell didn't, so he turned away. "I'm going upstairs."

"Did you get the job?" Tracy asked just as coolly, before he could limp to the stairs.

"Monroe said she'll call if she's interested." He wouldn't lose any sleep waiting up for the phone call.

"You showed up, didn't you? I know you ditched the last three interviews I set up for you."

He mumbled a vile curse he'd learned as a teen living in Germany and climbed the stairs to the apartment.

Tracy followed him into the galley kitchen. "Dylan, I can't take this anymore. You need to get a job and your own place."

He pulled a beer from the refrigerator. "I'm trying, sis."

"It's been a year since you were injured," Tracy said from the doorway. "You need to do something."

"I help with the bills." It wasn't his fault his disability payments were a pittance, or that Brenda had blown all of his savings before dumping him.

"I don't care about the money. I hate seeing you like this, and I don't like Bobby being around you when you're drunk. You need help. Zack Cartwright told me today about a group meeting--you know like Alcoholics Anonymous but for vets with posttraumatic stress disorder-- over at the VA hospital in Waco. Zack said meetings like those helped him after he got back."

He peered at Tracy. The wateriness of her gray eyes should have bothered him, but it didn't. "Good for Sheriff Cartwright. But I'm not going to any damned meetings where everyone cries on each other's shoulder."

"Why don't you make an appointment--"

"I'm not going back to the fucking shrink. I'm not crazy."

Tracy thrust out an exasperated breath. "Okay. But sitting here all day drinking yourself senseless won't help you get your life back."

"I told you I'll find work and a place of my own." *Someday.*

Setting her jaw, she lifted her chin a notch. "I'm worried about you. You're so different now." She paused and shook her head. "Okay, you don't want to go to the VA. Maybe you should see if Dad could get you a job with Homeland Security. You'd be good there with all of your experience with the Army. If nothing else, it would get you away from here and memories of Brenda."

"No." He turned away and drained most of the Budweiser.

"You'd have veteran's preference. Mom told me so. Why won't you even try?"

Shit, now she had their mother involved. "Because I refuse to be under a microscope." He pinned her with a glare over his shoulder. After the botched mess he'd made of his last mission, it was a miracle he hadn't been court-martialed, and a goddamned shame Congress pinned a Purple Heart on him. It made him sick to think he got it because he was General Bob Quinn's son. The last thing he wanted was his father pulling strings with his buddies in the higher echelon of government to get him a cushy job.

"I don't want to work for the government."

Tracy bit her bottom lip as he passed her to go into the living room.

"By the way, I'd appreciate it if the next time you set up a job interview for me, you don't mention Oak Springs Ranch again.' His feet felt heavy as he turned to face her, tripping him up. He grabbed the back of the couch to keep his balance.

Tracy averted her eyes and folded her arms over her chest. "I know you don't like Leon, but your experience working on the ranch was information Miss Monroe needed to know. When I was over at Oak Springs for dinner last night, Leon asked me to tell you to stop by."

"Hell will freeze over before I set foot on that ranch." He took a draw on the Budweiser. "So, did you see our step-grandmother off on her next great adventure? Greece this time, right?"

Tracy narrowed her eyes at him and pulled herself to her full height, which put her eye-to-eye and nose-to-nose with his six feet. "Have some respect. Maddie was married to our grandfather longer than our real grandmother was. She really cares about us."

He snorted and finished the beer. "Yeah, sure she does, as long as Mom was cut out of everything when Granddad died, and her son got it all."

"Uncle Leon would give you a job and a place to stay."

"That thief is not our uncle any more than that gold digger is our grandmother." He bit the words out between clenched teeth and took an unsteady step toward her.

Tracy moved back.

He didn't care she was afraid of him when he was drunk. "Leon stole our mother's land and took away our birthright. Oak Springs Ranch should be ours!"

Tracy shook her head, tossed her hands in the air, and walked away. "I have a customer in a few minutes." She glanced over the living room. "Clean up this pigpen before Bobby comes home from school."

Every thump of her steps hurrying down the stairs echoed through his head like a drum in a rock band. He tossed the empty beer can toward the trashcan by the computer desk. The can missed its mark by more than five feet, and the momentum of tossing it knocked him off balance.

He fell hard against the corner of the couch on the hip that metal and plastic had replaced after a piece of shrapnel had blown it apart. Cursing, he flipped over onto the seat and laid his head back. He squeezed his eyes shut. The white-hot pain searing through him reminded him of the flaming shards of metal and glass that tore through his men. Why the hell had he trusted the damned Afghani woman and her lies? He'd never be the man he was before he'd gotten his men killed.

He wasn't drunk enough to kill the pain or drown the memories or the dreams. But neither Brenda nor his last mission drifted through the fog of booze when he passed out. Charli Monroe's sexy orange toenails and the ghosts he'd seen swimming in her ocean-like eyes shimmered to life.

Chapter 2

The Longhorn Saloon was always crowded on Friday nights and tonight was no exception. The place tried to capture the flavor of the Old West, but mostly it reminded Dylan of every other honky-tonk he'd ever stepped foot in. Old sawdust and peanut shells covered the floor. The place smelled of stale liquor, sweat, smoke and fry grease.

As he pulled his old felt hat low over his forehead, he weaved his way past the mechanical bull and the jukebox. On the dance floor, an energetic group of locals and college kids were attempting to follow Ella Larson's cowboy boots as she scooted and boogied across the worn hardwood to Brooks and Dunn.

He headed for his favorite corner booth to find two barely legal boys sitting there. He pinned the college kids with his best tough-guy scowl. They got up and left so fast they had to stop and go back for their beers.

After sliding into the booth, he didn't have to wait long for Ella's younger sister, Julie, to come forward with a bottle of his usual. He handed her his credit card to cover the tab.

He'd thrown back a couple shots of Jack Daniels when a group of college kids shoved into the booth across from him. From the wild look in one of the boy's eyes, it had to be his first time in a bar.

Julie stopped by the table, checked their IDs and took their orders. He couldn't help but overhear the blonde, pressed up close to the wide-eyed boy, telling Julie today was his twenty-first birthday. After several minutes of teasing by the other boy, and giggles from the two girls in the group, Julie went to the bar to put in their orders.

Their drinks arrived and they toasted Birthday Boy with more laughter.

He didn't need this crap. Looking around, he found an empty spot at the bar and reached for his bottle.

Blondie next to Birthday Boy said, "Guess what Charli Monroe's doing tonight."

He slid a sideways glance at the table of kids, set the bottle down and stayed glued to the cracked vinyl.

The girl across from her laughed. "Oh, I can only imagine. She's in my psych class. I bet she's studying."

"Yep." Blondie played with the fruit balls in her prissy drink.

The boy beside the psychology girl lifted his beer and smirked. "She's one hot number. I've thought about asking her out, but something about her is just strange."

Psychology Girl, who looked too much like the boy sitting beside her to not be his sister, laughed. "I have to agree. She's weird. I don't think she even has any friends. She's been at Colton College since the beginning of the semester, and I've never seen her hang out with anyone. No wonder she's all the teachers' pet. As if the way she dresses wouldn't be enough to get their attention, she's a damned brainiac, and rich."

Dylan downed another shot of whiskey. His interview had been over a week ago. Charli Monroe hadn't called. No surprise there. Tracy was hounding him again to crawl to Leon Ferguson for a job. Lucifer would sit on the left hand of God before that happened.

When two familiar couples came into view, he was pouring another shot. His hand shook as he set the bottle on the table with a bang. What was his ex doing in here? At the sight of the skinny geek, Nick Dailey, with Brenda, he gritted his teeth as fire spread up his neck.

He had hated the pencil-neck geek since meeting him at a Christmas party a month before he'd shipped out to Afghanistan. Brenda, an English teacher, had become best friends with the science teacher after he started working at Killeen High School.

Nicky pulled out a chair. How long had his wife screwed around behind his back with her BFF before she ended up pregnant?

Brenda smiled up at her new husband before sitting. Nick took the chair next to her as Brenda's sister and her husband sat across from them. A few minutes later, Julie came over to take their orders.

Once the waitress left, he slid out of the booth. Somewhere in the fog clouding his good sense, he knew he shouldn't, but he was spoiling for a fight.

He half-limped, half-staggered to stand at the end of the square table.

Brenda's dark eyes widened when she noticed him. "Dylan?"

"Forgotten me already, Brenda?"

Sitting across from Brenda, her brother-in-law scowled. "I think you should walk away now."

"Howdy, Mike. Interesting that you have to stand up for your wife's sister, while her new husband sits there scared shitless." He nodded his head at the near replica of his ex-wife next to Mike. "Carrie."

"Leave now," Brenda growled.

"I'm crushed." He put his hat on his head to free up his hands. "I wasn't invited to the weddin'. I heard all about it, though. Gotta love the Colton Grapevine. Was it as nice as ours?"

She glared up at him. Her chest rose and fell in rapid breaths. "It was better, actually. The Country Club was remodeled since our wedding."

"That's something, I guess. Baby Geek doin' okay?" he asked, referring to Brenda's baby with Nick.

Brenda's plump red lips twisted into a cold smile. "He's doing exceptionally well," she said a little too sweetly. "We figure he'll make a great scholar someday. Strive for world peace, unlike the barbarians in your family."

He let the jab go regarding the Quinns' long military history, and moved around the table. He rested his palms on the table and leaned over them.

Nick pressed away, and his face lost most of its color.

"So, *Nicky*, how do you like sleeping in another man's bed? Livin' in another man's house? Oh, wait, that's right, you were makin' a baby with *my* wife while I was in Afghanistan getting blown up."

"Quinn." Brenda's brother-in-law stood, and Dylan straightened. Mike was taller by two inches, but he wasn't worried. He easily out-bulked the man by twenty pounds. "If you don't leave--"

Nick sprung from his chair. "If you want a piece of me, let's go out to the parking lot and go at it."

Brenda jumped to her feet and grabbed his arm. "Nick, don't be ridiculous."

Oh, how he wanted to punch this piss-ant into next week. He laid his hand on the other man's shoulder. The action looked friendly, until Nick winced in pain when Dylan applied pressure in the right places. "I think you'd better just sit right back down there, geek. I've killed bugs bigger than you. I wouldn't want the new baby to grow up without his papa."

His sharp tone gained the attention of curious customers sitting close by. Nick's face flushed, and he drew back his fist and let loose. Dylan saw it coming and nimbly dodged the sucker punch by grabbing the flailing arm. A heartbeat later, he had *Nicky* in a chokehold.

Brenda and her sister screamed, and Mike stepped closer. The bartender moved in with an old billy club in hand. "That's enough, Quinn. Let him go."

He looked over at the big man. "Aww, Sam, can't a man have some fun?"

Sam Larson slapped the billy club on the palm of his hand with a loud smack. "I'm not tellin' you again, Quinn. Let him go."

He glanced around. Every eye was on him. "Fine." But instead of letting go, he tightening his hold on Nick and said in the other man's ear, "Just a word of advice, *Nicky*. Don't get too comfortable in my house. If she cheated on me, how long do you think it will be before she throws you over?"

He let go of the gasping man, but Brenda grabbed Dylan's arm. She stood before him toe-to-toe. He looked over the curves the tight jeans and snug T-shirt outlined. What the hell had he ever seen in her?

Brenda fisted her hands by her sides and stood with her feet apart. "I never set out to cheat on you." Her voice pitched low, and her eyes flashed with rage. "But when I came to Fort Benning to see you off before you went to Afghanistan, you refused to even discuss us having a baby." Brenda swallowed and glanced at Nick, who was rubbing his neck and watching them. "I wanted kids. I was thirty-four and got tired of waiting on you to deal with your screwed up issues with your father." She returned to Nick and glared at Dylan over her shoulder. "Don't ever come near us again, or I'll press charges for harassment."

He snorted in response, turned away and stepped right into the path of Zack Cartwright.

"Shit, this night just keeps gettin' better," he mumbled.

The sheriff stood with his feet apart, hands on his waist above his service belt and scowled at him. "What's the problem here?"

He shrugged and glanced back at his ex-wife fawning over *Nicky*. "Nothin', Sheriff. Just congratulatin' the happy couple."

"That so?" Cartwright continued to throw off big-bad-lawman vibes. "Let's go, Captain."

He dodged the sheriff's hand before it landed on his upper arm. "You takin' me to jail?"

"Not tonight. I'm taking you home. You aren't in any shape to drive, but since you're still on your feet, I'll let Tracy deal with your sorry ass."

As they headed to the exit, he said, "Geez, Zack, you and my sister seem to be getting quite cozy these days. You rekindlin' those old flames?"

Zack stiffened and narrowed his eyes again. "You're a comedian when you're shitfaced, Quinn. Let's go. I don't have all night to deal with your bullshit. My daughter's home with a sitter."

* * * *

Charli sipped coffee from the Styrofoam cup she clutched, and stared at the beautiful house across the county road from where she'd parked. The afternoon sun rode high in the big clear sky and made the Italian single-story glow.

Spurred by a crazy impulse, she'd driven south to Killeen to Dylan Quinn's second reference. Almost two weeks had passed since she'd met him. She never let anything interfere with her schoolwork, but she'd nearly flubbed her criminal sociology exam--which meant she almost got a B--because she couldn't stop thinking about him. Even now, she should have been at the ranch unpacking. Instead, she'd left the moment the movers finished unloading the truck.

Whatever she'd been expecting, it hadn't been the yellow stucco house. With its red tile roof and arched entry, oddly it didn't seem out of place on a Central Texas ranch. In the background stood a barn painted the same buttery hue, and the metal roof was red to match the tile roof of the house.

She took another sip of the strong coffee. What inspired the house? The things she'd learned about Dylan Quinn since meeting him didn't jive with this place. This builder understood design and craftsmanship. The man who'd built such a beautiful home for his wife hadn't been the drunk Mrs. Pratt had told her was freeloading off his sister.

He glanced at her watch. Damn, she had to hurry. The last thing she wanted was to be late for her appointment with Leon Ferguson. After shifting her Lexus into gear, she pulled away, but not before taking one last look at the house.

On the long drive back to Colton, she tried to piece together what she knew about Dylan. Mrs. Pratt was totally against her having anything to do with him. The older woman was convinced Charli's interest in him stemmed from her studying to become a social worker.

Her mind wasn't on the drive and she nearly missed her turn onto Highway 6 as the GPS dinged at her. As she turned onto the northbound lane and headed back to Colton, her thoughts went back to Dylan.

There had to be a reason for a man, who had built a home for his wife and served his country for thirteen years, to fall so far.

What had happened to Dylan Quinn, and why the hell couldn't she stop thinking about him?

She left Highway 6 and turned down Oak Springs Road. The same country road went past her ranch. She paused before turning and stared at the elaborate wrought-iron sign over the gate of Oak Springs Ranch.

Heading down the long drive, she finally put thoughts of Dylan out of her mind.

She stopped the car and peered out at the antebellum-styled mansion. Manicured lawn surrounded the veranda. White Greek columns circled the house and held a second floor balcony.

"Holy crap. Guess that's what being an oil tycoon can buy you."

She cut the engine and got out of the car. Her own ranch would look like this someday. A lake, the focal point at the front of the property, had a manicured edge with a large gazebo overlooking the dock. Grand oaks and pecan trees shaded the drive and the lawn surrounding the mansion.

Somehow this place seemed larger than hers.

She headed for the front door and took one last look around. "I can almost smell the money."

The housekeeper led her into a formal parlor. The house had an air of wealth and privilege. Damned place reminded her of Hank's house.

The first time she'd seen her grandfather's home, she was ten days past turning fifteen and three days after her mother's death. She blinked, but the memories wouldn't relent. Before she could stop it, the painful scene from her past rushed her.

She stared out the window of the Silverado pickup at the hundreds of cattle grazing in the field. "You said we were on the Long Arrow. Where's the house?"

"We've been driving on the ranch for the past two miles. The house is just around the next turn."

She glanced at him. "Two miles? How big is this place?"

"Twenty-five-thousand acres."

"Is my grandmother at the house?"

"No. She died last summer. You sure ask a lot of questions."

She hadn't spoken more than a handful of words until his plane, with her mother's body and her precious few belongings in the cargo hold, landed at a local airstrip.

When the house came into view, she gasped at the size of the single-story. Later, she would count thirty-seven rooms.

He parked in the big ten-car garage where there were three sports cars and another pickup with the Monroe Farm Equipment logo painted on the side. Why did he need so many cars if he lived alone?

She followed her grandfather, Hank, out of the garage, down a hallway, and into the open foyer of the mansion. A chandelier made from a wagon wheel, with dozens of candle-like lights, hung from the high-beamed ceiling.

The only entry she had ever seen as big was in the bank where Momma had worked before she died in the car accident. The sudden stab of fresh grief took her breath.

Hank set his big hands on his hips. His hard face held no emotion but disdain. "I want you to know I've spent a lifetime collecting Old West art and artifacts and expect you to stay out of certain rooms. I won't have you destroying a million dollar masterpiece just because you want to romp."

She flinched at the harshness of his voice, but she wouldn't be intimidated. "Was Momma forbidden from these rooms, too?"

He turned and started walking away. "Yes. Come along, I don't have all day."

After showing her where she wasn't allowed to go in the house, Hank opened a door to one of the bedrooms. "This is your room. It was your mother's."

She looked around at the large bedroom. There wasn't a hint of her mom anywhere in the floral spread and white walls. "Do you still have some of Momma's old stuff?"

"No," he said at the doorway. "I got rid of it when she left with you."

"Why did she leave?"

"You don't know?"

She shook her head and shivered at his brusqueness. Didn't he care his only child was dead?

"I disowned her when she refused to give you up for adoption. I'd planned for her to marry a business partner of mine, but when she got pregnant by a saddle tramp, he bailed out of the deal. I lost a fortune because of your mother's whoring around." With a sneer, he left the room.

She wrapped her arms around herself and pushed the memory to the back of her mind by looking around the parlor of the Ferguson mansion. A vase in the corner reminded her of one of the famous Mings she'd learned about in an art history class. Several oil paintings graced the walls. One look at them convinced her they were originals, like Hank's Old West paintings.

At least she wouldn't have to look at his precious art collection again. After the last pieces sold, she was three quarters of a billion dollars richer.

When the pocket door slid open, she forced a pleasant smile as a man entered the room. Leon Ferguson was tall and lean. His dark suit had *designer* written all over its perfect tailoring. She guessed him to be in his early forties by the hint of silver at his temples. His tanned angular face, high cheekbones and dark, intelligent eyes hinted at Indian blood. He radiated masculine confidence by the bucketfuls.

"Miss Monroe, welcome," he drawled, taking her hand into his. A large ruby signet ring graced his finger, reminding her of royalty.

"Mr. Ferguson, hello. Thank you for meeting with me on a Saturday." After he let go, she clasped her hands in front of her. He moved his gaze over her. Why hadn't she dressed more conservatively instead of the short black skirt and her favorite periwinkle blue silk sweater? When a chill, which had nothing to do with the temperature of the room and everything to do with the heat in his eyes, skittered down her spine, she hugged herself.

"I'm sorry I'm late. I had an errand to run this afternoon."

His smile broadened as he turned toward the couch in the center of the vast room. "You must be extremely busy moving in. Besides, I just finished an important conference call. I'm in the middle of a land deal in Colorado." He faced her and held a hand out to gesture toward the silk-covered couch. "But you aren't here to be bored by my woes. Please sit and make yourself comfortable."

She gingerly sat on the edge of the ornate sofa.

Ferguson sat across from her in a matching wingchair. He rested his arms on the sides and folded his hands in his lap. "When you called, you said you were interested in entering a business arrangement."

The housekeeper entered, carrying a silver tray full of delicate cakes and a coffee set. She served them espresso and Leon dismissed her.

With shaky hands, Charli held onto the fragile china cup and saucer. "Yes, I'm wondering if you'd contract some of your ranch hands and equipment out to me. I'd like to get my pasture land cleaned up, a few fields planted, and my main corrals fixed. I'll pay ten percent above the going rate for the service. I don't want to waste any more time while I'm looking for a manager, and can hire my own workers."

Ferguson leaned back and sipped his coffee. His demeanor was the epitome of politeness. But some underlying magnetism of his dark eyes lured her in. She squirmed with apprehension and excitement at the same time.

He set his cup and saucer down on the low Chippendale table between them. "The old place needs a great deal of work. Quite overwhelming, I'm sure, for someone so young."

"I may be young, but I know what I'm doing. I helped run my grandfather's ranch for years."

"Of course, but Blackwell Ranch is a big investment." Leon regarded her with shrewd deep brown eyes as he sipped his coffee.

She held her saucer in one hand and laid the other on her thigh below the hem of her short skirt. When his gaze lowered to her legs, she tugged on the hem of her skirt and shrugged. The hot interest showing in his eyes shook her attempt at confidence. "I have a business plan and enough capital to invest. The house and most of the outbuildings need work, but I like the ranch and want to make Colton my home."

"These old mansions do hold a certain charm."

"Yes, they do, and I have plans for the house." She wasn't ready to share more of her ideas for the future.

"If I can be of service with the renovation, please don't hesitate to ask. Here in Forest County, neighbors watch out for each other."

Did she want Leon Ferguson watching out for her? What if he decided to look into her past? Hank had made sure if anyone tried to investigate her past, they'd hit a brick wall regarding her connection with Ricardo Rodriquez, a Las Vegas drug dealer, pimp and nightclub owner. But even Hank, with all his money and power, couldn't cover up Ricardo's serving a life sentence with no chance of parole for those crimes, as well as six counts of first-degree murder.

Her stomach twisted into a knot. No way could she drink the dark coffee. What if Leon somehow discovered her former cocaine addiction?

He made a weak gesture toward her cup with a flick of his hand. "Would you prefer something else? Tea, water, wine?"

She swallowed hard to get the stinging taste of anxiety off her tongue, and shook her head. "No, thank you, coffee's fine." Maybe one sip would appease him and get the hot pepper feeling out of her mouth. "Neighbors looking out for each other is one of the things I love about the area."

"Me, too. Colton and Forest County have a wonderful sense of community." He picked up his cup and took a drink. "I'll be more than happy to spare a few of the boys to get your place ready. It'll be easy to come up with a cost workup. Call you tomorrow to set up another meeting to sign a contract?" His smile eased her apprehension as he placed the saucer and cup back on the table. "A crew could start as early as Monday."

"Wow. That would be wonderful, thanks. You have a beautiful home."

"Thank you. It was built in 1867. A replica of the plantation house co-founder of the county, Dylan Ferguson, had left to come west with his cousins, Elijah Blackwell and Cole Cartwright, after the Civil War. Much of the art is my mother's. She's an art collector. In fact, she left for Greece yesterday for an auction."

She sipped more coffee. After the initial swallow, the rich brew did ease her nerves a bit. "Does she live here with you?"

"No, she moved to Dallas after my stepfather died." He leaned over his long legs and cranked up the intimacy of the meeting.

Okay, the nervousness was back, but in a different way. Leon was a handsome man. "This is a big house for only one person."

He laughed and held her gaze. "Yes, it is. I could say the same about the house on your ranch."

Heat of a blush prickled her cheeks, and she looked down into her cup. "I suppose it is."

"I know how daunting starting a business is. When I took over my grandfather's oil company, it was teetering on bankruptcy. I know how important it is to have the right help from the beginning. I'm willing to subcontract one of my foremen over to you to help manage the ranch."

He provided the answer to her manager problem. But should she take him up on his offer? She pushed a loose lock of hair behind her ears. Her chin came up, and she met his gaze. No, Dylan was perfect for the job. "Thanks, but I've found someone for the job."

"Of course." He leaned back, and for a split second, something cold hardened his eyes. "May I inquire who you're considering? I may be able to provide a reference."

"Your nephew." She crossed her legs and sipped the coffee.

"Dylan?"

Dylan had warned her about Leon; was Leon now going to warn her about Dylan? God, she hated all this family feuding crap. "Yes. He has an impressive resume."

"He worked here before he went to college and joined the military. His mother is my sister. Though, I guess, stepsister would be more accurate."

"What can you tell me about him, as a ranch hand?" She set her cup and saucer on the table.

"May I be blunt, Miss Monroe?"

Here came the bullshit about why she shouldn't hire him. She rested her elbow on her knee and stared him in the eye. "I should hope you'd be honest."

Shifting in his seat, Leon finished off his coffee. "Dylan came back from the war a changed man."

"He was injured and now has PTSD, I'm assuming. I was always under the impression multiple deployments like his didn't happen."

"I believe Dylan volunteered for the last two. He was wounded during the last one. His team was ambushed in a roadside bombing where four of his men were killed and the rest were injured." He shook his head and looked down at his folded hands. Regret? Had she misread him? "I hate to admit I didn't follow the war that closely, only its effect on the price of oil until then. We almost lost Dylan."

She folded her arms around her middle as a chill ran through her. "I'm guilty of not following the war, either. However, I'm discovering Forest County is very patriotic."

"Yes, it is. Another way we stick together." He sighed and averted his eyes. A regretful-sounding huskiness deepened his voice. "I offered him a job, but he refused it. Sadly, we don't see eye to eye. I hope he can turn his life around soon. He lives with his sister in Colton. I know Tracy is at her wits' end concerning him."

That sealed the deal. If Hank hadn't helped her when she came home after running away, she'd probably be dead. "I think he ll work out fine. I should be going. I can imagine how busy you are." She uncrossed her legs and stood. Holding out her hand, she smiled. "Thank you, Mr. Ferguson."

Leon took her hand, but instead of shaking it, he sidestepped the low table and bent over her hand, a real Southern gentleman. As he touched the back of it with his lips, she shivered. His gaze locked with hers, and her heart skipped a beat.

"Please, Charli, call me Leon. After all, we are neighbors and soon-to-be business partners. I hope we can also be friends."

"I'd like that, too, Leon."

* * * *

"Hello?" Charli called as she entered the reception area of Tracy's Classic Chic Salon the following Monday morning.

A tall, slender woman peeked around the archway of the adjoining room. "Oh, hi. I'll be right there.

"Hi. I'm Charli Monroe. I think I'm a little early for my appointment."

"Don't worry about it. It's good to finally meet you." Tracy said with a smile.

"Same here." She and Tracy had spoken on the phone a few times regarding Dylan, but they hadn't met until now. She stopped at the doorway into the salon parlor. An older woman sat in the chair patting her short blonde curls.

Tracy moved toward the other customer, but said to her over her shoulder, "Make yourself comfortable. I'll be finished in a few minutes."

"My dear, you are an artist," the patron drawled in a strong Texas accent when Tracy stood behind the styling chair.

"Aw, Mrs. Cartwright," Tracy said. "You say that every time."

Charli turned toward the floral couch in front of the double window, picked up a *People Magazine,* and began leafing through it. A few minutes later, the older woman and Tracy came out of the parlor.

"Tracy, dear, I really wish you'd come to the next planning session for the Forest County Charity Ball," Mrs. Cartwright said. "You have such wonderful taste."

"Thank you. I'll consider your invitation." Tracy punched the keys of an antique cash register to total the bill. "That's twenty-five dollars." She accepted the credit card and scanned it. "Isn't it a little early to be planning for an event that doesn't happen until July fourth?"

"My goodness, no!" the older woman gushed, aghast. "We have to make sure everything is perfect. Please think about it." She tucked her credit card into her Gucci handbag. "This year we're hoping to do something special for all the veterans in town. Too bad your brother is having such a hard time. He'd be perfect to speak at one of the committee meetings."

Tracy looked puzzled. "Why Dylan?"

"He was over there so many times and was part of the--oh, what are they called?" Mrs. Cartwright tapped her cheek with a long manicured fingernail a few times, then chirped, "The Green Berets. Zachery mentioned he's still drinking heavily. Must be so terrible for you, honey."

When Tracy glanced over at Charli, she looked down at the magazine in her lap. Damn, Tracy hadn't caught her eavesdropping, had she? She pretended to focus on the article about Brad Pitt.

In a reserved tone, Tracy said, "Dylan's getting better. It won't be too long before he'll be the man he was before his injuries and the divorce."

"He was such a good boy from what I remember of him when he'd visit with my son, Lance. And he did such a wonderful job helping you remodel this old house."

Dylan did this? She couldn't help but look around the lobby of the salon. The Victorian house was beautiful. The rich decor of cream, gold, olive green and rose complemented the rich, red tones of the wood flooring. Moreover, the carved molding was gorgeous, polished to match the unique floor.

Tracy's evenly spoken words drew her back into the conversation. "Dylan and Lance are still good friends." Tracy moved from behind the antique desk and spoke with obvious pride. "He's always been a talented craftsman. I wouldn't have been able to live here if he hadn't helped me fix up this place."

"When Zachery came back from Afghanistan two years ago, he was changed, too. I suppose Lisa's death and having to raise their little girl alone would change anyone, though."

Charli flipped the page of the magazine as Tracy glanced over at her again.

Turning back to the older woman, Tracy asked, "How's Zack doing? I only see him occasionally."

Was Tracy's voice wistful? Must be a story there.

Mrs. Cartwright sighed. "I think my dear nephew is burning the candle at both ends, if you ask me. The time of mourning is over. He needs a wife, and Amanda needs a mother. She's quite the handful."

"She takes after her father for sure."

The older woman laughed. "Yes, she does." She turned toward the door and smiled at Charli. "Oh, my, forgive my rudeness. Hello, I don't think I've seen you around." The woman held out her hand, and Charli stood and shook it. "I'm Winnie Cartwright. The mayor's wife."

Charli returned her smile. "Charli Monroe. Pleased to meet you, Mrs. Cartwright. I actually have a meeting with your nephew Zack tomorrow concerning some horses I'd like to buy."

"Oh, I hate the beasts. Never go near them." She placed a hand laden with jewels onto her ample chest and shivered to add emphasis to her dislike for horses.

How could anyone despise horses?

Winnie smiled and readjusted the strap of her purse. "I was thrilled when my son Lance finally decided to take over my husband's share of the CW Ranch. Paul, however, still gets involved because Lance is the senior partner of my father's law firm." Her brown eyes widened and her pink lips opened slightly. "Oh, you're the young woman who bought the old Blackwell place. I guess that makes us neighbors, too, since the CW and Blackwell Ranch share a boundary. You must tell me all about it. Jock was such a strange bird. He had bipolar disorder and refused to take his medicines." Mrs. Cartwright made a *tsking* sound and shook her head. "It was a shame how he cheated his boys out of the ranch, but then, I guess he had his reasons."

The older woman leaned toward her, her voice low. "I heard he did it because there's still oil under the land and didn't want them to reopen those oil wells, which makes no sense at all. Jock was always sinking his dwindling family fortune into one scheme after another." She chuckled at her own joke. "Have you met our neighbor, Leon Ferguson, yet?"

"Yes, Mr. Ferguson and I have met." She wasn't offering any more to the old busybody. She may not have been in town long, but she had been here long enough to know Winnie Cartwright was the tried and true queen of the gossip chain the locals called the Colton Grapevine.

Tracy cleared her throat. "Miss Monroe, I'm ready whenever you are."

Charli silently thanked her for the save and said to the mayor's wife, "If you'll excuse me?"

"Of course, dear." Winnie's lips compressed in displeasure, no doubt at being so easily dismissed. "We must talk again."

Settled into the chair by the shampoo sink after the front door closed, she smiled at Tracy. "Thank you."

"Not a problem. Winnie can be a bulldog if she smells a grape."

"A 'grape'?"

"A juicy story. The folks around here call them grapes--you know, like what grow on a grapevine."

She nodded her understanding, and Tracy turned on the water.

"You said when you made the appointment you wanted a trim?"

"I'd like to have my hair layered and shortened a little." At least, she hoped that's what she wanted. "Maybe see if you can do something with the front. I'm tired of pulling my hair back all the time."

"Sounds doable." After a few uneasy moments of silence, Tracy commented, "Your hair is such a pretty color. And the curl's natural, too, isn't it?"

She sighed. "I tried to straighten it once, but it didn't work. As for the color, I'm stuck with it, too. I have too many freckles and too pale a complexion for any other shade."

Tracy cocked her head to the side as she applied shampoo and worked it into her hair. "With your skin tone, I'd have to agree. But really, I like the golden red."

"Thanks."

The other woman worked with her fingers to massage her scalp. A butterfly clip held Tracy's twisted, golden highlighted brown hair at the back of her head. Friendly gray eyes were set in a face sharp with angles, much as her brother's, except Tracy's features were delicate, feminine.

Tracy rinsed the lather from her hair. "I can't imagine what the old ranch house must look like on the inside. I heard it was neglected for a lot of years even before Jock Blackwell died."

Tracy was hoping to harvest her own juicy grapes. Charli hated nosy people and suspected anything she told this woman would end up all over town. Nevertheless, she had to give a little if she hoped to get a little.

She sucked in a breath and let it out slowly. "It's in pretty bad shape, I'm afraid. Every day I live there, I find more needs fixing."

Tracy motioned for her to move onto the swivel chair before the gilt-framed mirror. "What are you planning on doing with the ranch? You're not married, are you? The house is so big."

"No, I'm not married." Nor would she ever be. She'd never trust a man with her heart again. Love didn't exist in a man's world, even when they professed it. They used those pretty words to get what they wanted from a woman, but they never gave any of themselves in return. She'd learned that too many times the hard way.

Biting back the bitterness, she repeated what was already public knowledge. "I want to get into the cattle business, possibly go organic eventually. I've done a lot of research on it, and there's a big market overseas for organically grown beef."

"Yeah, there is. If a rancher has the capital to put out, it's the way to go. So, that's why you moved to Colton?" Tracy didn't sound convinced. "Your landlady told me you were going to college. You definitely know how to stay busy."

Leave it to Aida Mae Pratt to share her personal information. Thank God, she hadn't shared much with the elderly woman.

She'd play along. "I would say I know how to make sure I lose my mind."

Tracy joined her in a laugh. "You're taking social work, right? Whatever made you choose that field?"

No one knew of her other plans--the real reason she'd bought the ranch. How would the people of Colton feel about those plans?

Measuring her words carefully, she said, "I want to work with troubled teens someday by opening a halfway house or summer camp. You know, for teenage mothers or for girls who just can't live at home anymore."

"Wow, sounds ambitious."

As Tracy finished combing out the tangles in her hair, Charli changed the subject. "So, how long have you lived in Colton?"

Tracy shrugged and reached for the scissors. "Since I was a teenager, but I consider Colton my hometown. I was born in England and lived all over. My father was an officer in the Army."

"Did your brother join the Army because it's the family tradition?"

She knew her question surprised Tracy by the way she paused in her work. "Partly. Dylan had hoped to inherit Oak Springs--not him exactly, our mother--but our grandfather decided to give it to his stepson. Dylan would have made a great rancher. He loves that kind of life. Going to the Army was the only other thing he could think of doing."

"Oh." She hadn't been expecting Tracy's straightforwardness, which made her suspicious. She remembered Mrs. Pratt's comments about Dylan mooching off his sister. Did Tracy simply want to get him out of her house? "I'm still looking for a manager."

Tracy scrunched her brows and concentrated on her hair. "I know. My brother applied for the job almost three weeks ago. You haven't filled the position?"

"No, I haven't filled it yet," she said as Tracy worked with the scissors, snipping at her waist-length hair. "I drove by the house he built near Fort Hood. It's beautiful."

"It is. He built it after he and his wife were stationed in Italy for a while. I don't know what you've heard about my brother, but he's not really as bad as the rumors claim."

"I spoke to Mr. Ferguson. He seemed surprised I interviewed him. He told me some of what happened to Dylan."

Tracy stopped in mid-snip of her locks.

Charli winced. She hoped like hell the woman knew what she was doing. She hadn't had her hair more than trimmed since she'd walked out of the Florence McClure Women's Correctional Center in Nevada four and half years ago.

With her bottom lip caught between her teeth, Tracy looked at her. "Leon and Dylan don't get along."

"I've heard. Was the oil business also your grandfather's?"

Tracy laughed, but it sounded a bit shaky. "My goodness, no. It came from Leon's grandfather on his mother's side. Leon changed the name and moved it to Dallas from Houston. Without having a son, Leon's granddad taught him the business and left it to him. But my grandfather was a major stockholder in the company when he and his father-in-law were business partners."

Tracy turned the chair until she faced her. As Tracy worked on the front of her hair, Charli looked up at the stylist. "What happened to Dylan?"

Tracy stopped cutting again and met her gaze. "He was in a bad situation in Afghanistan during his last deployment."

"I know he was injured." She remembered Leon's comment about Dylan having comrades who had died in the bombing. "He has PTSD."

His sister swallowed and nodded. "He's not suicidal or dangerous."

"He's an alcoholic."

Tracy stared at her. However, instead of confirming or denying the statement, she turned the tables on her. "I heard you lived in Las Vegas before moving in with your grandfather. Must have been something, growing up in Vegas. Are your parents still there?"

Her guts twisted into a frozen knot. How had anyone learned about her life in the city? Her life in Vegas was a closed book. No one could ever know what she'd done when she'd lived there. After finding her voice, she said, "No, my mother is dead."

"I'm sorry." Tracy furrowed her brow as if she knew she had avoided answering the entire question, but she didn't press for more about her parents.

Done cutting hair, Tracy exchanged the scissors for some styling mousse. They grew quiet as Tracy blow-dried Charli's hair, using a brush to style her new layered look. After she finished, Tracy turned the chair back toward the mirror. "What do you think?"

She didn't know what to think. She never had her hair this short in the front, except when it had all been short while she was in prison. She hated bangs, and now she had them.

"You don't like it?"

She ran her fingers through the back, liking the layers. "I don't know what I expected. I'll have to get used to the bangs."

"You have wonderful hair. It just needed a style that works with your curls, but I'm sorry if I missed the mark."

She met Tracy's gray eyes and smiled. "Not at all. It's just that I haven't had bangs since…for a long time. Thank you. I'll admit I only made the appointment to find out about Mr. Quinn. But I'm glad I sacrificed my hair for the information."

"I figured as much when you called." Tracy sobered, grabbed a vacuum broom, and swept up the hair clippings on the floor. "Dylan's not a bad man, Miss Monroe. I think he'd be perfect for Blackwell Ranch." Over the hum of the broom, Tracy went on, "He knows about starting up a ranch. He did it with his own place. As an officer in the Army he had to learn how to manage things and people. And you saw that he's got talent when it comes to building. He'd know exactly what needs to be done and if the job's being done right."

Tracy met her gaze, love for her brother shining in the misty gray of her eyes. She wasn't trying to pawn him off; she only wanted the best for him.

Charli's heart fluttered as she made her decision. "Tell Mr. Quinn to come by the ranch on Friday. I think he'll work out fine."

"I'll tell him. Thank you. All he needs is a chance."

Chapter 3

If Charli didn't soon take a break from cleaning the inside of the house to make the place livable, she feared she'd set a match to it. Why the hell hadn't she given Tracy a time for Dylan to show up?

As she headed off the back porch to the potting shed, she looked up at the fluffy clouds dappling the mid-morning sky. On such a warm day, she itched to be in the garden again.

Mrs. Pratt had spent two whole evenings telling her all about the Blackwell clan after she had mentioned she'd bid on the ranch last month. Did every small town have a crazy mixed-up history? Who would have thought the Blackwells, Fergusons and Cartwrights were all distantly related? From what she could tell, the clans despised each other.

But according to Mrs. Pratt, the county was founded when Cole Cartwright and his two younger cousins--Dylan Ferguson and Elijah Blackwell--won the tract of land making up the county in a poker game just after the Civil War.

Whether she wanted to know or not didn't matter to the landlady as she rambled on about the ending of the fifty-year oil partnership between the Blackwells and the Fergusons, spurring a feud between Jock Blackwell and Jason Ferguson.

However, what had interested her the most were Aida's stories about Penelope Blackwell. Jock's eccentric mother loved gardening and spent hours in the garden healing from her bouts with mental illness. An illness most people in town agreed had been passed down to Jock.

After Charli retrieved the tools from the shed, she placed them by the bed near the wraparound porch. She ambled around the six massive beds in the front yard and the weedy border along the tattered picket fence until she made her way to the small lake in the front. Maybe once she got rid of the neglect, the garden would be beautiful.

Wasn't that the story of her life?

Horsetails, cattails, water cannas and sweet flags edged the lake created by damming the creek running in the front of her property. A wooden dock, rotted and covered with green slime, jutted into the water. Someday she'd replace it. She could imagine the girls who came to her home to heal from life's hard knocks paddling around in small boats on the calm water, or fishing along the edge.

An old concrete bench sat on a stone patio near the water's edge. With the ivy and weeds, she wasn't certain the stone path wove through all of the large beds to the house, but here and there part of a path would materialize out of the overgrowth. For a half second, she considered sitting on the bench, until something slithered in the ivy and over the edge of the mossy rocks into the water by the lip of the lake.

Snake!

She shrieked and ran through the weeds and high grass to the porch steps, several yards away, clutching her heaving chest. Maybe a match wasn't such a bad idea after all. Hiring a bulldozer to level the place completely after the fire was an even better one.

She held her chest and waited for her breathing to return to normal. How many more snakes were in the garden? "Don't think about it." She gingerly made her way down the porch steps. "It was just a water snake."

What if it was poisonous?

Don't think about it!

She picked up the hoe and used it to poke in the weeds and ivy in a bed close to the house where she'd left her tools. Once she was sure there were no snakes hiding in the overgrowth to bite her legs off, she got busy pruning the shrubs.

With one eye on the lookout for another snake.

As she worked, a pang of grief sneaked up on her. She stopped for a moment and looked at the rosebush she was pruning. She missed her grandfather, not the man he'd been when she'd met him, not the man who worshiped his art and wealth, but the man he'd become after she'd run away. Pink roses would be a perfect reminder of him. She paused and stared at the new leaves unfurling on the stems. The day she'd ventured out into the garden at the Long Arrow for the first time soon replaced the vision of new growth.

When she had first gone to live with Hank, there hadn't been even a flowerpot at the ranch house. But sometime between when she'd left with the rodeo cowboy who'd taken her to Las Vegas and the day she'd come home after being released from the correction center in Nevada four years later, he'd taken up gardening.

She had wandered around the mansion for three days after coming home from the rehab in which she'd been treated for alcohol poisoning. Bored and needing to get out, she'd ventured outside. She'd been surprised to find Hank bending over a purple daisy-like flower meticulously snipping off dead buds.

"What kind of flower is that? It looks like something that would grow wild."

He straightened his back and put a big work-roughened hand on his hip. "Echinacea purpurea. Purple coneflower, and it is a wild flower."

Since when did the businessman have dirt under his fingernails? Had he retired from being CEO of his manufacturing business?

"When I lived here before, this garden wasn't here."

He looked down at the shears in his hand. "No, it wasn't. I never liked flowers, but after you left, Tonja Crow gave me a rosebush and told me to plant it. According to her, as long as I nurtured it and it bloomed, you'd be all right." He pointed the blades at a deep pink blooming rosebush in the center of the large bed. "It's over there. I probably would have let it die, if it wasn't for Tonja being an old Indian medicine woman." He lowered his hand and shifted his feet, but still he didn't look at her. "While I cared for the bush, I found myself enjoying taking care of it. That was the beginning, and I haven't stopped since. She was right, as long as I kept it blooming, you were alive, if not okay."

He wiped his brow with the back of his free hand. "Thing is, I found working with nature, along with finally opening up your grandma's Bible, helped me realize I haven't been very nice. I was a bastard to your momma and to you. I'm sorry, Charli." He finally looked at her, his blue eyes fierce with an emotion she had never seen before. Was it guilt? Was it regret? Could she possibly hope it was love? "I hope we can start over, but I know I'll never be able to make up for what has already happened to you."

She wrapped her arms around herself. "Hank--"

"No." He cut her off with a slash of his hand, but his voice was so gentle the shell around her heart cracked. "I hope you can forgive me, but I'll understand if you can't. Now, come here and help me. I'm not as young as I used to be."

"I don't know what to do."

He held out his clippers and a pair of gloves he'd had tucked in his belt. She was surprised to find they were just her size. She stared up at him. He hadn't been expecting her to come to the garden, had he?

His smile softened the hard angles of his face. "I'm going to teach you. Not just about the garden, but the ranch. Someday this place will be yours. You should know how to run it."

That day in the garden with her grandfather had become the beginning of her healing and a beautiful friendship with Hank. And had set her on the path leading her here.

She wiped away a tear as she finished with the rosebush. As she lopped off sucker growth from the large weeping cherry tree at the center of the bed, her mind stayed in the past.

Hank Monroe had changed the last few years of his life. He'd mellowed and become regretful of disowning his daughter, LeAnn, and of not understanding Charli's grief when she'd first come to live with him.

Damn, but it all didn't change the way he'd treated her before she'd ran away.

She paused in her pruning and wiped at her damp eyes with the back of her bare arm again, shuddering at the old memory. Why had he treated her so bad? Why had Momma died? The answers didn't come to her now any easier than they had nine years ago.

The sudden sound of a vehicle in the drive drew her back to the present. She lowered the pruning shears as Dylan Quinn stopped by the gate. He climbed out of the pickup and headed in her direction with a distinctive limp.

Shielding her eyes with a gloved hand, she smiled. "Hi. You're here. Good."

He stopped under the cherry tree and took in the entire yard with one sweeping glance. His inspection also included her, and something fluttered in her belly. "My sister told me you wanted to see me."

"Yes. You're hired, and I'd like you to start today." She pointed behind her. "There's a snake in the lake over there. It couldn't be too far from the edge. I want you to kill it. Then I'll show you around."

His lips twitched in a ghost of a smirk. "It was probably a little blotched or broad-banded water snake. They're harmless and common."

"*Little*? The thing was a good four feet long. And no snake is harmless." When the meaning of the rest sank in, she shivered as the blood drained out of her face. "Common?"

"Yep." He pushed back his dark brown Stetson, revealing some of his similarly colored short hair. "Water snakes are very common in this part of Texas. When I was a kid, I'd catch them from here and let them loose over on my granddad's place to torment his wife." His eyes twinkled at the memory. "Jock loved to watch me. You sure it was four feet long?"

She glanced at the lake again. "I don't know. Maybe it wasn't that long. Just kill it."

He shook his head, and his lips twitched further into a genuine lopsided grin. Who cared if he was making fun of her? The guy was gorgeous when he smiled. The hard angles and planes still provided structure, but now small crinkles added life to his silvery eyes, and a small dimple formed in his left cheek. The flutter in her stomach his assessment of her had started just got worse.

"No. Unless it's a cottonmouth." He picked up a hoe from where she'd dropped it. "I'll show you how harmless the water snakes are."

He went to the edge of the water and prodded around in the overgrowth of cattails by the limestone lip.

She jumped when he pulled the snake out of the water. It twisted around the end of the hoe.

He looked over his shoulder at her. "This little guy's a blotched water snake. I'm not killing it. Or any of his buddies in here either."

"It's a damned snake! Get rid of it. Now!" *Dear Lord, was the man nuts?*

He chuckled, the sound more than a little rusty as it drifted to her across the yard. "You aren't really afraid of this fella, are you? This guy's as harmless as a frog." He shook the snake off the hoe and probed around in the water for a few feet. Turning, he headed back toward her through the high grass and weeds. For a guy with a limp, he moved fast.

"Maybe it is as harmless as a frog, but I don't like them much either." When he stopped at the edge of the garden, she backed up a step, and her feet tangled in the vegetation. With an *ompff*, she landed on her backside in the middle of a clump of weeds, bluebonnets and, amazingly, yellow daffodils.

He laughed and held his hand out to her, which she ignored. With a shrug, he hooked his thumbs into the pockets of his jeans. "When I was on a mission in the South American jungle, pythons the length of my pickup would come into camp. We didn't have to worry unless we woke up in the morning with our feet in the mouth of one."

She widened her eyes. Was he serious?

He snorted and shifted his stance. "Of course that was better than our heads being swallowed first."

"Oh... *Oh!*" She struggled to her feet and brushed at her jeans. "If you aren't careful, you'll be fired before you even get started. I want that snake and any of his 'buddies' removed from my lake."

"I'm not killing the snake." He put his hands on his narrow hips, drawing her gaze to the way his jeans fit powerfully built legs. "If it was a cottonmouth, I would, but the water snakes keep down the populations of more unsavory critters like mice and rats."

"My, my, if this isn't a scene right out of the Bible." A smooth voice drawled from the opposite side of the flowerbed by the gate.

They turned to Leon Ferguson standing on the stone walk. She hadn't heard him drive up the driveway, and considering the thin line Dylan's mouth formed, he hadn't heard him either.

Leon had his hands in the pants pockets of his dark gray designer suit. His white Stetson cast his brown eyes in shadow.

"Ferguson, what are you doing here?" Dylan barked.

Leon ambled toward them on the stone path. "I'm saving a young maiden from torment. What are you doing here, playing the part of the devil?"

"I'm Miss Monroe's new manager." The deadly edge of his voice matched the flintiness of his eyes. "If there's anyone to save the young maiden from, it's you."

"Mr. Quinn, please." She turned to Leon. "Leon, is there something I can do for you?"

He smiled, showing off perfect white teeth in a face handsome enough to belong to an actor. "I was just passing by on my way home and decided to stop. How are the boys working out?"

Dylan's stance widened and his hands flexed at his slides. "What boys?"

"Charli and I have entered into a business arrangement."

She lost the battle with the urge to wrap her arms around herself. As much as she appreciated Leon's kindness, respected him, and was even a little attracted to him, something about him didn't sit right with her. He represented her peers in the community. According to Mrs. Pratt, besides the Cartwrights, she and Leon were undoubtedly the wealthiest residents in the county. No one in Colton could learn about her past. It would ruin her, and Leon, no doubt, had the means to dig up the dirt.

"Really?" Dylan stepped closer to her in a protective manner. Whiskey tainted his breath as the warmth of the exhalations tickled her cheek. "What kind of business arrangement?"

She could protect herself. Dylan Quinn wasn't any safer than Leon Ferguson. Stepping away from him, she forced her arms to her sides. "Mr. Quinn, I can handle this."

She faced Leon. "I'm amazed by how much the men got done since starting on Monday. The foreman told me last evening they'd be reseeding another fifty acres for hay this morning. And they have the corrals fixed and started on the fencing in the north pasture."

"Good, good." He glanced at Dylan. "I'll be going, unless you need a more reliable exterminator. I couldn't help but overhear about your snake infestation. I can give you the name of the company that has gotten rid of the snakes in our lakes over on Oak Springs for years."

Although he presented the perfect solution, she didn't the like way Leon had looked at Dylan as he said the word *exterminator*. "No, Mr. Quinn is quite capable of getting rid of the snake."

"Oh, I'm sure he is." Leon tipped his hat. "Let me know if there's anything else I can do for you, Charli." Dylan's jaw tightened as his uncle glanced at him. "It's good to see you up among the living again."

Leon headed back to his Porsche. With no pretense of lowering his voice, Dylan said, "Now, there's a snake no one wants in their garden."

Upon hearing the jibe, Leon's shoulders jerked in mid-stride.

Rattled by Leon's attention and the snake fiasco, she turned on Dylan. "You aren't off the hook. I want those snakes gone."

"We'll see."

"I hate snakes." She shuddered and put her hands on her hips. "Maybe I should have asked him who the exterminator is."

* * * *

Charli's glare had Dylan looking out over the lake. He followed the creek into the wild flower-filled pasture beyond the yard. Had he ever seen eyes as beautiful as hers before? "Leon Ferguson is the last person you should be doing business with. He wants this ranch. I'd wager that was the reason Jock Blackwell didn't leave a will. He knew none of his sons wanted the land, and he was afraid the one to inherit it would promptly sell it to Ferguson." He pointed toward the front of the ranch. "His first cousin Buck, who owns the ranch across the road, can't afford the ten-thousand acres he already owns. He would've easily lost it to taxes. Same goes for Jock's sister. Which means Leon would've gotten it for a song."

Determined to figure out what unsettled him about Charli Monroe, he looked back into her two-toned eyes. Their secrets were as hard to see as the murky bottom of the lake. "But Jock outsmarted Leon. He didn't leave it to any of his family. Because of his sons' greed, probate court held up the sale while the whole Blackwell clan fought over who should get the right to sell it until the judge decided they had to split the profits of the sale. I'm sure Leon was fit to be tied when you beat him to the bid."

She let out a long sigh. "I didn't know anyone else was even interested in the place. I went to Dixon Real Estate looking for a small ranch where I could have a few horses, but had a big enough house for what I want to do with it someday. I wasn't even considering raising cattle. By the end of the meeting, he'd shown me this place. He said it had just gone on the market that morning, but I had to make a bid soon."

She ruefully smiled, and his gut tightened, sending him in a tailspin.

"I went home and called him within an hour after seeing the ranch. I knew I was being suckered, but I liked the place." She glanced down at her arms where they crossed over her chest, and lowered them to her sides. After meeting his eyes, she lifted her chin a notch. "I had no way of knowing I'd stepped into the feud between Forest County's own version of the Hatfields and McCoys."

Damn, she was feisty. "Leon could have any land he wanted, but he wants this place." When Charli pursed her pink lips, he answered her unspoken question. "I don't know why he wants it other than because of his hatred for Jock, and he wants to add it to Oak Springs' twenty-five-thousand acres." He shifted his weight off his bad leg. "Why did you choose him to get your fields ready?"

"Mrs. Pratt was adamant he'd help, so I called him." She pushed wayward locks of gold-red spirals out of her face. "He agreed to contract the men I needed to get my fields planted and the corrals fixed. By harvest, I'll have my own hands and farming equipment. Once the work's done, my arrangement with Leon will be over."

Leon was far worse than even a cottonmouth in her garden. Dylan didn't want her anywhere near his mother's stepbrother. Leon might have swindled Oak Springs away from his stepsister, but Dylan wouldn't let the bastard to take Blackwell Ranch from some innocent girl.

"Look. Just let me handle him from now on. Okay?"

Nodding, she huffed in a breath. The action pulled her tank top taut over her breasts.

"That's what you're going to be paying me to do," he said, as he forced his gaze to hers and not on her breasts.

"I guess we'll need to talk about your pay."

"I figured we'd get around to it sometime today." Her interest in Leon hadn't eluded him, even though she wasn't completely comfortable with the oilman. If her fidgeting with her arms was any sign, she wasn't too comfortable with him either. He wanted to protect her from Leon, which meant making her self-sufficient. "I think on Monday we should take a trip into Fort Worth to do a little shopping."

Instant suspicion narrowed her eyes, bringing a smile to his lips.

"What kind of shopping?"

"Oh, I don't know. Let's see." Shrugging, he started counting off his fingers. "We'll need a tractor--actually we'll need at least two tractors--a few ATVs, a skid-loader with all the attachments, farming implements, hay mowers for all that hay you're sowing. At least one, maybe two balers, depending on the size of the bales. Feeding equipment, a combine, tack for those horses you bought from Cartwright..." He looked around at the tall grass of the yard. "A lawn mower. Give or take a few small ticket items."

By the time he finished with his list, she looked a little green under all her freckles. "Can't forget those small ticket items."

"You sure can't. The sooner you cut your ties with Ferguson, the better."

He looked toward the house. Several of the porch posts needed replacing and the broken and weathered shutters were unsalvageable. The roof looked relatively new, but he'd have to check it for bad shingles. The inside couldn't be in much better shape. Besides the surface repairs like painting and replacing flooring, undoubtedly there was bad plumbing and wiring, too. He looked back at her. She watched him with intensity again, stirring his blood.

He glanced back at the house. "If you don't mind, I'd like to do some of the carpentry work on the house."

Her eyes widened. "You would?"

Would he?

He took off his hat, only to reset it right back on again, then cleared his throat. "Yeah. I would. I'll subcontract for anything out of my expertise, and I have a couple of guys in mind to help out with the repairs on the ranch buildings and fencing."

"The work you did on Tracy's salon is beautiful."

He slid his gaze away and shrugged. "Like her place, this old house has good bones. Unfortunately, I'll need tools to do the work. I have some, but not enough. I hope you have a business account with liquid cash or a bank willing to give you a loan."

She simply nodded and sighed.

"Why on Earth did you buy this dump?"

"I wanted a place I could make my own." She looked at the ramshackle mansion. "When the realtor showed me the ranch, I knew it could be beautiful."

The sun played on loose coils framing her freckled, heart-shaped face and the deceptive youth of her make-up free profile. The rest of her long hair was pulled back into a snarled ponytail. With the overgrowth of spring green, bluebonnets and daffodils tangled around her feet, she reminded him of one of the fairy statues his mother collected.

Charli peered up at him with an ageless depth showing in her crystalline eyes. She had seen more than she should have for someone so young. He vaguely remembered the kids in the bar last Friday night and their conversation about her not having any friends. What had happened to her to make her so guarded?

He jutted his chin toward the house. "It was a beautiful place once. Built at the end of the eighteen hundreds, after fire destroyed the original place. The house was white and the shutters and trim were dark red--you know, like a brick color. And the gardens were spectacular until Jock's mother died about fifteen years ago."

"That's how I imagine the house."

The deep intensity of her eyes pulled him in as if he'd walked off the dock into the lake beyond the overgrown yard. He felt things he hadn't felt for a long, very long, time. Charli Monroe's appeal went deeper than attraction. What about her intrigued him so damned much?

When she spoke, her soft voice came to him like a whisper on the warm breeze. "I think of it like a caterpillar--a wrinkly, ugly worm with traces of dull colors on it. But when the worm metamorphoses, it becomes something truly beautiful."

As if conjured by a fairy's voice, a small blue butterfly fluttered by them. It lighted on a spire of bluebonnets. He stared at until it took off in flight to land on another flower. "Like a butterfly."

For a moment, he let himself drift back to the day he'd carried Brenda over the threshold of the house he'd built for her, and the dreams that had died when he read her letter two days before the mission.

In a flash, the memory changed. He stood along the roadside aiming an M-16 at the man behind the wheel of a derelict car. After the man refused to get out, he had ordered his men to surround the vehicle, and the Arab driver sneered. Then it exploded.

Nothing in his life would ever be bright and beautiful again.

* * * *

Later that evening, Charli set two mugs of coffee on the table and took the chair across from Dylan at the kitchen table. He tapped a pen on the wood top as he mulled over something. On a sheet of paper before him were listed several things he'd need from the home center.

She sipped from her mug. "So, where do we start? The horses I bought will be delivered the Monday after Easter. Sheriff Cartwright bred one of the sorrels to one of his prized stallions."

He stopped tapping and looked at her. "You're not fooling around."

She shrugged and looked into her cup. "Once I get the idea to do something, I jump right in and do it."

"I can see that." He leaned over his arms on the table. "The stables look pretty damned good, surprisingly. They're not as old as the other buildings. Jock added them about twenty years ago when he decided to raise cutting horses to irk my granddad. The stalls need fixed and it needs cleaned out. I'll take care of those first. I'd also like to call the men I told you about while we were on the grand tour."

"The carpenters?"

"Yeah, Tom Miller and his uncle, Jesse Riley." He picked up his mug. "Tom got out of the Navy not too long ago and worked for his father-in-law's construction company, but he recently went out of business. Tom's wife just had a baby, and I know he'd appreciate the job. He and Jesse have been doing handy work in the area, and both men have some ranching experience."

"Okay. Call them. They can work on the fences and then the barn."

He took a sip of his coffee. "I'll get the storage barn in shape for holding feed and hay. It'll be a mess to clean." He lowered the mug and arched a brow. "But thanks to Uncle Sam, I'm no stranger to bullshit."

She groaned and shook her head. "That's just bad."

His lips twitched into the rusty crooked grin, and as it had the other times she'd seen it, a quiver tickled her belly.

"I know. My jokes used to be funnier."

Somewhere the real Dylan still lurked inside the shell. Would working for her bring him out?

"Tracy told me about what you're planning to do with this place once you graduate." He leaned back in his chair. "I think opening up your place to troubled teens is a great idea. Noble."

Heat warmed her cheeks, and she looked down at the mug between her hands. "I hope I can get the support of the community. Without them, it won't work."

"Get the Cartwrights on your side and everything will be fine. If you haven't figured it out yet, they pretty much run this county."

She smirked at him. "They do seem to be pretty high up the food chain. The mayor's nephew is the sheriff."

"Not to mention Winnie Cartwright is the queen of gossip." He picked up the pen and started tapping again. "Where should we start in the house?"

"We?"

"Of course, we. Tom and Jesse will be set to work on rebuilding the barn and stringing fencing. But I'll need some help in here. I can teach you whatever you need to know. Mostly, I'll need a gofer."

"A gofer?" She sat back in her chair and crossed her arms. "Sounds boring as hell."

He stopped tapping the pen. "Probably is. I can hire someone else if you'd like. I figured you'd be interested in helping, otherwise you'd have hired a contractor and been done with it."

How did he read her so well? "Yes, I'd like to help. It'll be fun."

"Fun, huh?"

She shrugged and picked up her cup. "Sure. But let's take it slow. Rome wasn't built in a day. Besides, the gofer has classes on Tuesdays and Thursdays."

He grinned and set off the fluttering in her belly again. How did he do that?

"I suppose on those days I'll kick back and relax."

"Not if you want a paycheck." She drained her mug. "Where did you learn to be a carpenter? Was it something you learned in the Army?"

Shifting in his seat, he looked down at his hands. "No, I didn't learn carpentry or plumbing or electrical work in the Army." He toyed with the pen. "When I was a kid, Dad was stationed in Heidelberg, Germany. Right about the same time the Berlin Wall came down. Anyway, because my mother loved the city so much, we lived there instead of on base. Our landlord lived in the house next to ours and was a local carpenter. He took pity on me, I think."

Folding her hands under her chin, she rested her elbows on the table. "Why?"

He exchanged the pen for his mug. "I was always something of a loner. Tracy was often my only friend. Anyway, Karl saw that and decided to take me under his wing, I guess. In the three years we lived in Germany, he taught me everything he knew. Including a very colorful vocabulary of German curses."

"You learned enough to build the beautiful house near Killeen?"

"So, you went to the ranch?"

"Yes. Tracy said it's Italian."

Nodding, he looked into his mug, then took a drink. "Brenda and I were stationed in Italy for about a year before Nine-Eleven. It's a sized-down replica of a villa we saw there."

She had to press him despite the dangerous ground. Understanding his relationship with his ex-wife meant she'd begin to understand what happened to him. "How long were you married?"

He didn't look at her, and for a long time, he didn't speak. He tensed, and she knew she'd overstepped. She was about to tell him he didn't have to answer when he said, "Eleven years. We met my first day of high school. Brenda was the prettiest girl in Colton High and was the head cheerleader. I was the new kid no one knew, a geek actually."

"You, a geek? Never."

"Oh, I was. I may not have been the stereotypical geek with the thick glasses and a calculator tucked into my shirt pocket, but I was an outsider. I could speak German and a few other languages, too, better than I could ride a horse."

He stood and took his mug to the coffee maker beside the sink. His back muscles flexed under his t-shirt as he refilled his cup. An eagle and flag tat moved under his right sleeve as he slid the pot back on the hotplate. "Brenda and I had biology together. I loved it. She hated it. By the second term, I was her tutor and quite infatuated. By the end of the year, she was my girlfriend, and we both had a much better understanding of *biology*."

He took a long draw on the mug and turned to face her.

Dylan didn't enjoy talking about his ex, she could tell, but healing required discussing and dealing with the things causing the pain. Wasn't she still learning that lesson herself?

He leaned against the edge of the counter. "We broke up a half dozen times. The longest time occurred while I went to Texas A & M and she went to Texas Tech. The last time was when I told her I was commissioning into the Army. But we always got back together." He stared into his mug, and his already deep voice dropped an octave. "Now, she's married to another geek."

"High school sweethearts," she muttered. She couldn't begin to relate. Her *high school sweetheart* had been an older cowhand on the Long Arrow. Danny introduced her to sex and marijuana. With him, she could forget the grief and the hatred of her new life, but there was a price. She had to steal from her grandfather.

When Hank had caught her with him, he'd fired Danny and threatened to send her to boarding school if she didn't straighten out. He refused to provide for another whore like her mother. So, she pretended to be the model granddaughter while waiting for Danny to come for her. When the loser hadn't come, she'd run away to Las Vegas two months before her sixteenth birthday with an even bigger loser. There she'd met the ultimate loser, Ricardo Rodriguez.

Oh, yeah, she understood losers. Sweethearts--not so much.

He downed his coffee, put the mug in the sink, and turned to her. "After we get the stables ready, which room do you want to start in?"

She stood and tapped her fingers on the table's edge. "I think probably the bathroom off my bedroom. I want to totally remodel it. For a house as big as this one, I can't believe it doesn't have more modern conveniences."

"Jock's parents added the first floor master bedroom suite. But Jock never did anything more to the house after they died. Okay, we'll start in your bath." He paused at the kitchen door onto the back porch. With an unsteady hand, he removed the brown Stetson from the peg by the screen door. "Miss Monroe, thanks for the coffee."

"You're welcome, but please, call me Charli."

He nodded once and donned his hat. "Likewise call me Dylan or Quinn."

She held out her hand. "Sounds good to me, Dylan. So, Monday we go shopping?"

His hand shook as he took hers. The sensation of his callused fingers brushing against hers sent tingles to her wrists. His eyes locked with hers, and he held her hand a heartbeat longer than needed.

"That's the plan. I'll be here at seven. Be ready to go." He stepped through the door. "Goodnight, Charli."

"'Night."

His warm touch tingled in her hand even after the door closed.

Chapter 4

Dylan pulled into a back parking space of the Longhorn's parking lot a little before nine o'clock. Loud country music filled the warm evening with the twang of a steel guitar. His hands shook as he cut the engine and opened the door. He hadn't had a drink since morning. He couldn't remember wanting a drink while he was with Charli.

Something about her downright fascinated him. Especially the way she'd filled out those tight jeans and little tank top she wore today.

Had he totally lost his mind when he'd suggested she help him? He'd figured she'd balk and tell him to hire someone else in addition to Tom and Jesse. Now, he wished he'd suggested hiring another person. He'd never consider Tim the Toolman sexy, but Charli the Gofer could easily become the stuff of fantasies.

Dispelling the memory of her touch as he'd held her hand, he entered the honky-tonk. The place was packed. The local band, Texas Justice, played the stage by the crowded dance floor, rather than the jukebox providing the constant serenade of Strait, Garth, and Brooks and Dunn.

He made his way through the throng toward his usual booth, but a young couple, who looked happy in lust with each other, occupied his favorite dark corner. A cowboy nuzzled the neck of the redheaded girl in his arms. A redhead like Charli. Shit, he needed a drink.

He frowned at the couple who had taken his table. Someone called his name over Logan Cartwright's loud rendition of Travis Tritt spelling out all kinds of trouble. He turned and saw Zack Cartwright sitting at a table near the dance floor. The last person he wanted as a drinking buddy was the Coke-drinking sheriff.

Looking around the room again, he found nothing. Resigned, he took the chair at Cartwright's table. Funny how things happen. Zack Cartwright could have been his brother-in-law. Zack and Tracy had gone to high school together and had been crazy about each other during their senior year.

Until she'd started dating Zack's best friend Jake Parker--without telling Zack she'd dumped him. After graduation, Zack had gone off to ride the rodeo circuit and won a couple National Finals Rodeos. But when Nine-Eleven happened, he'd joined the Marines and, like so many young men and women, had ended up in the Middle East where his life changed forever.

Zack leaned back in his chair. "Hey, Quinn."

He settled in the chair across from him. "You conducting a stakeout in the Longhorn, Sheriff?"

The Forest County sheriff, looking every bit the part of a cowboy, flashed a grin. "I'm not on duty." He indicated the stage with a jut of his clean-shaven chin. "I'm here to see my little brother's band. Lance and Audrey were supposed to meet me, but something came up and they couldn't make it," he added, referring to his cousin and his wife.

"I should make time to stop by to see them sometime." Dylan looked around at the crowd and searched for a waitress.

Julie Larson was waiting on another table. She'd get to them. Her job also included collecting the cover charge and checking IDs, since there wasn't a bouncer at the door. He often wondered how she and her sister, Ella, kept track of everyone, but somehow they did.

"Lance and Audrey would like that." Zack took a drink of his Coke. "So, I heard you're working for the new owner of Blackwell Ranch."

"Affirmative. Started today."

"I'm glad you found something, Captain."

He pinned the former Marine with a glare. He didn't deserve the title or the respect in the sheriff's voice. "Don't call me that."

Cartwright shrugged and looked back at the band, which started the next set with a cover of *Ol' Red*. "I wanted to talk to you while you're sober enough to understand."

"Ha, ha."

Zack raised a blond brow. "You can't deny I'm usually dragging your ass out of here."

"No, suppose not." He shifted in his seat. His hip hurt like a son-of-a-bitch tonight. "What did you want to talk to me about?"

"I'd like you to talk at the Memorial Day banquet I'm planning at the American Legion."

He narrowed his eyes on the other man. "No."

Cartwright leaned his tall frame back and crossed his arms over his chest. "Why not? I'm talking, and Uncle Paul's speaking about his time in Nam. We even have old Henrietta Parker talking about her days as a WASP."

"Good for you. Sounds like you don't need me." Where the hell was Julie? He looked around the room again. "Besides, I'll be busy. Have a job now and all that."

"Wow. What a slave driver. You can't even have a few hours off."

He shrugged. Julie waved, and he gave her a nod of his head.

"What's she like?"

Julie stopped at the table and smiled at him, although he didn't miss her apprehensive glance at Zack. "Your usual, Dylan?"

"Yeah. Thanks." Once she left, he looked at the sheriff. "Who?"

Grinning, Zack lifted his glass and took a draw on his Coke. "The girl who bought the Blackwell place. She's made quite the stir by buying that old ranch. Usually, we don't know one college kid from the next until they do something to draw attention to themselves." His grin turned cocky. "Which usually only involves me and my department. But Miz Charlotte Monroe has managed to have the whole damn town wondering."

He drummed his hand on the table. Come on, Julie. Where was his drink?

"She buys Blackwell Ranch right out from under your uncle, and she bought four of my best quarter horse mares." Zack chuckled and shook head. "Knows more about good horseflesh than I would've ever given her credit for."

"I don't know anything about her." He shifted in his chair again, but this time, his hip wasn't bothering him.

Charli had surprised him with what she envisioned for the ranch. Downright impressed him, too, with her knowledge about raising cattle. Maybe she wouldn't want to give the calves sissy names, but he still couldn't imagine her mucking the stalls.

His lips twitched. Looking in the direction of the band to prevent Zack from noticing his amusement, he forced a matter-of-fact tone when he spoke. "Like I said, I just started today."

Julie handed back his credit card and deposited a highball glass of whiskey over rocks before him. As he lifted the glass to his lips with a not-so-steady hand, he looked over at Cartwright. What a way to ruin a good shot of Jack. He couldn't even savor the smooth burn that would help him sleep tonight.

After he lowered the glass, Cartwright pointed at it. "You aren't planning to drive home, are you? I know Julie indulges you by giving you a bottle. I reminded her the last time I dragged your sorry ass out of here, if you leave and kill some innocent person, her behind's in the sling same as yours."

Dylan swore under his breath.

Zack Cartwright never drank, at least not more than an occasional beer, and he never drank alcohol and drove. He'd lost his wife to a drunk driver, leaving him a single father of a little girl.

Damn it, all he wanted was a drink, which he wouldn't get at the Longhorn. Standing, he leaned over the table. "You know I don't drive when I'm drunk. I'll walk home first. But I've decided I don't want a drink after all."

On his way to the only another bar in Colton, Charli invaded his thoughts again. He never talked about his ex-wife, yet he'd told her about Brenda. For some reason talking about her with Charli made him feel almost relieved. Was he finally over her?

* * * *

"You sure you want to take your truck?" Charli climbed up into the F150 early Monday morning. Duct tape patched the leather seats in a few places. The faint smell of stale whiskey clung to the air. She promptly rolled down the window.

Dylan closed the driver's door and looked over at her. "Isn't my Ford classy enough for you?"

"Not what I meant and you know it." She snapped the seatbelt in place. "I'm willing to drive, that's all."

He started the engine and headed down the long driveway, dust churning up in their wake. "I know."

"You don't trust my driving."

"No, I'm sure you're as good as any other woman driver."

She glared at him. "That was quite a backhanded insult if I've ever heard one."

As they bumped over the steel bridge straddling the creek, he spared her a glance. "It's not your driving."

"Then what?" She crossed her arms over her chest. "You don't like my Lexus?"

"Bingo. Besides, showing up in a luxury car at a tractor dealership is like showing up at a fancy diner with dirt on your boots."

She refused to concede he possibly had a point. As she looked out the window, she muttered, "Maybe I'd prefer to drive anyway."

"I'm not drunk. I haven't had a drink since last night."

She should ask him about his drinking, but dealing with a pissed-off Dylan for almost two hours would be about as fun as sitting in the dentist's chair.

When he paused at the end of the drive, she looked up at the broken arch over the gate. One more thing she had to fix. She'd wait until she had a name for the place before replacing the weathered sign.

They were silent until they reached Highway 6. She patted her thigh, restless until she couldn't take the silence anymore. "Do you mind if I turn on the radio?"

"Not as long as you don't turn it to a country station."

In mid-reach of the radio dial, she froze and looked at him. "You don't like country music?"

He glanced at her. "Not particularly. Some of it isn't bad. I like Southern rock, but the twangy, cry-in-my-beer stuff, forget it. Before you say something asinine about cowboys always liking country music, let me remind you I grew up in Washington, D.C. and Germany. Country isn't what I listened to, and I've never acquired a taste for it after moving to Texas."

"I won't turn your station, but I like country. My favorite singer is Nate McConnell. I play his CDs to death." Someday, she'd like to meet the half-brother she'd never known she had until last summer.

"I've seen him in concert a few times, and Toby Keith, too."

"Over in the war? I know they do a lot of USO tours."

"Yeah. They both put on a good show and support the troops. I'll give them that. But McConnell is a bit too sentimental for me. Do you listen to anything else?"

"I grew up listening to The Beatles, Elvis, James Taylor and Carly Simon. My mother loved the music of the sixties and seventies. One of her favorite bands was The Sisters McGinnis."

Before she could turn the switch, he said, "Jackie McGinnis is your neighbor."

Realizing she probably looked like a fish the way her lips gapped, she promptly closed her mouth. "No way!"

He nodded and glanced at her. "She's married to Luke Cartwright and lives on the CW Ranch."

"The mayor's brother?"

Dylan looked back to the road. "Yep, one and the same. She's completely embraced the life of a Texas lady. Wouldn't even know she's from California. Their son Zack runs his father's half of the CW Ranch

Their younger son Logan is a lawyer, but is locally famous for his band, Texas Justice. Not a bad singer. " He wrinkled his nose. "But Logan insists on singing those crappy honky-tonk songs."

She laughed. "Here in the heart of Texas that's not unusual. Cowboys normally--"

"Ah." He clucked and shook his pointer finger at her. "I told you not to go stereotyping."

"In my experience, you're a rarity and that was even before I found myself on my grandfather's ranch." She turned on the radio, and a loud screech of an electric guitar blasted from the speakers. With a wince, she lowered the volume from ear splitting to tolerable. "Do you have any hearing left?"

"Can't listen to eighties rock without turning it up."

On the radio, Axl Rose squealed about his sweet child.

"I guess, but keeping your hearing is pretty darn important."

She leaned back in the seat, pulled her knees up, and wrapped her arms around her legs. The next song was slower, and she sang along with the guys from Warrant as they got a little closer to heaven.

At the song's end, she opened her eyes and glanced at him. The intensity he peered at her with heated her cheeks. "Sorry. I happen to like that song."

"That's okay. You're a good singer."

"Thanks. But I know to never pack my bags and head off to Nashville." Even if she could be as famous as her half-brother, she didn't want the attention.

Dylan turned his eyes to the road and cleared his throat. "Tracy mentioned you lived in Vegas. Did you grow up there?"

For a few heartbeats, the familiar need to protect herself rushed over her. How had anyone learned about Las Vegas? She let go of her legs, giving in to the urge to hug herself. As she concentrated on the heat devils floating in the distance on the flat, lonely road, she decided she had to trust him. If she wanted him to open up to her so she could help him deal with his depression, she had to answer his otherwise harmless questions about her own past.

Some of his questions, anyway. She would never be able to open her home to teens if anyone learned about what she'd done in Vegas. "No. I grew up in Tulsa. I only lived briefly in Vegas. I was fifteen when I moved to the Long Arrow, my grandfather's ranch." Fighting a tremor in her voice, she asked, "Who told Tracy I lived in Vegas?"

"I don't know who told her." He flashed her one of those fleeting, rusty grins that did funny things to her belly. "I pegged you for a city gal."

"I was." Although knowing someone out there knew about her living in Vegas bothered her, she relaxed a little with his teasing. He didn't know anything other than she'd lived there. How did he put her at ease so effortlessly? "The first time I tried to ride a horse, I fell off."

"Everyone does one time or another. I was about four the first time I rode by myself. Before then, my mother rode with me or I rode a pony. Scared her half to death when I took a tumble right out of the saddle. After the cast came off my arm, the first thing I wanted to do was get right back up in that saddle."

"I was fifteen, too old to ride with someone, too big for a pony, and I climbed up on the damned thing backward."

His full-blown laugh surprised her. The deep rumble sent all sorts of tingles through her. He looked at her with amusement shining in his silvery eyes from under his brown cowboy hat. The small crinkles at the corners of eyes and the dimple in his left cheek caused her heart to skip a beat.

"You really are something, Miss Charlotte Monroe."

She got the impression he hadn't laughed like that in a very long time.

Whatever his demons were, she wanted to exorcise them. Dylan Quinn deserved to laugh again, even if he directed it squarely at her.

* * * *

"I will honestly say, I'm impressed," Dylan said as they sat in a fast food joint not far from the Monroe Farm Equipment dealership.

Charli sipped her drink. "Why? Because I dropped a couple million dollars without having to mortgage the farm?"

After finishing off his burger, he shook his head. "No, because you were able to wheel and deal with the salesman. Those two tractors would have cost you nearly ten thousand more if you hadn't charmed him down. But I'm more surprised you never IDed yourself."

She popped the last of her french fries into her mouth, and lifted her shoulders in a shrug. "I didn't want him to know."

"He probably would've given you an even better deal."

Looking up at him, she flattened her lips into a frown. "Possibly. But I didn't think it was important for him to know. Besides, I doubt my telling him Hank Monroe was my grandfather would have made more of an impression than my threatening to take my business down the street to the John Deere place did."

"Would you've taken your business elsewhere?"

She wiped her mouth on a paper napkin, and her lips curled up vixen-like. "Hell, no. I still get quite a sizable dividend check for the stock I own in the company. But he didn't know that. Another reason not to show him all of my aces before I was good and ready."

He shook his head. "Remind me never to play poker with you."

"I'm not sure I'd like to play with you either. The way you looked at the guy scared him half to death."

"I don't think he knew what hit him."

"Nope. We make a pretty good team." By tacit agreement, they slid out of the booth to leave. She picked up her purse and followed him to the garbage can by the door. "I didn't even have to wear a miniskirt to get what I wanted."

Did she have any idea how damned good she looked in her skinny jeans and high-heeled boots, which made her legs go from Earth to Heaven? Not to mention, the nice cleavage she showed in the white shirt. He raised a brow, but didn't say anything. When she noticed his attention and wrapped her arms around her middle, he looked away.

He busied himself with dumping the remains of their dinner. More than once, she'd hugged herself in that uncomfortable, insecure way. "Do I scare you?"

She met his gaze and dropped her arms to her sides. "No."

"But I did."

They exited and headed for the truck. She fussed with putting the strap of her purse on her shoulder. "A little, when I first met you."

"What changed?

"I--I did some research."

"Research?" Once they reached the pickup, he opened her door.

She stepped into the space between the door and him. "Yeah, I learned about the Special Forces and saw your work at Tracy's and your ranch. I asked people about you and decided you deserved a chance. Then I hired you."

How did he respond to that? Charli stood so close he could see the blue flecks in her otherwise green eyes, and smell her soft perfume...like fresh peaches. Swallowing down the craziest notion he'd ever had in his life, he backed away before he proved himself nuts enough to kiss her.

"I think we should get going."

He pulled his keys out of his pocket. "Yeah."

Several miles of freeway flew past them before he lowered the volume on the blaring radio. "I'd like to move into the bunkhouse."

"It's in pretty bad shape."

"I know. But I need to get off my sister's couch. I thought I could fix up the manager's apartment. I'll need the office to run the ranch anyway. I'll do the work evenings and weekends."

"If you want to fix the place up, I don't care. Order the supplies you'll need when you put the order in for the other work to be done."

He glanced at her. "Why do you want to open the house to teenagers after you graduate? Why do you want to be a social worker in the first place? From what I understand, the money sucks."

Charli took so long to answer he almost told her to forget he'd asked.

"I don't want to do it for the money." She paused, and he met her gaze, if only for a beat, but in that second he saw her vulnerability.

What the hell was she hiding? What was she running from?

"My mother died in a car accident when I was fifteen. I want to help others the way I was helped."

His curiosity was more piqued than before; however, she obviously didn't want to talk about it. "I'm sorry I brought it up. But if what I think matters, you've got it pretty much together."

"Thanks. Sometimes I wonder if this whole ranching thing is a huge mistake. I'm not worried about the money. Hank left me a rich woman, but sometimes I hope I'm not getting in way over my head."

He slowed as he entered the outskirts of Colton. "Hey." When she looked at him, he went on, "That's why you have me. I won't deny I have my own problems. But I promise you I won't let you down."

Earthquakes, volcanoes and tsunamis had nothing on the smile she gave him.

Shit, he was in big trouble.

* * * *

Charli refilled her cup of coffee and headed for the kitchen table. Her psychology book lay open, but she ignored the fifty pages of reading she had to do. Personality disorders just didn't hold much interest for her tonight.

Before coming back to the ranch, she and Dylan had stopped at a local home center, bought most of the tools he'd need, and put in the order for the building supplies, which were to be delivered tomorrow morning. Was spending the amount equaling the gross national product of a small country in one day still considered just plain old shopping?

She groaned. Leon had been right about the ranch being a big investment.

Sipping her coffee, she remembered the day. Damn, she liked the ex-soldier and his dry sense of humor. While Dylan didn't mince words, as

Sara Walter Ellwood

the drive to had Fort Worth proven, he treated her with genuine politeness. A true officer and gentleman wrapped up in a cowboy's packaging.

Had she actually opened up with him? She never told anyone that much about her experiences. How had someone found out about her living in Vegas? The court documents outlining her criminal life while she worked at the strip joint were closed, and Ricardo Rodriguez, the man she'd thought had loved her, would be in prison for a long time.

As a horrible hiss-buzzing sound echoed from the front of the house, she sloshed coffee over the front of her favorite Ralph Lauren top.

"Damn." She grabbed the dishtowel from the sink to dab at the dark stain on the front ruffle of the white silk.

The terrible sound repeated down the hall. Giving up hope the towel could save her shirt, she rushed up the entrance hall before the doorbell rang again, flipped on the light, and pulled the sheer curtain back to look out the leaded glass of the door window.

What was he doing here at this time? She opened the door. "Leon, hi."

He tipped his hat. "I'm sorry if I'm calling at a bad time."

"Oh, not at all." She stepped out of the opening to allow him entry.

"These are for you." He held out a large bouquet of yellow jonquils and bluebonnets.

Tentatively taking them, she looked up at him. He brought her flowers? Why?

Leon chuckled and removed his white Stetson. "The other day, you fell into a bed of daffodils and bluebonnets."

"You saw that?"

"Yes, I did." He stepped closer and his expensive cologne enveloped her. "I'm glad I stopped by when I did. Sometimes I wonder if Dylan is mentally stable."

"I tripped."

"From my perspective, I thought he'd frightened you."

She stepped away. With his dark hair and eyes and the way his expensive suit fit him, Leon was a handsome man. But she wasn't attracted to him the way she was to Dylan's brooding good looks. "His pulling that snake out of the lake surprised me, but I'm not afraid of Dylan." She held up the flowers and smiled. "What are these for?"

"A housewarming gift." Leon pulled a bottle of Dom Perignon from under his arm and held it out. "I thought we'd celebrate."

She stared at the bottle of champagne and the too-hot peppery feeling of anxiety rushed over her tongue, making it hard to speak. "Celebrate?"

"Your ranch is ready, and you've formally moved in. That's reason enough for me."

"Oh." For the first time in months, she wanted a drink.

Leon frowned. "I'm sorry if champagne isn't to your liking."

She forced her eyes to meet his and curled her lips into a slippery smile she hoped wouldn't fall away. "I'm flattered, honestly I am, but I don't drink alcohol."

Sheepishly, Leon held up the bottle to inspect it. "I guess I should've considered that."

"How could you know? Come on into the kitchen. We can celebrate over a cup of coffee."

Leon grinned at her, showing a mouthful of perfect white teeth. "Sounds good."

As she led him down the hallway to the kitchen, she caught him looking around the cluttered foyer. "Sorry, about the mess. I haven't finished unpacking."

"Completely understandable." When she motioned for him to have a seat at the kitchen table, he remained standing. "I'm surprised you have so many things. Didn't you live at Aida Mae Pratt's boarding house?"

"Yes." She laughed and twisted the large bouquet of flowers in her hands. "I originally was going to sell most of this stuff, but just never got around to it. Most of it belonged to my grandparents and my mother." She looked down at the flowers in her hands. "Right now I'm glad I have it. I think I know exactly what to put these in." She laid the flowers on the table. "Excuse me."

After rummaging through a box in the formal dining room of her grandmother's crystal earmarked for auction, she returned to the kitchen. She took care of the flowers and served coffee, then she and Leon sat at the table.

A warm and secret glow burned deep inside her chest. She reached out and touched the satiny bright yellow petal. "I don't recall ever getting flowers from a guy before."

"I'm glad to have the privilege of being the first, then."

Her eyes widened at the horror of muttering the words aloud. Blood rushed to the surface and scalded her cheeks. "I--I didn't mean to..."

He chuckled and lifted his mug in a toast. "To neighbors."

At least, he had the decency to change the subject. With a shaky hand, she tapped her mug to his. "To neighbors."

Leon sipped his coffee, and she was aware of his intense gaze. "I was startled when your name crossed my desk last week."

Oh God! He knew she was an ex-con. When she'd applied to the college, she was bound by law to admit to her police record. He was on the board of directors of the college. They'd discovered her police record involved something more nefarious than shoplifting.

"What do you mean?" She worked to keep her voice from shaking.

"Oh, nothing ominous, I promise." He sipped more coffee, taking his good time to explain himself. "I'm impressed, actually. Your grades are exceptional." He chuckled and toyed with his mug, turned it this way and that. "What did you think I was going to say?"

She pulled her hands under the table and threaded her fingers together into a tight knot. "You...just caught me off guard." Swallowing hard, she forced calmness back into her voice. "Why would you see my grades? I doubt that's standard board policy."

"Your transcript was submitted for consideration for a scholarship presented to the student who shows the greatest academic excellence. Despite you not meeting the income requirement, the board had to officially reject your nomination." He rested his arms on the table and leaned over them. "We don't see grades like yours that often. A solid four-oh. Impressive, especially for someone who didn't graduate from high school."

Leon Ferguson knew too much about her from a source she'd never even considered. "I have my GED."

"I didn't mean to offend. You have something to be very proud of." His grin was Texas cowboy handsome with billion-dollar charm, and it swept her fear away, putting her at ease. "I realize you took care of your grandfather's ranch, I assume that's probably why you quit traditional high school and got a GED instead."

She nodded, agreeing with his reasoning, even though she would've graduated by the time she'd taken over the ranch if she'd stayed in school. She'd earned the graduation equivalent while in prison.

He took another drink of his coffee. "I think you could do better than a degree in social work. Have you considered business?"

"Not really." She'd already had it out with her grandfather once she started taking college classes online after leaving rehab for her bout of alcoholism. She wasn't discussing her reasons with Leon. "I have no interest in getting a business degree."

"Ah, but you do own one." Leon looked around the drab kitchen with a hint of disgust he didn't quite mask fast enough before she noticed. He looked completely out-of-place in his designer suit. Did he consider the scuffed linoleum and outdated appliances beneath him? Shame for her home was instant and painful. Someday her house would be as gorgeous as his, though for now, it wasn't more than a supersized hovel.

Despite her own wealth and designer clothes, the shabby house was her home. A memory of Dylan sitting at the same table came to her. He'd looked right at home, too.

Leon met her gaze and leaned over his arms again. "Ranching is very complex, especially the cattle business. You want to breed horses, as well."

"I know. That's why I've hired someone capable of helping me run the business end of things."

"Of course. Dylan. I'm sure, if he can get himself straightened out, he'll do well. However, one should never rely on others." His brown gaze held her captive. "Relying on others only sets you up to be dependent on them. I wouldn't want that to be the case for you."

She leaned back in the chair and peered at the open psychology book before her. How did he know one of her greatest flaws? She always relied on the wrong kind of person, usually some dirt-bag man who used her and then threw her away.

Or as with the case of loving Ricardo Rodriguez, she'd landed in prison when she'd fallen for his lies and threats, and led him to the men he'd murdered.

She curled her sweaty hands around her mug and forced her eyes to meet his. "I've wanted to be a social worker for a long time. I want to help others. I'll probably take some business courses along the way, but right now, I'm at the college because of its social work program."

Leon smiled, reached over the table and squeezed her wrist. He chaffed his thumb over the back of her hand. His touch wasn't uncomfortable; however, it inspired none of the sensations Dylan's had. "Whatever you do, I know you'll succeed."

When Leon let go, she clasped her hands in her lap again. She had to stop fidgeting or he'd figure out she hid something.

"It's late and you look like you were busy before I popped in." Leon stood and she followed, unsure of the swirling emotion he left behind, glad he was soon leaving.

She pulled her arms around her middle.

"Before I let you get back to your..." He glanced at the opened book on the table. "Psychology reading, I was wondering if you hired any hands besides my nephew?"

She forced her arms to her sides. "No. I have a few applicants, but I'd like Dylan to help with the interview process."

"Of course, but if you need anyone until then, I can spare a ranch hand or two."

"Thanks, but I think we can get someone hired before my cattle arrive."

"If you change your mind, let me know. Thanks for the coffee." Leon retrieved his hat from the peg by the door, and turned, twisting the white Stetson in his hands. "May I make a recommendation for the job, then?"

"Sure."

"I recently had to turn down someone who was looking for work on Oak Springs because I can't hire on anyone else. Kyle McPherson. He's a cousin of mine and Dylan's, and he comes from a prominent family here in Colton. He's a good worker and had been a hand on his grandfather's ranch before he sold it."

"I think he called me yesterday. I haven't had a chance to call anyone back. Thanks for the reference. I'll definitely call him first now."

Leon donned the Stetson and opened the kitchen door. "Remember, we're neighbors. Here in Forest County, Texas, neighbors take care of each other. Goodnight, Charli."

"Thanks. Goodnight, Leon."

Okay, Leon. What the hell are you about? She wasn't afraid of him. After all, if he knew about her past, he'd be all over it like crap on a pig. But was he really her friend? After a few moments of staring at the closed door, she shook her head and glanced at the table. Her gaze snagged on the bottle of champagne. She grabbed it and ran out the door.

"Wait! You forgot..."

At the edge of the porch, she stopped. The taillights of his Porsche bounced over the bridge in the distance.

With shaky hands, she raised the bottle in front of her face. The light of the floodlight in the porch ceiling played harshly over the elaborate script on the label. She hadn't had a drink in over three years and hadn't been high for nearly six.

What she would do for a drink.

One bottle. No one will ever know.

Once inside, she ripped the seal open and headed for the sink. "I won't give in. I'm better than this. I'm not that person anymore. I'll never be her again!"

She found a knife, and after three tries, got the cork out in pieces.

The fragrant white foam, cool and refreshing, bubbled out of the bottle and over her hands. A tear slipped onto her cheek.

Just one sip. That's all.

"No. Damn it!" She wouldn't sacrifice everything for that drink, despite the intense craving. Unceremoniously, she dumped the contents down the sink.

Chapter 5

Dylan banged on the door. He'd told her to expect him by seven o'clock. So, where was she? He was about to pound on the old wood again, when it swung open.

"What the..." The rest dried up and turned his tongue to dust.

Charli stood before him glaring icy spears. Her face was thunderous, and her flame-like hair tumbled around her shoulders as wild as a range fire. She looked like some avenging goddess interrupted from her slumber and not at all happy about it.

A woman had never looked so amazing. Then he noticed her clothing, or rather lack thereof.

"I heard you the first time you knocked." Her sleep-roughed voice burned right through him and boiled his blood. "You didn't have to continue beating on the damned thing for the next five minutes."

Had he heard her correctly? The turquoise, short, silky robe his boss wore demanded all of his attention. As she heaved a breath, he caught a glimpse of the side of a plump breast where the robe lapels slipped open. A lightning bolt couldn't have hit him as hard. He fought the knot of lust tightening his gut as his gaze slid down her body. Holy shit, her legs were long and gorgeous.

Imagining them wrapped around him, he swallowed hard. When her bare feet and metallic purple painted toenails spun away from him, the hem of her robe swayed only inches from the curve of her ass.

Jesus. How would he ever get that vision out of his head?

Charli marched through the kitchen to the hall leading to her bedroom, leaving him all but hyperventilating. "Since you're here, make yourself useful and put on a pot of coffee. You look like you need it more than I do."

"I--" The distant slamming of a door cut him off. "Damn."

He fumbled around looking through cupboards for the coffee and filters. By the time the coffee finished brewing and Charli reappeared, his hard-on had gone down. Her hair was tamed and styled around her face. Tight black pants and a long yellow shirt replaced the robe, but her purple toes peeked out of the high-heeled, crazy-colored shoes she had worn the day he'd met her.

He cleared his throat. "I see you aren't a morning person."

She stepped up beside him at the counter by the coffee maker and took his proffered mug of black coffee. After she sipped it, Charli looked up at him and grinned, but a grimace from an ice queen held more warmth. "Whatever would've given you that idea?"

How could she make him want to laugh as if his life wasn't a complete cesspool? Snickering, he shook his head. "I thought yesterday's bad mood was simply because you were about to make some other poor cuss rich."

"I didn't sleep well last night, and I have three classes today." She guzzled more coffee. "I'll be human after I have at least one cup of java."

"Uh-huh." When was the last time he'd had a good night's sleep not brought on by drinking himself into a stupor? He took a drink from his mug and pointed it toward the schoolbook-cluttered table. "The flowers weren't here last night."

She glanced over at them and smiled. "Leon gave them to me as a housewarming gift."

He set his mug down with a thump. "Wasn't that nice?"

Narrowing her eyes at him, she refilled her mug.

He sighed and leaned his good hip against the counter. "Look, I don't like Leon. I don't trust the man, and I don't understand his sudden interest in you."

As Charli lowered the mug, she jacked a glare that turned the green ice of her eyes to pure fire.

"Wait! I didn't mean that as an insult."

"Really? Sure as hell sounded like one to me. You know, if you'd get your head out of the bottle every once in a while, maybe you'd realize you're usually a jerk." She spun away and headed for the refrigerator.

He was a jerk for warning her against the greediest son-of-a-bitch he knew? "Now--"

She turned back to face him with her hands on her hips, cutting him off. "I think I should lay down one very important rule."

He crossed his arms over his chest. "What the hell is that?"

"As long as you're working for me, I expect you to show up sober and to stay sober the whole day you're here."

"And what if I don't?" He didn't intend to drink on the job, but couldn't guarantee he'd always show up not hung-over.

She yanked the door of the refrigerator open. "I find someone else. Leon has offered his man, Garcia. Maybe I should take--"

He moved over to her, grabbed her shoulders and spun her around before he realized what he was doing. Charli stood close enough for him to smell the sweet scent of peaches and see the flecks of blue in her wide green eyes. Her face, which had been flushed with anger, drained of its color until her freckles stood out in stark contrast to her porcelain skin. He let go and stepped back. "I'm sorry. I shouldn't have..." He swallowed and ran his hand through his hair. "I warned you more than once about Ferguson. I won't let you give him this ranch. I'll buy it from you first."

The surprise left her expression. She laughed a rough, shaky gurgle, nothing like her usual lyrical sound of mirth, which made his chest tight with odd pleasure every time he heard it. "You've got to be kidding. You'll buy the ranch? Hell."

She bent into the open refrigerator. It wasn't a secret he was broke, but her easy dismissal pinched his heart in an unfamiliar and uncomfortable way.

Over her shoulder, Charli burned him with the fire of her cat-like eyes. "I don't really give a flyin' fu--I don't care what your deal is with Leon. He's done nothing to me. He's a gentleman and only wants to be my friend." She turned back toward him with a carton of eggs in one hand and a jug of milk in the other. "So, if you can't accept that, I think you know what you can do. Goes for my rule about your drinking, too. Take it or leave it. The door's open."

After setting the eggs and milk on the counter, she bent into the fridge again.

Fuck this. He'd leave and never look back, but his feet wouldn't budge. If he didn't know Leon Ferguson better, he'd have no problem believing that his interest in Charli was sexual. God knew he had a hard time concentrating with her bent in front of him rummaging around in the lower drawer of the refrigerator.

The slimy bastard never did anything without an ulterior motive. Sex was probably on his agenda, but Charli was helpless when it came to what Ferguson really wanted. Stubbornly believing she could trust Ferguson would cost her the ranch. Something about her dream to turn it into that butterfly just wouldn't let him walk out the door.

She faced him with a green pepper and a chunk of cheese in each hand. "Okay. No drinking."

Her smile nearly outshined the sun. "All right."

He wasn't an overly religious man, but he prayed he could keep the promise.

She kicked the door of the old, dented refrigerator closed behind her. "Did you have breakfast?"

"What?"

"Breakfast? You know…the most important meal of the day. Or was it a liquid one?" She raised a perfectly arched auburn brow.

"No, I didn't eat."

After setting a bowl on the counter, Charli looked across her shoulder at him and opened the egg carton. "My mother had this saying--empty bellies make for empty heads. So, I'll make us breakfast while you set the table. Afterward, you can attack those stables, and I'll go to school." Smirking, she cracked two eggs and dumped them into the bowl. "But first, I make one hell of a mean omelet."

* * * *

After Charli left her last class, she made her way to the new Sinclair Plaza Mall on the outskirts of town. The shopping center consisted of two national retailers, a superstore grocery and several other smaller shops, most of them chains.

She parked by the grocery store and pulled her purse from her book bag. She'd been in town long enough to know the downtown stores had protested the modern mall, a sign of the times.

As she walked to the doors of the store, she looked to the right. On a slight bluff, a housing development was going up. The houses were large and beautiful, but all very similar in design and colors. Mrs. Pratt had complained about the "city slickers" moving into Forest County. The flashy construction sign declared the contractor LBF Construction--a company owned by Leon Ferguson.

While waiting in line after finishing her shopping, she picked up the latest *Country Music World*. Her favorite country superstar, Nate McConnell, was on the cover. Did anyone else ever see the resemblance? Were they anything alike?

The pang of loss and loneliness was sharp and sudden.

She didn't know her father and never would. He'd died last August. Two months after his death, she'd found a box of her mother's old letters tucked away in the attic. Either her grandfather had intercepted the letters before they were sent, or her mother hadn't mailed them to the Texan and rodeo cowboy named John McConnell. He hadn't known he had a daughter--a product of a wild extramarital affair with a rich Oklahoma beauty queen.

What would her half-brother think of her? She stared at the picture on the magazine cover. She'd never know. Contacting Nate would risk exposing her past. He was a favorite topic for the tabloids and already had a flurry of interest due to a recent scandal with a Hollywood starlet. The news of an illegitimate half-sister would set the entertainment gossip world into hyperactivity. The last thing she could chance was a nosy reporter snooping around in her past.

Blinking away the familiar sting behind her eyes, she placed the magazine on the conveyor belt and unloaded the groceries from her cart.

After leaving the store, she put the bags into the trunk of her car. Two teenagers stood by a lamppost a several yards away. The girl was dressed in ripped up black tights, short denim skirt and jacket. Although the male faced away from her, she knew he was older, more man than boy.

Finished with putting the grocery bags away, she closed the trunk and headed around the car, keeping close to the car so they wouldn't see her. She got inside and ducked down to watch them through the passenger side window as they continued their deal.

Money exchanged hands--the girl to the man.

A small bag passed from the man to the teenager.

She'd participated in enough street corner transactions, both as a junky and as a dealer, to know a drug deal when she saw one.

The girl nodded at the man. He walked away and got into a pickup. Charli quickly memorized the license plate number. The teenager glanced around again, sauntered toward the center of town, passing Charli's car. The girl couldn't have been more than fifteen. Why the hell wasn't she in school?

Charli snorted. During her sophomore year of high school, she'd skipped more school than she attended.

Without hesitation or guilt, she pulled her cellphone from her purse and punched in 9-1-1.

After anonymously reporting the crime, including the description of the girl and the license number of the truck, she pulled out of the parking space. As she drove past, the girl looked at her and scowled.

Oh, yeah, you have an attitude, don't you?

What if someone had turned her in just once?

Would her life have been different?

* * * *

Charli put away the groceries and changed into shorts, t-shirt and sneakers. After quickly eating the sandwich she'd bought at the grocery store deli, she grabbed another bottle of water and headed out to the stables.

Def Leppard's *Love Bites* blared on the radio in the corner and a gray, smelly dust cloud of God-knew-what formed in the air. Dylan must not have seen or heard her come in. He used a push broom to sweep the concrete floor of the breezeway. He'd cleaned out the stalls and removed the broken stall doors.

Muscles slid and bunched his in shoulders and back under the dark t-shirt. The eagle and flag tattoo on his arm flexed as he shifted the broom over the floor. The worn Army fatigues fit him snugly, outlining his narrow hips and a perfect behind. Heat flared to life in the pit of her stomach, and she swallowed against the desert in her throat.

He turned and pulled the dust mask from his face when he noticed her. Paused in his work, he leaned on the broom handle. "I didn't expect you back so soon."

Her heart did a little quickstep, fanning the flames melting her insides. She quickly extinguished the fire. What was she doing? He was an emotional mess and he worked for her. She had no business having the hots for him.

She had a hard enough time dealing with her own baggage.

"My classes are all in the morning. I brought you a bottle of water." His fingers brushed hers as he took the cold bottle. When a tingle shot up her arm from the contact, she let go.

"Thanks." He guzzled over half of the water.

She forced herself to look over his progress. "You got more done than I thought you would."

He lowered the bottle. "I'm not a slacker."

She folded her arms over her chest. "I didn't say you were. I'm just amazed at how much you were able to do. Did you take any breaks at all?"

"Just to eat."

Had she snorted one too many lines of coke? Nothing about the man before her should have been remotely sexy. Sweat stained his shirt and whitish dust covered his hat, clothes and scuffed work boots. "Do you need any help?"

His lips tugged up at the corners as he looked her over. Sweet mercy, did he know what he was doing to her?

"Sure do. Those duds aren't worth more than you're payin' me, are they? 'Cause you're gonna get dirty."

Dropping her arms to her sides, she looked down at the Abercrombie and Fitch t-shirt and jeans shorts. "Are you implying I'm too prissy to do manual labor?"

His eyes twinkled as he finished the water and shrugged.

So much for considering him hot. She put her hands on her hips. "I can do anything I damn well please. What do you need done?"

He tossed the empty bottle into a wheelbarrow holding broken boards and other debris. "You can start by grabbing the shovel over there and use it to gather up this--*crap*."

She eyed the dark gray and black pile, but retrieved the barn shovel from the corner near the open sliding door. When she returned, he handed her a pair of gloves and a mask. Together, they finished cleaning years of dust and litter.

Afterward, he lugged out two sawhorses and a rotary saw to measure and cut boards from the pile that had been delivered earlier that morning.

Once he had a pile of varying lengths of boards, he laid the saw to the side. "Now, we'll build a stall door."

"Just what I've always wanted to do."

Dylan cocked a brow at her sarcasm as he bent and picked up two boards. "Okay. Come here and I'll show you what you'll need to do." He held up one of the boards. "This is a two-by-four." Indicating a wider but thinner one, he said, "This is a one-by-six. Got it?"

"I don't know." She scratched her head and scrunched up her face. "Is there going to be a quiz later? Because if there is, I may need to take notes. This is pretty hard stuff to grasp."

He positioned the boards on the sawhorse and grumbled, "Smart-ass. Get another two-by-four."

She grabbed the board and handed it to him. "Takes one to know one."

He met her gaze and held it for a beat before chuckling and looking back at his work.

Two hours later, they'd built two stall doors, and she felt grimy and tired. They cleaned up, as best as they could, at the tack room sink before going inside.

She scrubbed the last of the crud from her hands and arms at the kitchen sink. Glancing at Dylan, she didn't want the evening to end. "Why don't you stay for supper?"

"I think I'd better go."

She stepped away from the sink to allow him his turn. "Aren't you going to work over at the bunkhouse?"

He nodded and lathered his hands. "Yeah."

"Without supper?"

He shrugged and picked up the hand towel. "I won't starve."

"Maybe not. But I got some chicken breasts and was going to make a casserole my mom used to make. I'll have more than I can eat. So, why not share it with you?"

He studied her as he slowly dried his hands. "Okay. I'll stay. Need any help?"

With her heart light with a fluttery joy, she moved to the refrigerator to get the ingredients she'd need. "Doing what?"

He leaned against the counter at the sink. "Cooking."

She set down the butter and vegetables. "You can cook?"

"Don't look so surprised. My mother is a chef. I may have picked up a thing or two."

"A chef, huh?" She handed him the package of chicken breasts. "What do you want done with these?"

"Cut them into thin strips."

"Got it." He put the package on the counter beside the sink. "Will I be quizzed? I never was good at tests."

"Jerk." She held a large knife out to him as they locked gazes. He wrapped his hand around hers on the handle. Heat suffused her cheeks as she pulled her hand from his, but neither of them looked away.

As they ate the simple chicken and rice casserole, she said, "I have a guy I'd like to interview Monday for the ranch hand position."

He took a drink of his sweet tea. "Who do you have in mind?"

"Kyle McPherson." No point telling him Leon recommended him.

"Kyle worked on the old McPherson place before Sinclair Development bought it and Leon's construction company turned it into a mall and fancy cookie-cutter housing."

After taking a sip of her own tea, she set the glass down. "You mean out there where new grocery store is?"

"It used to be a beautiful ranch. The Circle M belonged to my great-aunt and uncle. It's not the only place Sinclair bought up and Ferguson's construction company built on." He lifted a forkful of chicken and vegetables to his mouth.

She looked down at her own plate of casserole. "Is that why you think Leon wants my place? He'd subdivide it?"

"I think it's a good possibility." Dylan laid his fork down. "Even in this housing market, Leon's making money."

The thought of a subdivision of nearly identical houses on her land made her stomach hurt. She took a deep breath and shook her head. "You know I still can't believe it. Besides, a developer bought that ranch, not Leon. If he really wanted this place, why not just make me an offer? It's what I'd do."

He curled his hand into a loose fist beside his plate. "Charli, you don't know Leon."

"I didn't know you either, and if I'd listened to all the naysayers instead of my instincts, you wouldn't be sitting here eating chicken right now."

He didn't say more on the matter, but she knew he wasn't convinced.

After picking up his fork again, he pushed the food around on his plate. "Kyle's my second cousin. We'll interview him, but I don't know if he'll be a good fit for this place."

"I guess we'll decide that together, won't we?" She went back to finishing her dinner.

"You're the boss."

"Don't call me that."

"You aren't the boss?"

"Yes, but I don't like the way it sounds."

"Whatever you want, *boss*."

When she looked up at him, he grinned. Her heart did a little flip-flop, and her whole world tilted. Why did she feel like things would never be the same again?

* * * *

On Friday evening, Dylan climbed the stairs to the apartment he shared with his sister. He'd hoped to move out to the ranch, but the bunkhouse wasn't livable, at least, not without a major update. Charli and he had spent two hours every evening working on the place, but it was going to take a while to fix the manager's quarters. Blackwell had been a penny pinching SOB and never fixed anything if he figured he didn't need it.

Bone tired, he limped through the apartment. His leg and hip burned with a deep throb. For the past four days, he had accomplished more work than he'd done in a year. He was the soberest he'd been in about as long, too. While with Charli, it was easy not to crave a drink. The first couple of days had been tough, but at the end of today, he didn't have the shakes anymore.

Over the weekend, he planned to go back to the ranch and work on the bunkhouse apartment. He didn't understand the anxiousness to move out there, and tried convincing himself he wanted out of Tracy's house. But the real concern lay with Leon Ferguson and his obvious scheme to woo Charli.

Yesterday, Ferguson had showed up with another gift--a dozen multicolored roses. The poor girl acted as if she'd just won the lottery. Leon's setting his sights on Charli and her refusing to see through his neighborly act made Dylan crazy.

As he entered the kitchen, the shower went off in the only bathroom. Since his nephew, Bobby, wasn't bombarding him with questions, the boy must be with his father for the weekend.

A note tacked to the corkboard on the refrigerator informed him a plate of food waited in the oven. He rarely ate the food Tracy thoughtfully left for him. After sneaking a peek at the leftover mac and cheese and fish sticks covered with plastic wrap, he wrinkled his nose and closed the door. He loved his sister to death, but the woman couldn't cook worth shit. Amazing, considering their mother had trained at one of the best culinary schools in America.

The memory of Charli's breakfasts and her interesting, yet good, dinners came to mind. Damn, the woman could cook.

After snagging a Budweiser from the fridge, he headed to the living room. He stopped and looked at his crap lying all over the floor. When had he turned into such a pig? He'd have had his soldiers by the balls if they'd kept their barracks like this.

Before he even took a draw on the beer, he set it on the end table and cleaned the room. When Tracy entered, he was folding the blanket he used at night.

His sister stopped and peered at him. "I don't believe it. I've been after you for days to clean up this sty. Besides, it's Friday night. Isn't the Longhorn hopping?"

Instead of playing into her sarcastic comment, he looked over her outfit of faded jeans, boots and a Western shirt, which she only wore to honky-tonks. "Hot date?"

"No. I'm going down to Waco to watch Logan play." She headed toward the dining table. "Hey, I left you supper in the oven. I fed Bobby before Jake picked him up."

His stomach churned at her idea of supper. "Thanks. But during the week I've been eating over at the ranch."

She looked over her shoulder at him. "Really? She makes you dinner?"

Since he hadn't been able to keep a secret from his baby sister since they were kids, he shrugged. "Breakfast, too."

Tracy's mouth parted in surprise.

Time to change the subject. He picked up his beer. "You look good. So, are you and Logan Cartwright an item?"

"You know better." Tracy busied herself with getting her purse from the table and digging through it.

"I don't know anything." He sipped his beer. "You're dressed like a woman who's hot to trot."

Glaring at him, Tracy pulled a lip-gloss tube from the canvas cavern in which she carried everything from her wallet to extra socks he'd seen her whip out once. After she'd swiped the goop onto her lips, Tracy dropped the tube back into the bag.

"Logan and I are friends." She grabbed her doe-colored Stetson off the table, then settled it over her long brown hair as she peered into a mirror over the sideboard. "He's my best friend to be exact, since my big brother is a jerk these days." She fussed with the soft curls she'd ironed into her otherwise straight hair. "Besides, I happen to like his voice. I want to see him perform."

He raised a brow, and she flushed as scarlet as the cowboy boots on her feet and lace trimming her shirt. "Okay," he drawled. "But, sis, I don't need the particulars."

"Oh, you are impossible sometimes." Tracy rested her backside against the table. Her shoulders slumped like a balloon losing its air. "You know what I mean."

"Want to talk about it?" He surreptitiously leaned his shoulder into the doorframe of the galley kitchen, taking his weight off his bad hip.

"Not really."

Tracy had guy trouble, and he'd bet his paycheck the guy was a Cartwright.

"Zack gonna be there?"

"Logan said he'd try to come. Depends on whether he can find someone to babysit his little girl." Tracy jumped away from the table when he raised the beer to his mouth, but not before she caught sight of his grin. "You really are a bonehead if you're implying I'm dating Zack."

He drank his beer and studied his little sister. "Something's sure as hell going on between you and our good sheriff--or his country singing brother--or both. I hear that's all the rage these days."

"Now that's just totally sick." Tracy grabbed a denim jacket off a ladder-back chair. "Nothing is going on between Logan and me, or Zack and me, and you damn well know it."

"Is Bobby with Jake on Sunday?"

"Yes. I hate not having him for two major holidays in a row. Jake had him at Christmas, too." Scowling, Tracy jammed her arms into the sleeves of her jacket. "That jerk wanted me to meet him tomorrow night at some sleazy hotel while his mother colored Easter eggs with Bobby. Can you believe that?"

Knowing her ex, he did. After all, Jake Parker had manipulated and lied until he stole his best friend's girlfriend away from him. His sister knew better now, though. "You aren't going to fall for his sweet talk, are you?"

"A certain place slightly farther south of Antarctica would freeze over before that would happen again." With her jacket in place, Tracy fussed with straightening the collar. "How's the job going? You haven't said much about it. The boss makes you meals. Sounds interesting."

He inwardly groaned and headed into the kitchen, paused at the sink and glanced at her. Tracy would get all the mileage she could with that news flash. "It's good. The job, I mean."

She stood in the doorway, trapping him in the narrow galley. Tracy grinned and crossed her arms.

Trying to sound blase, he sniggered and shook his head. "Don't you go and get any ideas in that head of yours. She's my boss. And a kid."

"You forget I've met her. Charli Monroe is no kid. Besides, I hear dating the boss is all the rage these days."

"Now it's your turn not to be an idiot. I've never crossed that line, and I'm not about to now."

"True, but you aren't in the Army anymore."

He tossed back the last of the beer. While he'd been a second lieutenant in Airborne, a female sergeant in his unit had come on to him. Up until that night, they'd been friends. He'd been married, but so was she. He hadn't pursued the harassment case, but he made sure the sergeant understood such fraternization was against the rules.

Rules he believed existed between him and Charli, despite his growing desire for her. Their professional relationship wasn't the only reason he fought the lust. He'd never let a woman into his heart again. If he made love to Charli, he wasn't sure he'd be able to keep her out.

"It doesn't matter. Charli's my boss and a kid." Before Tracy had a chance to argue, he said, "We finished the stables today. Monday we're interviewing Kyle McPherson for the ranch hand position and her horses are going to be delivered." He glanced down at his empty beer can, surprised he didn't want another. "Then we'll tackle the house."

"We?"

"Yes, we. Who else is going to help? Tom and Jesse are starting on Monday, but I'll be putting them to work getting the pastures ready for the calves when they come. A lot of barbed wire still needs strung." He threw away the empty can and turned on the water. He filled a glass, opened a cabinet door and grabbed a bottle of Ibuprofen. "Charli's no different than you were when we fixed up this place."

Glancing at her, he dumped four painkillers into his hand and imagined the gears turning behind her gray eyes.

She leaned against the doorframe. "So, what do you *really* think of her?"

Charli was smart, had a great sense of humor, didn't put up with any bullshit and had determination by the bucketfuls. He more than admired her for her ambition to make it on her own and suspected her past hadn't been good. She was too street smart for an Oklahoma heiress from some hick town barely boasting five hundred souls.

He swallowed the pills with a swig of water. "What's there to think about? She's my boss. As long as her checks don't bounce, I'm happy as a clam."

The chiming of the clock saved him from more questions. Tracy looked at her watch. "If I don't want to miss the show, I have to go." She pointed a finger at him. "You aren't off the hook, big brother."

"And neither are you, little sister. There's something going on between you and Sheriff Zack Cartwright."

Tracy threw up her arms and let out a growl. The unfamiliar urge to smile at her exasperation tugged at his lips. Tracy peered at him for a moment before she crossed the small space and wrapped her arms around his neck, hugging him close.

He'd been a bastard lately, and for the first time in months, he was sober long enough to realize it. Holding her close, he spoke into her long brown hair. "You be careful, sis."

Tracy stepped away, her eyes watery. "I will."

Chapter 6

"They're beautiful!" Charli bounced on the bottom rail of the corral late Monday afternoon. Paul and Luke Cartwright unloaded the four mares from the back of a horse trailer.

Dylan leaned against the fence and studied her. "That they are." He glanced at Luke Cartwright and his brother Paul leading the mares into the corral. "You did well, picking from Zack's best mares "

"Thanks. I love horses. I want to have my own foals and train my own horses for shows." Charli swung her legs over the top rail and perched precariously. "I can't wait to ride one of them. To ride them all!"

The simple excitement she found in rebuilding the ranch pulled him in. Charli had a way of showing him snippets of the joy he thought had died in his life. Like reminding him of how much he loved horses, too.

The quarter horses, two sorrels, a bay and a black, calmed down. As Luke closed up the back of the trailer, Mayor Paul Cartwright, approached Charli.

She hopped off the top rail. Her custom snakeskin boots landed in the dirt beside Mayor Cartwright. Despite still looking like she belonged on the cover of a magazine, maybe a cowgirl hid under the designer jeans, after all. Charli beamed at the older man from under the brim of a cream-colored Stetson and held out her hand to the older man.

"Miss Monroe, my nephew wanted me to tell you it has been a pleasure doing business with you."

Luke, Zack's father, shook her hand. "You have four extremely fine mares here. They'll throw some nice foals, but they're also trained to work."

Charli smiled at the Cartwright brothers. The late morning sun glittered off the hot pink nail polish at the tips of her fingers as she propped her hands on her hips. So much for the cowgirl image.

"Cartwright horses are some of the best in this part of Texas. I couldn't go wrong, now could I? Besides, I believe in helping out my neighbors."

One of the sorrels ventured over. Charli held out her hand, letting the horse tentatively nuzzle it. Starting at the white star between the mare's eyes, she ran her hand over the horse's long face. "I think I'll call you Aurora for the Roman goddess of dawn."

The men laughed, and Luke said, "Just like a woman to come up with a name like that. You aren't into that New Age stuff, are ya? Tarot cards and crystals?"

She smiled. "No, I just like Greek and Roman mythology."

Dylan raised his brow. "You aren't going to name the others some kooky name, are you?"

She rewarded him with one of her fiery glowers.

"You are. Let me guess, you plan to name the calves, too."

She turned back to stroke the nervous horse. "Of course, I won't name the calves."

The other three horses came closer. He rubbed along the neck of the gorgeous black mare stopping next to him. The horse stomped her foot and let out a loud snort as she tossed her head from side to side a few times. As he stroked her neck and shoulder, she relaxed.

Luke ran a hand over the black's face. "Zack wanted me to remind you about speaking at his banquet on Memorial Day. He really would like you to join him. Many of the older veterans want to hear about your experiences over there in the desert. I know you boys had it a lot different than we did in Nam. I'm sure Miss Monroe could spare you for one day."

He saw the tactic a mile away. "I'm going to tell you the same thing I told Zack. No. Not interested."

"Why not?" Charli jumped right on in. "I think it's a great idea."

Of course, she would think it was a great idea.

"I don't like talking in front of people." He gave her a look hard enough to let her know to drop the topic, though she wouldn't. He'd learned that pretty quick with her. "Maybe sometime you could bring Jackie by. Charli's mama was a huge fan when she sang with her sisters."

Pink tinged her cheeks. "Dylan! I can't believe..."

The wrinkles in Luke's weathered face bunched on either side of his mouth, and his blue eyes twinkled. He grinned and tipped his hat at him. Tit for tat. Luke, an old rodeo cowboy and all around country boy, hated to be reminded his wife had been a rock star hippie.

Luke turned to Charli. "I'll see what I can do. Most younger folks don't even know she was famous back in a day. Our youngest boy, Logan, is more of a celebrity 'round here than she is."

The sorrel mare moved away. Charli rubbed her hands on her jeans. "I'd love to meet your wife, and I have to make it a priority to catch one of Logan's shows. I've heard he's really good, from the girls at Pratt's."

Luke smiled with all pride and good will. "He is. Dylan, think about the banquet. We'd better get going." He picked his hat off his head of nearly white hair and nodded like an old cowboy at Charli. As he glanced at Dylan, he stepped away.

Paul cleared his throat and shifted his feet. "Miz Monroe, I don't mean to pry, but before we go, I have to tell you my wife shared something with me that just, well, sort of amazed me."

"What have you heard?" A tremor sounded in Charli's voice.

"That you were a runaway."

Winnie Cartwright could have told Paul anything, but Dylan never expected that--

The older men looked at her with a mix of curiosity and admiration. The color drained from Charli's face; even her freckles washed out. Paul must have noticed her response and quickly back-pedaled. "I'm sorry if I brought up a bad memory...I'm sorry, ma'am."

She backed against the railing of the fence. Dylan stepped behind her and placed his hand on her shoulder, offering comfort for something obviously upsetting.

Her back immediately stiffened. "How do you know about my running away from home?"

Paul took his hat off and wiped his brow with the back of his gloved hand. "I'm sorry if I brought up something I shouldn't have. Winnie said she heard it from one of her friends. Where she got the information, I don't know."

"It's not something I talk about. Thank you for delivering the horses. Good day, gentlemen." Charli stiffly nodded and strode across the corral to the gate.

Paul sniffed and watched her retreat across the driveway. "I just wanted to tell her I'm amazed she's turned out so well. I've seen her grades at a board meeting at the college. She's an excellent student and obviously knows what she's doing here with the ranch. I wanted to let her know I'm..." Shaking his head, Paul moved away, patted his astonished older brother on the shoulder. At the pickup, Paul turned back to Dylan. "Tell her I'm sorry."

He glanced at him and absently nodded. Charli kept her back ramrod straight and hugged herself as she headed up the walkway to the back porch. Ignoring the brothers, he followed her.

She stopped on the porch and stared at the old screen door.

"Charli?"

With eyes filled with pain, she turned to him. "I was almost sixteen when I left. The rodeo was in town, and I talked this guy I met into taking me with him." She looked down at the peeling paint of the floorboards.

The reasons a man would take a fifteen-year-old girl away from her home sent a shudder down his spine. No doubt, she was lucky to be alive.

"That's how you ended up in Las Vegas."

Charli nodded, then looked at him after a moment of tense silence. He followed her into the kitchen, but assumed she'd clam up and didn't blame her. He didn't like discussing his past either.

She stood before the sink and stared out the window above. Not expecting her to say anything, he didn't know how to fill the void.

"I thought I was in love with the cowboy. We ended up in Vegas a few days later, where he dumped me after hearing an Amber Alert was posted for me." More of her mysterious past. "Apparently, someone saw me leave Arapaho Crossings with him."

"How old was this creep?"

"Old enough to know if they found me with him, he was going to prison. Especially since his payment was my dead grandma's diamond ring and...and me."

Charli licked her lips, and he looked away. The fiercely primal need to protect her slithered around his gut and twisted his heart, like a mother bear with her cubs.

"You stayed in Vegas?" His voice came out as a low growl.

"Yeah." The haunted look in her eyes made him want to pull her to him, but with nothing but more pain to offer her, he could never follow through with the desire. "I was eventually found, but I don't talk about what happened in Vegas. You know what they say..." The idea of her in the unimaginable situation of being a runaway in Sin City made him sick. "What happens in Vegas stays in Vegas."

What could he tell her to take away her pain?

He busied himself with pouring them both a cup of the dregs from the coffee pot.

She turned to him and let her arms fall to her side, but quickly brought them back up to hug herself again. "Now you know my deep dark secrets. What happened to you in Afghanistan?"

Sharing his past wasn't something he volunteered to do, but before he knew what he was doing, he took a deep breath and sat her mug on the counter beside her and spilled his guts. "I was the commander for a mission that was supposed to flush out a group of Bin Laden supporters in the countryside around Kandahar. Most of the mission is still top secret. I can say this, I should have suspected the woman giving us information seemed a bit too willing to help us, but I didn't have my mind in the game the way I should have."

He didn't tell her the reason he couldn't concentrate on his responsibilities. She'd only asked him what had happened in the cesspool, not about his failed marriage and the letter he'd received two days before the mission. "I ignored my warrant officer and first sergeant's warnings."

She waited for him to go on, but there was understanding in her eyes if he chose not to. Although he rarely talked about one of his biggest failures, he wanted to share something of himself with her.

With the memory of the four men who'd died that day weighing heavy on his heart, he tightened his hand around the mug and looked down into the black brew. "I should have listened to them. Hell, I should have seen it for myself. We walked into a trap."

"The bombing."

He met her gaze and nodded.

"That's why you drink so much. You blame yourself for what happened."

He sipped the old coffee. The bitterness in his throat may have been from the brew or the grief, he couldn't tell. For the first time in days, he craved a shot of whiskey. "Four of my men died that day. How can I not blame myself?"

"Oh, Dylan, I'm so sorry," she whispered, laying a hand on his cheek.

The soft touch served to remind him how much he wished he could be the man he'd been before his life went to hell. He stood very still and peered down into her eyes. He'd wanted to provide comfort to her, yet she'd ended up comforting him.

"What do you have to be sorry about?" He forced out over the lump in his throat.

Swallowing hard so her delicate throat moved up and down, Charli rested her hand over his rapid heart. "I'm sorry you had to fight. I'm sorry you got hurt. I'm sorry I can't take away the pain."

He stepped away from her and toward the door. "I better go take care of those horses."

He couldn't bear to look at her and the watery pity he'd surely see in her eyes as he let the rusty old screen door slap closed behind him.

* * * *

A week later, Charli swung the kitchen door open before he had a chance to knock. She had a frustrated twist to her lips and a frantic gleam in her eyes. "I'm glad you're finally here."

After Monday's confessions, they'd spent the following days quietly working together in the storage barn, neither of them mentioning the past again.

Her skimpy satin shorts and tank sent him into a tailspin. "I'm glad you're glad. What's going on?"

"I had to turn the water off." She moved away from the door. "The damned faucet broke off the sink last night."

Soggy towels of every size and color were scattered over the worn linoleum in front of the kitchen sink.

He put his hat on the hook beside the screen door. "I guess we start with the sink today."

While she dressed, he ran to town to get the supplies he needed to fix the plumbing. After he returned, they had a quick breakfast of toaster pastries and milk, and then got to work. Dylan hated plumbing, but he could do it, especially when she offered a great distraction leaning over the counter beside him. When he asked her to hand him a wrench, she retrieved it from the toolbox on the floor.

She rested her elbows on the counter and her chin in her hands. "I really didn't need this. I have a statistics test tomorrow, the last one before the final."

He turned the wrench a few times on the pipe fitting connecting the base for a new faucet and glanced at her. "When do you do your homework? I never see you with your nose in a book."

"I do it before I go to bed."

"When's that? Sometimes I don't leave here much before nine. And then Leon always seems to pop in." He jerked his chin toward the table. "I see he brought you another batch of flowers."

Charli glared. "So? He's my friend. He actually helped me understand one of my statistics problems."

He frowned. She never asked him for help. "He helps you with your homework?"

"Only this one time. I was studying when he came over."

"You could've asked me to help you."

She couldn't hide her disbelief. "You know statistics?"

He went back to twisting a wrench around the faucet base. "I'm sure I could've figured it out."

Laughing, she leaned farther over the counter on her arms. "If I didn't know better, I'd think you were jealous of Leon."

He concentrated on the stubborn plumbing and tried hard not to look at the fantastic view the crescent of her blue camouflage tank top provided of her freckled cleavage. "There's nothing that bast--he has I want." He looked at her. "I just know what he wants, and I'd hate to see you get hurt."

"I won't." She pointed at the faucet. "Looks like we're done."

He removed the wrench and took her cue to drop the subject. He didn't like how his skin prickled every time he thought of Leon visiting her at night. "Yep. When did this break?"

She started to gather up the tools and put them back in the box. "About midnight when I decided to make a cup of tea. I was getting ready to finish some sociology reading I had to do for tomorrow."

"What time do you go to bed, if you're still studying at midnight?"

"I usually go to bed between one and two. That's why I'm such a bitch in the morning." She dropped the last tool into the box and wiped her hands on the back of her short denim shorts. Her smile meant to be apologetic, but her eyes twinkled with mischief. "Sorry you see me at my best."

"Is not getting enough sleep the reason you answer the door half dressed?" The question slipped out of his mouth before he'd thought it through. His brain was stuck on the way she looked with her hands in her back pockets. His childhood fantasy girl, Daisy Duke, had nothing on Charli in short shorts.

The lilt of her laugh sent a sliver of anticipation through him. "I'm not ashamed of my body, Dylan. I'm sorry if the way I dress bothers you."

Shrugging, he leaned against the counter. "Not at all. I'm an open-minded kinda guy."

"Good. Because getting up before seven is a real killer for me. Now, go turn on the water. I want some coffee, and I'll make us a real breakfast."

* * * *

Dylan sat beside Charli at the large table of his friend's cabinetry store in Killeen on the third Monday of April. Her calves had been delivered last Wednesday. They were settled, and he didn't expect any problems. Before he began the remodel of her bathroom, he'd called his cabinetmaking friend and set up an appointment.

Charli pointed to a glossy photo of a custom-made kitchen. "I like this style."

The father and son team had made cabinets for a combined total of fifty years, and Dylan had hired them to build the kitchen and baths in his house. Normally, he stayed away from things reminding him of his ex-wife, but this kind of craftsmanship was hard to find.

After studying the picture, he couldn't argue the washed-out white oak in the farmhouse styling would be perfect in her kitchen.

The cabinetmakers scheduled a time to come to the house to get measurements and finalize the deal.

They left the shop and headed to a German pub he had frequented while stationed at Fort Hood. Over their meals of Bratwurst sandwiches and sauerkraut, he couldn't hold back voicing what had bothered him ever since his cousin started working on the ranch. "Kyle seems interested in you."

Charli set her sandwich on the plate and wiped her mouth with a paper napkin. The action drew him in like a fly to honey. What wouldn't he do to feel those lips under his? The possibility sent a jolt straight through him.

"I would never date a man like Kyle McPherson."

He raised a brow. "Why not? As far as I know, he's not gay, and the girls in town seem to think he's good-looking."

She shrugged and sipped her sweet tea. "I don't like men my own age."

A terrible wicked hope burned into his heart. Hell, he was only thirty-six, and that wasn't ancient. "Okay" was the only response he could muster.

Grinning, she gazed at him with eyes so blue-green they were like the ocean, forbidding and inviting at the same time. "I like older men. I find guys my own age to be complete immature idiots."

She looked away, leaving him hanging somewhere between drowning in the pools of her eyes and floundering in midair.

He crashed down when he realized he wasn't the only *older man* in her life. Leon might be forty-two to her twenty-four, but morals didn't matter to him. Moreover, the lack of financial security and fear of a broken heart didn't hold that old bastard back. "What about Leon?"

"I appreciate everything he's done for me." Charli picked at the sauerkraut on her plate. "I just wish he'd stop bringing me gifts every time he visits. I love the flowers, but I never have anything to repay him with."

The instant fire climbing his neck had him breathing hard and his gut turning cold. He growled at the image of her and Leon together. "I can tell you what he wants."

She put her fork on the plate and narrowed her cat-like eyes at him. "You aren't going to insist he wants my land again, are you?"

He shook his head and unlocked his jaw. Picking up his glass of cola to keep from fisting his hand, he kept his tone as blase as he could. "Not at all. I'd say first he wants you in the sack as naked as the day you were born."

Her mouth fell open and she spread her hands over the tabletop. "That is the most vulgar thing you've ever said to me. Whatever happened to the *officer and a gentleman* attitude among you military types? Because no Texas gentleman would ever speak to a woman that way."

"First of all, I'm not a 'military type.' Second, I never proclaimed to be a gentleman of any kind. I just like the facts straight up. There's no bullshit to wade through to get to the truth."

Charli looked out the window beside them and jutted her chin a notch. "Sounds like you're just a jerk to me."

"You don't think it's true?" After taking a much-needed gulp of his soda, he set the glass down with a thud. "Fine, in nicer language here's what I think. Leon wants you. He's wooing you, and you're falling for his crap hook, line, and sinker. And once you're reeled in, he'll take that land and leave you high and dry."

"I'm not falling for anyone's 'crap' because I've sworn off men after my last disastrous relationship."

What happened to you?

She changed the subject and asked about her bathroom remodel. Good move. He was starting to act like a jealous jackass.

* * * *

Charli heard another curse and cringed as she carried two glasses of sweet tea through her bedroom, heading for her en suite bath. For her to be able to hear it over the humming of fans and Kiss blaring from the speakers of her bedroom stereo, Dylan was incensed.

After fixing the kitchen plumbing three weeks ago, he'd replaced all the plumbing in the house. They'd had to pause in the work to get the calves in and order the new kitchen, but today, they'd started working in the bathroom. The new shower and garden tub had gone in easily enough. The sink plumbing, though, gave him trouble.

Sara Walter Ellwood

On top of it, yesterday's storms did nothing but increase the humidity level to unbearable, and her air conditioner had broken down during one of the violent thunderstorms.

"Dammit." A loud thunk sounded followed by "Ouch!" and a string of expletives--some of them German.

"Dylan, are you okay?" She rushed to the door, only to stop dead in the opening. Oh, sweet mercy! *Hot* didn't begin to describe the shirtless man lying on his back with his head buried in the cabinet. When she'd left him twenty minutes ago to answer the phone, he'd had his t-shirt on.

"Yes," he snapped. He strained, twisting a wrench on the old metal pipe. "This damned thing is...rusted...tight."

He let out another curse and more clanging followed. Bands of muscles rippled under the tan skin of his biceps and chest as he worked the wrench on the pipe. The eagle and flag tattooed on his upper arm took flight as he flexed the muscle beneath it.

Her gaze moved over the dark dusting of hair on his chest where he had another tattoo on his left pectoral--a green beret over a sword with some Latin words above it. Before she could figure out what it said, she noticed the jagged, silvery scars. Like some grotesque spider web glistening in the morning dew, they cut across his belly and down his right side to disappear under the edge of the faded Wranglers resting low on his hip.

Her eyes stopped at his belted waistband. The scars weren't ugly to her, but in that defining moment, she visualized his war injuries. Sadness, and at least a half dozen other emotions she didn't understand or want to analyze, bombarded her, quickening her heart. However, she couldn't ignore the instant liquid heat pooling in her belly.

"What did they say?" His muffled voice came from under the sink and drew her back to where his head should have been.

"Ah... The repairman can't come out until tomorrow morning." Her mouth was dry, and she gulped down some of the tea. The sudden spike in the temperature had nothing to do with her malfunctioning air conditioner.

He moved out from under the sink and looked at her. The fluid motion in which he stood--considering his bum leg--stunned her. He reached for the white t-shirt hanging over the towel rack. "I'm sorry. But it's hot as hell under there."

After setting the iced teas on the vanity top, she laid a hand on his arm to stop him. The sensation of his hot, damp skin under her cool palm overwhelmed her.

He turned blazing eyes on her and made no move to don the shirt.

Hadn't she sworn off men? Hadn't her life with Ricardo shown her men were nothing but total sadistic assholes? Didn't she vow she'd never fall for another lying jerk who'd only break her heart when he was tired of her?

Her body betrayed her good sense and her voice came out breathy. "Don't. It's a furnace in here. If you're more comfortable with your shirt off, it's okay."

His gray eyes darkened to a shimmery, bluish hue of a summer day. With jerky movements, Dylan opened the bottom of the shirt. "I don't think either of us would be comfortable if I went shirtless."

Oh, yeah, his working shirtless would make her squirm. When she'd first met him two months ago, his dark brown hair had been short, but now it fell over his forehead and curled around the tops of his ears. A small scar ran along the sharp angle of his right cheek under the dark shadow of beard he hadn't shaved that morning.

She let her gaze slip down over his work-toned body. His shoulders were broad, biceps muscular. The scars and tattoos gave him a dangerous edge she should run from, not eat up like eye candy.

As he pulled the shirt over his head, she reached out and skimmed her fingertips over the largest of the scars on his abdomen. Dylan shivered, yanked the shirt off before putting it completely on, and dropped it on the floor. He grabbed her wrist to pull her against him, and held her.

Her head spun, and her heart sputtered as his mouth lowered hard on hers. He licked at her upper lip, and she opened for him to plunge his tongue into the depths of her mouth.

Worlds collided, stars collapsed into black holes and whole oceans turned to deserts in their kiss.

His hands moved to her hips. Without breaking the kiss, he lifted her unto the edge of the sink. She wrapped her legs around him and crossed her ankles over his behind. When she pulled him as close as he could get with their clothing in the way, he groaned. She couldn't get enough of him and pressed her center into his impressive erection. He held her there, and somewhere in the cosmic haze, she realized they were dangerously close to giving in to the raw desire sizzling between them.

Her hands moved between their bodies through the soft curls up his chest. His hands molded over her breasts under her tank top. A moan escaped her when he flicked his thumbs over her aroused, satin-covered nipples. She wanted to touch him everywhere and wanted to be touched everywhere by him.

With a growl deep in his chest, he broke the kiss and pulled back. She opened her eyes to meet his. Why was he pushing her away?

The scowl twisting Dylan's flushed face wasn't that of a man who wanted to have hot, sweaty sex on the bathroom sink. He looked like he regretted every kiss, every touch, every utterance.

He untangled her legs from around his hips with hot hands. Once he was free, he lifted her off the edge of the sink to stand before the cabinet. Weak-kneed, she grabbed hold of the old ceramic top and leaned against it.

Stabbing both hands through his hair, he turned away with ragged breaths. "We can't. It's not right. You're my boss."

"Dylan, it was just a kiss, which we both wanted."

He bent to pick his shirt off the tile floor. "That wasn't just a kiss. And we both know it." With his back to her, he quickly pulled the t-shirt over his head. "I'm sorry. It won't happen again."

The growing dread of rejection and humiliation settled over her like cold, wet blanket. She stared at him for a moment, not believing he meant the passion in his kiss and touch. A muscle twitched in his clenched jaw and pain glowed in his eyes. Dylan desired her, but he wished he didn't.

"I'm not ready for this, Charli."

"Because of...your ex?"

He sucked in a breath, averted his eyes and nodded.

* * * *

"Aw, shit." Dylan ran his hands through his hair again and grumbled, "What the fuck do you think you're doing, Quinn?"

Like a monk, he'd fought the lust burning him alive since the first day she answered her door wearing nothing but a robe. As he worked, he hadn't missed the desire smoldering in her tilted turquoise eyes. Could even a monk continue to resist temptation with the knowledge an angel wanted him as much he wanted her?

When she'd touched him, a match ignited a fuse. Somewhere buried deep in the years of discipline he'd lived and breathed as a commander, he had found the strength to step away. But letting her go was as torturous as willingly walking a minefield. If he hadn't, he'd have stripped her right there on the bathroom sink and had sex with her.

The unbridled, raunchy kind they'd both regret.

Damn, what he wouldn't do for a drink.

In the kitchen, he caught up with her. Charli stood at the sink, staring out the window and hugging herself.

He couldn't hide in a drunken stupor concerning this mess.

She spun on him, but she didn't speak or accuse him of anything. As his boss, she didn't fire his ass for inappropriate behavior. Instead of staring up at him with her green-eyed glare as he'd come to expect, she hugged herself and sucked in her lip in the insecure gesture of a girl who didn't know how to face the world.

"Charli?"

She shook her head and sniffed. "Don't. I get it. You're not over your ex. Besides, I'm your boss and it was wrong." Her breasts rose and fell as she sucked in a deep breath, then she dropped her arms to her sides. He had seen the transformation before. "Forget it happened and chalk it up to the heat and humidity. Let's get back to work. I want the bathroom done by Wednesday."

Chapter 7

Charli had never been so glad to see Friday come. Besides being tired from the physical labor she'd done over the past several weeks, the tension between her and Dylan was as thick as the muggy Texas days since the kiss on Monday.

She set the last paintbrush on a paper towel beside the sink in the manager's apartment and looked around the room making up most of the living space. The kitchenette, a bathroom and a laundry-utility closet lined one wall. The manager's office adjoined the studio.

She hadn't held much hope for the bunkhouse apartment when she'd first seen it. Until Dylan had asked to move into the small, semi-detached manager's apartment, she'd considered having the bunkhouse demolished.

Instead, they had managed to transform the rat-infested mess into living quarters.

She went about cleaning the sink and wiping down the small counter space. When Dylan entered from the office, she asked, "Do you want to go to the mall over in Waco tomorrow?"

He dumped a ball of painter's tape into the trashcan. "For what?"

She finished drying her hands and shrugged. "I need living room furniture and this place needs furnished." She hung the towel over the oven door handle.

He puckered his brow. "I'll take care of the furniture for this place."

She crossed her arms over her chest and leaned against the oven door. "I can understand why you'd want to, but I'm willing to buy whatever you'll need."

His expression turned dark. "Stop."

She pushed away from the counter to face him and dropped her arms to her sides. "What?"

"Constantly psychoanalyzing me."

"I don't do that."

"Yes, you do. You do it all the time." He turned away and ran his hand through his hair, an agitated habit she'd noted when he was as upset with himself as with her. "I've ignored it until now, but dammit, I'm tired of feeling like a bug under a microscope."

"What the hell are you talking about?"

Dylan stepped closer and peered down at her. "You feel pity for me, so you think you understand me. You don't know jack-shit about me."

She threw up her arms and spun away. "Fine. Forget I suggested it. I was only trying to help. After all, this is still my property and I was going by the example my grandfather set. He always furnished the bunkhouse on the Long Arrow." She faced him. "But now I don't care if you sleep on the damned floor."

"Does that mean I can drink here?"

She wished he wouldn't drink alone, but she couldn't stop him. Drinking alone had almost killed her when she tried to drown her guilt over the murder she'd helped Ricardo to commit. "I don't care what you do here. But my rule still holds, if you show up drunk or drink on the clock. I'll find someone else."

He turned away and headed across the empty room. "Just wanted to make sure I have some freedom." His hands clenched into fists and unclenched at his sides. The muscles in his jaw ticked as he clamped down on his teeth. "I know what you're up to, Charli. I know you think you can save me from myself. Hell, that's probably the only reason you're so hot and bothered when it comes to me. You know, like when the doctor falls for the patient."

Not wanting to hear more, or say something she'd regret, she walked passed him. She was halfway to the office door when he said, "If I wanted a shrink, I'd still be going to the one Uncle Sam provided."

She forced the pain in her heart into anger and whirled around to face him. "You know what the hell your problem is?"

"No, but I'm sure you'll tell me." He went to the refrigerator and grabbed a bottle of water.

"Yes, I will tell you, you pigheaded jerk. I don't feel sorry for you. You do plenty of that yourself. Yes, I wanted to help you. I want you to be happy. Because I respect you."

He shut the door and stared over his shoulder at her. The portion of the eagle and flag tattoo showing under the sleeve of his t-shirt quivered as he flexed the muscle underneath.

"That's right, I respect you. I think you have an amazing talent for this kind of thing." She waved her hand, taking in the room. "I see how good you are with my animals and the men we've hired. Even with Kyle, though you can't stand him. You don't push, and you don't tell them to do anything you wouldn't do yourself. You're here every day before the crack of dawn to ride fences and often take care of things before the other guys show up. You've never taken a day off. Even on Easter, you were here, working on the apartment."

She paused and swallowed hard. Despite her vow never to do it again, she was falling in love with Dylan Quinn. "I'm sorry I crossed some invisible line the other day and ruined our friendship. I shouldn't have touched you, and I shouldn't have wanted you to kiss me. But dammit, I won't be sorry for the kiss."

Before she said anything else she'd never be able to take back, she turned and rushed through the office and into the early May evening.

* * * *

What the hell just happened? Dylan crossed the room to the office. Why did he get so upset when she suggested buying furniture for the apartment? The only excuse he could figure was letting her furnish his apartment further illustrated his financial status as compared to hers.

"Damn it all to hell." He looked out the window into the darkness and shoved his hands into his pockets.

She drove him crazy. He'd started drinking again at night. This time wasn't to forget the war or Brenda, but to forget how much he lusted after his twenty-four-year-old boss. A woman who he knew had the potential to break his heart if he let her.

He should talk to Julie Larson again. They'd planned to meet the night Brenda remarried, but he hadn't been able to bring himself to go through with it, and this was no different. He'd never slept around. While he'd been with Brenda, he'd been faithful. During the few times they'd separated between dating, he'd had other girlfriends and sowed his share of wild oats, but hollowness had followed those encounters. Making love to Brenda had made him feel alive.

He turned to face the screen door Charli had exited. The realization hit him square in the chest, making it hard to breathe.

Charli made him feel alive by just smiling at him.

* * * *

The house was a sanctuary from the tension she'd escaped, but Charli couldn't leave behind her realization.

Or the fact Dylan didn't feel the same about her.

After brewing a cup of herbal tea, she pushed thoughts of her moody manager from her mind. Somehow, she'd managed to help him with plumbing and painting the bathroom, redecorating the living room, and with his apartment, and still aced her finals this past week. She only had a paper due on Monday and the semester was over. At the table, she booted up her laptop to the research paper. She forced Dylan's rejection from her mind and focused on her work.

Lost in the effects of child molesters and sex offenders on society, she almost didn't hear the doorbell. After hitting the *save* icon, she went to the front door and looked out the window. Leon stood on the porch with a bouquet of red roses.

Oh, Leon, not another gift. But she couldn't deny she enjoyed her friendship with her neighbor. Every time he'd seen her, he'd given her a gift. Flowers, gourmet coffees, expensive teas--she would send him a small note of thanks and tried to discourage further gifts. Either she wasn't good at polite discouragement, or he was ignoring her.

She opened the door with a smile. "Leon, hi."

"Good evening. I thought I'd stop over to see how things are going."

Dressed in black jeans, a white shirt open at the collar, and ostrich skin boots, Leon Ferguson struck a handsome pose holding the roses toward her. But it was the megawatt smile that caused her to giggle. Could he be any more obvious with his intentions?

"You know you shouldn't keep doing this. Thank you. Come in." Taking the roses, she allowed him entry. As he removed his white Stetson, Leon looked through the doorway into the living room, which she and Dylan had painted earlier that day.

"You've been busy."

"We tackled the living room yesterday and today."

Leon followed her down the entrance hall to the kitchen. "I was riding this morning and thought we should go together sometime. I could either meet you here or you could come over to Oak Springs."

"Oh, I'd love to. I'm curious to see more of the famous Oak Springs Ranch." She sniffed the fragrant roses and sighed. "I wish I could do more riding, but I've been so busy. How're the negotiations in Colorado going?"

"Unfortunately, not well, but my lawyers are working on it. But enough about that. I like to leave my business in the office as much as possible." Leon hung his Stetson on a peg by the door and then leaned a hip against the counter by the sink. "Is Kyle working out?"

She filled her grandmother's crystal vase with water from the tap and arranged the roses. "Yes. He's great with the calves."

"How're the calves doing? The loss of one or more isn't unusual until they get settled in."

"They're good. I haven't lost a single steer. Not even one got sick. Dylan really made sure he took care of getting them settled into good pasture. I wish I could watch them more. They like to play and chase each other and are so darned cute." She glanced at him and heat prickled her cheeks. "I suppose that's an odd comment coming from someone who's raising them so they can become someone else's steaks and hamburgers."

"Hamburgers can be beautiful and a good steak is downright gorgeous." Leon grinned at her and shrugged. "To a hungry man."

She laughed and brushed a hand over her messy ponytail. "I must look a sight."

"I think you look like you've been working too hard. But even so, you're as lovely as ever."

Her cheeks burned, and she gestured a hand toward a chair at the table. "You and your flattery. You should know I'm immune to it."

"I've never flattered a single person, ever." Leon held up his right hand, three fingers extended. "Scout's honor."

"Were you ever a Boy Scout?"

"Oh, I think that would be telling on myself."

Shaking her head, she turned toward the old electric stove. "I was having herbal tea. Would you like some, or would you prefer sweet tea? Or I can make coffee."

"Sweet tea sounds good. Thank you."

After handing him the glass of tea, she refreshed her herbal tea from the teapot on the stove and they sat at the table.

"You haven't made much progress in your gardens."

Hugging her mug as she set it on the table, she sighed and shook her head. "One more thing I haven't been able to do. With school and working on the ranch and in the house with Dylan, I haven't had time to do much else."

Leon frowned and set his glass onto the oak top. "He isn't still insisting you help, is he?"

"He doesn't insist. I willingly help. We make a good team, too. Dylan and I did everything until Kyle, Tom and Jesse started."

"But you shouldn't have to." The knuckles of the hand encircling his glass grew white as if he was clenching his hand. A beat later, he relaxed his hand and grinned. His usual charm in place. "You should be watching your calves playing in the pastures, riding your beautiful horses, and working in your gardens." Leon brushed his fingertip across her cheek, and his voice lowered an octave. "You shouldn't be painting unless it is of a landscape while sipping tea."

She locked gazes with him and covered his fingers with her own. His touch was warm and gentle, but felt all wrong. She leaned back and out of his reach.

"I could help you out."

"How?" she asked a bit shakily.

"I own one of the best construction companies in the county." Leon looked around the kitchen. As a few times before, a disgusted frown pulled at his lips before he covered it almost as quickly as it appeared. Had she seen it at all? "A crew could have this place looking like a palace fit for a princess in a matter of a week or two. How long do you think it will take Dylan to do it?"

Should she take him up on his offer? But if she did, how could she help Dylan? He might not want her romantically, but he seemed to take pride in his work. Something she knew he hadn't felt in a very long time. She met Leon's gaze again and shook her head. "No, I want Dylan to work on the house. He's teaching me what needs to be done as we go, which I'm enjoying even if it means not doing other things I enjoy too. With summer, I'll have more free time. I really want this place to be mine. That was what drew me to it and why I didn't approach a construction company to begin with. I wanted to be part of the restoration, and I am."

"I'm pleased he's working out." Leon sipped his iced tea, but not before she caught the twist of his lips. But as before, he covered it so quickly she wondered if she'd seen anything at all. "Tracy and I talk regularly, and she told me Dylan has been acting more like himself since starting to work for you. We were all worried about how much he's been drinking. I guess he's lucky to be alive after what happened to him in Afghanistan. Has he told you anything about it?"

"He told me some of what happened."

"It is a shame. I can't imagine what it's like feeling responsible for one person's death, let alone four. All of it really should be blamed on his ex-wife."

"Because she had an affair while he was overseas?"

He blinked. Was he surprised Dylan had been so forthright with her?

"Yes. I was extremely saddened when I heard what Brenda did to Dylan." He sipped his tea and averted his gaze. "I don't think he will ever get over her betrayal. She sent him a Dear John letter only a day or two before the mission. He just wasn't thinking and led those men into a trap. He loved her. Still does, if Tracy can be believed."

She picked up her cup to take a drink, but her hand shook too much. Was there ever any chance for her and Dylan? After she lowered her mug, she touched one of the roses. "Really, you don't have to continue giving me flowers. I have the ones you gave me Saturday in my bathroom."

* * * *

"Aw, but I enjoy giving you flowers."

Dylan would recognize that pretentious Texas drawl anywhere and stopped short of stepping into the light spilling through the screen door onto the back porch. The kitchen door stood open, and he could see Charli and Leon sitting at the table, a bouquet of roses between them.

"Thank you. I do love them."

"Then why should I stop?"

Because she asked you to. He considered barging in until he heard Charli laugh.

"Got a point there, I suppose."

Leon took her hand from where it lay beside her cup. "I'm hoping you'll agree to have dinner with me next Friday night. I have some important business all week and won't be back in town until then."

"Oh." Would she tell the son-of-a-bitch where to go? "I think that would be nice."

"Wonderful. I'll send a car at seven sharp."

Leave. Something terrible kept him rooted to the porch step. His heart beat loudly in his ears, but not loud enough to block out the conversation inside.

"Where are we going?" Charli sounded excited, giddy with the way her voice shook. "Not that it matters, but so I'll know how to dress."

"The Creek Inn. The finest restaurant in Dallas."

Dylan turned and headed for his truck. He'd lost, and despite his best efforts at trying to protect it, his heart cracked. How would she want him over someone like Leon?

* * * *

Charli tossed in her sleep; her heart raced as the dream dragged her under.

"What are you doing here?" she asked as Dylan ambled toward her through the shadowy crowd. Dressed in a long, flowing gown, she stood before a massive fireplace.

"Taking you to dinner." He gazed into her eyes, and she saw his desire--and his love.

She held her breath. His lips lowered onto hers for an intense kiss.

"Hey, Bambi, get your cute little ass back on stage."

She cringed at the voice she'd hoped never to hear again.

A rough hand pulled her away from Dylan. The shadow crowd morphed into townspeople. They parted to reveal a stage with a metal pole in the center. The beautiful restaurant swirled into the smoky barroom of the Cat Call. Next to the platform, where she'd spent a wretched year of her life, leaned Ricardo Rodriquez.

"You're up, Bambi. Get over here, or you don't get this." Ricardo held a baggie of white powder in the air. She stared at the bag with a longing that surprised and frightened her. "My little deer loves her coke, doesn't she? I have a job for you."

Ric disappeared and a tall African-American man ambled toward her. When she recognized Tyrone Hodges, she gasped.

In her mind, she screamed, No! I won't do it. I won't lead him into a trap for you to kill him. With horror zipping through her, she was powerless against purring, "Hello, handsome."

Tyrone looked her over. "Aren't you Rodriguez's woman?"

She sidled closer and ran the too-long acrylic nail of her index finger over his shoulder. "I don't work for Ric no more."

Tyrone reached for her, and she soon found herself in his muscular arms. He smiled, his teeth showing brilliant against his dark face. "I could use a girl like you."

"That's why I'm here."

Inside her mind, she sobbed and wished she could get away from him, but she had no control over her actions. She was an observer of the events rather than a participant, even though she was within her own body. She could not change the events from happening.

"Let's get out of here." She ran her hand over the gold chains and smooth chest showing though his open silk shirt. "I'm willin' to show you what I can do."

When she cupped his growing erection, he growled. "Oh, baby. I've heard you're a wild one."

In a blink, she stepped into the room of a rundown apartment building. Ricardo's biggest rival in the illegal businesses of drug dealing and prostitution stopped and pulled her into his arms toward the bed. Although the room was Tyrone's, somehow they were on a movie-like set. She looked up to the terrifying view of the townspeople, Dylan and Leon watching her with widened eyes and open mouths.

Tyrone pulled her toward the bed and unlaced the corset top she wore. She was incapable of stopping her hands from unbuttoning his shirt.

"I can definitely see why Ric keeps you around, Bambi."

She met his gaze and shook her head. "He ain't keepin' me forever."

He flashed his white teeth again, and bent to nip at her neck. She shivered with revulsion, knowing what she had to do with this man. When the door to the room crashed inward, Ricardo burst through the opening.

"What the fuck?"

Tyrone pulled her to him to use as a shield and fumbled for the gun on the table beside the bed.

She screamed. She'd been tricked as much as Tyrone. Ricardo aimed his piece at the other man and fired before Tyrone had a chance to. The bullet buzzed by her head and entered Tyrone's skull between his eyes. As the man fell backward onto the bed, she collapsed onto the floor, sobbed hysterically, and crawled away from the dead body.

Dylan stood beside the bed and looked at her with a grimace of disgust and disbelief. "You murdered him."

"No!" She struggled to free herself from the icy skeletal fingers of the dream. "No! I didn't know Ricardo would kill him. I didn't know!"

"I can't believe you'd do this." Dylan looked at the dead man sprawled across the bed. "You killed him in cold blood."

"Dylan, please, I'm not a murderer. I'm not!" She sobbed.

"Shut up, bitch." Ricardo grabbed her by the upper arms and shook her. "You are exactly that. I want Tyron's territory. You know that. You led me to his secret hideout."

He sounded loud in the quiet room of stunned people. She recognized the older Cartwright brothers, the mayor's wife, Mrs. Pratt, Tracy, Zack and so many other people, who could never know what she'd done, all watching as if she acted out a play.

"I could never love you." Dylan turned away from her.

She struggled against Ricardo's hold on her. "Don't go, Dylan! I'm not like this anymore."

"C'mon, baby, I'll always take care of you. You don't need these people."

"No!" Shaking her head, she tried to resist his grip.

Leon appeared on the stage and held out his hand to her. "Come to me, Charli. I'll take care of you. With me, you'll be nothing but the wealthy woman you were meant to be. I can protect you."

She reached for his hand, but the distance was too great. "Leon!"

Ricardo laughed in her ear. "No matter how expensive your clothes are or how high and mighty you try to be, you're nothing but a whore. My murdering whore."

"No!"

Then he hit her.

She woke screaming and to the sound of the phone ringing. Gasping for breath, she reached for the receiver just as the machine picked up.

She glanced at the clock. A big red 3:25 stared back at her. As she continued to shake off the nightmare, she spoke into the receiver. "Hello?"

"Miss Monroe, this is Zack Cartwright." The deep voice on the other end echoed in her ear.

Instantly on alert, she sat on the edge of the bed. "Sheriff, what can I do for you?"

"I brought Dylan Quinn in for public drunkenness. I tried to contact his sister, but she's not answering either of her phones. I know he's working for you, so I'm hoping you'd take him home."

She ran her fingers through the snarled mess of her hair. "I'll be there as soon as I can."

"Thank you, Miss Monroe." Zack hung up.

"Yeah," she breathed into the dead receiver. The dream came back to her, and she shivered. She pulled her legs up, and wrapped her arms around them. Curled into a ball, she rocked in the middle of the bed and cried.

She nearly gave into the despair, but then remembered the call. Sighing, she pushed herself off the bed and got dressed. Dylan could never love her for what she'd done, but he needed her.

* * * *

"Thanks for coming down at such an ungodly hour, Miss Monroe." Sheriff Zachery Cartwright led Charli into his office.

She sat down on the edge of the chair in front of the sheriff's desk. "Dylan isn't just my employee, he's my friend."

"I'm glad you feel that way." Cartwright cleared his throat. "So, he's working out?"

"Dylan is a very talented carpenter, and he has a good sense of business."

"Seeing him like this doesn't sit right with me. I understand why he tries to drown in a bottle of whiskey, but that's not the way to go." Zack moved to the coffee pot in the corner. He held up a Styrofoam cup and the pot of strong smelling brew. "Want some?"

She could use a cup of coffee. "Yes, black, thank you." Zack handed the steaming cup to her. "You were in the war?"

Zack sat behind the utilitarian desk, set his coffee-stained *World's Greatest Daddy* mug on the wood surface, and stirred three teaspoons of sugar into his coffee. Several frames holding pictures of a beautiful dark-haired, blue-eyed little girl sat on the corner of his untidy desk.

On the wall behind him were more photographs. The one to draw her attention was of him with two other men in uniform in front of a Humvee with a desolate desert in the background. They held military guns and stood shoulder-to-shoulder with smiles on their faces.

Beside it was a picture of a smiling cowboy accepting a large silver belt buckle in a rodeo arena. From the size of the crowd pictured, she assumed it was taken at the National Finals Rodeo. At first, she couldn't believe the cowboy was the same man as in the other photo. Or the same man sitting behind the desk.

She looked at him as he said, "Afghanistan, Iraq, and then Afghanistan again. Marines. I was MP--military police. After coming back the last time, I lived in the bottle myself for a while. I was involved in a similar situation to Dylan's at a checkpoint on the border of Afghanistan and Pakistan."

"Oh." She sipped the pungent coffee. "I'm sorry." What else was she supposed to say? "Thanks for serving."

Zack nodded and sipped his coffee. After he set his mug on the desk again, he leaned over his folded arms. "I watched my buddy get shot after he pulled me to safety. I should have died. Instead, my friend did, leaving behind a pregnant wife. Then six months after coming home, my wife was killed by a drunk driver. I found myself a single father to my four-year-old daughter. That's how I know what Dylan's going through."

She swallowed hard. No one ever spoke about what had happened to the mayor's nephew. She remembered her dream and the horrendous cold-blooded murder she'd helped perpetrate. Whether or not she had known Ricardo's intent was irrelevant. She should have known. Both Zack and Dylan had killed men, but their actions were honorable and sacrificial.

Hers were out of misguided love for a greedy man and addiction to cocaine.

"The best thing that has happened to Dylan in a long time was going to work for you, Miss Monroe. I just want you to know. He needs to realize he's not to blame for the deaths of those men. The enemy is."

"Sheriff, I want to help him. But I'm not sure he wants it."

The sheriff chuckled and finished his coffee. "I didn't want help either, but I had a daughter to raise. I couldn't wallow in self-pity, or she would've been taken away from me. Sometimes we all need a good kick in the behind, Miss Monroe. Let's go get Dylan out of here."

Behind the bars of one of the two holding cells, Dylan lay on his back on a cot, the cell's only furniture. A toilet and a small sink stood in the corner. A combination of disinfectant, urine, stale booze, and vomit clung to the air. She wrinkled her nose as they walked down the short hallway between the cells.

When he glanced at her, she nodded, and Zack called through the bars, "Hey, Quinn, wake up. Your ride's here."

Dylan groaned and mumbled something intelligible. Zack slid open the unlocked door and entered the cell. For a heartbeat, she hesitated before entering and wrapped her arms around herself. The last time she'd been inside a jail cell hit her between the eyes and sent a shiver through her. Her accommodations at the Florence McClure Women's Correctional Center in Nevada had been more comfortable than this. She swore the day she was released she'd never spend another second inside a prison cell. Here she was willingly stepping into one.

"It's time to check out of my fine establishment."

Dylan responded to the sheriff by trying to turn over onto his side away from him.

"C'mon, you know the drill. If you stay the night, I have to cite you."

This time Dylan's voice was stronger when he mumbled in response, but she didn't understand the words.

"Aw, c'mon, Captain, I really don't want to have to book you."

Dylan opened his eyes and growled, "Don't fuckin' call me that."

Zack's lips drew into a fine line. "You will always be a captain, Quinn, just like I'll always be a gunnery sergeant."

"Fuck you, Cartwright."

"Geez, Dylan, I think your momma should've washed your mouth out with soap more often. You should know that's no way to talk in front of a lady."

"Tracy's my sister." He sluggishly rolled to a sitting position with his head between his hands. "She's heard me cuss plenty of times."

"I wasn't referring to Tracy."

The look Dylan narrowed at the sheriff should have scorched his blond hair. Charli's breath caught when his blistering gaze moved from Zack to her. "What's she doing here?"

Zack bracketed his waist with his hands and widened his stance. "I couldn't get hold of Tracy, so I called Miss Monroe. She was kind enough to come down here to get your sorry butt out of the clinker."

Unsteadily, Dylan stood and moved around the sheriff to stop before her. "I don't need or want your help."

The stench of whiskey burned her nose and twisted her already uneasy belly. She straightened her back. "That's just too damned bad, isn't it?"

He locked his eyes onto hers for a long moment before turning away with a huff and dropping on the cot. "Why don't you just go back to your ranch and leave me the hell alone. I quit."

The sheriff looked upon him with a careworn expression.

She said, "Sheriff, would you please excuse us?"

Zack regarded her for a moment with his lips pressed into a thin line before nodding and leaving them in the open cell.

She put her fists on her hips and squared her shoulders. "I won't let you quit. I need you to fix my house and run my ranch."

After standing again, he took a threatening step toward her, but she matched his glower with one of her own. "Why do you care? Hell, why are you even pretending to fix the place up? Ferguson's gonna get it anyway."

"What is that supposed to mean?"

He shrugged and ran his hands through his disheveled hair. "Oh, come on, Charli. The flowers, the constant checking up on you...the date."

"How do you--"

"It doesn't matter." He cut her off and stepped so close she could see the bloodshot veins in his wintry eyes. "Leon Ferguson's a parasite. The longer he's there, the more hold he has on the ranch--and on you."

She worked to keep her anger from her voice. "Leon isn't going to get my ranch. He wants me, not my land."

For a moment, he looked as if she'd slapped him. He shook his head and let out a bitter laugh. "You aren't all he wants. Trust me on that one, sweetheart. Ferguson wants your land, and if he gets a woman almost half his age in the sack in the bargain, it's just one more perk. Shit." He shook his head and backed away. "If he can't swindle you out of the land, he'll marry you for it, and when he's tired of you, he'll throw you away. But he'll make damn sure he keeps the ranch."

He turned away from her for a moment before looking back. "I never expected you to be a woman who could so easily fall for a smooth talker like Ferguson."

Her anger boiled over. "You're a jerk. Leon has been nothing but a gentleman." She spun on her boot heel and headed for the open cell door. "And if something develops between us and leads to marriage...so be it."

She should just fire him and cut her losses. Maybe if she tried, she could love Leon. Damn it, she didn't want to love any man, not Leon and, especially, not Dylan Quinn.

Zack Cartwright's words echoed through her mind, reminding her of her promise to herself to help Dylan.

She moved through the cell door and glanced over her shoulder. "Come on. I refuse to jeopardize my dreams because my manager is a total jackass."

Chapter 8

Charli sat on the very edge of the luxury seat and gaped out the tinted window of the limousine. A gold-painted helicopter, with the black logo for Ferguson Industries on its tail, readied for takeoff.

After the limo came to a stop in front of a portico, she waited for the driver to open the door.

Leon helped her out of the car. "Good evening, Charli."

"So, this is how we're able to get to Dallas and still have time for dinner."

With his hand resting on the small of her back, he led her toward the helicopter. "You didn't think we'd drive to Dallas, did you?"

"I sure as heck didn't expect to fly there."

Leon laughed as they stopped just outside the swath of the blades. A crewmember rushed forward and helped them board.

Once inside and buckled in, Leon spoke to the pilot through the microphone of a headset. Soon they rose quickly into the air.

When the helicopter turned and headed north, Leon removed the headset and leaned close. "You're a vision."

At first, she didn't grasp his meaning. "Thanks. I must have tried on ten dresses."

"The dress is lovely, but not nearly as beautiful as the woman wearing it."

A giggle escaped from her lips before she could corral it. Heat burned her cheeks, and she ducked her head to look out the window by her side. With the setting sun in the west, the vista was breathtaking. His come-ons were laughable, and she wasn't falling for them. However, she'd play along. She couldn't deny she enjoyed hearing his flattery just as much as she loved his gifts. "Oh, you. Flattery will get you nowhere."

"I state only the truth." As he spoke, Leon pulled a long jewelry box from his suit pocket. "This is for you."

She stared at him before slowly reaching for the black box. "Leon, whatever this is, you shouldn't have."

"Yes, I should. I did. Now open it."

Her hands shook as she opened the velvet lid. She gasped and put a hand to her mouth. "Oh my God! Leon, I can't accept this."

Leon reached over, took the delicate strand of gleaming diamonds and held it up. "Yes, you can. I'm giving it to you. I ask nothing of you in return, except the chance to get to know you." He leaned closer and put the necklace around her neck. Their gazes locked, and Leon was close enough to kiss--if she yearned to do so. She trembled as his fingers brushed her skin under her hair while he fastened the closure.

Although the hunger in his eyes frightened her a little, excitement filled her as his lips met hers for a passionate kiss. Despite all her vows of not wanting a man, she wanted to fall for him. He was the right man to love, unlike the one she was so afraid she'd fallen for.

He deepened the kiss as he pulled her into his arms. She wrapped her arms around his neck and kissed him back, but she couldn't make her heart follow her head.

* * * *

Dylan's gut twisted as Charli drove away in the limo. He pounded his fist into the doorframe of the stable and headed into the dim interior. He had to do something, anything to get her off his mind. He'd tried to keep his distance the past few days, but she was still there, wanting to be his friend.

Maybe she did.

He wished she could be more.

Aurora, Charli's usual mount, whinnied several times as he led the black mare out into the breezeway. When the sorrel kicked at her stall, he called out, "Sorry, girl, Charli's not riding with me. She's too busy being wined and dined out of her clothes and her land."

His belly did that twisting thing again. *She doesn't want you, hotshot. Face it and let it go.*

He went about saddling the mare Charli had named Artemis. He swung up into the saddle, and his phone rang as he trotted out into the cool evening. After looking at the caller ID and not recognizing the number, he put the phone back into his jeans pocket and headed for the pasture to check on the calves. A few of them had acted odd when he and Kyle had ridden out onto the range to check on them earlier that afternoon.

The sun had set and daylight was fading fast. Calves bawled in the distance and night insects chirped in the grass. A coyote howled somewhere in the descending darkness. Artie snorted and he checked for the .357 stashed in the belt of his jeans at his back. "Sorry, girl, I should've taken one of the four-wheelers out here."

They'd plodded along another hundred yards when he noticed the outlines lying in the tall grass.

"Whoa." He reined in beside one of the dark lumps. After dismounting, he patted the nervous horse on the shoulder. "It's all right, Artie."

The calf lay on his side, attempted to lift his head and bawled pitifully as Dylan knelt beside him. Big, dark eyes rolled back in the calf's skull. "Hey, buddy, what's the matter?" He gently placed his hand on the steer's heaving, bloated belly. It struggled to breathe, coat damp with sweat. "Hang in there. I'll get you help."

He stood and examined the other ten calves lying in the grass. Some seemed unusually agitated while others panted like dogs in the dead of August heat, but the evening was cool for this time in mid-May.

Although he didn't hold much hope for the steers, he pulled out his cellphone and called the veterinarian, then dialed Kyle's number. When he didn't pick up, Dylan left a frustrated message, and then called Zack Cartwright.

* * * *

"Sir! Sir, you can't barge into the dining..."

Dylan ignored the maitre d' just as he'd paid no attention to the man's reprimands for not having the proper dress when he rushed into the exclusive hotel and restaurant. He didn't want to think about the place being a hotel, and prayed Charli was still eating her fancy dinner.

Leon had flown her to Dallas in his private helicopter, but that was over three hours ago. Dylan hadn't actually considered the time until he pulled into the parking lot and threatened the valet when he warned him he couldn't park his truck in the lot unless he had reservations at the inn.

Every head in the place turned to stare at him as he rushed through a glitzy dining room. Several women even gasped and covered their mouths with bejeweled hands. Did his dirty cowboy boots and jeans disgust them?

When he didn't spot Charli among the late diners, he turned on the frail-looking man following him. "Where's Leon Ferguson?"

"That's privileged information--"

"Don't give me that bullsh--" He interrupted himself when another round of gasps filled the air thick with expensive perfumes and rich foods. It wouldn't do to be arrested before he even found her. He forced a semblance of cold reason and the authority thirteen years in the Army had bestowed on him into his voice. "I'm the manager of the ranch Mr.

Ferguson's companion owns. There's an emergency. I need to speak to Miss Monroe immediately."

The maitre d' still hesitated. When Dylan wouldn't budge, the penguin suit relented with a sigh. "This way."

He followed him down a hall to the private dining rooms. They stopped before an ornate double door, and he didn't wait to be announced. He pushed past the maitre d' and headed into the room.

The intimate ambiance spoke of Leon's wealth and success. Dylan ignored the string quartet playing soft music in the corner, the flowers and the candles. Leon stood and glowered at him, while Charli sat there with wide eyes and her mouth hanging slightly ajar.

The penguin rushed in behind him and groveled to Leon about the interruption of his dinner.

He ignored both men. "Charli, I need to speak with you."

"What are you doing here?" Leon asked stiffly.

She blinked and closed her mouth. He realized, with a jolt, she didn't look disappointed or even angry at seeing him. She seemed surprised mostly, and then he noticed a hopeful twinkle in her turquoise eyes.

You're crazy, Quinn. She's not glad to see you. She's thinking of ways to fire your ass. He got down to business. "You have to come home."

She frowned. "How did you know where to find me?"

He swallowed the thick lump forming in his throat. "I overheard you talking the other night."

"What's so important you couldn't have called?"

"I didn't want to call about this. The calves..."

"My calves? Dylan, what's happened?"

He kneeled beside her chair. She might not have named the steers, but she cared about her calves. He'd caught her watching them play in the pastures more than once. "Some of them are sick. We think they were poisoned."

"Poisoned?" Her voice went shrill and then broke. "How?" She swallowed and puckered her brow. "Who's *we*?"

He took her hand into his. Her grasp was moist as she clasped his fingers. "Dr. Evans, the vet, thinks they got hold of some jimsonweed."

"Jimsonweed?" She turned in her chair to face him fully. "I thought it was some kind of hallucinogen drug."

He took her other hand and held both of them as they trembled within his. "It is. Or can be used as one. Sometimes it's called thorn apple or devil's trumpet. If livestock eat enough, it could kill them." He squeezed her hands, willed her his support. "Charli, your horse, Aurora--"

"Is she sick, too?" Her eyes misted, but she blinked before the tears splashed onto her pale cheeks. She wore very little makeup, but then, she didn't need it.

"Yeah." He would tell her later about Doc Evan's prognosis concerning the mare's new pregnancy.

"Kyle never said anything after feeding the horses today. Where could my calves and horses get this stuff?"

Leon had stood quietly watching them until now. He placed his hand on her shoulder. "Usually in pasture, especially overgrazed pasture. The other place is in feed--silage and hay."

Charli looked over her shoulder at Leon. "But my pastures aren't overgrazed."

"Hay, then."

"The hay you bought last week." She snapped her attention to Dylan. The accusation in her gaze and voice stung more than he'd ever admit.

He could only nod and looked down at their clasped hands.

"But the calves haven't been fed much hay, have they?"

"Not much, but with all the rain the past week, some of the better pastures are too wet. I had Kyle supplement with hay."

The dark green of the sheath dress made her eyes all the more luminous. Candlelight twinkled off the diamond necklace around her neck. He was sure she hadn't been wearing it earlier when he'd seen her before she'd left in Ferguson's limousine.

"I have to get back to the ranch." She stood and looked at Leon. He slipped his hand around her waist.

The large ruby signet on his ring finger glittered in the yellow glow of hundreds of candles. The ring had been passed down for generations in the Ferguson family and by all rights should belong to his mother. The sight angered him, but not as much as Leon touching Charli fired his gut. Possessiveness for her boiled through him.

She looked up at Leon, but didn't step away. "I'm sorry, but I have to go."

"Of course, we can leave immediately." Leon retrieved his phone from his suit pocket. "Let me call the driver to meet us and have the helicopter ready for takeoff."

Dylan had broken every speed law between Colton and Dallas to get there in an hour and a half. Leon could have her home within a few minutes.

He headed for the door. "I'll see you back at the ranch."

"No. Dylan, wait."

He turned, and she stepped out of Leon's embrace. Charli took Leon's hand and smiled, but it looked forced. "Thank you, Leon, for a wonderful evening. But I'll go home with Dylan. After all, he came all the way into the city to inform me of the emergency, and on the way back, he can tell me what we need to do to fix it."

"Hopefully we can have dinner again," Leon said pleasantly, sliding the phone away.

Dylan jerked his head up at the challenge in the older man's eyes when Leon glanced at him.

"Yes, I hope so, too. I had a great time." Charli turned to Dylan and took his hand. "Let's go."

"Charli," Leon called, and she paused to look at him. "Let me know if you need anything. I'll do whatever I can."

"I'll call you. Thanks for everything." She touched the necklace at her throat.

Dylan's heart sank a little farther. He'd never be able to afford such a gift. He tried to let her hand go, but she clung to it as she tugged him through the door.

He led her to the old pickup that looked as out of place in the parking lot as he had in the dining room where she had sparkled as much as the crystal.

Chapter 9

Neither Dylan nor Charli spoke much during the drive home. He waited for her to ask him how any of this could happen, but she never did. As soon as they pulled into the driveway, she asked, "Who took care of my sick animals while you came to Dallas?"

He parked the truck in front of the garage. "When I couldn't get hold of Kyle, I called Zack Cartwright."

"The sheriff? Do you think someone did this to my animals?"

He hoped she didn't fuss about him not calling Ferguson's men. "No, I guess you could say I asked Zack to help us out. He's your neighbor, too. Did you forget you share a four-mile boundary with the Cartwrights?"

She shook her head.

He cut the engine, leaned against the steering wheel, and stared out into the darkness. "I needed someone to move the calves in closer to the barn while I came to you. I trust Zack and his men. The sick ones are quarantined in the barn corral, and the others are in the pasture behind the bunkhouse where I can watch them for signs of sickness."

"Have any of them died?"

He met her imploring eyes. "Not yet."

"But you think some will."

"I don't know."

She got out of the truck and headed for the stable despite the shimmery cocktail dress and sky-high shoes.

He'd bet her outfit had a price tag at well over a thousand dollars. He caught up with her. "What are you doing?"

"I'm checking on my horses." She looked up at him. "How's this going to affect Aurora's pregnancy?"

He slid his gaze from hers.

"Dylan?"

"Doc Evans expects her to abort."

A single fluorescent light burned in the breezeway of the stable. The three healthy horses flicked their ears and nickered a curious hello.

Aurora's stall was empty. Charli turned to him. "Where is she?"

"In the corral. The best thing for her is to walk. If she lies down, she probably won't get back up."

She immediately headed out the other door into the corral, and he followed. Zack Cartwright led Aurora around the outside of the rail fence. The horse would stop, paw at the dirt and shake her head, but he'd tug on her lead to force her to keep moving. When Zack noticed them, he led the mare over to the door.

"How is she?" Charli rubbed her hand along the horse's sweat-dampened neck. Aurora tossed her head.

Zack patted the mare's shoulder. "She's getting tired. Doc gave her a shot of Banamine and said she should start calming down in about an hour or so. Now, we just wait for the poison to work out of her system. He doesn't think she had enough to kill her, but she's colicky." When the sorrel dropped to her forelegs to lie down, Zack tugged on the line. "Oh, no, girl, we need to walk."

Dylan reached for the lead. "I'll take over, Zack. Thanks, buddy, for coming out."

Zack relinquished the rein and patted the mare's shoulder again. "I'm glad I was off duty and could help."

Charli stopped stroking the mare's neck as he led her away. "Yes, thank you. I have no idea how I can repay you."

"Promise me when you decide to buy more horses, the CW gets your business, and we'll call it even."

"You've got a deal. I still feel bad, though. Where's your little girl?"

"She's with my mother. Don't you worry, ma'am." Zack glanced back at him and the mare. "Aurora's a strong horse. Her sire and dam were good horses. She'll be all right."

After Zack bid them a good night, Charli stumbled over the rough dirt to Dylan and the mare in her crazy strappy shoes. The floodlight cast the area in a harsh blue-white light. Mindless of her expensive dress and high-heels, she fell into step with him.

He pointed to her shoes. "You're going to break your neck in those things."

She stroked the mare's neck as they moved along the fence with the horse's head between them. "I'm used to waking in heels."

"Not in dirt and horseshit, you're not. Go change. I'll keep walking."

She hesitated for a moment and rubbed the restless mare's shoulder. "Okay, I'll be back."

She picked her way over the rutted ground in those stilts she called shoes. How the hell she walked in those things was beyond him.

Ten minutes later, she returned wearing jeans, a t-shirt and boots. Now, she looked like she belonged in a barnyard. He hadn't expected the intense twist of desire tying him up into knots so tight he ached.

She took her place on the other side of the mare's head. "How much longer do you think we should walk her?"

"Until all signs of the stomachache pass. Another hour at least. Here." He handed her the lead. "I'm going to call the rancher who sold the hay."

"But it's two in the morning."

He shrugged. "If I sold bad hay, I'd want to know."

"I see your point."

"Don't let her lay down."

He made his way back to the office and found the information he needed. At first, the rancher was rather indignant about being forced from his bed, until he explained the situation.

"You're sure no one else had trouble?" he asked when the rancher adamantly denied any other reports of poisoning.

"I'm sure. I'm feedin' my own livestock from that batch and ain't got any problems, but I'll talk to the folks I sold hay to. I'm sorry. Call me tomorrow morning, and we'll talk more about this. I don't want a reputation of sellin' bad hay. I'm robbin' Peter to pay Paul now as it is."

He assured the rancher there were no hard feelings and hung up.

When he returned to the corral, he stood back in the shadows. Charli softly murmured to the mare. Aurora plodded along with her head low next to her mistress's shoulder.

Charli might have shimmered and looked every inch the part of a Texas lady in the lap of luxury of that fancy restaurant in Dallas. But did she know she belonged here with her cattle and horses instead?

He walked through the gate and came up beside the woman and horse. "She seems better."

"Yeah. She's calmed down over the past ten minutes. What did the rancher say?"

He related the call to her.

When he finished, she asked, "How much hay was fed to the animals?"

He looked away. "The calves had some yesterday and today, the horses for a little longer. As soon as we--Doc and I--suspected it was the hay, I removed it all from the feeders. Zack brought some from the CW for the horses when he showed up with his men."

"Why wasn't Kyle here?"

"I don't know where he is. He never returned my calls. And I needed to get to you..."

"I--I appreciate you coming for me."

A tense silence settled between them as they kept the horse moving.

After another half-hour of walking, they were exhausted, and the horse had finally calmed down enough for her to return to the stall. Dylan checked on the other three mares, making sure none of them was getting sick. She stroked Aurora's face and neck. The mare nickered softly, and Charli let her nuzzle her palm.

"It's gonna be okay, Aurora. Please, hang in there."

When the sob broke loose, he looked at Charli. She'd held up well until now. The horse wasn't out of danger, but they'd gotten over a significant hurdle. She let out another sob and the tears started.

He gathered her in his arms, holding her close. "Shhh," he murmured into her hair. She smelled of sweet, summer peaches. He moved with her out into the breezeway, closing the stall door behind him. "She'll be okay, Charli."

Please, God, don't let that be a lie.

She wrapped her arms around him and rested her head on his chest. "What if they die? What if I lose them all?"

He rested his cheek on the top of her head. "Doc Evans is the best vet in three counties. He's treated jimsonweed poisoning before."

"I guess we should stay with her tonight." She swiped at the tears with the backs of her hands, getting her emotions under control.

"Yeah. But we can take turns." When she would have pulled away, he held on. He responded to her closeness and knew she'd notice the growing bulge in his jeans, but he couldn't let her go. "Let's go in and have some coffee and decide who's taking the first shift with her. Now that the medicine kicked in, she should be good until morning."

Charli shifted away, turning to lean on the top of Aurora's stall door. The mare nuzzled her hand. "Will Dr. Evans return in the morning?"

"Yes."

Satisfied they could safely leave the horses, she led him across the driveway and into the back of the house. She made coffee while he paced the kitchen. He should have stayed in the stable. His desire wasn't the only thing bothering him.

Naturally occurring livestock poisoning wasn't common. The conversation with the rancher replayed in his head. Something about the entire thing didn't sit right with him. And it was that *something* keeping him in the kitchen.

She poured two mugs of coffee. "Who's taking the first shift?"

He stopped in his trek across the floor and faced her. "I'll stay in the stable tonight."

She held out a cup of coffee. "Hardly seems fair. I can take a turn."

"I know, but I don't mind. I'll drink this and take a cup with me. I'll let you get to bed."

The cornflower blue of her t-shirt highlighted the blue flecks embedded in her green eyes, making them appear aquamarine. "I'm afraid, Dylan."

He set the cup on the table and wrapped his arms around her. She clung to him, pressing every soft curve against him. Fear and worry pulled the skin taut over her forehead. Hunger blazed to life in the depths of her eyes.

Just step away before you make a huge mistake. She didn't let him retreat. Charli ran the tips of her fingers along his stubbly jaw and down his chest between them. He swallowed as the lingering touch slammed into his groin.

"Stay with me for a little while." Her voice was warm as good Southern whiskey and just as intoxicating. "I don't want to fight this thing between us anymore. I don't want to be alone."

"Me either." Slowly, he slid his hands over the soft cotton covering her back. She shivered and her lips parted.

He lowered his mouth to hers, and she opened to accept the full thrust of his tongue. She tugged on his t-shirt, and skimmed her hands over the skin under the hem. He groaned deep in his chest as she raked her nails over the small of his back, jolting his already excited erection.

When he tried to retreat from the battle of dueling tongues, she sucked on his, wrenching a long, deep moan from him. His hands held the curve of her behind, but it wasn't enough. He wanted to touch her flesh.

She broke the kiss long enough to pull his t-shirt over his head. Before he knew what she was doing, her hands were on his belt. He caught her by the wrists and stripped her of her shirt and bra. She tugged off her boots and shimmied out of her jeans between gut-twisting kisses.

She stood before him wearing only a diamond studded belly button ring and a pair of stretch lace, pink panties. Freckles, millions of them, speckled the creamy porcelain of her skin. Like springs caught in a blacksmith's fire, her red-gold hair fell around her face and shoulders and down her back to her waist. The sexy pout puckering her lips and the heavy-lidded eyes caught and held his.

He knew she wasn't innocent, but something about the way she looked made him think she was far more experienced than he'd initially thought.

"Are you sure we should do this?" His voice came through as a low rumble.

Charli flashed him a wicked grin. She skimmed her right hand over the Special Forces tat and the puckered nipple on the left side of his chest. He shuddered when she leaned in and flicked her hot tongue over the point and ran her hands down his body to the fly of his jeans. She'd already opened the belt. She lowered the zipper and purred against his skin. "Don't you dare get all noble on me now."

"I wouldn't think of it." He toed off his boots and shucked his jeans.

"If you don't have a condom, we can--"

"I have one." He pulled his wallet from the pocket of his jeans and removed a crinkled packet.

"How long have you been carrying that thing around?"

"For a while." He looked down at the battered foil paper. He didn't want to think about the night Brenda remarried, when he'd put it in his wallet. The night he'd almost slept with Julie Larson. Thank God, in the end, he couldn't do it. He'd forgotten about the condom until the kiss in the bathroom.

"I guess we have everything we need." When she squeezed his hard-on, he groaned and the only thing he could think about was burying himself inside her soft heat. Charli ran her lips up his neck, along his jaw. She licked the shell of his ear. Her warm breath on his damp sensitive skin caused him to shiver again as she whispered, "Right or wrong, good or bad, I want to have sex with you right here and right now."

Then she stroked the length of his erection.

He sucked in a hissing breath and tugged at her panties. They fell to her ankles, where she stepped out of them. Thinking beyond the primitive need pounding through his veins was impossible. He lifted her onto the edge of the table.

"Dylan." She moaned, arching into him, when he nibbled first one taut nipple and then the other. Her fingers flexed in his hair, holding him close to her.

Under his hand, the skin of her inner thighs was buttery soft. He stroked her hot, slick sex. She arched into his hand and called his name again when the first quakes of orgasm shattered her. He let her ride out the waves until his erection pulsed with painful need.

With unsteady hands, he sheathed himself in the condom. While he kissed her long and deep, she wrapped her legs around his hips. He thrust forward the same time she pulled him to her. They both groaned at the connection, breaking the kiss. He moved within her fast, hard and deep.

Her head fell back, and she gazed at him through heavy-lidded eyes. The erotic beauty of her lips parting on a moan, the long auburn lashes over passion-darkened eyes, and the hungry flush of her freckled cheeks made his knees weak. Fire boiled in his low belly. She flexed her fingernails into his shoulders, and her muscles tightened around him, drawing him deeper.

He caught one of her rosy nipples between his lips again, pulling the hard raspberry into his mouth. She clutched at his shoulders, let out a high keening sound, and shuddered around him as he pounded deep inside.

She was slick and so hot that he thought he might burn up before the end. Combined with the contractions of her inner muscles, the sensations wrenched a release out of him that curled his toes. He cursed and trembled as he emptied himself into her. Struggling to fill his lungs with air, he rested his forehead on her shoulder, afraid he'd slide to the floor in a boneless heap.

She turned her face and placed a kiss next to his ear. "Wow. That was amazing."

"You feel so good. I want you again." He kissed her.

She held him close and sucked on his tongue. When she moved on him, she felt *too* good.

He pulled away and stared down into her eyes. "Damn. Please tell me you're on some kind of birth control?"

"I wish I was. I want you again, too."

"That isn't what I meant." He pulled out of her.

A slow pucker troubled her brow when she looked down at his softening erection.

"Shit."

* * * *

Her breath caught as he muttered the curse. Charli swallowed hard and stared at the broken condom, mentally counting days. "Oh, no."

He moved away and grabbed his clothes from the floor. After hopping off the table, she gathered her things, then followed him into her bedroom. Dylan went into the bathroom, and she picked up the silk robe from the bottom of her bed, quickly pulling it on. She wrapped her arms around herself and paced the floor.

When he came out, he was dressed, except for his boots. His eyes narrowed on her, and he growled, "So, let me get this straight--right now millions of my little soldiers are marching upstream hoping to find the princess at the castle?" His remark didn't warrant a response. He turned and ran his hands through his hair. "How possible is it you could get pregnant?"

She trembled and tightened her arms around her middle. "I had my period not quite two weeks ago. What are we going to do? You know... if..."

He strode past her, his hands fisted. "I can't believe it. I knew this was a mistake. The last thing in the world I've ever wanted was a kid."

She flinched at his words, but when he stopped and turned on her, she jumped back at the wintery hardness of his eyes.

"How long have you been planning this?"

"Planning what?"

He took two steps toward her. "The grand seduction. Almost every morning you answer the damned door looking like something from my fantasies. You come on to me tonight. You didn't get Ferguson in bed, so you settled with me, is that it?"

"No!" Tears of humiliation and fear scalded her eyes, but she'd be damned if she let them fall. Squaring her shoulders, she fisted her hands by her side and skewered him with a glare. "I won't deny I wanted you. But don't you dare blame this all on me. It was your condom that broke. Dammit!" She grabbed the hair at the side of her face and spun away from him. "I sure as hell don't want a baby any more than you do. Not now."

"What's going on with you and Ferguson?"

The crushing pain pinching her heart caused her anger to crash and burn out like a meteor falling to earth. Did he honestly think she'd sleep with Leon?

She faced him and fought the tremor in her voice. "Nothing is going on between Leon and me. I went to dinner with him, but nothing else would, or has ever happened between us. I'm as concerned as you are that right now, as you so eloquently put it, your 'little soldiers' are swimming upstream, hoping to hit the jackpot. But you don't have to insult me. I'm not a slut."

She sniffed, but a tear rolled over the dam of pride with which she'd tried to hold back a tidal wave. "The last thing I've ever wanted was an unwanted pregnancy, especially since *I* was one."

His face lost some of the hardness, and his voice was gruff. "That's why you never mentioned your father. You don't know him."

Sara Walter Ellwood

"My mother was nineteen when she and a rodeo cowboy from Texas had a fling. I didn't know my father's name until after Hank died. It was among a box of Momma's letters I found. There's an old Polaroid in there of my sperm donor, too. I look a lot like him."

"Charli..."

She held up a hand. "I'm a big girl. We had sex, and we both knew the consequences going into it."

She blinked to keep more tears from slipping past her crumbling self-control. She'd wanted Dylan, and she'd gone after him, probably confirming his belief she was capable of indiscriminate sex. Hugging herself again, she tried to keep the sharp pain from ripping her apart. "I'm sorry I seduced you."

"Charli," he rasped when she turned away.

She didn't face him.

"If the worst happens, I won't do what your father did to your mother. I would never abandon my responsibilities."

Closing her eyes at the ache in her heart from the conciliatory words, she paused in the doorway of her bathroom. "Don't worry about it. Good night, Dylan."

Once the door closed behind her, she slid down it and cried.

Chapter 10

Dylan left the house, and after checking on Aurora, retrieved a bottle of whiskey from the bunkhouse. For the rest of the night, he sat on a bale of hay in the breezeway of the stable with the horses. When a storm came up, he listened to rain hit the tin roof and the wind howl around the corners. What he wouldn't do to get rip-roaring drunk.

All he could think of were Charli's parting words last Friday night about her respecting him. He lifted the bottle to his lips and snorted. "I doubt you have an ounce of respect for me now."

Hell, he didn't have that much for himself. He had no right to lash out at her. Their blunder affected her as much as him, if she turned up pregnant. Even if she didn't conceive, how could she ever forgive him for the way he'd treated her afterward? Instead of holding her and telling her that he loved her, he'd become a coward.

Afraid of fatherhood. Afraid of love. Afraid of rejection.

When the horses started to stir with the wakening of a new day, he checked on Aurora again. She was restless, and from the trace of blood on her tail, it was a safe bet she'd aborted. Ironic how one life could be lost, while he and Charli might have created another.

Not wanting her to see the evidence of the loss of her first foal, he fetched some warm water from the tack room sink and a rag.

After he cleaned the blood from Aurora's tail, he made sure the mares had the fresh hay Zack had brought, and water. Working hadn't prevented the same question from circling around in his head.

Why would he accuse her of sleeping with Leon?

Although she'd been on a date with him, she had left with Dylan. She'd come on to *him*.

In his only defense, he'd been scared shitless by what could come of his moment of recklessness. He didn't want kids. His constant postponing of having a family was a major reason his marriage fell apart.

So, what do you do if she's pregnant, hotshot?

He didn't know the answer.

When the veterinarian arrived around six AM, he called Charli on his cellphone rather than facing her.

He couldn't, not yet, but when he did, he intended to tell her somehow they'd make things work.

The bay she'd named Athena showed signs of poisoning. After the vet checked her out and gave her a shot, Dylan led the mare out into the corral to walk her.

Charli made her way out to the stables and took over walking the sick horse. Not more than a few words passed between them, before he headed back into the stable.

Zack and his men had gathered the contaminated hay into sacks. He planned to destroy them, but the same gut feeling of something being *wrong* grated on him like desert sand in a combat boot. He tied the sacks closed and grabbed two more to gather some chunks from unopened bales he chose at random.

Afterward, he headed to check on the calves in the barnyard. He stood under the short overhang of the barn with the vet. "How're they doing, Doc?"

Evans pushed back his beat-up straw hat over his white hair. As long as Dylan could recall, the older man had never worn anything but jeans, a fringed leather jacket over a Western shirt and worn shit-kickers.

Doc squinted at him over his shoulder. "They aren't out of the woods, and this damned rain isn't helping, but I think they'll make it." The vet patted him on the shoulder. "You did right fine, Dylan. If you'd waited 'til morning to ride out into that pasture, you'd've found them dead. But I can't imagine why on God's green Earth you were riding around in the dark."

He couldn't tell the veterinarian the only reason he'd been riding out on the range was jealousy. He swallowed and nodded. "Thanks, sir."

Charli checked on the sick calves and spent most of the day in the stable with her horses. They spoke with Evans before he left, but they hadn't spoken more than a handful of words to each other. However, he knew they had to talk.

The rain had turned the day gray, damp and dismal. With the collar of his old M65 field jacket turned up, he tilted his hat over his forehead against the mist. He headed for the house after she left the stable later that afternoon. When the flashy black Porsche cut off his path, he wasn't surprised as much as angry.

Leon got out and looked around. "I'm surprised you haven't resigned--or been fired."

"Go to hell."

Leon buried his hands deep into the pockets of a custom-tooled leather jacket. If only Dylan could wipe the cocky smirk off his face. "You *are* responsible for Charli's livestock losses."

He clenched his hands into fists at his sides and worked at unclamping his jaw. "We haven't determined where the poison came from. Besides, she hasn't lost anything. Fortunately, I'm a hands-on kind of manager."

Yeah, right. He'd had his hands all over his boss.

Leon shrugged and looked around again. "When you aren't too drunk to stand up, maybe you are. But I can smell the whiskey from here."

Dylan pushed by him, but he hadn't gone two steps before Leon said, "A woman like Charli may be attracted to someone like you. Hell, she may even have a fling with you, but she'll never settle for a broken down drunk with murder on his hands." He moved in behind him and spoke near his shoulder. "You can't win against me. I want her, and I'll have her. She left with you last night, but she called me today."

He jerked at the news.

"What can you give her? You're penniless and a drunk." Leon provided the answer already echoing through his head. "Nothing. Just remember that, Quinn. Not a damned thing but heartache."

Dylan had to work at unclenching his hands and back teeth long after he'd left the ranch.

* * * *

"Leon." Charli opened the door on the first knock, hoping it was Dylan.

"Hello." He stepped through the opening into the kitchen. She looked past him as Dylan sped by in his truck. She sighed and closed the door.

The molding was partially stripped of coats of old paint, and boxes sat on the counter where she'd been wrapping dishes that previous morning. She caught him looking and said, "We started the remodel in here on Thursday. My new floor and cabinets are coming next week."

Leon took her hands, and she relaxed into his gentle touch. "I wanted to see how you were doing, not your house."

He peered at her with intense brown eyes as dark as his hair. Why hadn't she fallen for him? Leon obviously cared for her. She sucked in a deep breath, and let it out slowly. "I'm okay." She stepped away toward the coffee maker on the counter. "Want some coffee?"

"Sounds good. Thank you."

After she served coffee, she led him into the living room. She couldn't sit at the same table where she and Dylan had had sex, especially not with Leon. Not the morning after.

He settled on the couch beside her. "I'm hoping we can have dinner again."

She looked into the coffee mug she had both hands wrapped around. She'd spent hours crying. Although she could be pregnant with a child Dylan obviously didn't want, he also didn't want her. Not once had he tried to talk to her about what had happened. He'd avoided her all morning by calling her when Dr. Evans arrived. She hoped he'd come to her. Her speech was all planned out. She'd lay her heart out there for him. But it never happened.

Instead, he'd left, no doubt, to drown his sorrows in a damned bottle of whiskey.

She pasted on a smile. "I'm sorry. I can't go out with you. Not now. But, I could really use a friend. I don't have many."

Leon reached over and ran the back of his fingers over her cheek. Angling his head, he looked into her eyes. "I *am* your friend. I'm here for you. What are you going to do now?"

"I guess we wait and see what happens." She almost laughed at the double entendre.

Leon leaned back into the couch and sipped his coffee. "If I may give you some advice..."

"Yes?"

He set his cup on the end table. His expression solemn, he folded his hands in his lap. "Dylan failed you. I just saw him outside. He reeked from that swill he drinks. If you continue to rely on him, he'll lead you to ruin."

She bristled so fast she wasn't sure of what to make of her own response. Squaring her shoulders, she shook her head. "No, he hasn't. If he hadn't called the vet when he did, my calves and horses would be dead. Yes, he purchased the hay, but anyone could have done that." She took a deep breath. "Dylan is also my friend, and I need him right now as much as I need you."

* * * *

Dylan sat in his usual corner of the Longhorn and nursed a bottle of Jack Daniel's. No matter how much he drank, like the broken George Jones track playing on the jukebox, Leon's parting words played over and over in his mind.

What can you give her? Not a damned thing but heartache.

Would Charli turn to Leon now? He lifted the bottle to his lips and drank. The thought that she'd choose the oilman made him not only fighting jealous, but sick to his gut.

The bastard could end up raising *his* child.

He would fight him with everything he had before he let that happen, even if Charli had slept with Leon and paternity was called into question. The son-of-a-bitch had taken Oak Springs from him, but he'd fry in hell before he'd let Leon take anything else from him.

Did that include Charli? She'd come to him; did she feel something more than lust for him?

But it wasn't him she'd called.

"If she wants Leon, let her have him." He winced and clenched a fist against the painful twist to his heart.

She'd never want a failure like him. She had beauty, both inside and out, she was admirable, smart, funny and classy--in her own fashion magazine way.

He wasn't good enough for her. He'd never be the man she deserved, especially since he was to blame for the poisonings.

"What a way to totally fuck up, Quinn," he muttered and took a long draw on the bottle, hoping for oblivion.

"Captain, when are you gonna realize you can't drown your sorrows in a bottle of Jack?"

He leveled the man standing beside his booth with a glower. "Cartwright, if you weren't wearing that tinfoil star, I'd--"

Zack chuckled and slid into the booth across from him. "What? Deck me? Bring it on. You special ops types think you're so damned tough." Zack's laugh turned into a shit-faced grin. "I could kick your ass any day of the week."

He set his bottle on the table with a thud. "To what do I owe this displeasure? Aren't you supposed to be wasting taxpayer money somehow?"

"I am. Your sister called, and I'm here checking out her complaint. Tracy saw your truck out front and couldn't stop because she had her boy with her. She's been trying to get a hold of you since this morning."

"You can tell her I was too busy to answer."

"A little early to be drinking, isn't it?"

He picked up the bottle and sloshed some of the amber liquid into a shot glass. "It's never too early."

Zack leaned back and whistled low between his teeth. "I'm almost afraid to ask how things are out on the ranch."

After throwing back the shot, he wiped his mouth on the back of his hand. "Then you have no reason to ask."

Cartwright just sat there waiting with his arms crossed over his chest.

He huffed. "Charli hasn't lost any calves. The sorrel aborted early this morning, but seems to be doing better, however, twenty more calves and the bay mare are now sick." He wasn't telling him the real reason he was here.

Zack finally lost the stupid smirk. "How's Miss Monroe holding up?"

He shrugged and lied. "She's okay." Charli wasn't okay; she was scared and vulnerable. Just the way Leon wanted her.

Whose fault was that?

"Let me take you home. I think you're probably needed more there than here." Zack stood and waited. He wouldn't take no for an answer.

Dylan dragged himself out of the booth. "You know, Zack, you're a royal pain in my ass."

"Yeah, yeah. And dealing with you isn't a day in the park either."

As they moved through the sparsely occupied bar, he swallowed hard. He didn't have many friends, but Zack was probably the closest thing he had to a best friend. "I wanted to thank you again for helping out last night."

Zack pushed open the door. He squinted against the bright late afternoon sun. "No problem. Someday you can return the favor." He held out his hand. "Give me your keys. I'll drive you back to the ranch. Dawn's on patrol out your way, I'll call her and have her pick me up."

He dug for his keys. "I've been meanin' to ask."

"Yeah?" Zack took the keys and opened the passenger side door for him.

He probably should have taken offense to the way Zack was taking over, like a damned mother hen, he thought belatedly as he climbed in. "You and my baby sister aren't tryin' to get me on the straight and narrow, are ya? 'Cause you both should know it ain't gonna work."

Laughing, Zack closed Dylan's door and got in on the driver's side. "Tracy and me conspiring on something like that? Now I know you don't have any brain cells left."

As Zack pulled away from the curb, Dylan shook his head. "Nah. You're right. Hell would freeze over first."

Zack glanced at him. "Speaking of hell suffering a cold snap, are you going to speak at my banquet in two weeks?"

"I may be drunk, but I'm not drunk enough to be coerced into saying yes to your dinner. That's one favor I won't repay you with."

* * * *

On Monday morning, Charli sat at the table and sipped a cup of coffee, waiting for Dylan to come work on the kitchen. She'd seen very little of him since Friday night.

He'd only spoken to her when it was necessary, and said very little. She didn't have to have a minor in psychology to know he blamed himself for what was happening to her animals. His total avoidance of her did surprise her. They had to talk about what had happened between them.

Did he now think she'd expect him to marry her if she turned up pregnant? He didn't love her, his actions afterward and the way he avoided her clearly proved that. If it was his fear of marriage keeping him away, he needn't worry. She had no intention of ever getting married. One farce of a marriage was enough for anyone.

When she answered the soft knock on the back door, Dylan wasn't on the other side. Tom Miller shuffled his feet with a shy smile pasted on his round face.

She moved to let the bear-like man in. "Where's Dylan?"

After taking off his cowboy hat, he hung it on the hook beside the door. "Quinn's gonna mow one of the hay fields today. He wants to make sure you have good hay. Told me to finish up in here."

She stared at the former sailor for a moment before she realized what he'd meant. Tom passed her, heading toward the doorway leading into the dining room. He began assessing what needed done to the door molding. "He's giving me a break from the weather for a while." He glanced over his shoulder and gave her another shy smile. "And Uncle Jesse. His cantankerousness could test the nerves of a saint."

The only thing she could do was nod. Dylan didn't want anything to do with her. She pressed a hand to the center of her chest and wrapped her other arm around her middle, but the pain in her heart was still unbearable.

When Tom reached for a dust mask on his tool belt, she finally found her voice. "What would you like me to do?"

Tom paused, looked at her and shook his head. "Dylan said you'd probably want to help. You don't have to. I'm used to working alone." He picked up the electric sander Dylan had placed by the wall, and glanced at her. "I'm going to sand this old paint off."

Taking the hidden suggestion within the comment, she nodded and forced herself to move away. Tom didn't want her around either.

She wanted to get as far away from her ranch as she possibly could. After dismissing the idea of calling Leon, she found Tracy's number and gave her a call.

* * * *

"Where the hell have you been all weekend?" Dylan asked the moment Kyle McPherson exited his classic Mustang.

Kyle looked around, pushing his hat back over his shaggy sandy blond hair. "I had things to do, people to see, cuz. I was off, remember?" His grin turned cocky. "If it'd been the boss callin', I'd've paid attention."

Heat raged up Dylan's neck as fast as fire in dry brush. He struggled to unclamp his back teeth. "I called you. Several times, in fact. And the last time I checked, I'm still running this place. Next time I call, you'd damn well better pay attention."

Kyle squared his shoulders and his scruffy jaw twitched. "I'll keep that in mind. So, any of the calves die?"

"No. And I want to keep it that way. They are, under no circumstances, to be fed any hay. There's enough pasture for them and the sick ones are under the care of Doc Evans. I'll take care of the horses."

Kyle's blue eyes narrowed. "Are you implying I'm responsible for this?"

"As far as I'm concerned no one is responsible, but I don't want any more to get sick, and I sure as hell don't want any of them to die."

He ordered Kyle to clear out the storage barn of all the hay. He'd hired a truck to haul it away, and when Kyle finished, he could have the rest of the day off. He didn't want to deal with the kid.

As he passed the barn, Dylan went inside. The roof had been replaced, the walls fixed and the inside gutted. Charli hoped to buy more horses, but the stables could only hold eight at most. The barn had room for twenty horses, plus a large tack room, and special areas for foaling.

"Howdy." Jesse Riley, Tom's wizened uncle, bent over a stall door in the breezeway, glanced at him and continued to hammer in nails. Several more stalls remained to be built.

"Jesse, I need to ask you a question." He had long ago learned Jesse Riley was as nosy as Winnie Cartwright and not much got past him, but unlike the mayor's wife, Jesse usually kept what he knew under his hat-- key being *usually*.

"Yeah." With his hand on his back, Jesse stood up and laid his hammer aside. "What do you want to know?"

He looked around at the construction and piles of boards lying on the concrete floor. "Have you noticed anything odd going on with Kyle?"

Jesse laughed, a nails-rolling-around-in-a-coffee-can sound. "There's always been something *odd* about that boy. I think his mama and daddy should've stopped while they were ahead before having him."

"Did Kyle give Marlin and Jeannie a hard time?"

Again that laugh, as Jesse grabbed a two-by-four off a pile. "Did he ever. Marlin McPherson is a good man, but he spent the last ten years getting the boy out of trouble. Old Sheriff Madison should've put him in juvey hall years ago." Jesse looked at him and shook his head. "Leon Ferguson wouldn't give him a job because he didn't trust him, in fact."

"That's a glowing recommendation." He thought for a moment. "Jesse, keep your eyes and ears open, will ya? I didn't want to hire him, but the boss did."

Jesse tipped the bill of his ball cap. "You got it."

* * * *

Tracy settled across from Charli in a booth at Ella's Diner later that day. "Oh, that's just terrible." Charli had told her all about the poisoning as they walked to the restaurant. "Dylan hasn't talked to me. What I've heard mostly came from Zack and the infamous Colton Grapevine."

Charli reached for a menu. "The sheriff's been a wonderful neighbor, but I wish Dylan would just ask Leon for help. I know he'd be more than willing. I haven't brought it up because I know how he feels about your uncle."

She also hadn't brought it up because Dylan was avoiding her.

Tracy fussed with the napkin-wrapped silverware. Her face pinched in a frown. "Are you seeing him now?"

"Who?"

"Leon." Tracy set the paper napkin and silverware down. "I've heard about the date."

She leaned back into the red vinyl seat. "Wow, does anything stay private in this town?"

Tracy snorted and shook her head. "Nope. The telephones were ringing off the hook Friday after Leon flew you to Dallas. You've become the envy of a lot of women who've been trying to lasso my uncle for years."

"They can have him, because I'm not dating him."

A young waitress stopped by their table. Charli recognized her immediately from the drug deal in the grocery store parking lot.

Tracy voiced her surprise. "Annie, what are you doing here? Shouldn't you be in school?"

The girl stopped short of rolling her eyes. "Mom pulled me out and decided to home school me. What do you want?"

Tracy ordered a burger and fries without looking at the menu. Charli ordered a chicken salad sandwich and fresh fruit. The girl walked away.

"Who's her mother?"

"Ella Larson, the owner of this place and co-owner of the blasted Longhorn Saloon." Tracy made a *tsking* sound and pushed her long hair from the side of her face. "Annie's a troublemaker with a capital *T*. She was arrested on drug charges a month ago. A shame. She's a smart girl." Tracy shook her head and played with her silverware again. "Her mother and father divorced abruptly a couple of years ago, and afterward, her daddy completely ignored her. I heard through the Grapevine he found out he's sterile and probably had been since a horse kicked him when he was a kid."

Charli looked back at Tracy, her meaning dawning. "She doesn't know?" Tracy shrugged, and she turned her attention back to the teenager behind the counter. "How old is she?"

Tracy thought for a moment. "Fifteen or sixteen, I'm not sure."

Annie brought their lemonades, and Charli studied the girl. Her hair was bleached white with the short, spiky tips dyed bright pink, but her roots were dark. Enough black makeup for at least five people surrounded her deep brown eyes. She had a stud in her nose, a hoop in her bottom lip, plus numerous other piercings. Her baggy black pants and t-shirt screamed *bad attitude*.

She felt Annie's anger and resentment sizzling under the surface like some primitive volcano, and remembered the anger all too well. If something wasn't done to help defuse it, her intervention of calling the cops that day would have been for nothing.

"So, what's going on with you and Dylan, then?"

Sipping her lemonade, she stalled as long as she could. "Nothing's going on."

Tracy puckered her brow again, but didn't say more on the matter of either man.

Their meals came, and they ate in silence for a few moments until a woman stopped at their table on her way through the restaurant. "Hello, Tracy."

Tracy narrowed her eyes at the petite brunette carrying an infant carrier by her side. "Brenda. I guess Zack can't keep all the riffraff out of town."

Brenda? As in Dylan's ex? Charli studied the woman closer. Brenda wouldn't ever be a supermodel, but she was prettier than she had imagined. Her dark hair was styled into an attractive pixie cut, her eyes dark and intelligent.

Brenda laughed humorlessly. "Oh, Tracy, you always did have a sick sense of humor. You know what they say... Those in glass houses shouldn't cast stones. When's your next class reunion? You, Zack Cartwright and

Jake Parker all in the same room--I'd buy tickets for that show." Brenda turned to her, holding out a hand to her. "Hi, I'm Brenda Dailey. I don't think we've met."

They shook hands. "Charli Monroe."

"Oh, the owner of the old Blackwell place. My mother told me my ex-husband works for you."

"If your ex-husband is Dylan Quinn, then, yes, he's my manager." She glanced down at the bundle in the carrier. "Is this your baby?"

Brenda's fake smile turned soft, and she pulled the blanket away from the infant's sleeping, chubby face. "Yes, this is Nicholas, Junior. He's almost eight months old and growing like a weed."

"What do you want, Brenda?" Tracy sounded as if she chipped the words from the coldest ice cube she could find.

The woman shrugged. "I just saw the two of you and thought I'd do the neighborly thing and say hi. I'm supposed to meet Mama for lunch." Brenda turned to her again--fake smile bright enough to short-out a power plant.

Anger ripped through Charli. How could anyone hurt someone as badly as Brenda had Dylan? Though he didn't talk about the reasons for his divorce, she had heard enough to know. Brenda's baby had been conceived while he'd been, not only still married to her, but in Afghanistan fighting for his country.

Brenda shifted the carrier from one hand to another. A big diamond on her finger glittered in the sunlight coming through the window. "I'm a bit surprised Dylan is still working for you, Miss Monroe."

Besides the jealousy burning a hole in her stomach, she didn't like this woman with a mile-long vicious streak. How could Dylan have loved someone so self-absorbed? How could he still love her? "Why are you surprised? He's an excellent manager."

"I've heard about his buying poisoned hay. He was probably drunk."

"I haven't lost anything because of Dylan."

"Now that surprises me." Brenda waved at an older woman--probably her mother--as she entered the diner. "Dylan cares only for himself."

She speared the woman with a glare. "You're wrong."

"Excuse me."

Charli placed her napkin beside her mostly empty plate and slid out of the booth. Brenda stiffened when Charli went toe-to-toe with her, and towered over her by a good four inches. "A man doesn't fight for his country voluntarily and struggle with the type of guilt Dylan does because he doesn't care. If you ask me, he cares too damned much about a lot of things."

After picking up the check from the edge of the table, she looked at Tracy, who regarded her with something akin to stunned admiration as she stood. "Are you ready? I better get back."

"Yeah." Tracy adjusted the strap of her big canvas purse. "The clientele of this place just hit an all-time low."

They left, leaving Dylan's ex staring after them with her mouth hanging open.

* * * *

Dylan stopped the tractor and lifted a bottle of water to his lips. Damn, he didn't mind grunt work, but he hadn't expected to be the one mowing hay when he signed on as Charli's manager. He needed to do something besides sitting around waiting for her animals to die or her to fire him.

He also had to clear his head. Something about the whole poisoning had been eating at him since he'd found those poor critters lying in the field. The more he thought about it all, the more he suspected something more malicious than bad hay.

His gut told him not to trust Kyle McPherson.

However, his gut had been wrong before.

Four good soldiers were dead and five more wounded because he'd trusted his instincts.

He put the water bottle away and shifted the tractor into gear as he looked over the neat rows of mowed grass, and snorted a chuckle. How fickle were the wishes of a farmer? After several terrible drought years, the recent storms were more than welcome. But now, he hoped the weatherman was right and the rain held off for a few days until he got the hay baled and stowed in the barn.

On the way back to the equipment shed, he looked out over the pasture bordering Oak Springs Ranch on the right. Two old derricks sat rusting away in the center of the field. On the other side of the fencerow, another loomed in what had been a jointly run oilfield for fifty years. Most of the modern Ferguson and Blackwell wealth had come from that field.

The Fergusons had invested wisely. The Blackwells hadn't. Bad blood between the clans resulted, which only escalated when the drilling abruptly stopped forty-two years ago. The rumor from the time claimed Jock Blackwell put a stop to the drilling when Dylan's grandfather, Jason Ferguson, married his second wife, Maddie. Jason had insisted the drilling stopped because the oil ran out.

Dylan looked back to the rutted path leading to the barn when a slight movement in the brush around one of the capped oil wells caught his attention. He swung his gaze over to the old oilrig just in time to glimpse a telltale flash of sunlight reflecting off a rifle barrel.

Instinct kicked in. He ducked down just as the whirl of a bullet passed through the cab of the tractor, displacing the air where his head should have been.

He stopped the tractor as another bullet whizzed by, scrunching his eyes closed against visions of fire, flying dirt and shredded metal. Of men's screams of pain as they were blown to bits. He gasped at his own pain--some imagined, some real--in his bad hip. Forcing his eyes open, he focused on the instrument panel of the tractor to stay grounded in the present and not back on the mountain road outside Kandahar.

He crouched as low as he could get in the cab between the seat and the controls, reached under the seat and pulled out the .357 he'd stashed there that morning. Having lived in Texas long enough, he knew to pack heat when riding the range. In the past, it would have been for situations such as he found himself in now, but mostly, he carried the gun to kill rattlesnakes and scare off an occasional coyote.

He removed his hat and peeked over the edge of the door. Despite not seeing anything, he aimed the pistol and fired in the spot he'd first seen the flash. If nothing else, whoever was out there would know he was armed and had sharpshooter aim.

The low rumble of the tractor engine became deafening in those moments of waiting. After a few minutes, he determined the shooter had slunk back to whatever hole he'd crawled out of.

Dylan eased the tractor into gear and moved forward several yards before sitting in the seat and heading in as fast as the Monroe Special 1025 could move.

* * * *

After Dylan parked the tractor and mower in the equipment shed, he headed for the house.

Sure enough, a black Porsche parked in the drive. Upon hearing Charli's laugh, he headed toward it. She and Leon stood in the yard by one of the flowerbeds. A pile of weeds and lopped-off overgrowth lay next to it. She held her gloves in one hand, which rested on her hip in a relaxed manor. She motioned with the other, laughing at something Leon must have said. Who would've thought the bastard could be so funny?

Hidden in the shadow of the house, he stared at Charli. A big straw hat cast her face in shadow, but he could hear her just fine.

"Thanks again for stopping by, Leon. Honestly, we're fine. Dr. Evans believes my animals are on the mend."

Leon took her free hand. "Let me know if you need anything, anything at all."

Her bright smile hit him as hard as a kick in the balls. "I will, I promise."

With the tenacity of a pit bull, he headed in to break up the happy couple. "Charli, you need to go inside now."

Her brow puckered, and she pulled her hand from Leon's. "What on Earth for?"

He peered at Leon before answering. "Someone just took a couple of pot shots at me out by the old derricks."

"*What?*" Her face lost color. "Someone *shot* at you?"

"Yeah." He glanced at Leon, who was dressed casually in jeans, a Western shirt and that white Stetson--like some spaghetti Western good guy. "None of your cowhands would be *poaching*, would they?"

Leon slipped his arm around her waist. She didn't move away. "I highly doubt it. Are you sure they aimed for you?"

"If I hadn't seen the sun reflect off the barrel, someone would be planning a funeral right about now."

Charli looked a little woozy. She stepped out of Leon's embrace, hugged herself and moved closer to Dylan. "We have to call the sheriff."

He fought the urge to wrap his arms around her by clenching and unclenching his fists at his sides. "I already did. But I really would like if you went inside."

She nodded and looked at Leon.

He rested his hand on her shoulder and she leaned into it. "You should go in and stay in until Sheriff Cartwright gets to the bottom of this. I'm sure it's just a hunter poaching on either your land or mine, but one can never be too cautious. I'll stay if you want."

"No, I'll be okay."

"All right." The sight of Leon placing a kiss on her forehead about sent Dylan into the stratosphere. Leon drawled, "Call me."

She smiled and nodded. "I will."

After they went inside the kitchen and she brewed a pot of coffee, he paced while waiting for Zack. He couldn't take the silence. "What's going on between you and Ferguson?"

She poured two mugs of coffee. "He's one of my few friends."

"He looked damned *friendly* out there a few moments ago." He hated coming off as a jealous idiot, but damn it, she could be pregnant with his baby. Besides, being shot at was enough to make anyone prickly as a cactus.

"Maybe we were. What's it to you?" She jutted her chin. "You already think I've slept with him, so maybe I should. He's more than a little interested in me."

"Yeah, he is. When are you going to see through his lies?"

"Leon is not lying to me. He's nice to me, which I could say your idea of *nice* needs reevaluating."

The front doorbell sounded before he could respond, and she stomped down the hall to answer it. Zack Cartwright and his lieutenant, Dawn Madison, entered the foyer.

Zack pulled out a notebook from his pocket. "Tell me what happened."

* * * *

"That bastard would've killed me!" Kyle McPherson paced the teak flooring of his boss's office later that evening.

The SOB leaned back in his chair and stared out the window behind his desk. "You should have had better aim."

"If you want Quinn dead, you fuckin' do it. Sombitch is as crazy as a three-legged armadillo. He couldn't've seen me, but if I hadn't moved, I would be the one dead."

The boss snorted and stood. "Now, that would have been a damned shame."

Kyle jumped when the boss grabbed him by the front of his shirt, shook him for good measure, and gritted out between clamped teeth, "You will do exactly what I order you to do."

"Why don't I just finish off the calves? Or those mares? A little more jimson or some other weed will do it. Hell, I could even set it up to look like Quinn's doing the poisonin'."

"Why not? Because you're being watched, you fool." He let go of his shirt with a shove and stepped away. "Get the hell out of here. I'll be in touch. You still owe me."

He beat his hat on his thigh before plopping it on his head and leaving.

Chapter 11

Charli entered the diner and made her way to a booth. The place was empty. She'd timed her visit just after the breakfast rush and before the lunch crowd's arrival. A moment later, a blonde woman, who appeared to be in her early forties, approached her table. "Hi, honey, what can I getcha?"

She returned her smile. "Sweet tea, please."

"Comin' right up."

When the woman returned with the beverage, Charli asked, "Would it be possible to speak with Ella Larson for a few moments?"

The women shrugged and folded her arms over her red apron. "Sure. That's me. What can I do for ya?"

"Can you have a seat?"

"Sure." She slid into the booth across from her. "I'm not busy at the moment."

Charli swallowed hard and mentally plunged. "I'd like to talk to you about your daughter, Annie."

Her eyes widened. Annie had obviously learned how to apply makeup from her mother. "What about Annie? Are you from the Department of Family and Protective Services? I swear if that son-of-a-bitch is trying--"

"No," she broke in, "I'm not from DFPS. My name is Charli Monroe. I'm the new owner of Blackwell Ranch."

Ella narrowed her brown eyes at her. "What do you know about Annie?"

She took a much-needed deep breath and gulped a sip of tea to settle her nerves. It didn't work, but she trudged on. In spite of everything going on in her own messed up life over the past week, she couldn't stop thinking about Annie since seeing her again on Monday. "I know she's recently been arrested for drugs."

Ella laughed, but it was bitter sounding and raspy, as if she'd smoked one too many cigarettes. "Hell, everybody knows that. What do you want?"

"I made the call. I saw Annie buying drugs in the mall parking lot."

Ella scowled and shifted forward. "My daughter could go to jail because of you."

She wouldn't let Ella intimidate her. "Yes, she could, but I'm hoping it was an intervention. If it was her first offense, she'll most likely get off with a fine and probation. And if she's lucky, it will turn her life around."

"So, you think because you were a runaway and ended up in Vegas, you're an expert."

She took a deep breath. It would be so easy to let this all go, to turn away and never think about Annie Greenberg again. Her past would remain where it needed to be--in the past. But she couldn't let Annie continue down the path she was on. She had to do everything she could to stop Annie from making the same horrible mistakes she had made. She'd promised herself when she got out of prison she'd do everything possible to make sure another misunderstood teenage girl *never* lived the horrors she had.

"Yes, I lived on the streets of Las Vegas." A lump lodged in her throat, but she forced it down and the quiet words out. "I've seen what addiction can do to a person, Ella. I had friends who died there. Most times no one even knew their real names. Their families never knew what happened to them."

Although trepidation replaced Ella's scowl, her voice remained indignant. "Who the hell do you think you are? You think you know what my daughter's going through. You have no idea."

As Ella got out of the booth, Charli fisted her hand under the table. "Has she been in any kind of treatment at least? Is she talking to someone? I heard the rumors about your husband. Does she know why her father doesn't want anything to do with her?"

Ella looked back at her. "How do you know about that?" Her eyes narrowed again. "You're seeing Leon Ferguson, aren't you?"

What did Leon have to do with anything? "He's my neighbor, that's all. Ms. Larson, I understand Annie better than you can ever imagine." She paused and her heart raced. "I--I never knew my father, and I hated him because I thought he abandoned me. My mother raised me until she died when I was fifteen. When I came home after running away, my grandfather found me help, and I was able to sort through the pain, grief and anger. Annie needs that--she's hurting."

A resigned frown pulled at one side of Ella's too-red lips. "Look, I don't know what you think can be gained by this, but Annie is on a runaway train straight to trouble, and there's not a damned thing anyone can do but pick up the pieces after the crash."

"What if you could prevent the crash?" She had to make her see her point. "Has she ever run away?"

Ella scowled her for a long moment. Then she slid back into the booth and slumped over her arms on the faux marble tabletop. "She's run away twice now. One of these days I'm so afraid she'll...get hurt." She looked away and muttered, "Especially if he gets hold of her."

What did *that* mean? "Annie needs help."

Ella met her eyes again. "I know. She refuses to talk to a shrink. Aren't you some kind of doctor?"

"Goodness no. I'm majoring in social work at the college and would like to help girls like Annie eventually." She pressed her hands onto the table to keep them from shaking. "And, although it's a long way off in the future, I can't stop thinking I can help Annie somehow. Where does she stay while you're at the Longhorn?"

Ella squared her shoulders. "She's at home."

"Alone? Or is she on the streets?"

Ella averted her eyes again. "Yeah."

She didn't have to ask her to clarify the breathy answer.

Her temper flaring again, Ella leaned back against the seat and fisted both hands where they rested on the edge of the table. "I'll deal with Annie any way I see fit. Why do you care what happens to her?"

"I care because I know what's out there, Ms. Larson." She gathered her courage. She'd already told Ella more than she ever wanted anyone to know about her past, but Annie's life could hang in the balance. "I'd like to talk to Annie, that's all." She handed the woman a business card. "Please, think about it and call me. I'd hate for Annie to get into trouble. I called the cops so she could get help. Find a good therapist and get her to talk. I think we both know Annie's problems are deeper than just drugs."

Ella looked at the card, and after a while, nodded. "Okay, I'll think about letting you talk to her."

* * * *

Charli walked Leon down the steps of the porch to his car. "Thanks again for dinner."

He turned and smiled at her. "Since you won't agree to go out to dinner with me, I have to bring dinner here."

Heat infused her cheeks and she sighed. "I really do appreciate it. It's been a long week and a half. You've been wonderful through it all. Thank you."

"There's no need to thank me, Charli." He took her hand, and she squeezed. He'd been here for her since the poisoning.

He gently pulled her to him and wrapped her up in his arms. Before she could hug him back, she felt the distinct bulge of an erection and tried to pull away. "Leon, I can't."

"Please, let me hold you. I would never force you to do anything against your will." The gruffness of his voice rang all sorts of warning bells in her head. "But I..."

She should have known this was coming. "Leon?"

He cleared his throat. "Charli, I'm falling in love with you."

She sucked in a breath and stared up at him. *Holy shit!* Now what was she supposed to do?

His chuckle seemed forced as he ran the back of his fingers down her cheek and cupped the side of her face. "I know you don't feel the same, but I hope someday you will. We could be so good together. Our combined ranches would be the most profitable in all of Central Texas. Our wealth unmatched. You could staff this place and open that home you told me about. You'd be the mistress of Oak Springs, a member of the Junior League, if you wish. With me, you'd be a lady of society and no one would *ever* think of speaking against you. I'd take care of you."

Oh, God. When she opened her lips to speak, he touched his thumb to her mouth. "I don't want any answers tonight." Leon paused and swallowed. "I have to go to Denver for a little while."

"The land deal?" She sucked in a breath of relief, so not ready for any of this, but she didn't want to hurt him either.

He nodded. "The negotiations have hit a major snag over the mineral rights of the tract of land I want. My lawyer thinks I should show up and explain to the sellers what my plans are. I hope to pound out a deal that's agreeable to all concerned parties in a few days."

"I'll miss you. You'll be careful?" She wanted to wrap her arms around him, but she couldn't make her arms respond.

He placed a soft kiss on her forehead. "Of course I will. I have the most beautiful woman in the world to come home to. I love you, Charli." Before she could respond to him, he kissed her long, hard and with passion enough for them both.

* * * *

"...love you, Charli." Like the whisper from the devil, the raspy words floated to Dylan.

The kiss that followed went on for an eternity and glued him in the dusky place between the barn and stable watching it.

So, she'd made her choice.

Maybe he needed to make one, too.

* * * *

Dylan reread the faxed report and tossed it onto his desk. After glancing at the letter to Charli he'd written earlier, he turned the chair around to look out the window at the pasture. He shouldn't care what the report said, but he did. If he truly planned to resign, as he declared in the handwritten letter, he wouldn't struggle to make sense of the fax, would he?

As her herd nibbled the rich, green grass in the field, his mind continued to clear from the alcohol he'd tried to drown in last night.

Hadn't Brenda taught him women couldn't be trusted? He'd been a fool to let himself get involved with Charli emotionally. Yet, he couldn't let go.

He focused his thoughts on the report. The toxicity of the calves' blood showed the amount of poison only found in green jimsonweed, and a great deal of it at that. However, the only place they could have gotten the weed was in the hay, which made no sense. If they had ingested more, they would've died from it.

Someone had fed the animals the fresh jimsonweed and made it look like it came from the hay. He turned his chair around and dialed the sheriff's department.

After explaining to the answering officer he needed to speak to the sheriff, he was transferred. The younger man answered on the second ring.

"Zack, it's Dylan."

"Captain, to what do I owe this pleasure?" He heard the smile in Zack's voice. "Is someone else using you for target practice? Or have you reconsidered my invite to the banquet on Monday?"

"No, and I won't." The man never gave up. "And no, no one is shooting at me." Despite the teasing tone, the sheriff had taken the threat seriously, and neither of them thought it was a poacher. Someone had aimed to kill, but left no evidence behind to track. "I got the report back from Doc Evan's lab. I'm convinced Charli's cattle and horses were intentionally poisoned."

"Do you have any of the hay left that was fed to the animals?"

"Affirmative." He glanced at the sacks of hay leaning against the corner of his office and told Zack his suspicions.

"Bring it in to the department. I'll send it to the Rangers' lab ASAP. It would take a helluva lot of jimson to make that many calves and two horses sick, so if it did come from the hay, there has to be more of the stuff in it."

"I'll get it to you by noon with a copy of the report."

"Do you know if Miss Monroe has any enemies?"

The same question had plagued him. He didn't know much about her For all he knew, she could have been part of a gang or even the mob in Vegas, but he did know of one enemy who was a lot closer to home.

The memory of the kiss he'd witnessed churned the acid in his belly. Unlike when Brenda had slept with her fellow teacher, getting herself pregnant in the bargain, he knew Charli was being tricked. Leon didn't love her, he'd bet his life on it. Somehow, he had to get her to see it.

"I don't know if she has any enemies or not. But I think it would be best to keep this between us until we know what *isn't* in the hay."

Zack hesitated only a moment. "Roger, Captain. I'll do it your way for now. If you find out anything, let me know."

"I will." He hung up the phone.

He picked up the letter of resignation and looked at the short handwritten note. When had he become such a coward? He'd been avoiding her, knowing they needed to talk about what had happened, and just as importantly, what it meant.

By avoiding her, he'd left the door open for Leon. She could still choose Leon, but before that happened, he intended to prove to her Leon wasn't all he pretended to be.

He was more determined than ever to make sure he atoned for all the bad decisions he'd made over the past couple of weeks. Even if it meant sticking around and discovering Charli felt nothing for him despite the child they may have created together.

He stood and tossed the scrap of paper in the general direction of the trashcan under his desk. After he made a copy of the fax, he grabbed the sacks of hay gathered from the feeders and headed out. The sooner he got the answer back from the Texas Ranger forensics lab in Austin, the sooner he could set a trap to catch the two-legged snake in the garden.

Chapter 12

Dear Charli,
By the time you read this, I'll be heading for Denver and thinking about you. I wish I could be there right now. I already miss you. Call me.
Love, Leon

Charli lowered the embossed card and stared at the large bouquet of deep red roses.

She'd spent all night trying to convince herself she would be better off with Leon. Dylan would just have to accept Leon being in his child's life. However, no matter how much her brain tried to reason out all the good things that could come out of being with Leon, her heart wouldn't listen. It steadfastly belonged to Dylan.

The realization cleansed her soul of indecision and confusion. She crumpled the letter and carried the roses with her when she left the kitchen. At the trash receptacle on the other side of the garage, she tossed them and turned toward the bunkhouse.

When Dylan didn't answer the knock on the screen door of his office, she turned around and looked out over the pasture. Her cattle nibbled on the tender green vegetation. Was he working on the range?

She turned back to the door. Perhaps, he was inside eating lunch, or he'd seen her approach, and like a coward, hid from her. He wouldn't be hiding from her for long.

Taking a fortifying breath, she opened the screen door and turned the knob of the solid door. After she entered the small room, she peeked around the frame of the open door separating his living space from the office. "Dylan? Are you in there?"

Her only answer was the low hum from a window air conditioner. She stepped into the darkened room serving as his living area and bedroom. At the bottom of a futon, a blanket and sheet were tangled into a ball.

A small square table and two chairs made up the rest of the apartments furnishings. She stared at the empty bottle of whiskey sitting on the tabletop. Swallowing hard, she turned away.

No sign of the man who occupied these sparse quarters.

She heaved a sigh of disappointment and turned to leave the way she'd come. On the desk, she noticed a letter with the official letterhead of Sam Evans' veterinarian clinic.

She picked up the fax and read the report that told her nothing she hadn't already known. Her calves and horses had gotten sick from ingesting the toxic plant datura stramonium, commonly known as jimsonweed.

The sheet of paper fell from her hand and landed back on the desk. She noticed another paper on the floor partway under Dylan's desk as she moved away. The letter was addressed to her in his strong handwriting. She picked it up.

Charli,
I quit.
If you are pregnant with my baby, I hope you'll let me know before you and Leon do anything. My sister will know where to find me. I'll do what I can, but I can't be there.
Dylan

She had to read the letter twice before the full impact of its meaning hit her hard enough to shatter her heart.

Dylan was just like every other man she'd ever loved. He'd used her and thrown her away.

At least Leon wanted her. Maybe she shouldn't have been so hasty with throwing away his note.

Too bad, he wasn't the man she wanted.

"Charli?"

At the sound of Dylan's voice, she sniffed back the tears, but didn't turn to face him. She held up the letter. "So, this is what you want?" How could she face him? But she had to. He stood inside the door. "When are you leaving? Tonight? Like some coward!"

"I'm..." He took a step toward her, and the screen door closed with a bang.

"Don't." She held out her hand. "Just don't. I don't want you to be sorry. I don't want to hear your excuses." She tried to rush past him, but he caught her around the waist.

"I'm not going anywhere." He pressed so close, and despite what he intended to do to her, his touch was like a balm on a sore nothing else would heal.

She tugged free of his grasp and flailed the sheet of paper at him. "That's not what this says."

Dylan dropped his hands to his side, his face full of chiseled regret.

He turned toward the desk and tossed his hat on it. As he shoved his hands through his dark hair, he gruffly said, "You were never supposed to see that letter."

"Oh. So, were you just gonna take off and I'd never see you again?" She hated the brittle sound of her voice and the fear crashing over her. The pain in her chest made it hard to breathe, and she wrapped her arms around her middle. He didn't love her, but she'd never believed he'd abandon her.

* * * *

Dylan turned and hated what he witnessed. Charli backed away from him like a scared little animal. How could he cause her so much pain and fear? He took her into his arms and pulled her close to him again.

She didn't fight him, but she made no move to hug him back.

"I'm not leaving you. Unless you tell me you don't want me. I wrote that letter this morning while I was still drunk." When she looked up at him, he wiped at the wetness on her cheek with his thumb. "I'm scared I can't be the man you deserve." *I'm afraid you don't love me.* "I never wanted kids. I don't think I'll be a good father. My own father was never around, but he was around enough for me to know I'll never measure up to Bob Quinn." Muttering, he added, "I never did in any other way."

"I'm scared, too." She slipped her arms around him. "Too much is going on at once. What are we going to do?"

"I don't know. But I told you I'd be here for you, and I will. When do you expect to get your...eh..."

Charli swallowed and tears shimmered in her eyes. "I'm late, if that's what you're asking."

Nodding, he glanced away and his shoulders slumped. *Damn.* "Charli, I can't play games with you. I saw the kiss the other night." He met her widened eyes. "What does Leon mean to you?"

"Nothing. He has feelings for me I don't return." She paused and swallowed so hard her throat moved. The pulse fluttered at the side of her neck. "What does Brenda still mean to you?"

"Not a damned thing." *What do I mean to you?* But he couldn't get the words past his tight throat. "But even if you are pregnant, I'm not ready for marriage again." He couldn't let himself get in that deep. Marriage to a woman who didn't love him was the last thing he wanted.

Charli slowly nodded and turned away. She wrapped her arms around her middle and looked out the screen door. "And I--I don't want a marriage either. I won't be trapped in a marriage for a child's sake. That's worse, in my opinion, than living separately. Actually, I never want to get married. I'll never let a man have that much control over me."

Her words cut through his heart like a mower through grass. But didn't he feel the same way? He forced air past the knot in his throat. "Are you going to take a test?"

She faced him again. "I will, but I've been late before. I'll give it a couple more days." He nodded his agreement, and then she jutted her chin toward his desk. "I saw the report."

He cleared his throat before turning toward the desk. "Yeah. Jimsonweed poisoning."

"Are you going to come back to work on the house?"

He wanted to. He missed her, their meals, the conversations about everything to nothing, her icy glares, her sunny smiles and her fiery arguments. She made him feel alive, and because of the joy she found in his work, he could take pride in something again.

To flush out the tool who'd poisoned the animals and to prevent any other calamities, he had to work alongside him. "No. Isn't Tom working out?"

"Tom's okay." She moved away and faced the window behind his desk. "But he doesn't let me help and doesn't work as fast as you. I really want to get the house done. You'd told me Kyle could handle the ranch work."

He looked down at the floor and clenched his fist. He hated not telling her the whole truth. "After the poisoning, the work has doubled. I won't buy hay again, and getting it in from your fields takes both of us."

"Oh." She sniffed and didn't look at him. "Maybe I should just hire a general contractor to do the work. Leon has offered his company."

At the mention of the name, he turned her to look at him. "No. Not Ferguson." Despite her glare, he headed off her argument. "If you want to hire someone to come in and do the work, that's fine. As long as it's not Ferguson."

Her expression remained defiant. "What if I want Leon's company to do the work? I've seen some of the houses his company has built. They're beautiful."

"And shoddy."

She shook her head and pushed his hands away. "Dear God, Dylan, I know you don't like him, but it's not like Leon himself will be driving the nails and painting my walls."

"No, he wants you on your back and your deed in his name." He stepped away with clenched fists. Heat crawled up his neck. "Maybe he's already gotten you into bed, but I won't let him take this land the way he swindled my grandfather out of his." The moment the words were out, he regretted them.

"I can't believe you! Do you have any idea how insulting that is?" Charli shot him through with blue-green fire. "Yes, Leon wants me, but I haven't slept with him. I don't want to! And I can't believe you still think he wants my land. Why? Why the hell would he want my ranch when he can buy whatever land he wants?"

"You can't be this blind or naive. Think! You know everyone in town was shocked when you took the bid for this place out from under Leon. In all the years I've known him, he has never gone after a local woman, and then you show up and suddenly he's all over you. Is being socially accepted by this town so damned important, you'd willingly fall for his act?"

The tears misting her eyes extinguished the fire. Damn, he didn't mean to hurt her.

"But why? Why does he want my ranch so badly?" She hugged herself again. Her face went pale, and she sat in the old chair in the corner by the door. Finally, he'd made her think.

He leaned his backside against the desk, facing her. "I wish I knew why. I only know Leon has wanted this place for almost as long as I've known him."

He looked down at his crossed boots. "When we were kids, my family came to Oak Springs for Christmas. I was about seven, Leon was twelve or thirteen, I think. Anyway, we were fooling around like boys do, and we snuck over here. He wanted to check out those old derricks. When we got to the bridge, Leon stopped the four-wheeler we were riding. I looked toward the house and saw old Jock standing on the front porch with one of his girlfriends and Johnny--Jock's first son. He's about the same age as Leon. And I figured they probably knew each other."

He stared into the past as he spoke. "Jock looked up at us, and it was almost as if there was some silent exchange between him and Leon. After a moment, Leon looked at me with so much hatred in his eyes it scared me."

As he submerged himself into the long ago scene from that mild winter day, he remembered the way Leon's face turned hard at seeing Jock with his family. Something tripped in him. He looked up to find her watching him. "We were about halfway back to Oak Springs when he said to me, 'I'll own that ranch someday.' I laughed and said something about Jock's kid, and Leon looked at me and said, 'His bastards don't matter. Blackwell Ranch will rightfully be mine.'"

He paused, his mind buzzed with a hunch so outrageous he didn't believe it himself. "I didn't think anything about it until I'd heard about Leon firing three of his lawyers and his secretary when he discovered you beat him to the bid on this place. Then it slipped out he'd been trying for years to buy the ranch from Jock. Then Jock destroyed his will. The consensus at the time was he was just being a son-of-a-bitch by not giving it to his sons and letting it go to probate. Everyone chalked it up to his craziness. I'd say it's because the last person Jock Blackwell wanted to have this place was Leon and that's who would have bought it from the Blackwell boys." He kneeled before her. "Suddenly those childish declarations didn't seem so silly. Don't trust him, Peaches." He skimmed his fingers over her pale, damp, cheek. "I don't want you to get hurt."

I don't want to be hurt if you turn to him.

* * * *

Four days later, Dylan invited Tracy out to the ranch. After they'd eaten the burgers she'd picked up from Ella's on the way over, he'd suggested they go riding. Bobby was content to stay and torment Jesse as he finished up for the day in the barn. He saddled the black and the sorrel Charli had named Ceres. The bay, Athena, seemed healthy enough, but he didn't want to take the chance by saddling her.

Tracy reached over the stall door and rubbed Aurora's long white-splotched face. "She's a beautiful horse."

He tightened the cinch on Artemis. He hated her name, and had a tendency to refer to her as Artie when Charli wasn't around. Who named horses after Greek and Roman goddesses anyway? The answer made him smile as he patted Artie's graceful neck. Only Charli. Over his shoulder, he looked at Tracy. "She's had a rough couple of weeks."

"Is she the one that was sick and aborted?" Tracy took the reins of Ceres, who waited in the breezeway, saddled and anxious to go.

"Yeah, but she's doing better. Let's go. I need to talk to you." He swung up into the saddle and led the way out of the stable.

As they headed toward the southeastern side of the property, he gathered his thoughts on the way. Once they came to an unused pasture full of wildflowers, he stopped.

Tracy pulled up beside him. "Okay, big brother, what's going on?"

He leaned over the saddle horn and pushed his hat back over his forehead. "What do you know about Kyle McPherson?"

"What do you want to know?"

He straightened and turned to peer at her. "Remember I haven't lived in Colton for thirteen years, sis. What was he like as a kid? Jesse told me he was a troublemaker. Tell me what you know. You know almost everything that goes on in this town before it even happens because women like to talk when they get their hair done."

Tracy furrowed her brows and looked away. "I know Kyle had a few run-ins with the law when he was a teenager, but his father always got him off the hook. He worked for his grandfather on his ranch until Uncle Jim sold it to the developer. He always has a flashy car and likes to buy his girlfriends expensive jewelry. Just the other day, Jenny Garret showed me the impressive emerald bauble he'd given to her."

"Do you wonder where he gets the money? Charli isn't paying him that much. Her wages are fair, but they aren't gonna make a man rich."

She shrugged. "Maybe it's not real or his credit cards are maxed."

"Maybe." He frowned. "Was he ever in trouble for drugs?"

"I don't know." Tracy looked at him. "Wait. I think he was. Got himself in trouble over in Waco about a year and a half ago, but his daddy pulled strings with Sheriff Madison, right before the old man retired, and they got the charges dropped or lessened. Shouldn't you already know this? He is *your* employee."

He took a deep breath. "He legally doesn't have to tell an employer anything if the charges didn't stick. Damn, if I'd known that, though, he wouldn't be working here. I knew I should've called Wyatt before I hired him." Wyatt McPherson was Kyle's older brother and a Texas Ranger. Maybe he should still call his old friend.

"Did he steal something? What this is all about?"

"I think he's responsible for the poisoning."

"*What?*" She shook her head. "Kyle's a spoiled brat, but I don't believe for a minute he'd poison horses and cattle."

He glanced away and dismounted. After moving away, he waited for Tracy to follow him to the ground. "I know McPherson did the feeding the morning the stock got sick. According to Jesse, Kyle acted jittery for a few days before the animals got sick. The morning before I found the calves, Kyle started the feeding before five-thirty. I don't think the boy has ever been here that early. I also know jimsonweed is easy to buy on the street."

She stared at him for a moment. "Why would Kyle poison Charli's animals?"

"On the orders of someone willing to pay him enough to afford fancy emeralds for his lady love." He raised a brow, and as soon as Tracy added two plus two, she widened her eyes. But in case she still had trouble coming up with four, he added, "And who in this county has more money than morals?"

"You don't really think Leon is behind it, do you?"

"I wouldn't put anything past that snake. Including murder."

His sister shrieked, "You think he's behind the shooting, too!"

"Tracy, Leon wants this land. And he wants me out of the way."

"But *why?*" She shoved her fists to her hips and squared her shoulders. "Your insistence on this is going beyond crazy. Accusing anyone of such crimes is serious business, but our uncle--who just happens to be one of the richest men in Central Texas--is downright ludicrous."

Although he'd lived in Colton as a teenager and for the past year, Leon hadn't been around much during his high school days. He'd been off at Harvard, and after Leon graduated, he'd gone to work for his grandfather in Houston. Tracy, on the other hand, had never left Colton since moving here. She'd gotten pregnant her first year at Colton College and dropped out to marry Jock Blackwell's nephew, Jake Parker. Possibly, she knew a great deal more about Leon and Maddie Ferguson than he did.

He ran his hand through his hair. "What do you know about Leon's real father?"

Widened eyes replaced her frown, and she thoughtfully sucked on her bottom lip. "Not much. Maddie doesn't talk about him. I've never even heard the man mentioned by name. Dylan, what the hell are you thinking?"

He looked out over the drifts of yellow, white, blue and red flowers. "Something beyond crazy."

"Dylan?"

He glanced over his shoulder at her. "Yeah."

"Why do you care if Leon gets this place or not? Rumor has it Charli and Leon are seeing each other."

"Because Charli has worked too hard for this place to have it swindled away from her by sweet talk and bouquets of roses."

Tracy gently touched his shoulder. "You're in love with her, aren't you?"

"I'll never let a woman do to me again what Brenda did. Charli's just a good person who has had a tough life and deserves a fair chance to make it."

Tracy snaked her arm around his waist and laid her head against his shoulder. "Oh, Dylan."

A white butterfly swayed gently on the wind over the field. He had to save this land from Leon's greed. If he couldn't give his kid a normal family where Mom and Dad lived happily ever after, he'd make damned sure he or she had a home.

He moved away from Tracy and mounted Artie. "Let's get back."

Charli had had her few days. By now, she should've pissed on a stick. And he'd know if his life was about to become a whole hell of a lot more complicated.

Chapter 13

Charli stepped back from the wall, admiring the painting she'd purchased from an antique dealer in town. It was a beautiful seascape with one of the famous lighthouses along the southern coast in the foreground. She tilted her head to one side and retreated another step to admire her handiwork. The picture was perfect.

Tom worked somewhere upstairs. He never asked for help, and if she didn't hear the sounds of an occasional saw or hammer and the twang of his radio, she'd wonder if he was even around.

After Leon left for his business trip, she'd decided to redo her bedroom. Tediously, she'd stripped the woodwork and repainted it a pure white, then painted the walls azure. When she'd pulled up the putrid green carpet, she uncovered red oak in reasonably good condition. She'd polished the flooring as she and Dylan had done in the living room.

Now as she looked at the once drab room, pleasure tingled through her. She'd done this. All of it. Before she'd met Dylan, she wouldn't have known where to start.

He'd gotten under her skin the first day they'd met and stayed there.

As she looked down over her flat tummy, she tried to imagine herself pregnant. She couldn't, didn't want to. How could she ever be a mother? She'd been close to hers, but Momma died when she just started needing her mother the most.

She forced the wave of grief down and went into the bathroom. After taking a quick shower, she changed into a clean pair of shorts and a t-shirt before heading back into the bedroom.

She admired her handiwork for a few more minutes. She had to talk to Dylan and stop stalling.

"Is this another one of your butterflies?"

She slowly turned at the sound of his deep voice. Dylan stood in the doorway of her bedroom. Thick, dark brown hair fell over his forehead, the skin tanned from the sun. Broad shoulders filled the opening, and he had his hands tucked into the pockets of his faded jeans. He took her breath away.

Meeting his silver eyes, she gave him a small smile. "You could say that. This room was ugly before I started on it."

"Yeah, it was." He stepped through the door and looked over the room as he moved toward her. The dimple in his left cheek deepened when he grinned. "I'm impressed."

She shrugged and clasped her hands before her, uncomfortable and, yet, pleased with his praise. "I only redecorated it. Wasn't all too difficult."

He chuckled low, and it vibrated through her. "Who are you kidding? I remember teaching you which end of the paintbrush to hold."

It was too painful to look up at him and know she was about to destroy whatever might have been. She wrapped her arms around her middle. "I--I'm pregnant."

Unable to hold back the tears, she turned away from him, not able to bear watching his teasing admiration turn to hatred for trapping him in unwanted fatherhood. When he didn't speak, she squeezed her eyes shut against the hollow ache. In a voice so soft she doubted he'd hear it, she whispered, "You don't have to be involved if you don't want to be."

"No." His arms engulfed her from behind and turned her to face him. The disbelief in his eyes surprised her. "I told you I'd be here. Neither one of us may have wanted this, but we created a life together." His voice broke and he swallowed hard. "I said the other day I'd never measure up to my father. I know I never will if I walk away from you and our baby. I'm not like your father, Charli, and I won't let another man raise my child."

She wrapped her arms around him and buried her face into his shoulder. He smelled of horses, leather, and sunshine--and she never wanted to let him go. Her tears fell in as much relief as anything else. "I'm not sure I can do this alone."

His breath warmed the side of her neck where his face pressed. "You won't be alone as long as you want me here."

She pulled back, and he gently brushed away the tears on her cheek with the pad of a thumb. The gesture was so tender and his eyes were so full of emotion, she could almost imagine he really cared for her.

Of course, he cared. Dylan cared for everyone whom he felt responsible for. But it wasn't love. Ricardo had told her he cared for her, but he'd only cared as long as she did what he'd coerced her into doing. Danny had promised to take care of her, but he'd only cared for her as long as she stole from her grandfather to support his drug habit.

For Dylan, it was his sense of honor. He'd knocked up a girl. Of course, he'd take care of her because it was the *right* thing to do.

He smoothed his hand over her damp hair. "When was the last time you ate?"

She shrugged a shoulder. "I don't know. I think it was sometime yesterday. I haven't had much of an appetite."

"I'm going to fix you something. You need to eat."

She nodded and followed him out to the kitchen. He rummaged through the new stainless refrigerator. "I like the way the kitchen turned out." He faced her with a carton of eggs and a package of bacon and set the items on the new island in the large kitchen.

Dylan finished stockpiling ingredients on the granite countertop. She pulled out one of the bar stools and sat down to watch him. He took two pans down from the rack above the workspace and went about making an omelet and frying bacon.

When he set a plate of food before her, she smiled up at him. He took the stool beside her, his own plate piled high.

"This looks--interesting." She picked at the green pepper and cheese omelet that looked more like scrambled eggs with green chunks and splotched with gooey cheddar. The bacon was extra crispy and slightly burnt on the edges. "Your mother's a chef, huh?"

"Okay. So, I'm not a *great* cook, but I haven't starved." He shrugged and took a forkful of food. "It's no worse than some of your concoctions." After swallowing, he gave her a squinted look. "In fact, this is one of your concoctions."

"I suppose it is." He'd really cooked for her? She ate the meal he'd made. Leon had brought her food from some of the most expensive restaurants in Dallas, but none of those meals had warmed her as much as this fare of burned bacon and too-cheesy omelet did.

When he pushed his plate away, she glanced at the uneaten food. "You can't be full already."

He took a sip of his coffee. "I ate supper earlier. This was just a snack."

"Some snack." When Dylan wasn't drinking, he had quite a healthy appetite. "What did you have?"

"Tracy brought burgers from Ella's. We took Artemis and Ceres and went for a ride. Hope you don't mind."

"Not at all. Tracy and I had lunch a couple of weeks ago at Ella's." Watching him closely, she paused and took a sip of the milk he'd poured for her. "I met your ex there."

Dylan stiffened and looked away. "Her parents and sister still live in town."

"She was meeting her mother." She swallowed when he picked up his coffee mug, only to set it down again. "She had her baby with her."

He sniffed and looked at her.

"I decided I don't like her much."

Dylan snorted and picked up his mug. This time he took a drink. "Brenda always was high-maintenance, I guess. But she wanted kids, and I didn't."

"Dylan." She waited for him to meet her gaze. "I'm sorry this happened."

He gave her a crooked smile. "Hey, I think I'm as much to blame as you are. As the old saying goes--it takes two to tango. If anyone should be sorry, it's me." He glanced down into his mug. "I acted like a jackass afterwards." He met her gaze. "I guess I freaked."

"I understand." She ate a few more bites of the omelet. "I wonder if this is how my mother felt when she found out she was pregnant with me."

He set his mug on the granite counter. "Have you ever looked up your father? You said you know his name."

She shook her head and rubbed her hands on her thighs. "No."

"He didn't want anything to do with you?"

She shook her head. "He didn't know about me."

"Your mother never told him?"

"No. He went back to his rodeo life and his wife." Sighing, she leaned over her folded arms on the countertop. "I did a Google search and found he had a ranch near Paris, Texas. I thought about contacting him last year after I found the box of letters, but then found out he was dead." She sighed. "It's for the best. Meeting him would have only caused a tabloid mess."

His brow wrinkled, then his eyes widened slightly. "He's someone famous?"

She would have laughed if her heart didn't squeeze so painfully. "He won a few silver buckles, but he's not famous. My half-brother is. Country singer Nate McConnell."

"Ah, that's why you like him so much." Dylan finished his coffee.

She nodded and sipped from her cup. "I wish I'd have known my father."

Maybe she wouldn't have ever ended up in trouble if she had.

He faced her. "Our son or daughter will never wonder who I am. Even if…" He swallowed so hard his Adam's apple bobbed. "Even if things don't work out, I'll be there for our kid."

She blinked at the sudden wash of tears. "I know."

"You should ask Tracy who her doctor is. I know it's someone local."

"I suppose I should go soon. You don't mind me telling her?"

He smiled, and her heart stuttered over a beat. "No. Tracy and I have never kept secrets from each other. She'll be thrilled she's going to be an aunt. Let me know when you get an appointment."

"Why?"

"Because I want to be there."

His interest in her pregnancy filled her chest with hope and wonder. He might not want kids, but he wanted to be involved. Her mother had been all alone in her pregnancy. She'd lived at home, but her parents had refused to have anything to do with her. They'd wanted LeAnn to give her up for adoption. At least, Dylan hadn't wanted her to do that--or worse, have an abortion. She couldn't ever do that either.

"If it's what you really want."

He feathered his fingers over her cheek, his gentle touch soothing. "Charli, I want to experience this with you." He paused, and his eyes settled on her lips. "You make me feel things I haven't felt in a long, long time."

She held her breath and stared into his beautiful eyes. It wasn't a declaration of undying love, but something in the way he looked at her made her heart take flight and soar. She turned on the stool and faced him.

Her bare knees and thighs brushed against his denim-covered legs and a shiver tickled down her spine. Unable to resist their closeness and her own needs, she reached up and skimmed her fingertips over his right stubble-roughened cheek and the scar at his jaw line. His eyes darkened with desire, and heat pooled in the pit of her belly.

"I want to be with you, too," she whispered and laid her hand on his cheek. If the only part of him she could have was his lust, she was willing to settle for that. It was better than nothing at all. "Stay with me tonight. I don't want to be alone."

He wrapped his hand around her nape. Though his kiss was tender, it ignited a passion like no other. Her heart ached from her love for him.

Before she could wrap her arms around him, he pulled back and took her hands into his.

Maybe he didn't want her after all. He smiled and laced his fingers with hers. The simple act of holding his hands seemed as intimate as the kiss. His voice was rough with desire. "After I clean up this mess, let's go outside and enjoy the evening." He kissed the tip of her nose and chuckled at her puzzlement. "Then we'll try out those new sheets."

Once the kitchen was spotless again, he took her hand and led her out the front door and into the garden. They walked around a few of the garden beds hand-in-hand before he broke the silence.

"I'm surprised you got so much of the garden done."

She looked over the beds as they meandered through, heading for the lake in the far front of the yard. "I had to stay busy after school was over. I guess it's over for a while."

"Charli?"

She looked up at him. "I just realized school will have to wait." Even in the waning light of late evening, she saw his countenance melt a little. She tried to force a smile, but failed. Surprisingly, though, the reassurance rang true. "I didn't say I was quitting. I'll go back when I can. After the baby is older."

Until then she'd be a mother, a rancher and whatever he wanted her to be to him. Only the threat to her promise to help Annie twisted her heart. She was still determined to do what she could for the girl. Something about Annie wouldn't let her go.

"If you want to go back in the fall, I'll be here. And after the baby is born, I'll be here. I know how much being a social worker means to you."

She squeezed his hand and this time the smile was easy. "Thank you."

Once they got to the edge of the water, she warily peered around for snakes. He chuckled and the tension dwindled, at least a little. She glared at him.

Dylan pulled her down beside him on the stone bench. "Relax. I'll protect you if one of the snakes decides to take a bite out of you."

"If that was supposed to reassure me, it was a lousy attempt."

His chortle filled the evening, and he wrapped his left arm around her shoulders. His right hand enveloped hers. He had big hands, work roughened and strong, perfect in their comforting warmth. She couldn't help relaxing into the latent strength of his chest and shoulder.

They sat there for a few moments just watching the occasional ripple in the dark water as the evening turned to night. The purple sky swallowed the last rays of sun. While stars twinkled to life above the trees, fireflies danced closer to earth. Frogs and insects filled the night with a symphony of delightful music. A woodpecker added percussion, a trio of whippoorwills and an owl from the woods gave voice to the night song.

"It's beautiful out here." He didn't bother keeping the awe from his rough voice.

"Yes, it is. I fell in love with this place during the day. If I'd seen it at night..." She let the statement trail away.

He took his arm from her shoulders and leaned his elbows on his thighs. He stared down at their hands clasped together.

She knew enough about Dylan Quinn to fall head over heels in love with him. But what made him tick? "Why do you believe you won't measure up to your father?"

He glanced at her and drew in a deep breath. Concentrating on their hands again, he pressed hers between his palms as if he was sizing her much smaller one to his bigger ones.

At last, he heaved another long sigh. "Robert Quinn is a retired brigadier general who now works in Homeland Security. He's had the kind of career most officers wish for. Dad has done so much. He was in Nam at the very end, and in Germany during the fall of the Berlin Wall, he was a battalion commander in the Gulf War and was sent to Bosnia. There he helped track down war criminals as a commanding member of the security force."

He met her gaze. She rested her free hand on his forearm. The muscle bunched under her touch. "On Nine-Eleven, Dad was in the Pentagon, and he was one of the first to deploy to Afghanistan, where he was a senior officer under General McNeill during the early days. That's where he pinned on the star. From there he took a divisional command in Iraq."

Dylan got a faraway look in his eyes. His pride in his father was evident, but there was something resentful under it. "I was in Iraq at the same time and went to the change-in-command ceremony. Dad introduced me to a few of the brass. When they asked me what class I'd graduated from, you would've thought Dad's officers had asked how long I was in the state pen by the look on my father's face. He was ashamed when I told them I didn't go to West Point."

She was only about half following the military lingo. "Why?"

He snorted. "I'm my father's number one disappointment. Not only didn't I graduate from his school, I'm something of a hothead. So, I didn't rise up the ranks as fast as Dad would've liked either."

"But why should he be disappointed? You were in the Army and served the country well."

"My family can trace its military history like a rancher can trace cattle breeds back to the first sire and heifer."

He paused and she thought he was finished, but then he sighed again. "Dad never wanted Mom to come back here. He would've preferred she stayed in Washington with his family. Dad considered Granddad Ferguson a bad influence on me in particular. I loved horses as a little kid, and on our visits to Oak Springs, I practically glued myself to Granddad's side, learning everything I could about the ranch. Granddad had taken an instant dislike to Dad. Thought he was a pompous Yankee ass." Dylan chuckled and looked at her.

"You see, my dad had been raised in the military. His father lived and breathed it. Granddad Quinn would've pinned on a star if a heart attack hadn't killed him during the waning days of the Cold War. I have roots clear back into the Revolution and beyond. One of my ancestors supposedly fought in the Crusades beside King Richard the Third."

He pressed his lips together. "All I ever wanted to do was be a rancher."

"There's nothing wrong with ranching. Besides, you were in the Army and an officer. Your father should be proud of you. I know I am."

His face softened, and he kissed her fingers. "I only joined the Army because my grandfather willed Oak Springs to his stepson instead of to his daughter."

He let go of her hand and stood, shoved his hands into his pockets, and stared out over the dark lake, leaving her bereft of his touch.

She clasped her hands between her thighs. "You were hoping to run Oak Springs, weren't you?"

He nodded, but didn't look at her. "When Mom moved back here, I hated this place at first. This place just seemed so...I don't know...backward. I'd lived all over the world, had just spent three years in Germany and before that we lived in D.C."

She looked down at her clasped hands. "I understand perfectly. I felt the same way when I was fifteen and my grandfather took me back to the Long Arrow after Momma died."

Dylan turned. "You know we probably have more in common than either one of us would like to admit."

"I doubt that. Other than both being fifteen when we were plucked from our lives to be dumped on a ranch." They stared at each other for a moment, and she thought about his guilt over the deaths of his men. She remembered her own role in the murder of Tyrone Hodges and his guards. Maybe he was onto something with his assessment.

She cleared her throat. "So, when did you decide ranching was what you wanted to do with your life?"

"I was only here for a few weeks before I fell in love with the place all over again. Granddad was happy to teach me about the ranch. It was the unspoken assumption Mom would inherit Oak Springs. Leon was away at Harvard, and I assumed I'd run the place when Granddad retired. Mom didn't want the ranch, and Dad was more interested in war strategy than breeding cycles.

"I was a cocky teenager who thought I had it all. I went to college and majored in ag-business, all ready to take over once I graduated. Then Granddad had a stroke my junior year of school and died."

"And he left Oak Springs to your uncle and not to your mother."

He looked at her. She didn't need to see his eyes to know how much pain would be in them. His voice quivered with it. "I didn't know what to do, so I joined ROTC and when I graduated was commissioned into the Corp of Engineers. Dad was disappointed when I didn't want to be a career military man, but he hated his only son chose to become an officer by not going to West Point. I broke a tradition going back as far as West Point's first class."

His father wasn't the only one he was trying to live up to. From the sounds of it, he was trying to live up to a standard set beyond too high by his whole family tree. She stood and put her arms around his waist.

He looked down into her face, and she held him close, loving him, wanting him. "Dylan, you are your own man. You have to do what feels right for you, not your father--or anyone else."

"Psychoanalysis mumbo-jumbo?"

She shook her head. "No, my grandfather. When I came home after running away, I had to find myself. I felt like a complete failure, always comparing myself to my mother. Despite her mistakes, she was a great woman who succeeded. She had nothing when she got to Tulsa, except a month-old baby and a few thousand bucks, but she got a job in a bank because they had a daycare, and she saved and learned. By the time she died, she was the manager."

He smiled. "You take after your mother, I see."

She shook her head. "No, I may have learned from her, but it happened only after I stopped comparing myself to her--or to anyone else, for that matter. I can't be my mother any more than you can be your father."

Sara Walter Ellwood

Dylan stared at her for a long time with a light in his pewter eyes she'd never seen before, and then he captured her lips with consuming passion, sweeping her away.

He ended the kiss and brushed his lips over her temple. "Let's go in and try out that fancy bed."

Chapter 14

Charli led Dylan into her bedroom, paused in the middle of the room, and turned to face him. A vibrating energy slivered through her, quickening her heart with a forbidden desire melting her insides.

She'd never stripped for a man who she truly desired--except Ricardo. However, she'd never loved him as much as she did Dylan, and she wanted to do something sexy and seductive.

She puckered her lips into a wanton pout she'd perfected so many years ago. It felt a bit rusty, but she must have pulled the seduction off if the sudden fire in his eyes was any indication.

When he took a step toward her, she backed away, shaking her head. "Uh-uh. I want to do something for you."

"You're already doin' plenty," he said in a perfect Texas drawl. "You're driving me crazy. What do you have planned?"

"You'll see, cowboy."

He grinned. "I like that."

"Good," she purred and gave him a sassy smile, backing away by placing one foot directly behind the other so that her hips swayed in a slow roll. "Because it's exactly what you are."

She pulled the rubber band from her hair. With a careless flick of her fingers, she tossed it in the general direction of the dresser. She fluffed the curls with both hands and gave the mess a toss.

She kicked off her sandals--one at a time--then grabbed the bottom of her tank top and slowly lifted it over her head. She flung the shirt at him, hitting him in the chest. He held it to his nose, taking a deep breath.

"You always smell like peaches." His gruff voice snagged over her nerves, causing her to shudder.

After a few belly dancing moves, she ran her hands over the satin bra and down her stomach, drawing his eyes down. She gave her hips a provocative shake and turned around. He wanted to protest; she heard it in his groan. But when she shimmied out of the denim shorts, he hissed in a breath of sweet torture. Her bra fell to the floor, and she danced to imaginary music. She looked over her shoulder as she slipped her thumbs under the elastic of her panties and pushed them to her ankles, letting her hair fall to the floor and shaking her ass.

A primitive growl escaped him. He moved behind her, his hands pulling her up and turning her into his arms. His mouth consumed hers as a starving man might a feast. By the time they came up for air, she feared she'd melt into a puddle.

"Your turn."

She grabbed the bottom of his t-shirt, pushed it up over his chest, and ran her hands through the dark curls.

He yanked the shirt over his head, then pulled her to him and covered her mouth with his again. She sucked on his tongue, nipped at his lips, and worked at his belt buckle and fly. When she broke the kiss, he tugged off his boots and socks and kicked out of the jeans. His harried movements made her grin.

"Okay, I suppose I could have done that with more finesse." When he saw her expression and where she was staring, he lost his grin. "I know the scars... We can turn out the light, if you'd..."

She met his eyes and a love so deep and overwhelming filled her heart to overflowing. Tears pricked her eyes and she fought the urge to let them fall. It wasn't as if she hadn't seen him naked before. So, what was the problem now?

"Dylan, you're beautiful." She couldn't tear her gaze away.

After clearing his throat, he took her into his arms again. He chuckled against her lips. "I must say, I've never been called that before. You're the one who's beautiful."

She relished the fissions of her soft and smooth body against his harder and rougher one.

When she opened her mouth under his, he deepened the kiss in a tangling duel with her tongue. She tightened her arms around his neck, rolled up on tiptoe, pressing herself into his lean strength and potent hardness.

After drawing back the blankets, he lifted her, bridal style, and laid her onto the crisp sheets.

Stretched out beside her, he possessed her with hot caresses, covered her breasts and gently kneaded them. When he brushed his thumbs over her taut nipples, she tightened her hands on his biceps. They were as hard as stone under her touch.

He moved his lips along the column of her neck to the racing pulse. She moaned when he nipped at the sensitive skin and gently suckled it, not enough to mark, but enough to send fire dancing through her veins. She writhed under him as he caught and drew alternately on her nipples.

"Dylan, please..."

He moved from her breasts to her belly, lighting butterfly kisses on the hot surface. The muscles beneath bunched with anticipation. His hands weren't idle--they were busy brushing along her inner thigh to find the center of the needy ache. She buried her hands in his hair as he gently parted her with his fingers to touch her.

When his lips and hot, wet tongue replaced his fingers, the orgasm came on her fast and furious like a summer thunderstorm. She shuddered, bucked against him, and moaned his name on a long breathy sigh. After bringing her gently down, he again brought her to the height of pleasure. Then again. She'd never have or need another orgasm. Then he kissed his way up her body.

He found her lips again and plunged his tongue into her mouth in a direct imitation of what would come next. She arched up into his body, eager to join with him, aching as if he hadn't already given her the sweetest pleasure. He soon obliged by shifting and settling into the cradle of her pelvis.

When she met his heavy-lidded gaze, his eyes burned her alive. She placed her hands on either side of his ruggedly handsome face and wrapped her legs around him. He didn't rush his entry as she'd expected him to. He stared down at her and slowly pushed himself into her starving body one incredible inch at a time, filling her to the core of her being. Buried in her body, he groaned and moved--pulling almost completely out before thrusting in again. Soon the coil twisted and lifted her up again.

When she tightened around him, his breath hitched, his strokes became faster, harder, and deeper, as though he wanted to fuse them together forever. Spasm after spasm seized her, and she clawed at his shoulders and back, clinging to him, afraid she would fall into nothingness.

He didn't relent on the intense friction until he dove into her one last time and growled as his own release crashed over him.

When it was over, he rolled onto his back, pulling her with him. She landed astride him in a tangle of legs and arms and a blanket of sweat-dampened hair.

They held each other while their hearts slowed, breathing evened, and senses returned.

Smiling, he brushed her hair from her face. "Now *that's* what I wanted to do to you before."

She returned his satisfied grin, but she didn't have the strength yet, or the will, to lift her head from his chest. She enjoyed listening to the rhythm of his breathing and the hard, steady thump of his heart.

"I'm still trying to put my body back together."

Tightening his hold around her back, he chuckled. The soft rumbling vibration caused her to shiver. She remembered the man she'd met not so long ago. The unsmiling, dead-eyed cowboy. The ex-soldier who'd blamed himself for the deaths of men under his direct command. She wasn't sure what came about in Dylan that transformed him into a man who could smile and whose silver eyes now occasionally twinkled with fiery vitality. Whatever it was, she was happy to see it.

The memory of the last time she'd stripped before a man--or rather an entire room full of drunk, horny men who had watched from smoky tables--flickered into her mind. Her gut twisted as she remembered their degrading calls and leering eyes. For some reason, stripping for Dylan had been more sexually exciting than any foreplay she'd ever experienced.

Although she was certain she'd do it again for him, she prayed he never figured out where she learned her moves. He might forgive her for being a stripper, he might even forgive her for being a hooker, but helping to kill six men in cold blood... How could he forgive that when she couldn't do so herself?

She stopped the flow of thoughts. The last thing she wanted was to deprive herself of this afterglow. Dear God, the man knew what he was doing in the bedroom.

She traced the sword, the beret and the Latin words of the Green Beret tat that had intrigued her since the first time she'd seen it.

"What does this mean?" She shifted over him and read the Latin words. "*De oppresso liber.*"

He caught her hand and held it against his heart. "The translation isn't perfect, but it roughly means 'to free from oppression.' The motto for the Special Forces."

"To free from oppression." She looked at him. "You really lived by that motto, didn't you?"

He untucked his arm from under his head and rubbed the back of his fingers against her cheek. "I tried to."

Not wanting to bring up bad memories, she looked at his right bicep, where he had the tattoo of a bald eagle with its wings spread and carrying the U.S. flag in its talons. She gently skimmed her fingertips over the flag, and the steel band of his bicep contracted with her touch. "Is this a Special Forces tat, also?"

"No. I got this one when I finished jump school." He explained, "Parachute training. Before I joined the Special Forces and after my short stint in the Corps of Engineers, I was part of the Army Airborne."

She sat up and stared at him. "You jumped out of airplanes?"

He laughed again deep in his chest. His fingers grazed over her exposed breasts, causing her to shiver with need all over again. "Yes, I jumped out of airplanes and helicopters, too, sometimes with food or tanks and other equipment falling with us. I think the longest jump I made was in Afghanistan when we jumped at thirty-thousand feet after I became a Delta."

"You and the lingo." She shook her head. "English, please. What's a Delta?"

He touched the tip of his finger to her nose. "Special Forces. Delta Team. Green Berets. They're all names for the same thing."

"Now I know you're crazy." She shook her head. "I--I can't imagine falling out of an airplane from thirty feet. I'm glad you don't do that anymore."

He raised a brow. "Would you be worried about me, Peaches? Worried my 'chute wouldn't open?"

"Damn straight, I'd be worried. You *are* the father of my baby." She lost the teasing tone. "But I'd also be proud of you because you were possibly sacrificing your own life for others." When she stroked the tattoo on his chest again, the muscle underneath quivered. "Personally, I'm glad you gave up the green beret for a cowboy hat, even though the choice wasn't completely yours or without a lot of heartache."

He stared at her for a long moment. Sadness flashed across his rugged features. Had she overstepped by bringing up something so painful to him? Before she could apologize, he pulled her down on top of him again and kissed her thoroughly.

Soon they were free falling, but neither of them needed, nor wanted, a parachute.

* * * *

The next morning, Dylan knew he was in way over his head and the reason had nothing to with the mouthful of peach-scented, red, curly hair. He awoke early, as usual, but he didn't get up to go riding around the ranch. No, this morning he held onto a real live angel who had the magical touch of turning the ugly things around her into butterflies.

Sara Walter Ellwood

Charli sprawled over his chest, warm, soft and sexy. He lightly pushed her hair out of his face and away from hers and watched her sleep. Damn, she looked so young. There was a twelve-year age difference between them. Deep down he knew he ought to marry her and raise their baby. After all, it was the *right* thing to do. How could he, though, when the *right* thing could very well be the *wrong* thing?

I won't be trapped in a marriage for a child's sake.

Her words still hurt. He was certain she felt something for him, but whether it was love or just lust, he didn't know. He'd thought Brenda had loved him, too, when she'd come to see him off to Afghanistan the last time at Fort Benning, Georgia.

That night before he'd shipped out had been one of the most passionate he and his former wife had spent together. He'd been a fool not to realize she was telling him good-bye. She'd decided to leave him for her best friend. He'd read her Dear John letter so many times, he remembered every word.

I'm sorry, Dylan, but I can't live like this anymore. I'm in love with Nicholas and we're going to have a baby. I've tried to be a good wife. I even tried to love you again when I came to see you ship out.

But I couldn't stop thinking you've spent most of our married lives on the other side of the world fighting someone else's war. You never stopped to realize how much I wanted you here with me, or how much your not wanting kids hurt me. When I left you at Fort Benning, I realized I haven't loved you for a very long time.

Wasn't one one-sided marriage enough? Especially when he was the one left with the broken heart?

The sun rose over the trees and slanted warm sunlight between the curtains at the bay window. Splinters of light bounced off the dust particles floating in the glowing shaft.

Charli shifted, rubbing her soft body over the length of his, and purred like a cat as she woke. Damn, she was one hot number, even in the morning.

She mumbled something unintelligible and smiled brightly at him from under the tangle of hair.

He burst out laughing. When her smile faltered, he held her close. "You know this is the first time you've ever smiled at me in the morning and meant it--and it's only a little after five. I must have done something right."

The frown turned upside down and wicked. "Maybe you did." Charli slithered up his body, touched him in all the right places, bringing him from semi to hard in a heartbeat.

She looked down into his face, and for a moment, he thought he saw a light in her two-toned eyes that hadn't been there before. Could he be more to her than just another sex partner? Before hope could catch hold, she kissed him, and in one amazing motion, took him into her sweet, warm body.

An hour later, after they had taken a long shower together, he closed his jeans and came up behind her at the vanity in the bathroom. She finished blow-drying her hair and tried to tame the wild waist-length curls. With each stroke of her brush, he wanted to mess it all back up again.

She met his gaze through his reflection and smiled at catching him watching her. "What do you have planned for today?"

He shrugged. "I was thinking about taking a run up to the Fort Worth Livestock Auction. Check out what's selling these days."

She turned, her brow puckered. "Why?"

He couldn't keep his hands off her and pulled her to him. "I want to check out some cattle for this place. Now that your stock is on the mend and we'll soon have more than enough hay in and good pastures, I was thinking it might be a good time to look into getting more cattle. Ten thousand acres of range is a lot for a hundred calves and four horses."

"Do you mind if I tag along? Last weekend, I saw the ad in the paper for the auction." She grinned like the Cheshire Cat. "I'll keep you company."

He couldn't hide his surprise. "I have a hard time imagining you at a dusty, smelly cattle auction."

She narrowed her eyes at him and huffed. "Hell, Dylan, who do you think bought the calves in the first damned place? I'm no stranger to a livestock auction."

He kissed her nose. "Okay, it's an official date. You keep me from getting lonely, and I'll spring for lunch while we're there."

"Wow, our first date is chilidogs at the Fort Worth Livestock Auction."

Heat exploded up his neck like an oil well blowing its top. "I'm sorry I can't afford to fly you to the Creek Inn."

Her eyes widened, and then they burned him with green fire. "That wasn't what I meant and you know it, you jerk. I was joking. I guess that's not possible around you."

Aww...shit.

Charli passed him and headed for the mussed bed. She tugged the sheet and blankets up in jerky, vicious motions.

Sighing, he ran his hands through his damp hair and moved in behind her. "I'm sorry. I just feel like I can't--"

He cut himself off. The pompous asshole couldn't give her what she needed either. Although he still was convinced that Leon's attentions weren't noble, she had to choose. "What do you really want, Charli?"

She faced him. "I want you to be a part of our baby's life. I know what it was like to not have a father around. But I can't force you to stay. I'm not going anywhere. This is my land. The real question is what do you want, Dylan?"

You.

He took hold of her upper arms. "I'm a first-class jerk who used to jump out of airplanes to fight other peoples' wars. I don't have a dime to my name, so I can't offer you or our baby a damned thing, but..." *My love.*

"But what?"

He couldn't say it, not when she didn't feel the same for him. Maybe if he never spoke the words, he could protect his heart. "I want you, Charli, for as long as you'll have me. I'm not going anywhere, either. I'll help you any way I can to make this ranch profitable and a home for the baby."

"Then let's see what happens. If you want to stay here--at the house, I mean--you can. Or only part of the time." He got the translation loud and clear--*Or when you want to share my bed.*

He was making a huge mistake when it came to his heart. "You don't mind all the tongue-wagging that'll go on if we live together?"

"I can't say it thrills me to be the center of gossip, but I'd like to share my bed," she paused and peered up at him, "and my life with you."

It wasn't *I love you*, but maybe she suffered the same case of cold feet he did. *Yeah, right.* Even if she'd said the words, it didn't mean she meant them. Brenda obviously hadn't.

"You can start moving in right away if you want." Her smile slipped a little. "After all, in a few months, tongues will be wagging anyway when I start looking like I swallowed a watermelon whole."

A vision of Charli very pregnant flitted across his mind. With it came the nugget of speculation that would, no doubt, be on the lips of the gossipers as they wondered who the father of Charli's baby was.

He would squelch the whispers right now by making it appear he and Charli were together. But what if he wasn't the father? No, he had to trust her. He forced a smile. "I suppose you're right about that. Hell, I can move in now. I only have my clothes, and I can grab those while you make breakfast."

His presence in her bed would most likely irritate Leon when he came home. He had heard about his trip to Colorado from Tracy. *What a bitch to be so high up on the corporate food chain only you can make the deal.*

Her pulling him down for a soul-bending kiss hid his smirk. Wouldn't the son-of-a-bitch be surprised to see him answering the door when he visited? He would find great pleasure in shoving Leon's bouquet of roses into his face. On the high from a night of the greatest sex of his life, he held her to him and took over the kiss. She surrendered when he explored her mouth. He wanted to make love to her one more time, but there was a rap on the back door.

Charli groaned and eased out of the kiss. "That's Tom."

He nodded and rested his forehead against hers. "Why did I tell him to work today?"

Giggling, she pulled away. "Because he's off Monday."

"We may as well go let the cat out of the bag, so to speak. I was hoping to sneak out before he got here."

"Now, you can make yourself useful by putting on the coffee instead." She took his hand and led him into the kitchen. "Then you can move in and we'll have that date."

Maybe they actually had a future together.

Or maybe she'd end up breaking his heart when Leon returned.

Chapter 15

Things had to be too good to be true, but Charli didn't stop to analyze what was going on. Dylan moved his meager belongings into her bedroom before they had breakfast.

He plopped a camouflage duffle bag, which had seen better days, onto her bed. She stood in the doorway and raised her brows at him when he faced her.

"That's it?"

He shrugged and glanced back at the bag. "All that matters."

"You don't have any more *stuff?*"

He shook his head once and crossed the room. "Nope. I'm not a packrat, and for thirteen years, I wore the exact same thing every day. Besides, divorce took care of the rest."

She didn't miss the pain that darted across his face at the mention of his divorce. Forcing her attention to the bag lying on the bed, she said, "I was wondering how the heck I was going to find room in my closet for your things. I guess I shouldn't have fretted. C'mon, breakfast is ready."

After they'd eaten, they jumped into his pickup and raced up the highway to Fort Worth.

Over the loud squeal of AC/DC paving their highway to hell, she said, "You know we should probably buy a truck for the ranch."

"You don't like my trusty old Ford?"

"You don't like my Lexus."

"Oh, sure, now that's the prissy-assed vehicle of choice."

She glared at him, and he grinned.

"Hank gave me my dream car after I took over his ranch. Sometimes I miss it."

"Which was?"

She smiled, remembering. "A Jaguar. Bright red convertible with black leather interior, fully loaded." She sighed. "I loved that car."

His shock vibrated the truck. "You're kidding."

"Nope. I traded it in."

"You traded a Jag in for a *Lexus*?" His incredulous expression would have been funny if they weren't in the middle of late morning rush hour traffic. A semi-truck cut across two lanes of highway directly in front of them.

"Dylan!"

He easily avoided a disaster by plying the breaks. Once he stopped consigning the driver to hell, calling in to question his manhood, along with a few things about his mother, he winced as if in pain. "Why would you trade a fine piece of automotive mastery like a Jaguar in for a Lexus?"

The frantic beat of her heart slowed as she held a hand over her breast. "I wanted something more practical to move to Texas with. Hence, the Lexus."

As if bewildered by the circumstances, he shook his head. So, the rough and tough cowboy had a soft spot for fast, little sports cars.

After a time, he slid a mischievous look her way. "Maybe it's a good thing you got rid of the Jag. I can imagine how sexy you'd look in one. It drove me crazy resisting you in those little robes you wear. Combined with a fast car..." He shook his head and groaned.

"I really tormented you by answering my door in a robe?"

"Hell, yeah." He tossed her another glance. "Thank God you'd stomp off to your room to shower and dress, because I needed the time to calm my raging hard-ons."

She laughed and admitted, "I never realized you were so attracted to me. Until the kiss in the bathroom. I would lay awake at night wondering what you were like in the sack."

"Well?"

She tried to pretend indifference by shrugging, but she couldn't stop the sly smile. "I wasn't disappointed."

He fidgeted in the seat and took a deep breath. "That's something, I guess. I think it's time to change the subject. My jeans are getting mighty uncomfortable."

She laughed again and went back to the original topic of discussion. "The ranch probably should have a company pickup."

"Probably. Although I don't mind driving my truck." He eyed the lane-hopping minivan in front of them. "The Ford isn't new, but it's reliable. We can take a look into getting something later."

What would he do if she surprised him on his next birthday with a brand new, shiny pickup truck? It wasn't a Jag, but that could come later, maybe their first anniversary.

First anniversary?

Boy, wasn't that putting the cart before the horse? They probably wouldn't last the day. There was still a gulf between them. Did he believe she'd slept with Leon? Did he still love Brenda? The image of Brenda and her baby popped in her mind and a terrible suspicion bored into her heart.

She looked at his profile. He was so handsome, so strong and honorable. Yet, something vulnerable hid below the tough-guy skin. "When are you going to tell your parents and Tracy about the baby?"

He didn't look at her. "Tracy will find out soon enough. As for my parents, I think we should wait a little. Just to let us get used to the idea. Maybe, tell them after you see the doctor."

Sure, there was no use getting their hopes up about a new baby if something was wrong with it and she had a problem.

Or Dylan decided he didn't want to stick around, after all.

"Charli, it has nothing to do with not wanting the baby," he said when she didn't speak. "A lot of people wait until the third month to tell folks. We should have some time to come to terms with what's happening."

She nodded and looked out the window. "You still think the baby might not be yours."

When silence met her statement, she looked his way. His jaw flexed, and he didn't look at her. "The thought has crossed my mind."

"Dylan." She waited for his gaze to meet hers, if for only a second. "I swear I never slept with Leon. Before you, I haven't had sex since I was eighteen." She closed her eyes and swallowed, knowing she had to tell him something. But she couldn't tell the truth, at least not all of it. "After I ran away, I met a man in Vegas. We--we got married."

He looked at her again with wide eyes. "He's the reason you don't want to get married again."

"Yes."

"Did you love him?"

Averting her eyes to her hands in her lap, she shrugged. "I thought I did. He took me off the streets, gave me a place to live."

"And beat you."

She nodded and sucked in her bottom lip. "Yeah. Our marriage was annulled after my grandfather found me in Las Vegas."

It wasn't the total truth, but it was close enough, and all she intended to divulge. She and Ricardo Rodriguez hadn't been legally married, since they never applied for a license. The facade of marriage had been his way of controlling her, and she'd been too young and naive to realize it.

She looked at him. His hands gripped the steering wheel until his knuckles whitened.

"I would never hurt you, Charli." His voice came from a place so deep, it rumbled.

"I know."

He met her gaze with eyes so fierce they frightened her.

She assured him, "I haven't seen him since I left Vegas." She'd already said enough about her life with Ricardo. "I suppose waiting to announce the baby will be okay. That way the Grapevine won't completely exhaust the juicy grapes all at once."

He deftly switched lanes to merge onto the correct ramp off the Fort Worth beltway.

"No, we definitely want to make sure there're enough 'juicy grapes' on Winnie Cartwright's grapevine." The sarcasm fell as flat as his forced smile did.

For the rest of the trip, an uneasy silence descended upon them. By the time they arrived at the auction, she was determined to not let the shadows in their relationship or of her past ruin the day. They pulled into the parking lot crowded with livestock trucks, pickups, and SUVs--many of them with trailers.

She turned to him and touched his arm as he killed the engine. "Dylan, I know it's hard to trust me, but I'm not a woman to play games. To me Leon was never more than a friend. Yes, he wanted to be more, but he wasn't. It's you I want. It's your baby I'm pregnant with."

He skimmed his fingers over her cheek. "And I want you, Charli. I guess I--I can't help but wonder why you chose me."

"Don't wonder." They locked gazes, and her fingers closed over his, resting on her cheek. "C'mon. The auction's about start, and I want that chilidog you promised me."

They got out of the truck and headed toward the office to claim a bidding number.

A few moments later, they scanned the pens of cattle. When she found two pens of year-old Angus heifers offered by the same rancher, she said, "How about these? They look healthy and would be good for breeding."

After coming up beside her at the metal railing, he leaned over his arms on the top and surveyed the heifers with a critical eye. He pushed his hat back and looked at her. "You know more about this stuff than I've ever given you credit for. It's time I stop underestimating you." She raised a brow, and he said, "These are good. So, you're done playacting at ranching, huh?"

"What's that supposed to mean?"

He took her hand in the natural way of new lovers. The action about stopped her heart. "Now don't get your tail feathers all in a ruffle, although you have very nice tail feathers." He leaned back to glance meaningfully at her jeans-covered ass. She poked him in the chest, and he pushed her Stetson back over her head a little and met her gaze. "It means I've been waiting for you to decide to actually raise some cattle on the old place."

He might not trust her, but he had faith in her. She often wondered what he truly thought of her, especially when he'd make the kind of smart-ass comments like the one from that morning about her going to a livestock auction. For a long time now, she'd figured he was waiting for her to break a nail and run away like some prissy bitch.

Whose fault was that?

She'd cleaned herself up over the years, given up massive amounts of makeup for a more natural look and traded trashy clothes for designer names. Although she still sometimes showed more skin than most people were comfortable with, no one ever questioned her wealth or her sense of high fashion.

But she was a rancher, not a runway model.

"You really believe in me?" Her voice dipped and nearly cracked.

He squeezed her hand. "Yes."

She fought the sting behind her eyes, and the heat racing into her cheeks had nothing to do with the temperature of the late May day. She sniffed and turned away before she made a fool out of herself by crying.

They moved along the aisle to find seats in the auction arena. "I've been thinking of changing the name of the ranch."

"I wondered when you'd get around to it. What are you thinking?"

She looked up at him and snorted. "I haven't the foggiest, damned idea."

He snickered and held out the cardboard placard with their number on it. "Do you want to do the honors?"

"Oh, I think you've got it covered. I'll just sit here and keep you company." She patted his thigh and stroked the area in a slow circular motion with her fingertips.

His eyes darkened. He leaned over and whispered in her ear, "Keep it up, and I'll forget what I'm bidding on. You'll end up with those alpacas we saw, instead of cattle."

She inched her hand up a bit, leaned over, and purred in his ear, "I trust you to make the right decisions now. And later when I get you home alone, cowboy."

She squeezed the flesh to the inside of his thigh bare inches from the bulge his hardening erection made.

"Now stop. They're starting and people are staring." He took hold of her hand and pinned it farther down on his lean leg, near his knee. In a voice that got progressively huskier as he spoke, he whispered in her ear exactly what he intended doing to her when they got home.

The day suddenly got a whole lot hotter, causing her to squirm on the metal bleacher. She didn't care if he bought the sorry-looking alpacas, just as long as he hurried up.

By the end of the auction, she was the proud owner of a hundred head of Angus, fifty Herefords and two registered bulls--an Angus and a Hereford. The cattle would be delivered Wednesday. She groaned as she wrote a whopping check from the business account. He was right. If she was serious about raising cattle, she had to stop playacting.

"What do you think of Zeus and Jupiter?" she asked on the drive home.

He glanced at her. "Please tell me we're having a conversation about astronomy or mythology, and you aren't thinking up names for something."

She smiled. "The bulls. I'd like to name them, just for fun. The Angus can be Zeus and the Hereford Jupiter."

"Why not something like George or Bubba?"

"Those are so boring. Actually, the names are for the same god. Zeus is Greek and Jupiter is the Roman version, but either way, he was the father of most of the other gods, plus heroes like Hercules. Besides, it seems appropriate to name my bulls after a god who liked to transform into a bull to seduce human women."

He looked at her with his mouth slightly ajar. "You've got to be kidding?"

"Nope. I personally don't see the allure. But, hey, maybe ancient Greek and Roman women were a little desperate or something."

"Or more likely were into bestiality." He let loose with a belly chuckle that had her laughing with him. Once he was able to get a breath again, he said, "Okay, you can name the bulls after some horny Greek god, but for the love of God, promise me you won't name our kid after some mythological person."

His words stilled her heart, and they locked gazes for as long as possible considering the traffic. She swallowed the lump in her throat. He believed her baby was his.

"I promise, as long as you don't insist on Bubba." Her voice cracked despite her best efforts to keep it light.

"Hey," he smiled and his voice was gruff, "Bubba is a noble name."

She rolled her eyes at him and laughed, and the tension shattered.

It was almost six o'clock when Dylan drove over the bridge to the clearing in the trees. The sun shone directly over her house. The glow looked like a crown on an aging royal holding court with the various ranch buildings set off to the side and behind.

This was the home she hadn't had in a long time.

His amused voice cut through her sentimental ponderings. "Get ready."

"What?" she asked a little wobbly while he'd parked the truck beside a red Taurus.

He unbuckled his seatbelt and jerked his hat brim toward the porch. Tracy stood between the porch pillars with her arms crossed over her chest. Her right foot tapped an agitated tattoo at the top of the steps. Bobby, Dylan's ten-year-old nephew, was at the edge of the lake, but as soon as he noticed them getting out of the truck, he raced up the yard, weaving around the garden beds.

"Hey, sprout," Dylan called to his nephew and led the way through the open gate of the picket fence.

"Hi, Uncle Dylan!" Bobby tacked on a sing-songy, drawn-out warning, "You are in so much trouble."

Tracy came off the porch as Dylan ruffled the boy's dark hair affectionately. "Is that so?"

"Is that so?" Tracy parroted, all puffed up like a prizefighter despite her willowy figure. At six feet, she was as tall as her brother. She faced Dylan, and for a moment, Charli actually thought she was going to deck him. Then she caught the delighted twinkle in Tracy's gray eyes. "Why is it I had to learn my big brother has moved in with his boss from Sally Miller?"

He leaned toward Charli. "Tom's wife, another notorious town gossip. Thrives on *juicy grapes.*"

"Ah." She smiled at Tracy. "I'm beginning to wonder who doesn't."

"So..." Tracy looked from her to Dylan. "Is it true?"

Taking her hand, Dylan passed his sister. Her mouth fell open and her eyes went wide. As they headed up the steps to the porch, Tracy squealed, "You are living together!"

Charli unlocked the front door. They entered the coolness of the large entry and headed down the hall.

He ushered his sister and nephew toward the kitchen. Tracy stopped in the arched doorway and gaped at the room, slowly taking it all in. "Wow! This is beautiful."

"Mom, can I go back outside?" Bobby asked in that whiney way of little boys.

Tracy blinked and turned to her son. "Sure."

Bobby instantly bolted to the front door.

Tracy called over her shoulder, "But stay away from the lake. There're snakes in it."

Her reply was the door closing with a bang.

Charli turned to Dylan. "See! You are the only one who seems to think those snakes are harmless."

"They are." He tossed his hat on a hook by the back door. He went to the sink, washed his hands, started a pot of coffee, then retrieved the baking pan with the steaks they'd planned to make for supper out of the fridge.

She motioned for Tracy to sit at the table. "Would you like to stay for supper? Dylan's making steaks."

"Okay."

He grabbed another package from the freezer and tossed it into the microwave to thaw.

While he put four potatoes into the oven to bake, she fetched mugs and the fixings for the coffee. When he finally came to the table and poured the dark brew, Tracy quivered like a kid at Christmas deprived of opening her gifts until everyone else woke up.

Dylan sat beside Charli and met her gaze briefly. She smiled in reply to his silent question. He looked across the table at his sister. "Yes, I moved in. But it only happened today."

"What brought this on?"

She took a deep breath. "Dylan and I are gonna have a baby."

Tracy stared at them for a moment as if she didn't quite comprehend. When it sank in, she opened her mouth, quickly covered it with both hands, and let out a squeal louder than the one earlier. She leaped out of her chair and into his open arms and fiercely hugged him.

"I'm so happy for you." Tracy hugged her. Tears glistened on her cheeks, and she fanned her flushed face with her hand. Dylan grabbed the Kleenex box from the shelf on the corner cabinet, and Tracy plucked several tissues from it to wipe her face. She sat down and noisily blew her nose. "I'm sorry... I'm just... Oh..." At last, she found enough composure to ask, "When are you due?"

She smiled and shrugged. "February, I guess. I just found out."

* * * *

Dylan knew what Tracy's next question would be probably before his sister did. Just as the microwave beeped to announce the steaks were finished defrosting, Tracy expectantly looked from Charli to him. "When's the wedding?"

He let go of Charli's hand and stood, wanting to put some distance between the women and himself at the moment. He took the steaks out of the microwave. "There isn't going to be a wedding."

He could feel Tracy's eyes boring into his back. "What? Why not?"

"Because." He faced the two women. "We decided not to get married. Marriage doesn't make a family, Tracy. You of all people should know that, considering how bad yours turned out."

If the jibe about her ill-fated train-wreck of a marriage bothered Tracy, she ignored it. She glanced at Charli and crossed the kitchen to stand across the island from him. "Dad and Mom won't like you not getting married."

He shrugged, then put the two extra steaks in the dish of marinade and turned to a cabinet for a platter. After facing his sister again, he spoke more casually than he felt. "When did that ever stop me from doing what I wanted? If I remember correctly..." He flipped the additional steaks a few times in the goop and locked gazes with Tracy. "They were none too happy I got married the last time."

"That's because Mom pegged Brenda from the first time she'd met the selfish bitch. I remember Dad telling you it wouldn't last."

He could remind her that their father had said the same thing about her and Jake Parker, too.

Whether they were ready or not, the steaks were finished marinating, and he plopped them onto the platter. He needed out of this conversation as fast as possible. The last thing he wanted was to discuss his ex, or how right their father always was, or his feelings for Charli. "I guess General Robert Quinn was right about that and a few other things, too. Your marriage lasted what--four years?"

So, he'd gotten his jab in anyway. What kind of respectable big brother would he be if he hadn't? Tracy narrowed her eyes on him, but she didn't say anything else on the matter.

He picked up the plate of steaks. Heading for the back door to the porch, he glanced at Charli, who seemed riveted by the conversation. He wasn't having any more of it in front of her. He smiled and winked in a way that he hoped would let her know this was how things usually were between him and Tracy.

As he went about getting the grill ready, the doors, both the solid and screen, closed and he glanced over his shoulder. Tracy had followed him out and watched him with her bottom lip sucked between her teeth.

He took a deep breath and fiddled with the gauge on the front of the grill to set the correct flame, then closed the lid and faced her. Before she could say anything about hearts and flowers and happily-ever-afters, he pinned her with a no-nonsense glare. "Look, Tracy, I don't really give a damn what Mom and Dad think, or anyone else for that matter. I'm going to do everything I can to be a decent father and the man in Charli's life for as long as she wants me. I was a husband once, and according to the former Mrs. Quinn, I wouldn't've won a husband of the year award. Maybe shacking up is the way to go. That way if Charli decides she's had enough of me, she can just kick me out and be done with it."

Before she came out of her surprise at his frankness, he said, "Why don't you go help Charli with the salad she's fixing. I think this conversation has gone on long enough, don't you?"

Tracy let her shoulders fall a bit as the fight went out of her and probably the hope, too.

"And Tracy, I don't want Mom and Dad to know about this until I'm damned good and ready to tell them. Got it?"

She opened her mouth to protest, but instead, bit her lower lip again and nodded agreement, then went back into the house.

After the grill was hot, he placed the steaks over the flame. As he waited for them to cook, he leaned over the railing and looked out over the spacious backyard without seeing it.

Yeah, sis, I'm in love with her. But I'm too much of a coward to marry to her.

Chapter 16

Charli rolled over onto her side and ran her fingernail down Dylan's sternum. He shivered, but he was far from cold. Only a touch from her set him on fire. He looked up into her face and smiled.

"So, what are we going to do today?" She shifted until she was directly above him.

"I could think of plenty of things I'd like to do, but I have horses to feed and cattle to check on." Rolling with her, he reversed their positions. He'd put that pink glow in her face just a few moments ago.

After kissing her so thoroughly Charli moaned, he shifted his weight off her and sat up. She sidled up behind him, hugged him from behind, and kissed his shoulder. "It just keeps getting better."

"It sure does." He glanced over his shoulder at her. Her liquid eyes and the long, auburn lashes veiling them entranced him. He'd never seen eyes like hers, and when they were soft and satisfied, he could get lost in them. He shook his head. "Horses. I have to feed the horses."

Charli moved away and stood. Once she'd retrieved a bra and pair of panties from the dresser, she went into the walk-in closet. When she returned, she leaned a naked hip against a wing chair with her clothes dangling from a hand.

Damn, she was beautiful. He prayed she never got tired of him.

"You didn't answer my question. What are we doing today?"

He shrugged and stood to pull on a pair of jeans. "It's Memorial Day. I know there's a parade in town. Tracy's church has some kind of bazaar which usually includes lots of baked goods and homemade quilts." Grinning, he looked her up and down. "Or we could spend the day like we did most of yesterday. Right here in this room."

She headed to the bathroom. "As much as I enjoy having sex with you, Dylan Quinn, I'd also like to do something else with you." Charli paused at the door. "When Tracy and Bobby were here Saturday, she told me about the banquet tonight for veterans."

"What about it?"

"I'd like to go. She said you could bring a guest."

"I'm not going." *Just drop it.*

"Tracy said you were being stubborn about this. You served this country like the rest of the folks there. Actually, I don't understand why you *don't* want to attend." Before he could argue, she turned and closed the bathroom door in his face.

He stared at the white-painted slab of wood for a moment and listened to the water coming on in the shower. With a shake of his head, he turned and grabbed a t-shirt.

In the kitchen, he put on a pot of coffee, tugged on his work boots, and headed to the barn. After he fed the horses and cleaned the stables, he took a brush off a shelf in the tack room and began grooming Artemis. He needed to think.

With gentle strokes, he brushed the mare, bringing her coat to a black luster. "I just don't understand what the big deal is, Artie. I don't want to go to that dinner."

The horse flicked her ears at the sound of his voice, but offered no opinion.

Was he the only one who understood that he didn't belong there? Cartwright's banquet at the American Legion was to honor those who had served proudly and lost their lives. Not for those whose mistakes caused the causalities.

He thought of the four men who'd died that day. Kent, a pain in the ass if there ever was one, had been his chief warrant officer and second in command. They'd served four years together in the same Delta Team. He left a wife in Kansas with four kids.

There was Wagner, the kid of the team. He'd just joined Special Forces, a staff sergeant, and eager to learn everything he could. He was working on a degree, hoping to be commissioned someday.

Finished with Artemis, he put her out into pasture, then entered Ceres' stall. He began rubbing down the smallest of the four mares. She nipped at his hat, and he patted her shoulder. "Hi, girl. I'm glad to see you, too."

As he brushed her chestnut coat until it shined, the memories continued. He saw Zabinski's laughing face as he pulled yet another practical joke on some unsuspecting SOB. The first sergeant, who liked to disagree with him at every turn, only had six more months until retirement. He'd never gotten to walk that daughter he'd left in Pennsylvania down the aisle.

He sniffed back the pain twisting his gut, but a tear slipped past his defenses as he remembered the last man. Fisher had been the medic of the unit for six years. He and the sergeant first class had a lot in common, and of all his men, Brad Fisher had been his closest friend. Brad had found him in his barracks crying like a girl the night he'd read Brenda's letter. Brad had gone through a divorce himself and offered his ear when he wanted to talk.

They'd never gotten the chance to have that talk.

He left the stall, leaned on the door and pinched the bridge of his nose as he sobbed. He cried for the friends he'd lost and for the lives cut short.

After getting himself under control, he finished with the horses. He wanted a drink, but there wasn't a drop of the stuff on the place.

When he entered the kitchen, Charli was at the stove, wearing a sundress and looking sexy. She sang along with the radio in perfect harmony with that country singer, half-brother of hers, as he crooned out a ballad about his woman being only a memory.

He listened for a moment as Nate McConnell declared that in the end all we had of those we care about were just memories.

The good and the bad.

He remembered his friends and realized he had many good memories, too, of men worth honoring.

When the song ended, she looked over her shoulder at him, and he didn't want that drink anymore.

"Okay, we'll go to the banquet, but under no circumstances will I get up and talk."

Charli smiled and her eyes got shimmery.

Don't you dare start crying.

"Go wash up, cowboy. Breakfast is almost ready."

* * * *

The banquet hall in the American Legion on Houston Street was decked out in red, white and blue bunting. Round tables, where everything from weekly bingo to wedding feasts happened, were festive with white paper tablecloths, hurricane lamps and miniature flags. In the background Lee Greenwood sang *God Bless the U.S.A.* over the sound system.

Dylan and Charli circumvented a crowd of people gathered around Mayor Cartwright, and they found a seat at a table near the back. People looked their way, a few of them waving in surprised greeting. Dylan responded with a nod of his head.

Zack Cartwright ambled over. He looked spiffy in jeans, a white Western shirt and bolo tie. "I don't believe my eyes. Why, if it isn't Captain Dylan Quinn. Is the devil wearing long johns these days?"

Dylan couldn't quite hide his grin as he shook the other man's hand. "Don't ever quit your day job and take the act on the road."

Chuckling, Zack bobbed his head at Charli. "Ma'am. It's good to see you again."

"This is really nice, Sheriff."

"Thanks." He sat down in the chair across from them. "But please call me Zack."

She smiled and nodded. "Okay. Zack it is. And I insist you call me Charli."

"Will do." He looked at Dylan. "I'm glad you're here. I need to talk to you later."

Dylan glanced at her. "All right."

After a few moments of chitchat, Zack stood. "I've got to make sure the Larsons have everything they need in the kitchen."

"The Larsons?" she asked, taken aback. Most of what she'd heard about the family hadn't been good. Siblings, Sam, Ella and Julie were admired for their shrewd business sense. But most people remembered their rough upbringing with an abusive stepfather and an alcoholic mother, which led to all three of them getting into trouble as teenagers.

"Yeah, they volunteer every year," Zack said. "Sam tends the bar, Ella caters the shindig and Julie manages the dining room. Their real daddy was killed in Vietnam." He said his farewells and headed off toward the kitchen.

Soon enough, people settled around the tables. Tom Miller and his wife, Sally, sat with them. A few moments later, silence fell over the hundred or so people gathered as a woman in the dress uniform of the Army stood and headed for the podium. As she passed a beautifully set table near the podium, she paused and saluted the six empty plates.

She cleared her throat and solemnly began speaking, riveting Charli with her words. "Set for six, the empty places represent Americans still missing from each of the five services--Army, Navy, Marine Corps, Air Force, Coast Guard--and civilians. This Honors Ceremony symbolizes that they are with us, here in spirit..."

Charli looked around as everyone stood at the woman's request. She sensed Dylan stiffen beside her and glanced at him. He stood tall and straight, as did Tom and every other former or current service man or woman in the place. Even those whose old backs were normally stooped by hard work and age stood with pride. As the officer read from an index card, the "Honor Guard," consisting of Zack, his uncle, Ella Larson, Tom Miller and two other men, each placed hats from the five branches of the military on the plates. Ella placed a cowboy hat on the sixth.

She had never witnessed such a moving service before. By the end, she wasn't the only one sniffing back tears and reaching for tissues. Many of the men were, too.

She glanced up at Dylan and took his hand. He met her gaze with gray eyes swimming in unshed tears. When a tear dripped off his long dark lashes, she squeezed his hand.

After a few moments of reserved silence, Toby Keith's *American Soldier* came from the speakers and quiet conversations resumed. Julie, Ella and several other waitresses from Ella's Diner and the Longhorn began serving the meal of roast beef with all the fixings.

Sally Miller, who was the complete opposite of her shy husband, leaned over the table, her brown eyes wide with expectation. "I heard Rachel's home on leave because she's deploying to Afghanistan in a few weeks."

"Rachel?" She looked up at Dylan.

He nodded toward the redheaded woman who had narrated the ceremony. "Major Rachel McPherson. One of Kyle's older sisters. She's an Army nurse. Doesn't come home much. Bad blood between her and her older sister, Audrey Cartwright."

"Oh."

The meal was good, and Tom and Dylan talked about the ranch and the work on the house. While the men talked, Sally filled her in on all the old gossip for the reason why there was *bad blood* between the McPherson sisters. Of course, she had already guessed it--Lance Cartwright, Zack's first cousin and son of Mayor Paul and Winnie Cartwright. The thrill of the telling gone, Sally pulled out pictures of her five-month-old son.

"He's beautiful," Charli said of the Easter photo of little Tommy, Jr., who, in her opinion, had been aptly named.

She couldn't help but wonder who her own baby would look like. Would he have her red hair? Dear Lord, she hoped not. Would he look like Dylan? Or some hybrid of them?

She handed the picture back and caught Dylan gazing at her. He rested his hand on her thigh under the table and gently squeezed. Was he wondering the same thing?

After the meal, the speeches began. They weren't long, and she found ninety-one-year-old Henrietta Parker's adventures as a female pilot during WWII hilarious.

Charli noticed Ella standing near the bar and stood. "Excuse me."

Ella looked up with a tentative smile on her lips. "Hello. It's good to see Dylan here."

"Yeah. I think he needed this." She glanced at Ella's older brother.

Sam nodded his head. "Can I get you anything, Miz?"

"No, thank you." She shook her head and met Ella's eyes. "Is there somewhere we can talk?"

Ella put out her cigarette in the ashtray. "Here's fine."

"How's Annie?"

"I've had her to two shrinks in Waco. She refuses to talk to them."

"Have you considered my offer to speak with her?"

Ella looked beyond her, and Charli glanced over her shoulder to find Dylan standing behind her. Ella said, "She thinks you're just another shrink."

"How about we surprise her?"

Ella shrugged. "Knock yourself out. What do you have in mind? I'm at my wits' end. She stole a hundred bucks out of the cash till." She sighed, and the woman's exasperation shot through Charli clear to her toes. "I know she bought drugs with it."

She caught Dylan's look of concern from her peripheral vision, but she ignored him. This was between her and Ella. She had to help Annie, who was so much like she'd been at that age, there was no way she could turn her back. "Is she still waiting tables at your place?"

Ella snorted. "When she shows up."

She took a deep breath and let it out. "Call me some morning when she's at work. I'll swing by at the lull between breakfast and lunch."

Ella's lips twisted in a sad half-smile, and she looked at Dylan before answering. "All right." She slid off the barstool. "I'd better get back to work." She headed for the kitchen door with her shoulders stooped.

Sam stepped close and leaned over the gleaming bar. "That girl means the world to my sister, Miz Monroe. If there's anything you can do to help her, I'd appreciate it." He nodded at Dylan. "Quinn, it's good to see you somewhere other than in my honky-tonk."

Before Dylan or she could respond, Sam turned to take an order from a couple of older men.

Dylan narrowed his eyes, and she squeezed his hand. "We'll talk about it later, okay?"

After a beat, he nodded.

* * * *

Dylan found Zack talking with Rachel McPherson and a uniformed National Guardsman. Rachel smiled at him and stepped forward to hug him. "Hello, Dylan."

"Welcome home, Rach." He stepped back from his cousin. "But I hear you're going back to Afghanistan."

She shrugged and brushed at wisps of bobbed auburn hair that had fallen into her face. "I'll be in a field hospital near Kabul. Hopefully, this is my last trip over there. I hope to get promoted to light colonel and go to the War College in Pennsylvania next year. Then I can take a stateside command."

"I never thought you'd make a career out of the military. Why don't you get out? You could get a civilian job anywhere."

She patted his arm. "Someday I may. Hey, you take care of yourself."

"You too, Rachel."

After she left and Zack completed his conversation with the Guardsman, he turned to Dylan. "I got the results back from the Rangers."

"I figured."

"Just as we suspected. Only a trace of poison, which was only in the hay from the feeders."

He glanced over at Charli, who was having an animated conversation with Zack's once-famous, ex-hippy mother, Jackie McGinnis Cartwright. He looked back at Zack. "Now what do we do?"

Zack thrust out a breath and stuffed his hands into the front pockets of his jeans. "Nothing but wait. We don't have any evidence that it's Kyle--or Leon."

"Then I suggest we find some."

* * * *

Dylan helped Charli into the passenger side of her car and then got behind the steering wheel. After they were on the road, heading to the ranch, he said, "Annie Greenberg is a troublemaker. I'm not so sure it's a good idea for you to get tangled up with her."

Charli sighed, and when he glanced at her, she averted her eyes to her lap. "Annie's exactly the kind of kid I want to help someday."

"Maybe, but that's someday. You don't even have your degree yet. But it's my opinion once a kid starts doing drugs..." He paused and shook his head. "I wish you'd just let this one go."

"I can help her."

He looked at her for as long as he safely could on the winding country road. "You were like her, weren't you?"

She wanted to tell him the truth, but when he looked back at her, something in his expression froze her tongue. She looked out the dark passenger window and spoke a half-truth. "I've been where she is. After my mother died, I was angry and hurting. That's why I ran away. Annie doesn't even realize her actions only make the pain worse. It's a terrible, vicious circle--made worse with drugs."

"What do you plan to do for her?"

The dimness of the car hid his profile, but she saw his jaw flex. Was he wondering if she had done drugs? She cleared her throat. "First, I just want to get her to talk to me. Eventually, I'd like to convince her to come to work for us." He narrowed his eyes on her, and she quickly added, "I know how working on the Long Arrow helped me. She can help me get the gardens cleaned up and with the house. Painting, cleaning, things like that. I know Jeremy Greenberg works as a horse trainer over on the CW. I'd bet she knows a lot about horses. Horses are great therapists. They listen and never judge you. But mostly horses love you unconditionally, no matter what you've done."

He let out a curse. "Charli, you're talking about taking on a big responsibility while you're pregnant. I really wish you'd wait."

She looked out the side window again as they turned down the driveway of her ranch. Visions of a terrible life exploded with brilliant reminders of what could happen to a girl like Annie searching for love and willing to do anything to get it.

She remembered Ricardo bursting into the sleazy room where Tyrone Hodges had taken her. Ricardo's goons had eliminated Tyrone's five guards while she'd had sex with Tyrone. She swallowed back bile at the memory of the bullet buzzing by her head to hit Tyrone between the eyes.

At last, she croaked out, "Maybe I should, but it would be too late for Annie."

Chapter 17

Charli sat in the curve of Dylan's arms on the old porch swing Wednesday evening. Her head rested on his shoulder while he idly twisted a lock of her hair around his finger.

He shifted a bit and looked down into her face. "I'm still miffed you'd risk yourself by riding with us this morning."

Rounding up the nervous cattle and getting them to the back pastures and keeping the two bulls separated had been a challenge after their delivery earlier that day.

She'd witnessed many roundups at the Long Arrow, but she'd never participated in one. Her initial stint on a horse aside, she was an excellent rider. But she hadn't *worked* a horse before.

"I was a little out of my element, I guess."

"You *guess*?"

"Okay." She exhaled a long breath. "I shouldn't have ridden, but I was needed. You can't deny it."

"We could've handled it. Kyle's a shithead, but he's good in the saddle and with cattle, and so is Tom. If I thought we needed more riders, I would've contacted Zack Cartwright and asked him to help us out."

Looking back, she wondered how much she'd really helped them.

"I was afraid you'd get hurt out there." He pulled her into his lap and held her back close to his chest, burying his face in her hair. After he splayed his hands over her still-flat belly, she understood. He'd been afraid for their baby.

Dear God, she hadn't even considered what could have happened if she'd been thrown or otherwise injured.

She turned and locked gazes with him. He really cared about her and their baby. "I'm sorry."

He glided his fingers over her cheek. "I know. Just don't do something like that again. I don't know what I'd do if you got hurt."

His words jolted her, and she thought about her idea again. The plan would keep him around, even if he didn't want her anymore. She had the power to give him exactly what he'd always wanted.

She shifted so she could wrap her arms around his neck. "I won't, I promise. I'm still getting used to this being pregnant thing."

His hands settled on her waist, and the tension left him. "Did Tracy give you the name of her doc?"

"Yeah. I'll make an appointment tomorrow."

"Good. Let me know when it is." He kissed her long, deep and thoroughly, just like he made love to her. The world disappeared with Dylan.

She raked her fingers into his hair and straddled his thighs. He was so hard, and she shamelessly pressed against him, mimicking what she was certain would happen once they found the will to leave the porch for the bedroom.

She'd given plenty of lap dances in her short career as a stripper and prostitute. She knew exactly how to touch and entice men with her body, but a lap dance had never excited *her.*

His fingers moved to the closure of her bra under her tank top the same time a sound from the driveway found its way into her fogged mind. She vaguely recognized the sound--gravel crunching on the drive.

He broke the kiss. "Ferguson."

She turned to find Leon getting out of his Porsche. Oh, God! Dylan shifted her beside him, keeping his arm around her waist.

Leon came up the steps and moved through the growing shadows of the porch to stop a few feet away from them. Thank God his hands were empty. She would have died for sure if he'd brought her flowers, or some other I'm-interested-in-you gift.

The darkness, under the brim of Leon's white Stetson, swallowed his eyes. "How are you, Charli? I hope you received my notes and gifts."

She couldn't answer. Shame rippled through her. She should have told him she wasn't interested.

"Charli?" Dylan jerked his attention to her, but she ignored him. She'd deal with him later.

She stood before Leon. "We need to talk. Would you like some coffee?"

Leon glanced at Dylan. "Yes, I think we *do* need to talk."

She headed into the house and hoped Dylan wouldn't follow them.

After they entered the kitchen, she turned to face him. Leon's eyes were dark and completely unreadable. "So, you and Dylan...."

She wrapped her arms around herself and swallowed. "I'm sorry, Leon. I didn't want you to find out like this."

He looked out the window behind the table. "How long?"

"Since before the poisoning." She went to the coffee pot and poured two cups. She held one out to him. When he didn't take it, she set both mugs on the table. "I tried, Leon. I enjoyed our time together, but I couldn't feel more for you than friendship. You've become my best friend since the poisoning, and I appreciate everything you've done for me. I'm sorry I didn't tell you before you left. I know I should have, especially when you told me..."

The muscle at his jaw twitched. "How're your cattle doing?"

Taken aback by the abrupt change in subject, she nodded and cleared her throat when no sound came out. "They're good. I didn't lose any, and Doc Evans gave them a clean bill of health today when he stopped by. We--Dylan and I--also bought a sizable herd Saturday. How was the trip? Everything okay?"

"Yes. The land's mine and so are the mineral rights." He took a deep breath and let it out. "I'll see you around, Charli." He headed for the back door.

"Leon." When he looked over his shoulder at her, she said, "I--I need to return something."

She ran into her bedroom and pulled the diamond necklace he'd given to her from a dresser drawer. As she looked at it, her mind flooded with all the scenarios she'd come up with for what she'd tell Leon since Friday. She'd avoided answering her phone and hadn't returned his calls, but she hadn't wanted to hurt him, either.

She held out the black box when she returned to the kitchen. "Here. I can't keep this. You gave me it with the hope we'd...be together."

Leon looked at the box. "No, I gave it to you." He smiled but it never reached his eyes. He may have been hurt, but she sensed anger. If he was jealous of Dylan, why wasn't he fighting for her? Why wasn't he proclaiming his love for her? Why wasn't he trying to convince her she'd be better off with him? Leon wouldn't give up this easily.

Better get used to men sayin' they love you to get what they want, baby. Only fools ever mean it.

Ricardo's words whispered through her mind like a freezing breeze through a humid tropic. Leon didn't love her. He'd only wanted her land and now he'd figure out some other way to get it from her. She shuddered at the thought.

"Consider it a token of my friendship."

Swallowing hard, she nodded once. She didn't want the necklace. "Okay."

She didn't need an enemy like Leon Ferguson.

Leon headed for the door. She waited for him to drive down the driveway before leaving the kitchen and returning to the porch. Dylan wasn't there. She tracked him down in the barn.

* * * *

Dylan was working on the last of the shelving in the tack room when Charli entered. He glanced at her and finally unlocked his jaw. He believed she hadn't slept with Leon, and she hadn't gone running to Leon. Possibly, she did want him over Leon, but his jubilation was tempered.

Now, Leon would go for her throat with everything he had. He suspected Leon's angle had been to marry her to get the place. After all, she was beautiful and a wealthy woman in her own right. A few more bucks in the Ferguson coffers couldn't have hurt, either.

"What did you do with his gifts?" He laid the hammer on the workbench and faced her.

"I tossed them. And I didn't tell you because I knew how you'd react. I didn't want to give you more reason to think you aren't the father of my baby." She rested her hands on her belly. "Dylan, I don't want Leon, I want you." As Charli glided toward him, she pulled her t-shirt over her head. "I--I want only you. I think we need to pick up where we left off, cowboy."

He didn't care if his grin was cocky. For now, Charli Monroe was his. "I can't agree more."

He drew her to him and kissed her. Her mouth was sweet, warm and inviting as she opened under his. She tugged his t-shirt from his waistband and ended the kiss. With his help, she pulled the shirt over his head.

She backed away from him, her hips doing a provocative roll. When she came up against the workbench, she shimmied out of her jeans and removed her boots and bra.

"C'mere, cowboy," she purred and gestured with her index finger.

He took her into his arms and kissed her eyes, her temple, and slid his lips to her ear. "What have I done to deserve you?"

Before she could comment, he kissed her lips and pushed her panties to the floor. He picked up his shirt, spread it over the top of the bench and lifted her to sit on it. He slid his mouth down her throat to her speckled shoulder. He wanted to kiss each freckle, though there were thousands of them, millions, and every single one was beautiful.

He devoured her breasts, first one and then the other, until he had her writhing. Her hands fisted into his hair, holding him to her breast.

Charli spread her legs, and he moved between them. She worked the belt and fly of his jeans open and pushed them down his legs. When she stroked his erection, he groaned. Jesus, she was a wild woman!

His fingers moved up her inner thighs to the smooth skin at the heart of her physical femininity. She moaned, and her eyelids fell closed as she arched her back. Her hair cascaded around her shoulders in breathtaking flame.

"You are so beautiful," he whispered and parted her with his fingers. She was wet and ready.

"Dylan, please, I want you inside." She wiggled when he stroked her silky center.

"Then I won't keep the lady waiting." After taking hold of her hips, pulling her to the very edge of the bench, he entered her with one swift stoke. She clung to him and bucked against him as he dove into her, deeper and faster with each thrust.

She screamed his name, and her nails bit into him in delicious abandonment.

"Charli," he gritted out as she quaked around him. She was so tight, so hot and wet. With one last hard, deep thrust, he let go and emptied himself inside her.

Moments later, he held her against his chest, stroked her back and listened to her rapid breaths. He brushed her hair from her face. When she pulled away to meet his gaze, he said, "I want you to know I have no intention of leaving you. I may not be ready for marriage again. I don't think I ever was a good husband, but I'll do everything in my power to be here for you."

Her breaths came in a raspy gasp, and she stared up at him with eyes as deep as a tropical ocean. "I know we haven't been together long, but you are living with me and we are going to have a baby together."

He tensed and warily asked, "Yeah?"

"Go into partnership with me--regarding the ranch. I know it's sudden and probably now isn't the best time to bring it up, but I want you to know...I...I want you to have an equal say in the ranch."

"You can't be serious." He stared at her, his heart raced in the back of his throat and his breaths stuck between his ribs, making him dizzy. His chest was bare, his jeans were down around his ankles, and he was still buried inside her. If she'd asked him to marry her, he wouldn't have been more surprised.

But she hadn't told him she loved him.

"It makes sense, doesn't it? You and I have equal shares in Blackwell Ranch and equal say in what happens to it. Shouldn't we both have a say in what our child inherits?"

He moved away from her, yanked his jeans to his waist. She sat there on the workbench still naked. He thrust his hands through his hair.

"I don't have anything to give our baby, Charli." He turned away. "Nothing. Brenda cleaned out my bank account long before she decided to divorce me. Not that I had much to begin with. Even with my hazard pay, I wasn't ever gonna get rich in the Army. I sunk all of what I inherited from my grandfather Quinn into the ranch she weaseled me out of during the divorce." He faced a wall of bridle hooks and every muscle sagged as if dipped in lead. "I don't have the capital or the collateral to even think about going into a partnership with you."

Charli hopped off the bench and wrapped her arms around him from behind. She laid her head on the back of his broad shoulder. He relaxed, the tension leaving his body as he leaned into her.

She whispered near his ear, "Dylan, I'm not asking you to sink money into the ranch. I'm asking you to make a commitment to this land and to our baby without the complications of saying 'I do' to me."

He turned and swallowed her up with his arms. "Are you sure about this? What if things don't work out between us?"

"I guess we had better make damned sure things do work out."

Did she understand what she was offering? If things went south between them, he could fight her for half of the ranch or half of the profits from the sale of it. Not that he'd do it, but it would be well within his right as her business partner. When he found his voice, it was a hoarse croak. "I'll think about it. But if I do agree, it won't happen until the baby's born. I want to give you time to back out if you decide to."

Charli swallowed and slowly nodded. He'd given them both an out if they wanted it. "Okay."

"There's one more thing."

"What's that?"

"This place needs a new name."

Her laugh was watery. She laid her head on his shoulder, holding him close. "I've been thinking about that since the auction. I still have no idea."

He turned in her embrace and wrapped his arms around her shoulders.

She smiled up at him and her eyes glittered in the slanted evening light from the window. "Maybe Monroe and Quinn? M bar Q?"

A memory drifted to him of them standing in the garden when a tiny blue butterfly fluttered by. The house and ranch had been crumbling, the fields hadn't seen cattle in years, and he'd been a broken down drunk who hated his life. Now, the ranch was on its way to new life. And he'd been given a second chance at a beautiful life.

He thought about the girl, Annie. Charli would turn her into one of her butterflies, too. She had done it to herself, hadn't she?

It was so obvious, he chuckled. The delighted sound brought a sharp sting to his eyes and a look of concern from her.

"What about Butterfly?" He ran the pad of his thumb over her soft freckled cheek, still flushed a lovely pink from pleasure. "You've transformed this place, just like you wanted. The ugly worm has become the butterfly."

"You remember that? My crazy thing about caterpillars and butterflies?"

"Yeah. I think it's perfect."

Her eyes swam in unshed tears. "Butterfly Ranch it is. You sure it's not too sissy for you?"

He nuzzled her neck and held her as tightly as he dared. Her soft naked breasts fit perfectly against his hard bare chest. "Nah, I'll just claim you came up with it. No one will ever question the assertion. After all, you named the horses after Greek and Roman goddesses and the bulls after a horny god who can't decide what his name is."

She giggled and pulled away to meet his gaze. "You still having trouble with your horse's name? You'd have probably called Artemis something lame like Blackie."

"Damn straight. It's bad enough they're moody mares."

Charli shifted out of his arms and dressed. She moved with the quiet grace of a dancer. When she caught him watching her, he snickered and picked up his shirt from the concrete floor where it had slipped off the bench.

"You know, I think we just christened the barn, so to speak." Dressed again and looking very much like a cowgirl, she ambled over to him. She laid her hand on his cheek and gave him a sexy-as-hell pouty grin. "I think it's time to go buy some horses. What do you think, cowboy?"

Then she kissed him.

* * * *

"You were supposed to be making sure she wanted out of the cattle business, not buying more," he ground out and held his cellphone in a death grip. He rarely angered, but when it came to Blackwell Ranch, he did so often.

"How the hell was I supposed to know she'd buy more cattle?" Kyle McPherson's whiney voice raked over his nerves. "I couldn't kill the calves. The damned old man, Jesse Riley, watches me like a hawk. It's Quinn. He's pushing her to do this. They shacked up together. Today when she was riding in the roundup, Dylan acted like a lovesick puppy because she was with us. Tom told me he thinks she's knocked up. Now, the bastard really acts like he owns the damned place."

He ran a hand through his hair. The jewelry box weighed down his suit pocket. Flipping open the lid, he looked at the diamond ring. Snapping the lid closed, he tossed the five-carat bauble across the room. He never, *ever* lost a conquest, and he wanted Charli Monroe more than he liked to admit. The fact Dylan Quinn was the one warming her bed damn near had him seeing red.

"Do something about it. I'm paying you to make sure Charli Monroe signs over that ranch to me."

"What the hell do you want me to do? I can't kill Dylan. I already tried."

He reached into the depths of his being and found calm against the seething rage making it hard to breathe. He'd long ago learned never to let extreme anger or fear show in the business world. To do so was a weakness the enemy could easily exploit, a lesson his grandfather had taught him.

"Come up with something, Kyle." He paused to make sure his point got across loud and clear. "I want the ranch. I still have the evidence I'm sure your Texas Ranger brother or the Dallas police would love to get hold of."

A loud, disgusted curse sounded down the wire. He let a predatory smile touch his lips. The young fool was right where he wanted him. "All right," the younger man said, resigned. "All fuckin' right."

He disconnected the call and looked out at the night. He'd get what he wanted and avenge the wrong done to him when that crazy bastard abandoned him long before he'd been born.

* * * *

After making love in the barn, Charli and Dylan went inside. She listened to his even breathing as he spooned close behind her. Hugging the arm holding her, she stared at the wall. She should have told him she loved him when she offered him the partnership. She'd told Ricardo she'd loved him, too, and he'd even married her, or so she had thought at the time. But he hadn't ever loved her.

And neither did Leon. She doubted he was even truly her friend, and that hurt. Every man she'd ever cared for had used her or planned to steal from her by bending her emotions to fit their purposes.

Was Dylan doing the same? Why hadn't he ever told her he loved her? But when she'd offered him exactly what he'd always wanted, a ranch of his own, he didn't take it. What else could be holding him here? If he was only with her for the baby, why didn't he want to marry her so their baby would never carry the stigma of being illegitimate? What would he do if he ever found out about her past? Would he take her baby from her? The thought terrified her. She could never give up her baby.

Sniffing back a sob, she closed her eyes against all the questions buzzing in her head. When sleep finally came, she was no closer to having the answers to any of the questions. Then the dream flickered to life.

"I can't stay here," she said as she threw clothes into a duffle bag. "You shot him when he was right beside me. What if you would've missed, Ric?"

He laughed, tossed the bag across the room and grabbed her wrists. "You'd be dead, I guess."

Her knees turned rubbery and bile boiled in her stomach. She couldn't fight his grip.

"You think I care about you?"

"You told me you'll take care of me. You told me you loved me." Her brittle voice cracked. "You married me."

The harsh chortle hurt as much as his tightening grip on her wrists did. "Shit, how many of your Johns tell you the same thing, Bambi? The only reason I even keep you in my bed is because you're a good fuck. The reason I take care of you? The reason I married you? Guys know you're my girl, so they're willin' to pay some major bucks to fuck you. You're an investment. I'd be a moron not to make sure you have clothes and food and plenty of coke to keep you happy. I love you making me a rich man. I love the way you give a blowjob, but that doesn't mean I'm in love with you. Better get used to men sayin' they love you to get what they want, baby. Only fools ever mean it."

She yanked on her arms, trying to get free. Her heart, what little hadn't already shattered, crumbled to dust. "I'm not doin' it anymore! I'm leavin' you."

"Where the hell do you think you'll go? Back to the farm?" He pulled her close and his face twisted into a frightening glower. "No one will ever want you. You're nothing but a coke addict and high-priced hooker who helped me kill six men."

When she shook her head, he scoffed, "Oh, you forgot about Hodges's guards. I had them killed, too, you know. You led me to Hodges's hangout. You're as responsible for those deaths as you are Tyrone's."

"No!" She sobbed and fell to her knees before him.

He picked her up by her wrists and tossed her on the bed. "Who will buy your drugs, Charli? You have no idea how good you have it, being my personal slut. You get to have the pick of Johns, live in my apartment, and I provide you with all the nose candy you want. All I ask is I get to fuck you whenever I want." He ripped her shirt and bared her breasts. "Like right now."

"No, Ricardo, no!" she screamed, but fighting him was useless. She'd learned that lesson a long time ago.

Dylan gathered her in his arms, murmuring soothing words into her hair, and held her until morning.

Chapter 18

Two days later, Ella called Charli. Annie was at work. When she entered Ella's Diner, the place was empty. Ella nodded in greeting and brought her a glass of sweet tea.

A few moments later, Annie stopped next to her table. "Mom said you want to talk to me."

She smiled and gestured to the seat across from her. "Yes, please sit down."

Annie remained standing with her arms crossed over her black t-shirt. "I don't want to talk to you. I saw you that day at the mall."

She returned the girl's stare. "And I saw you."

Annie put her hands on the table and leaned over them into her personal space. The skull pendant of her necklace swung forward and *dinged* off the untouched glass of iced tea. Charli calmly moved the glass and continued to stare into the girl's scowling face.

Annie snarled, "I could get fined and have to do stupid community service and rehab for a fuckin' year because of you."

"You sure could," she evenly said. "Rehab isn't a bad thing and neither is community service. It's your first offense and you're a minor. If you were older, like your friend who sold you the drugs, you'd be doing jail time."

Annie cursed again and straightened to stand over her. "I'd have to be caught first."

"Like you were when I called the sheriff?"

Annie growled and turned away.

"I only want to talk, Annie."

With her face flushed and her hands fisted, Annie spun around. "I don't need a shrink."

She shrugged. "I didn't think I did either."

The words had the effect she hoped they would. Annie glanced over her shoulder. "What do you mean?"

The tea was cold and sweet, but it did very little to calm her nerves when she took a drink. "Sit and I'll tell you."

For a tense moment, they locked gazes. Then Annie slid into the booth. "I'm sittin'."

Charli smiled and sat back. "How long have you been smoking pot?"

Annie lifted one shoulder up in a half-shrug. "Everyone knows pot is harmless."

"Really?"

"Hell, they want to make it legal."

"Sure. For medical purposes. Are you suffering from some disease?" She leaned forward. "Annie, marijuana is far from harmless. It's addictive. Since the authorities don't usually threaten rehab and jail time unless something a lot more potent than marijuana has shown up on your drug test, you've done more than just smoke pot. I know it was coke in the bag."

Annie shifted in her seat and looked away with a sneer. "Why the hell do you care? I know who you are. You're the heiress who the whole damned town's talkin' about just because you bought some stupid ranch."

She had to be honest with the girl or nothing she said or did would make a difference. She took another sip of the iced tea. "I care because I was where you are when I was fifteen."

"What's that supposed to mean?"

"I grew up in Tulsa. When I was fifteen, my mother died in a car accident. My grandfather, whom I'd never met, took me back to his ranch in western Oklahoma. I hated him, and I was angry my mother died leaving me alone. I got involved with one of the ranch hands on the ranch. Danny. He was only four years older than me, but I thought he hung the world."

Pausing to drink more tea, she prayed she wasn't making a mistake by telling this girl one of her deepest, darkest secrets. But she knew it was now or never to save Annie from making the same painful mistakes.

"What does that have to do with anything? So, what? You lost your virginity, and he didn't love you." Annie scooted across the seat to get out of the booth.

"Yes, I lost my virginity to him." Her quiet words stopped Annie. "I also stole from my grandfather for him, and in return, Danny introduced me to drugs. First, marijuana, and then I graduated to coke."

"You did drugs?"

She squeezed her shaky hands into fists under the table. "Yes."

Annie stared at her for a few heart-stopping moments. She half expected her to run and announce to every gossipmonger in town she'd been a drug addict. Instead, Annie leaned in over the table. "You said your mom died. Why didn't you live with your dad?"

How personal did she want to get? Somehow, knowledge about her being a runaway and living in Vegas had become common. She'd just admitted to drug use, but only Dylan knew about her mother or that she was illegitimate.

"I never knew my father."

"Why not?"

"He didn't know about me."

"Why did you do drugs?"

She leaned over her arms and peered into Annie's dark eyes. If she'd read her correctly, she should hit a chord with her next statement. "I wanted to escape the pain and anger of losing my mother. I felt alone, and I didn't understand why she was taken away from me. I ran away from home two months before my sixteenth birthday and ended up on the streets of Las Vegas. I was furious with my grandfather and blamed him for my mother's death. She'd moved to Tulsa because he disowned her after she got pregnant with me. In my messed up thinking, I figured, if we had stayed at the Long Arrow, Momma wouldn't have been going to work in Tulsa that morning."

She took a breath and looked down at the fake red and white marble of the table. "We had nothing for years. Momma worked in a bank and lived partially on welfare, but she still barely had enough to cover the rent. She'd go without lunch for months before Christmas just so I'd get whatever overpriced, foolish toy I wanted that year from Santa Claus. It hadn't been until about two years before her death things started looking up for us because she'd gotten a management position at the bank. Then she died."

She paused and swallowed back a ton of old hurts and pain she'd long ago thought were resolved.

Deep inside, she still wanted Hank to take it all back. "I'll never forget the day I saw the sprawling ranch house. Twenty-five thousand acres of land, cattle everywhere. The foyer of the house was bigger than the condo my mother had scraped and starved to pay for. Then I found out just how rich my grandfather was. I hated him."

After a moment of fighting back the pain from the old memories, she cleared her throat and met Annie's gaze. "Annie, I know you're hurting, too."

"Nothing's hurting me. You don't know me. You tell me some sad sob story. Boohoo." On the defensive, Annie shifted to get out of the booth again.

"I know your father and mother are divorced, and since then, he won't so much as talk to you. I'd bet you blame your mother and can't understand what happened."

Annie narrowed her eyes on her, the tension as thick as Ella's famous biscuit gravy. "Every nosy old biddy in this hick town knows that. My dear old dad wanted a son but got me instead." She shrugged and looked down at the table. "He decided he'd wasted enough time on waiting for me to grow a dick."

She had done some research on Jeremy Greenberg. "He works as a cowboy on the CW and trains their horses."

Annie looked up. "Yeah. So what?"

"Can you ride?"

"Depends on how cute he is." Annie's lips twitched.

"Did your dad teach you how to ride a horse?"

"Yeah. Dad taught me." Annie lost some of the hostility and her shoulders sagged a little. She was looking for something more than she had right now. "I learned how to train horses, too. I wanted to work on the CW someday."

She swallowed her heart, which was stuck in her throat. Jeremy Greenberg had no right hurting this girl whether he was Annie's biological father or not. "I hope you and I can be friends."

"Why?"

"Because I think we have a lot in common."

"My mom won't let me talk to any of my real friends, and I don't want to be friends with you."

"Are these 'real friends' the ones supplying you with drugs?"

Annie shrugged and narrowed her eyes.

She should talk to Ella first, but she'd made progress and what she was offering was harmless enough. She wanted to save Annie. "I'll have to discuss it with your mom, but if she says it's okay, I'd like you to come out to the ranch and ride with me. In fact, I want to buy some more horses, and who knows, I may need a trainer someday."

Annie's shrug was meant to look indifferent and bored, but the sudden gleam in her big brown eyes betrayed her very real interest in her offer.

Charli stood and smiled. "You think about it."

* * * *

Two weeks later, Dylan drove out to the CW Ranch to purchase at least five more horses, which he intended to give real horse names--like Traveler and Trigger and Geronimo.

When he drove up to the main corral at the old homestead, Zack Cartwright, dressed in the tan uniform of the county sheriff, stood by the railing. He had a boot resting on the bottom rail and leaned over his arms on the top one. Zack turned his official Stetson-covered head to watch him exit his truck.

Once he headed toward him, Cartwright said, "Captain."

He bristled, but let the nickname slide. "You told me I'd be meeting with either Luke, Paul or your cousin Lance because you were too busy playing lawman."

Zack pushed back his hat and stepped away from the railing. "Lance has a meeting in Dallas, Uncle Paul has a meeting at the Mayor's office and Dad refused to meet with you. He reminded me in not too many uncertain terms he's retired and these horses are mine." He pasted on a shitty grin. "I think it was their back-handed way of reminding me I own the ranch, despite the fact I should be sitting out on Highway 6 trying to catch today's crop of speeders. I have a budget to meet."

Maybe it was another incredible night spent in bed with the most amazing woman he'd ever known, or perhaps he just found the comment funny; whatever the reason, he laughed. "Are you still resisting the inevitable?"

Zack shrugged and looked out over the corral full of some mighty good-looking horseflesh.

"I suppose old habits really do die hard."

Zack Cartwright had been a hell raiser who wanted nothing to do with his half of the ranch.

"You know..." Dylan leaned against the railing. "I never quite understood why the hell you never wanted to run this place." He looked across his shoulder at the slightly taller man. "First, you were a damned rodeo champion, even back in high school. Second, it's in your blood."

Zack shook his head and peered out into the distance above the horses. "I suppose I'm a lot like you."

"Me?"

Zack met his eyes. "The military's in your blood. Your father's a general, but you came to Texas a spoiled Army brat and decided you wanted to be a rancher. I'm a hayseed ranch kid who decided he didn't want the ranch anymore."

"Why'd you join the Marines? You were getting rich rodeoing. Even had your mug in one of those stupid girlie calendars."

Zack let out a long sigh and leaned over the rail again, mimicking Dylan's relaxed pose, but he had a feeling Zack was no more relaxed than he was. "Nine-Eleven happened."

"So? Most people tied yellow ribbons on their trees and stuck bumper stickers on their cars. They didn't join the Marines."

Zack smiled and glanced at him. "I was in Cheyenne and met Lisa. Her dad was a veteran of Vietnam and her brother is a Marine."

"Don't tell me you signed up to impress a girl?"

"Yep." He laughed, but it didn't hold much humor. "I guess I did. She'd only marry me if I gave up the rodeo. No way in hell would I have stayed on her daddy's ranch. And I sure as hell wasn't coming back here. I needed a job and the Marines seemed like a good choice. I bought the whole spiel--hook, line and sinker."

Zack's sad smile told him everything. "I suppose it did set me on a career path. I wouldn't have gotten my job if I hadn't been a MP." He shrugged. "What can I say? I felt compelled to do my patriotic duty."

"And you got the girl."

"We got married two days before I headed for boot camp. Next stop, Afghanistan." He grew reflective. Dylan knew the rest of the story. Eerily similar to his or, more likely, the damned terrorists had no originality. "My unit was ambushed by a group of Taliban supporters. The next thing I knew everything went to hell." Zack met his eyes. "Kinda like what happened to you."

"Not quite." He broke eye contact and looked back at the horses, prepared to say no more about the subject.

"Dammit, Quinn. Don't you think we know your story? All about the nasty divorce and the bombing and the way things went down? Come on, this is Colton! The damned walls talk. Yet, we still respect you. We still care about your sacrifice. I think it's time you start thinking about all the times you *weren't* wrong. Start thinking about how many times your team, under your leadership, saved hundreds, maybe thousands, of lives. Who knows, maybe your sacrifice helped SEAL Team Six get that bastard."

He jerked back. *Just walk away and take the business elsewhere.* There were plenty of horses in Texas. The Cartwrights didn't own them all.

Zack heaved a breath that raised and lowered his shoulders. "I know you blame yourself for those men's deaths, but not talking about it isn't doing anyone any good."

He scowled at Zack and balled his fists at his side. "You're right. Talking about it isn't helping anyone. It sure as hell won't bring those four good men back or reattach legs and arms."

As he turned away, Zack grabbed his arm and stared down at him. With the dual bearing of one of the Marine Corps and the big ego of a Texas cowboy lawman, Zack Cartwright probably intimidated more than his share of lesser men. Dylan wasn't a lesser man. He balled his hand up to punch the sheriff.

Charli's quiet words whispered in his mind, *De oppresso liber...*

To free from oppression.

You really lived by that motto, didn't you?

I tried to.

He *had* lived by the motto. A memory flickered of the girls his team rescued from the mountain cave in Afghanistan early in the war--on yet another hunt for the devil who'd started it all. Those half-starved, battered women would have surely died in that stinking hellhole if it hadn't been for him following a hunch.

His hunches had usually panned out.

Until the day when they'd walked into a trap.

He took a long breath, let it out slowly and lowered his fist.

Zack dropped his hand from his arm. "Tracy told me about the woman who gave you the intel."

He peered out over the horses. "I should have picked up on the trap. I fell for everything that damned woman told me. I should have told my commander I wasn't fit to lead the team."

"So, why didn't you back out of the mission?"

He snapped his attention to Zack and stared at the hotshot's stony certainty for a long time. "Because I was trained not to let personal stuff get in the way of the job."

A corner of Zack's lips curled up. "Exactly."

"What the hell is that supposed to mean?"

Zack shrugged in a whatever-you-want-it-to-mean way. "You thought you had your head in the game. We all do that, Dylan. The night before the battle that ended my illustrious career in the Marines, Lisa had rushed Amanda to the hospital because her appendix was about to burst." He leaned on the top railing and looked out over the horses again. "I wanted to be there so damned bad, if I could have, I would've gone AWOL to be there. Moments before the truck exploded, I was mad as hell because I was sitting on a rock holding an M-16 instead of my wife while our baby was in surgery."

Zack looked over his shoulder at him. "But the moment that truck came into the checkpoint, I shoved thoughts of home and Amanda to the back of my mind and became a soldier. I did what I was trained to do, and so did you when you took your team and led them."

He moved away from the rail and faced him. "You were only doing your job. Should you have suspected the trick?" Again a shrug. "Who's to say you'd have seen it even without the emotional baggage? Was there even a trick?"

Dylan shifted his feet and flexed his hands at his side. "Cartwright, don't ever become a shrink."

"The truth always has to be swallowed with a bit of pride."

Zack rubbed his neck and looked down at the ground. When he met Dylan's eyes, Zack said, "You know my mother and aunt have a hand in planning the shindig over the Fourth of July. Anyway, they wanted me to ask you to speak during their last meeting, the Friday before the party. I thought we could go together."

He glared at Zack and moved toward the gate into the corral. The sooner he found the horses he wanted, the sooner he'd get the hell away from Zack. "No. I showed up at the Memorial Day thing, but I'm not talking to a group of ladies."

Zack shook his head and followed him. "Why not? They don't want you to talk about the blood and gore." He moved to block him from opening the gate. "They want you there because they respect you. They want to hear about your life as a soldier. You don't have to talk about the bombing. You were in Bagdad and Fallujah, and you were in Afghanistan. You were in on the plans to bring down Bin Laden."

"Yeah. Call the SEALs. They toasted his ass, not me."

Zack lifted his hat off his head and shoved his fingers through his short blond hair, then jammed the hat so far back on his head Dylan expected it to fall off. "They want to know they sent their young men and women over there for a good reason. They want to know you and I and Rachel and a dozen others in this county have risked our lives for something."

He stared at Zack. Had it been a trap? The woman who had confronted them with the intelligence seemed so scared, so righteous. She'd told him Bin Laden had killed her son and husband. Even claimed to support the Americans. The American forces had built schools and hospitals and provided jobs.

His warrant officer and first sergeant hadn't believed the woman. He thought about the men in question. They had been teamed up for a long time. There had been plenty of times those two hadn't agreed with him. Times when he'd been right on the money.

As if knowing exactly what he was thinking, Zack said, "What if the woman was telling you the truth and your luck just plain ran out?"

"Shit happens?"

Zack nodded once solemnly. "All the damned time. My daughter would still have her mother if it didn't."

Maybe his luck had just run out. He cleared his throat. "Okay, hotshot, I'll speak to the ladies, but you're going to be there or the gig's off."

"Wouldn't miss it." The younger man slapped him on the shoulder, opened the gate, and flashed him the same kind of grin a shady used car dealer might. "Now, can I interest you in some fine Cartwright horseflesh? The best in all of Central Texas."

* * * *

While Dylan went to buy horses, Charli and Tracy went shopping. They left the quaint boutique, on a side street of downtown Waco, and headed down the sidewalk to an Irish pub on the corner of the street. Tracy insisted the place had the best corned-beef sandwiches in the entire state of Texas. Charli doubted it, but she had to admit Tracy knew exactly where to find the perfect wallpaper for the baby's room and all the stuff to go with it. She'd collected samples and had a bag full of stuff to take home to show Dylan.

After settling into the booth by the window and ordering their late lunch, Tracy took a long draw of her Guinness. Charli had driven, so she didn't mind if Tracy drank a beer.

Tracy set the mug on the scarred table. "Aren't you a little worried about doing the nursery this early?"

"Why?"

"Because you aren't very far along, that's all. What if you change your mind, or something..." Tracy let her voice trail off.

"If Dylan leaves me, the ranch is still mine."

"No." Tracy shook her head. "That's not what I mean."

Then she remembered Dylan telling her Tracy had miscarried her first pregnancy. "You mean if something is wrong with the baby?" Tracy nodded, and she swallowed. "I guess I'm a little excited, but I want to get the nursery done before I get too big. If something happens... I--I'll just redo the room."

As she put a hand over her belly, she shuddered and looked down at the table. She loved her baby. What if something went wrong? "I have a feeling, once I start showing, Dylan won't let me do a damned thing."

A tentative smile touched Tracy's lips. "Did you get an appointment with Dr. Hawkins?"

"Yes." She shook off the grim thoughts. "I couldn't believe we got in so quick. My appointment is Friday. I also made an appointment with a lawyer."

Tracy's expressive gray eyes widened. "A lawyer?"

"Yes, to draw up paperwork making Dylan a full partner in the ranch."

Tracy blinked and then blinked again. "He bought into the ranch?"

She fussed with her napkin. "Not exactly. I offered him a business partnership. It's logical, considering we're living together and going to have a baby. If something happens to me, I wouldn't want Dylan to... You get the idea. He wants to wait until the baby is born to sign the papers and insists on paying me for it out of his share of the profits."

After she put the napkin down, she picked up her glass of sweet tea and shook her head. "He doesn't know it yet, but I'm not taking any of his money. I'll put it into a trust fund for the baby. The other thing we need a lawyer for is to make the new name of the ranch official."

"What's the new name?"

"Butterfly. Can you believe Mr. Tough Guy came up with it?"

"Dylan?"

"Yep."

They both laughed.

Tracy leaned back into the booth and folded her arms over her chest. "You must really love my brother."

"I've never known a man like him."

Tracy's face was as bright as a supernova, but suddenly a great shadow eclipsed it. "He doesn't know."

It was a statement, not a question, but she answered anyway. "No, he doesn't. I'm not sure how he feels about me either." Many times she'd thought she'd felt his love, but she'd been convinced the other losers she'd been with had loved her, too.

Tracy regarded her for a long time before bending forward and placing her arms on the scruffy tabletop. "Charli, Dylan cares a great deal about you."

Unable to meet Tracy's eyes, she played with the condensation on her glass. "I know. He feels something for me, but I don't know if it's love.

I've never been a good judge of love. I'm no stranger to being the one in love and the man just playing me for a fool."

"I've done that myself."

Charli looked up at the other woman. "Your ex?"

Tracy picked up her beer. "I never really loved him, and he never loved me. To him I was the grand prize in a game. I meant not being able to judge whether someone loves me."

Tracy took a deep breath and let it out. Her shoulders slumped as she leaned more into a slouch. "When Zack Cartwright and I were seniors in high school, we were quite an item. He was a bad-ass junior rodeo champ who had probably ridden as many girls as he had broncos." Charli blinked at her bluntness, causing Tracy to laugh, but it was a sad sound. "Sorry."

Tracy sipped her beer and continued with her story. "When we were in seventh grade, Zack gave me a nickname most guys around here still refer to me as--Olive Oyl. But something happened the fall of our senior year. Zack went after me with both guns, and I was too caught up by the idea of Zack Cartwright wanting me, to think straight. We went out, and before the night was over I'd given him my most prized possession--my virginity. Hell, the boy was only seventeen and had a special pocket in his wallet for condoms. Good thing though, because after that night, we couldn't stay away from each other."

Folding her arms over the table and leaning in, she said, "I didn't realize Zack loved me until it was too late. I never knew how he felt. But I didn't want to be the one with the broken heart, so I decided to be the one to cut my losses and get out. He and a barrel racer by the name of Dawn Madison"--at her puckered brow, Tracy added--"yeah, his lieutenant--always seemed to be at the same rodeos together. I knew she wanted Zack and let my imagination, along with Jake Parker's lies, cloud my judgment. Late in the summer after graduation, Zack and Dawn had competed in the same two rodeos together. Jake, Zack's best friend, told me a bunch of lies, including that he had always loved me and wanted me. That I deserved better than Zack." She looked away and murmured, "On our third date, I let things go too far."

Tracy took another sip of beer. "The day Zack returned home from Houston, he came over to Oak Springs where my mom and I were living at the time, to see me." She snorted and drained the beer. "He saw me, all right. He found Jake and me in the barn--together."

Tracy looked out the window beside their table, and she couldn't mask the wistful regret in her voice. "I broke Zack's heart and didn't realize until it was too late I broke my own heart, too. All because I was too afraid to tell him I loved him."

"You still love him?" she asked after a few tense moments. "Zack, I mean."

Tracy looked up at her, and said a little too quickly, "No."

Their food arrived, and to her delight, the corned beef sandwich was the best she'd ever eaten.

Tracy wasn't ready to put the conversation about past loves to bed. She pinned her with intense pewter eyes. "Dylan was hurt by Brenda. Just like I hurt Zack. I found out later he'd bought me a ring with prize money he'd won from the rodeos. He'd come over to the ranch to ask me to marry him, only to catch me with his best friend."

"Ouch."

Tracy smiled and it seemed oddly placed in the story of broken hearts and lost love, especially since she suspected Tracy was still very much in love with Sheriff Zachery Cartwright. "But you know what? Zack got over me. He met a woman in Wyoming when he was riding the professional rodeo circuit. They fell in love and had a beautiful little girl together."

If Tracy regretted the fact, she hid it well.

Tracy pointed a ketchup-covered french fry at Charli. "Dylan has never been able to hide his feelings from me. I know he loves you, even if he hasn't told you. I'd bet my paycheck on it." Tracy wiggled her perfectly arched eyebrows at her, stuffed the fry into her mouth and quickly chewed.

Charli laughed and shook her head. "I think you're crazy."

"A common enough speculation." Tracy sipped the glass of water the waiter had brought with their meals. "Tell me, has my brother called our parents with the news they're gonna be grandparents?"

"I don't think so." She rearranged her fries on her plate. Tracy's conviction that Dylan loved her didn't send relief washing over her. Was he still afraid the baby wasn't his? "He told me that he wanted to wait a little while."

"He's an idiot."

She laughed, but it was choppy-sounding even to her. "I usually call him a jerk."

"He's that, too. Don't let his putting off telling Mom and Dad about you and the baby bother you, Charli. He hasn't talked to our parents more than two or three times since coming back to Texas. Hell, I had to remind him to send Mom flowers on Mother's Day. He feels like he's let Dad down or something."

"I hope they can accept me, since Dylan and I won't be getting married."

"Married or not, I know they'll love you. You changed my brother's life. And for that I'm grateful." Tracy reached across the table and squeezed her hand. The gesture and Tracy's words brought the sting of tears to her eyes. "I've always wanted a sister. Welcome to the family, Charli."

"I've always wanted a sister, too," she croaked, realizing just how lonely she'd been before Dylan Quinn had driven into her life.

Chapter 19

Two weeks after Charli picked out wallpaper and paint samples at the boutique in Waco, she had the small nursery beside their bedroom completely redecorated. Dylan helped with stripping the paint and ripping up the grungy carpeting, but she'd been determined to do most of the work herself.

The sound of a vehicle crunching on the gravel of the driveway drew her attention out the open window. She didn't recognize the Jeep Wrangler and was surprised when Ella Larson got out.

She climbed off the stepstool and put away the electric screwdriver with which she'd been attaching hardware for a curtain rod. The doorbell chimed as she headed toward the front door.

Ella gave her a shaky smile after she opened the door. "I'm sorry if I'm interrupting something."

Returning Ella's smile, she stepped out of the opening. "No, not at all. Please come in."

Ella looked around the freshly painted foyer with its new molding and hardwood floors and spiral staircase. "This is really nice."

"Thanks. The guys just finished it two days ago. Would you like something to drink? I just made some coffee a little while ago."

Ella fidgeted with her oversized leather purse. "No, thanks."

Charli led her into the living room, and after they were seated, Ella said, "Annie ran away again."

The breath left her lungs, and she had to struggle to get enough back in to form words. "Oh, no."

Ella swallowed hard and looked down at her clasped hands. "My brother found her hitch-hiking along Highway 6. She's home again, and I've locked her in her room."

"You know that's not going to work."

Nodding, Ella sighed. "I don't know what else I can do." Ella looked away again and sheepishly said, "Annie got mad at me because I wouldn't let her come out here. She told me you offered her a job."

Charli leaned back into the couch cushion. After speaking with Annie, she had talked to Ella, but she'd never mentioned that part of the conversation. She'd only told Ella about inviting Annie to go riding, which Ella wasn't sure about allowing.

"I wouldn't say I offered her a job." She brushed loose hair from her face. "I did say I may someday need a trainer for my horses, but I didn't mean...now. Mostly, I offered her my friendship."

Ella locked gazes with her. "You'd want to spend time with her? Her stinking attitude is costing me business at the diner. But it's the only way I can keep my eye on her."

"I know her father works over on the CW. I saw how her eyes lit up when I invited her riding." She gripped the arms of the chair. "Annie misses that as much as she misses him. If you let her come out here, I know I can help her."

Ella looked down at the purse she held in a death grip. "If I tell you something, will it be kept completely confidential? Like a doctor?"

"Yes, of course."

Ella hesitated, obviously debating whether she could trust her.

She leaned forward and clasped her hands together, locking her gaze to Ella's. "Ella, I'm a professional--or at least will be when I eventually graduate. I also hope you count me one of your friends. I'm not a gossip. Lord knows there're things in my past I don't want broadcasted, and I would never repeat anything you tell me. I don't want Annie to end up on the streets. It's not a good place."

Ella toyed with the strap of her purse. "When I was twenty-seven, I did a few things I'm not very proud of. One of them was cheating on my husband."

"And Annie was the result of the affair."

Ella nodded and averted her eyes. "Annie doesn't know Jeremy isn't her father. She idolized him, and now he won't have anything to do with her. We tried for years to have a kid, and when I got pregnant, he was so happy. He'd wanted a son, but he loved Annie. Then we tried again and again to have another kid." Ella swallowed and blinked at the moisture in her eyes. "We went to a doctor in Waco. We found out he couldn't..."

"Did you know he wasn't Annie's father?"

Ella sucked in a deep breath and let it out. "Yeah. I got pregnant when Jeremy was at the Futurity in Fort Worth as the rider of Jason Ferguson's champion cutting horse. But I lied to make him think it happened when he got home."

She didn't judge Ella. Her mother'd had an affair with a married man when she was nineteen, which resulted in her existence. "Annie thinks Jeremy doesn't love her. She blames herself for the loss of that love. It's ripping her up inside, Ella." She rubbed her hands on her legs. "I hated my father because I thought he didn't want me. I didn't know he was never told about me. Annie's hurting for the same reason. Maybe the time has come to tell her the truth?"

Ella's breath caught as she stared at her. "I want to help her, but I'm afraid to tell her the truth. I'm afraid to let her know who her father is because she'll want to see him. Annie can't ever have contact with him. He'll turn her into what he is--a snake who can't be trusted. He's done things. Terrible things, to get what he wants."

She closed her eyes for a second. *Lord, help me get through to this woman.* "Annie deserves to know the truth."

Ella's made-up face lost all color under the layers of foundation and blushing powder. She jumped to her feet. "No. Annie can never know the truth."

While Ella paced before the couch, wringing her hands, Charli remained sitting. "Ella, lying to her is only making the pain and hurt worse. So, you don't want to tell her who her real father is, then don't-- for now. Just explain to her your ex-husband isn't her father. She deserves to know that much."

After a long time, Ella stopped moving and peered at her. "I'll let Annie come over. I know you're right. But if her paternity is ever revealed, certain folks will have their lives rocked to hell and back."

* * * *

The last Tuesday of June was hot, but Charli was glad to be outside. Dylan and Kyle were loading the last of the hay into the completely refurbished barn. Tom and Jesse were building the new porch. The house would be painted and the last of the outside work was scheduled to be finished the following week, after Independence Day.

Earlier that morning, she had gone riding with Annie for the first time. To her delight, Annie was quite an accomplished rider. They hadn't talked much, but she was thrilled just to have her on the ranch. After Julie Larson picked up her niece, Charli spent the rest of the afternoon working in the border garden along the lake.

She was still afraid of the snakes making the water their home, but as long as she didn't see one, she was okay. Dylan had finally relented and set some traps to catch some of the vermin to release them in the other lakes on the ranch.

She finished trimming back some of the ivy and stood to stretch her back. She tired so quickly the past couple of weeks, and now she felt like she'd puke. Maybe she needed to lie down. The morning sickness had caught up to her a week ago and was becoming an all day thing. Spending the early mornings with her head in the toilet was already getting old.

After she gathered her tools, she headed for the potting shed in the backyard. Jesse waved as she passed the construction going on at the front porch. "Giving up already?"

With her hand resting on her belly, she smiled at the older man. "It's too hot out here, and I'm not feeling well. Would y'all like some sweet tea?"

"Hope you feel better soon. The tea sounds good. Thank you kindly, ma'am." Jesse smiled and went back to work when Tom moved in with a new floorboard.

After taking two glasses out to the guys, she was pouring herself a glass when the screen door opened. Believing the person was Dylan, she said without looking, "Oh, Zack called..."

"Hello, Bambi."

She spun around and dropped the glass.

Barely able to force enough air past her numb vocal cords, she wheezed, "Leon... H--how do you know about that name?"

Leon laughed as he moved toward her.

She backed away until she came up against the counter.

He shoved at the mess on the floor with the toe of his boot. "I know a lot of things, Bambi Deere. I know how you got that extremely unimaginative moniker, for one." Leon went on, "I know you were tried as an adult in Nevada and sentenced to five years for possession of cocaine, prostitution and accessory to murder. You ended up serving only a year in Florence McClure Women's Correction Center because you were paroled on good behavior at the ripe old age of nineteen. By the time you were twenty-one, you were admitted into rehab for alcoholism. Hence, the reason you don't drink."

She was beyond sick and wrapped her arms around herself. "Dylan was right about you all along. I defended you! I didn't want to believe him, even when I knew he was right."

Leon laughed again, the sound grating along her nerves.

"What do you want?"

"I think you know what I want, if Dylan was so right about me."

She grabbed hold of the granite countertop to keep from falling to the floor. How could Leon do this to her? Her voice rattled when she demanded, "Why do you want my ranch?"

"That has to remain a mystery, I think."

Leon had played her for a fool. After drawing a deep breath into her constricting chest, she narrowed her eyes on him and let her shock and pain over the betrayal turn to anger. "You were leading me on." She stepped away from the counter, and though her knees were weak, she moved toward him. "You told me you were my friend!"

The crack of her hand slapping his cheek was loud in the large kitchen. Leon slowly pressed his hand over the red mark and looked down at her. His eyes burned with an insane fire. He grabbed her and pushed her against the counter. The memory of the times Ricardo had grabbed her and forced himself upon her rushed to the surface. Before she could scream, Leon held his hand over her mouth.

Leon shook her until her teeth rattled. "You led me on, too, whore. If you scream, you'll be sorry," he warned before taking his palm away.

She wiped her mouth with the back of one hand. "I never claimed to be more than your friend."

"I want this ranch, and you will sign it over to me, or your past becomes public knowledge."

She glared at him. "Never!"

With his breathing heavy and his voice low, Leon calmly asked, "What do you think Dylan will do when he finds out about your past?"

Her heart stumbled over a few beats. She had to believe Dylan loved her enough to forgive her.

Leon must have seen her thoughts in her eyes because he snorted. "You think he loves you. You thought I loved you, too. You thought Rodriquez loved you, and the cowboy Danny Palmer. Love is a fickle thing, Bambi."

How did Leon know about her first love? Hank had fired him, but if Danny had truly loved her, he would have come back for her. Danny had known how much she hated the Long Arrow and her grandfather.

Dylan had never even hinted at the words.

"Let me tell you what Dylan will do." Leon broke into her racing thoughts. "My dear self-righteous nephew will dump you so fast your head will spin. He's the type of man who would never settle for a woman like you, no matter how much in lust he is with you or how much you think your money and designer clothes have changed you. You're still a whore. No better than his ex-wife. And the baby you're pregnant with--"

"H--how...do you..."

Leon cut her off as if she never uttered the disjoined words. "He'll definitely not want you after I tell him it's mine."

"I'll have a test done!"

"A test?" He sneered. "Money can buy me anything I want, Bambi."

She fought against him. "No! I'll tell Dylan the truth about my past. I won't let you take my land. I'll tell him about you. He'll believe me because he knows what you are. He's been warning me about you ever since we met."

Leon seemed taken aback, but not for long. "You think that will stop me?" He gripped her upper arms and shook her again. "I'll just have him eliminated and pin the murder on you. It wouldn't be the first time I got rid of an obstacle to something I've wanted. Who wouldn't believe you'd kill your lover? You've already served a year in prison for your role in having a man killed. The only reason you weren't charged for helping murder Hodges's five bodyguards was a technicality. It would be so easy to make it look like Dylan found out about your past and threatened to leave you. Out of anger and fear, you kill him. A crime of passion."

Bile, boiling out of her stomach, scalded her throat. "Stop! Just stop." She had to breathe. She swallowed the bitterness and forced unsteady air into her lungs. "What do you want?"

"You know what I want, Charli. I want you to sign the ranch over to me after we are married." Her eyes widened, and Leon snickered. "Saturday night, the Charity Ball will take place at the Country Club. You will be my companion, where I'll publicly propose to you and you will say yes. Don't worry, I'll take care of you. You'll still be my wife and mistress of my ranch. A member of society. No one needs to know you're my personal whore. And the bastard you're carrying... Just one more thing I'll take way from Quinn."

She fought the dizzy haze threatening to snatch her consciousness away. "Fine. I'll give you the ranch, but I'll never marry you," she growled, shaking her head. "I won't do it."

"No, Bambi. It's not just the ranch I want. I want you, too." Leon let her go and she fell against the counter, her legs no stronger than a five-minute-old foal's. Leon looked around the kitchen. "It's truly amazing how dangerous ranching is." He left the way he'd come. The banging of the screen door was loud as a gunshot.

* * * *

The Dodge Ram extended cab pickup rolled to a stop near the barn. Dylan had spent all day working in the heat of a hay field and the barn.

He just wanted to go into the house and get a tall glass of Charli's sweet tea and something to eat.

Zack got out of the truck, looking more like the rodeo cowboy he'd been as a younger man than the county sheriff he was now. He paused and opened the back passenger door, then helped a black-haired little girl of about five or six from the backseat.

"Hey, Captain," Cartwright greeted as he came toward him, but something was off with his usual cheerfulness.

He scowled at the other man. "How many times do I have to remind you I'm no longer in the Army? Were you kicked in the head one too many times by a bronc, or did those prissy Marines warp whatever brain you had?"

"The Marines are great!" The little girl stared up at Dylan with her chin sticking out. She held a naked Barbie doll in her free hand and had a small backpack on her back with another doll sticking out of the open zipper. "Daddy was the best Marine ever." The narrow-eyed conviction she'd pinned him with snapped him out of his bad mood.

"That's right, baby girl, you tell him." Zack snickered and yanked on the girl's single ponytail atop her head. "*Captain*, like it or not, you're a retired officer and I was enlisted. It's what's done."

Dylan looked at the younger man and shook his head. He, of all people, knew all about military etiquette. Hell, he called his own dad "General" if other military personnel were within earshot. Despite the fact, he muttered, "That's just plain stupid."

Zack and his little girl fell into step beside him as he headed across the driveway.

"You're not on duty, so I can gather no one's under arrest," he observed from the casual way Zack was dressed and the rug-rat hanging onto his hand.

At the sight of Amanda--dressed in denim short coveralls and miniature cowboy boots--something tingled in him. In less than seven months, he would be a father, too. Would his kid stare down complete strangers if they ever called his honor into question?

"I came to talk to you. Is there someplace we can go--private?" Some of the natural amicability seemed to go out of Zack, instantly pulling him back from the sentimental sinkhole.

After a moment, he nodded. "My office."

Zack instructed his little girl to stay in the yard and play with her dolls, followed him into the ranch office and looked around. The nosy hotshot even looked into the apartment.

Zack whistled low. "I don't think my barracks at boot camp were this sparse."

He pushed past the other man into the living room. "You're behind the times, Sheriff." At the refrigerator, he pulled out two bottles of Coke and held one up. "Want one?"

Zack nodded and easily caught the bottle he tossed across the room to him. "Thanks. What am I missing?"

He limped back across the room. Pain shot up through his thigh and hip, which didn't make him in any better mood.

"I'm surprised your aunt hasn't been singing about this news from the roof tops. Don't tell me the queen of the Grapevine is losing her touch?"

"My aunt is happy as a lark you agreed to talk to the Forest County Charity Ball Committee." Zack followed him into the office again and his eyes flashed at him. "What else have you done she'd be gossiping about?"

Despite his crappy day, he grinned. "Charli and I are living together."

Zack raised a brow and lifted his Coke to his lips. Before he took a drink, he smirked. "Oh, right."

"What the hell is that supposed to mean?" he snapped and sat behind his desk.

Zack pulled the rickety chair from the corner and spun it around. After sitting on it backward and resting his forearms over the back, he shrugged. "I heard the news from Tracy. About time, I reckon. I saw it coming since the night at the Longhorn right after you started working for her. Besides, she was your date for the banquet."

"Go to hell."

"Probably." Zack removed his hat and hooked it on the bend of his knee. "By the way, I haven't had to drag your sorry ass off to the hoosegow to sober up for a while."

Dylan glanced out the door to watch Amanda play in the dry grass under the pecan tree just off the small porch. What would his child look like? Amanda didn't look much like Zack, except maybe for her big blue eyes. Her black hair must have come from her mother, because Zack's was golden blond. He imagined *his* little girl with her mother's wild red hair, and her incomparable spirit.

Dylan drank a long draw of the Coke. "I haven't been in there since the poisoning."

Zack lost the cockiness, and his expression turned much too hopeful for a pain-in-the-ass sheriff. "Did you stop drinking?"

He sniffed and shrugged. "I guess you could say. Oh, there are times I really want a drink, but Charli won't allow the stuff near her."

"Former alcoholic?"

He narrowed his eyes at Zack for figuring out so easily something Charli desperately wanted to keep to herself. He'd suspected the alcoholism from her insistence on his not drinking and her own aversion to alcohol. He'd figured out she was probably a former drug addict after they'd argued about her helping Annie Greenberg. Now, he wondered what else Zack knew--or had guessed. Whatever her past contained, he didn't want it to come back and hurt her.

"Signs are there. She was a runaway. Lived as a teenage girl in Las Vegas."

Zack visibly shivered. Dylan had done that more than once when he considered Charli living on the streets and relying on some dirtbag who beat her.

"I've been there with the National Finals Rodeo, remember? I know I did some harebrained things while in Sin City as a twenty-something know-it-all kid. I can imagine her doing a lot, including drugs."

"Do you have a purpose for today's social call, Sheriff?" He admired Charli more than she'd probably ever know. She'd pulled herself out of the gutter, but he didn't want to discuss what had been swimming in the cesspool with her.

Zack's brows drew together as he averted his eyes. He made a fist with his free one before taking a deep breath and looking up. "Yeah. I do. Actually, I'm here for two reasons. I've got something on McPherson."

"Go on."

"Turns out he was the main suspect in a burglary in Dallas in March. According to the initial report, he got away with a hundred thousand dollars worth of jewelry, electronics and cash."

Dylan whistled low in his throat, then scrunched his brow in confusion. "How'd his father manage to get him off for it? Give back the loot and pay off the owner?"

Zack shook his head. "No. The charges were dropped by the owner of the house McPherson allegedly broke into, the day he was apprehended by Texas Ranger Wyatt McPherson."

He jerked in surprise. "His own brother arrested him?"

Zack nodded once and sipped his Coke.

"Who the hell would drop the charges?"

"Elizabeth Sinclair."

He puckered his brow. "Any relationship to Sinclair Development and Land Management?" The urban development company was grabbing up ranches around Forest County and the neighboring counties like candy from a broken pinata at a kid's party.

"The CEO."

"Wow. She dropped the charges?"

"After Leon Ferguson presumably talked to her. Seems Ferguson and Miss Sinclair had been having dinner at Ferguson's Dallas penthouse when the call came in the thief was apprehended. Anyway, according to Wyatt, Ferguson accompanied Sinclair to the Dallas PD. As soon as he found out who the burglar was, Leon and Sinclair asked the detective questioning them if they could talk privately. Afterward, she dropped the charges, saying she'd found the missing property. Despite the fact Kyle had already sold the electronics." Zack shook his head and sneered. "With her denying the proof, the cops had to let him go.

Although the news should have shocked Dylan, it didn't. "We all should know Ferguson has the developer in his back pocket. He's gotten every construction contract in the county. Put a few of the smaller operations right out of business."

Zack chuckled. "I'm not sure *back pocket* is the right analogy here, but I have to agree. The rumor Wyatt heard is they're more than just business partners. I'd bet my shiny tin star Leon is holding a noose around Kyle's neck. You're probably right to be worried."

Dylan swore under his breath. "I should fire his ass."

"Does Charli know you suspect him of poisoning her cattle?" Zack glanced out the door again. Amanda wandered away from his line-of-sight. He got up and went to the door. After reminding her to stay put, he came back and took his seat again.

"No. I haven't told her." Dylan took another swig of his Coke. "Uh... we were going through some personal stuff, too, at the time, and I didn't want to add to her worries."

"Fair enough. I think you should mention it now. She's cut her ties to Ferguson, I presume."

"Affirmative. What do you have on that son-of-a-bitch?"

"That's the other thing I wanted you to know." Zack rubbed the dark growth of beard on his chin and took a deep breath. "I had an interesting visit from Ella Larson this morning."

"Ella? What does she have to do with anything?"

"She told me something that, if it's true, could change a lot of things."

"Will you stop beating around the bush?"

"According to Ella, sixteen years ago she was Leon's lover. She told me something about your grandfather's will."

"What the hell are you getting at, Zack? What does one have to do with the other?"

Zack cleared his throat and looked out the door at his daughter. "Leon forged your grandfather's will, Dylan."

He leaned heavily back into his chair, the breath whooshing out him. "You know what this means if it's true, don't you?"

Zack twisted the half-empty bottle of cola in one hand for a moment before pinning him with a meaningful gaze. "Pandora's Box is about to fly open. What are you going to do?"

"Afraid I'm going to break the bastard's neck?"

Zack scoffed. "Thought has crossed my mind. You special ops types always have been half-crazy."

"Tell me exactly what Larson told you."

Zack glanced out at Amanda before responding. "About seventeen years ago, Ella worked on Oak Springs."

"Yeah, she was a maid in the house and did some of Granddad's paperwork. She witnessed his will. Jeremy Greenberg trained Granddad's cutting horses before your dad stole him away from Oak Springs."

"When your granddaddy had his stroke, Leon wrote up a new and improved will. A forger signed it as Jason Ferguson, and since Ella had witnessed the original, Leon approached her to sign the forgery."

When he found his voice, he growled, "That's how she could afford to open the diner."

"Probably. She agreed to never go to the police, if he promised to never lay claim on her daughter."

"Annie?"

Zack grinned, though it never reached his eyes. "Yep. She's Leon's. And apparently, he'd wanted to raise her as his protege."

"Holy shit."

"And then some."

"Where does this leave Mom, Tracy and me?"

Chapter 20

For a long time after Zack left, Dylan sat at his desk and stared out the window at the pasture behind the old bunkhouse. A mile and half away, as the crow flew, Oak Springs Ranch lay out beyond the gradual roll of the land, and bordering both ranches to the west was the CW. At one time the three ranches were a whole lot larger and joined to form one of the biggest ranches in this part of Texas.

In 1865, three cousins--Cole Cartwright, Elijah Blackwell and Dylan Ferguson--returned to Texas from the Civil War half-starved and disillusioned. They'd found themselves in the cowpoke town of Dallas, hoping to find a way to buy enough land to raise longhorns. Dylan, the youngest of the trio from the cotton country of East Texas, talked his cousins into pooling what little money they had, and Cole, the eldest, agreed to play in an epic poker game. The gamble paid off. Cole won over one hundred-thousand acres of land--what later became Forest County. They'd gone into business together and Cole's Town, which eventually became Colton, soon followed.

Dylan shook his head. How did things get so messed up?

Greed. He answered his own question. Greed and the loss of the family connection that had kept three cousins alive while fighting on the losing side of a war and made them rich men raising cattle.

He didn't understand that kind of greed. He knew it existed and had seen it in places far more desolate than Colton, Texas. However, being on the possible losing side of such greed made him fighting mad. The real inheritor of Oak Springs might be his mother, or it might be Leon's mother, but he would bet it wasn't, since Leon had forged the will.

He reached for his cellphone. After noticing it was dead, he picked up the receiver of the desk phone and dialed his parents' number. He needed some advice and hoped his father was the man to give it. His mother answered on the second ring.

"Hello." Eileen's soft Texas accent resonated down phone lines and bounced off satellites, bringing a smile to his lips. Even after all the years away from Texas, she'd never lost the twang in her voice.

"Mom, it's me."

"Dylan! It's good to hear from you. I got your flowers for Mother's Day. They were lovely." He sent her flowers every year, although he would have probably skipped this year if it hadn't been for Tracy's reminder two days before the holiday. "Thank you."

"I'm glad you liked them. How're you doing?"

"We're fine. Dad's out in the yard with the pooches. I just got home from golfing with some friends. How are you, Dylan?" She softly asked. "The job working out?"

"I'm okay."

"Really?"

"Yeah. The job's perfect." He chuckled. What an understatement.

"Dylan?"

Sobering a little, he assured her. "Mom, don't worry about me. I'm better than fine. I actually have some news." He'd originally wanted Charli to be with him when he announced the baby and their living together, but now might be better. Besides, his mother wouldn't stop bugging until he told her something about why the job was going so well. 'Great news."

Just as he was gearing up to tell his mother he was going to be a father, a loud ruckus sounded in the background on his mother's end. He recognized the noise as his mother's two Yorkshire terriers. The thought of his father riding herd on the two sissified dogs made him smile. His mother spoke to his father, then to him, she said, "Here's Dad, I'm going to put you on speaker phone."

"Hello, son," his father said after she'd pushed the appropriate button on her phone. "Your mother told me you have good news?"

"Hi, Dad." Taking a deep breath, he plunged headfirst. "Yeah, I do. I'm seeing someone. She's the best thing that has ever happened to me."

"Oh, Dylan," his mother gushed.

"Who is she?" his father asked. Leave it to Robert Quinn to sound suspicious.

"No one either of you know." He paused again. Why did he feel like a teenager asking to borrow his parents' car to take a girl out for the first time? "She's my boss, actually. Charli Monroe. We're living together."

"Your boss?" The general didn't keep the disapproval out of his voice. "Sounds serious, and damned complicated."

"We're going to have a baby," he said as if it would explain everything.

"Oh!" his mother choked. Crying? "We are so happy for you."

You may be, but Dad's already wondering how long it will last and how his son could ever cross the line of propriety by falling for his boss. He forced the negative thoughts out of his mind.

His parents hadn't even met Charli, but there wasn't anything about her not to love. She was caring, loving and the most sincere person he knew. Sure, she had probably done things that were illegal, but her persevering despite a possible hellish past on the streets of Las Vegas was admirable--and one of the things he loved most about her. She inspired him to rise above his own hell.

"We're pretty happy about it, too." He had stopped doubting the baby was his, and couldn't wait for him or her to be born. He might not ever be a great father, but if he did his best, that was all anyone could hope for.

Maybe his father had done his best, too.

His mother got her tears under control. "Put her on."

"Charli's not with me at the moment, but I promise I'll call back as soon as possible so you can meet her."

"Good." His dad cleared his throat. "When's the wedding?"

His mouth was as dry as a West Texas summer. "We haven't decided to get married--yet."

"Why the hell not?" his father barked. "If you're living with her and you're happy about a baby, why aren't you getting married? I know times have changed and people live together all the time, but dammit, you owe it to the baby to give it a stable home and your name. You aren't not marrying her just because of that ridiculous idea of yours not to have kids, are you? If you aren't man enough--"

"Bob, please." His mother broke in. "This is Dylan's life and we have to let him live it."

"Marriage is the right thing to do," his dad said.

He tried to unclamp his jaw. Now, he remembered why he hadn't wanted Charli around when he told his parents about them. He'd known his father would react like this. "I think the decision is between Charli and me, sir. We've both been burned. Badly. So, we decided not to rush into marriage. I didn't say we'd never get married. We're just waiting to make sure it *is* the *right* thing to do."

He should stop, but before he knew what was happening, he said, "I never was man enough for you, was I, Dad? Never the perfect son." He tightened his hand around the receiver. "Have you ever considered the fact that maybe you aren't perfect yourself?"

Silence. Had his parents hung up on him? "I know I'm not perfect, son." His father's deep voice rumbled over the phone. "I missed so much of yours and your sister's lives. I could have been a better father. And I'm sorry you thought I--" He paused for a moment, and he could almost *see* the general run his hand through his hair--a habit Dylan had when he was nervous. "I swore I'd never become a pompous, overbearing ass and treat my own kids like my father treated my sister and me. I guess I broke that vow."

Had his father admitted to being wrong about something? He wasn't sure he could take many more surprises for one day.

He cleared his throat and got down to the business he'd called about. "There's another reason I called." He closed his eyes. How to explain? He'd always been a straight shooter, so why change now? He turned his chair around and looked out the window. "The sheriff has come by information suggesting Granddad's will was forged."

"*What?*" his parents said at the same time.

He reined in his hatred for Leon and his frustration with his father and explained how he'd come by the information.

His dad was the first to recover on the other end of the phone. "If this is true, there may be grounds to contest the will."

"I should have known Daddy wouldn't have completely cheated us out of an inheritance." Eileen's voice was as hard as he'd ever heard it. "Daddy had often talked about you running the ranch, Dylan. It shocked and hurt me when Leon got the place lock, stock and barrel."

He may have Butterfly Ranch with Charli and their child, but Oak Springs was in his blood. He was more Ferguson than Leon ever could be. His namesake was the youngest of the lucky poker-playing cousins.

He gritted his teeth as his mother said, "I should have contested it after he died. Why didn't I?" She broke down, and he heard her soft sobs in the background. This time the tears weren't happy ones, and they poked at the hatred twisting his gut for Leon Ferguson.

After his father murmured comforting words to his mother, Dylan loosened his jaw enough to ask, "Dad, do you think you could help us out? You have contacts I don't. Zack Cartwright is already doing what he can as the sheriff, but I don't trust anyone else, except for maybe Lance and Logan Cartwright, if I need a lawyer."

Bob Quinn didn't hesitate. "I'm already thinking about it. I'll let you know as soon as I find out anything. But I think you already know, finding the real will is crucial, or everything will either be held up in the Texas courts or will go to Madeline."

The last thing he wanted was his grandfather's widow getting the place. "Affirmative." He gave him Charli's landline number. "Thanks, sir." "Dylan."

"Sir?"

"We aren't in the Army anymore, son." His father's words sank in, his voice gruff. "I hope everything works out with you and Charli. You deserve to be happy. I never got along with your grandfather, but I never thought Jason would do something as cruel as build up your dreams of running the place just to shoot them down. If the ranch is supposed to be yours, I'll do everything in my power to make sure you get it." He was quiet for a moment. "Son, I just want you to know, I'm damned proud of you."

He couldn't fight the sting in his eyes and blinked several times to clear his vision. Before he found his voice, the phone on his parents' end went dead, but he spoke anyway. "I'm proud of you, too, Dad."

He hung up the phone and sat there for a long time replaying his father's admissions in his mind. He thought about his reasons for not wanting kids. Were they really because he was afraid he wouldn't be a good father, or were they because he hadn't met the woman with whom he wanted to have kids? Had he always known Brenda wasn't right for him?

He wanted to marry Charli. He loved her more than he'd ever loved Brenda, and he even wanted more than one kid with Charli. If only he knew for certain how she felt about him.

He shook his head at the Chinese puzzle laying before him. He was afraid to tell her he loved her, without her telling him first that she loved him. If she hoped for him to say the words first...

They could be together sixty years and have a passel of great-grandkids before either one of them said those three little words to the other.

But before he could contemplate a diamond ring and words of love, he had to deal with Leon.

* * * *

With her arms wrapped tightly around herself as she considered Leon's threats, Charli paced the kitchen floor for a solid three hours after he'd left.

She didn't doubt he'd do everything in his power to carry them out.

Leon Ferguson might have wealth, he might have the respect of an entire state, but he was the same kind of lowlife Ricardo Rodriguez was. Motivated by greed and cruelty, men like Leon and Ricardo intimidated and controlled by force to get what they wanted, and when that didn't work, they committed murder to get it.

She paused and looked out the window behind the table. The barn stood across the wide driveway, freshly painted white, the new metal roof gleaming dark red in the setting sun. Only four short months ago, she'd looked out over at that same barn and wondered if it would ever be functional again.

Now cattle and horses grazed in the pastures. Her house was again beautiful and her gardens bloomed.

When she saw Dylan heading around the stable, her heart skipped a beat and her breath caught. If he hadn't believed in her, she'd have fallen for Leon and all of his crap. She smiled at that. Dylan liked things straight up, he'd said, no bullshit to get to the truth.

She lost the smile.

Dressed in old Wranglers, cotton plaid shirt, scuffed work boots and a battered brown hat, Dylan limped toward her. She loved him, and she knew without a doubt he loved her. He wasn't like any other man she'd ever known. Greed didn't motivate him. He wasn't power hungry or cruel. He lived by a code of ethics and had impeccable honor and honesty.

Could he ever forgive a liar such as her?

When he entered the kitchen, she met his gaze and knew she couldn't risk losing him by *not* telling him about her past and Leon's threats.

However as they stared at each other, she couldn't force the words over her frozen vocal cords. After his arms swallowed her whole and his mouth came down onto hers, hard and hungry, she could do nothing but give and take in the soul-healing kiss.

Words were impossible.

Much later, as they lay within each other's arms, Dylan said, "I called my parents this afternoon and told them about us and the baby."

She lifted her head from his shoulder and looked down at his face. "What did they have to say?"

He shrugged and shifted his eyes away from her. He wasn't telling her something. "They're thrilled and can't wait to meet you. I bet Mom's already picking out baby clothes and telling all her friends she's going to be a grandma again."

She had to tell him about Leon. "Dylan..."

Taking her hand, he looked in her eyes. "They will love you, Peaches. They're happy for us."

"How can you know that?"

He rolled them over until he was above her. As he nuzzled her neck, he murmured, "Because you are the best thing that has ever happened to me."

Her breath caught and she gripped his biceps. Shock and tingling excitement zinged through her. Her eyes burned and moisture gathered in their corners. *Tell him!*

His soft gray eyes looked down into hers and a smile touched his lips. "Charli, I should have told you this a while ago, but--" The phone rang, cutting him off, and he cursed. "I have to get it."

He rolled over and sat up on the edge of the bed. Why he hadn't let it go to the machine?

"Hello?" He paused and then he barked, "What the hell do you want?"

She sat up behind him and laid a hand on his shoulder, but he jerked away.

Dylan stood and thrust the receiver at her. Taut contempt replaced the love she'd seen in his expression only seconds ago. "Here. It's for you."

Trying to calm her racing heart, she glanced at the clock; it was only a little past nine. With an unsteady hand, she took the phone and held it to her ear. "Yes?"

Dylan headed into the bathroom.

She flinched when the door slammed shut.

"My sweet bride-to-be, I'm just checking to make sure you and the baby are okay."

"Go to hell." She glanced at the bathroom door and spoke in a low voice. "I never want to talk to you again."

"Oh, Bambi. I do like your spirit. I'm sure it was the reason Rodriguez could demand hundreds of dollars for a night of pleasure with you. I can't wait until you're in my bed."

She gripped the receiver with a sweat-slickened palm. "I will die before that happens."

Leon chuckled, and she shuddered at the mocking sound of it. "What if Dylan was out of the way, would you reconsider then?"

"I intend to tell him, Leon. I'll tell him everything--about my past and your threats."

"Do you know how Jock Blackwell died?" He didn't wait before providing the answer. "The former owner of your ranch didn't want to sign the ranch over to me, either. Then one day he went riding out on the range and fell off his horse. He hit his head and was dead for two days before his youngest bastard come by looking for him. I heard it was a gruesome sight. Quite remarkable, too, since Jock was a rodeo bull rider in his younger days. I wonder what a lawman of the caliber of Zack Cartwright would do, if a similar fate befell his friend. I doubt the sheriff would rest until he discovered who killed him, Bambi."

Slamming the receiver into the cradle, she trembled with anger and terror at the picture Leon painted. If she told Dylan about Leon's threats, Dylan would go after him. Protecting him meant she had to remain quiet, but she had no intention of letting Leon win. She just had to figure out what she could do.

But she couldn't tell Dylan she loved him without telling him about her past. And about Leon.

Dylan came back out of the bathroom, wearing a pair of shorts and nothing else. Every toned muscle in his beautiful body was tight with a lethal combination of hatred, jealousy and anger. "What did the bastard want?"

She swallowed and shook her head. "Nothing. Come here." He obeyed, and she took his hand. As she pulled him back onto the bed, she said, "He won't be bothering us any longer."

Before he could question her, she ran her hands up his chest and wrapped them around his neck to bring him down into a passionate kiss. She intended to show him how much she loved him, even if she couldn't tell him.

* * * *

Charli fitfully slept beside Dylan. Something was up with her. What did Leon want? The bastard hadn't called or shown his face since he'd caught them on the porch. Whatever it was, it had upset her. She hadn't said a word after she pulled him back into bed.

When they'd made love that time, she'd clung to him as if he was a raft in rough seas.

Caught in a dream, Charli mumbled, "Ric, no...no!" She tossed away from him, but settled and her breathing evened out before he had a chance to wake her from the nightmare.

He got up and pulled on the jeans he'd discarded the night before. He needed some air to clear his head.

After pulling on his boots, he went out onto the back porch and leaned over the railing. The house was nearly finished and he was glad. Maybe when it was done, he and Charli could finally have some peace. At least, they could after he figured out what recourse his family had regarding his grandfather's will.

The cool air was refreshing against his bare chest. However, the breeze did nothing to clear his senses. What had Leon said to upset Charli? Had he heard about the baby? Ferguson had already been denied one child when Ella kept Annie from him. Did he believe her baby was his?

But if Leon thought that, it meant Charli had lied about not having sex with him.

No. He couldn't accept it. Charli wasn't a liar. She hid her past, but she had never lied to him about things that mattered to him.

While he peered into the darkness, a ruckus from the stallion stabled in the barn shattered his thoughts. He glanced in that direction and a cold lump formed in his gut.

All the other horses were in the stable, but it only had room for eight. The paint had been a little skittish at being placed in the big barn alone. He didn't want the horse kicking the new stall to hell because he was lonely.

He was halfway across the gravel drive when he smelled the smoke. As he crossed the distance at a jog, he noticed a dark silhouette move between the barn and the stable, skirting the corral at the back of the barn in the darkness. The full moon was high, and he'd long ago developed good night vision.

Crouching in the shadows, he changed directions and followed the figure. As he circumvented the side of the barn, the odor of gasoline mingled with smoke.

Damn, the barn was on fire.

He stopped when the figure--definitely a man--moved into a splotch of silvery light. The horse inside the barn frantically whinnied and kicked at the stall. Flames shot up the back wall to the dry hay in the loft. Smoke was thick and getting thicker, but he continued to watch the man.

He got to the side of the stable and moved along it to the entrance. Once he was at the open sliding door, he pressed his back against the door and took a deep breath of the smoke-heavy air. In a few more moments, it would be too thick to breathe.

If he hoped to save the horse in the barn, he had to hurry, but he had a sinking suspicion he had to stop the intruder or the stable would go up in flames next. With the comforting surge of familiar adrenaline, he peered around the doorframe into the darkness.

At first, he didn't see anyone, but the horses had. A few snorted and nickered in greeting. When the intruder moved into a shaft of moonlight, he recognized the arsonist. As Kyle McPherson--the youngest son of the Forest County Fire Chief--poured gasoline over the hay stacked in the breezeway, Dylan rushed in on silent feet.

Like a snake strike, he came up behind his younger cousin, grabbed him around the neck in a chokehold he'd used hundreds of times. McPherson tried to struggle, but he applied pressure to the back of Kyle's head with his free hand.

Next to his ear, Dylan said, "I would suggest you stop trying to move. I've killed men with this very same maneuver." To prove his point, he pushed on Kyle's head. Despite the pain the kid had to be in, Kyle didn't show it. "Just a little more pressure and I'll crush your throat."

"Go to hell." Kyle choked and sputtered.

"How much is Ferguson paying you to torch the place? Was the house next, Kyle? You planning to add murder to your rap sheet of burglary, livestock poisoning and attempted murder?" He had to speak loudly over the roaring and crackling of the blaze and the worried horses.

Kyle clammed up. An eerie orange glow filled the void outside the door. The air was growing hot. If he planned to save the paint in the barn, he had to disable Kyle. In another lightning fast jujitsu move, he laid an unconscious Kyle on the sawdust-covered floor.

Once he made sure Kyle was still breathing but out for the count, he grabbed a couple burlap sacks and ran back toward the burning barn.

* * * *

The roar reminded Charli of the Amtrak rail, which ran by the Cat Call. Was she locked in a nightmare again? What was that smell? Smoke? She bolted upright. "Dylan?"

She flipped the bedside lamp on. Where was he? She rushed out of bed, tripping on the sheet tangled around her legs. After grabbing the clothes Dylan had stripped off her the night before, she dressed and ran from the room.

"Dylan! Where are you?" When he didn't answer, she headed to the kitchen. She saw the blaze through the window behind the table and stopped dead in her tracks. "Oh, God, no!"

She sprinted from the house and partway across the driveway, despite the gravel cutting into her bare feet. When she heard the bloodcurdling squeal of the horse in the barn, she feared Dylan was trying to save it.

"God, no! Dylan!"

She ran as close as the heat would allow. The snapping and crackling of old oak boards and dry hay devoured by flames hurt her ears. The hellish light burned her eyes, while she choked on the bitter smoke.

"*Dylan!*"

Hunching over and pulling on the halter of the big paint stallion, he appeared in the doorway, like an avenging angel from the bowels of hell. What looked like a feed sack covered the horse's head. Another draped over Dylan's head with a corner held over his nose and mouth, scantily protecting him.

She called to him again, and he looked in her direction. Dylan coughed and wheezed as he approached. He pulled the sack off the horse's head. "Did you call nine-one-one?"

Unable to grasp what was happening, she shook her head.

"Go! Call!" A violent cough raked him for a moment, bending him over. He struggled for air so badly his body shook from the need of precious oxygen. When he caught enough breath, he said, "And tell them it's arson."

"Arson?" She coughed on the polluted air. In the crimson light, she noticed a red welt on his upper back. "You're burned!"

"I'm fine. Some hot hay fell on me. It's nothing," he barked and struggled to hold the halter as the horse thrashed his head from side to side and stomped the ground. "Get back, I'm going to turn him loose."

She backed toward the picket fence. Dylan pulled the sack from the nervous paint's head and let go of his halter. He took off like a racehorse from the gate, jumped the pasture fence and disappeared into the darkness.

Would she ever see that beautiful horse again?

"Charli?" Dylan's croak brought her attention back on him. "Go! If this fire spreads, we'll lose everything. I'm going to turn the other horses out."

As if outside her body watching the events unfold, she ran into the house and called for help. When she came back out, Dylan was leading the last horse out of the stable. The frightened animals circled each other in the pasture. He entered the stable again, and when he came out, he was dragging someone beside him. When he reached the edge of the yard by the driveway, he dropped Kyle McPherson unceremoniously onto the grass.

She rushed off the back porch. "Is he hurt?"

"Not permanently." Dylan's voice was hoarse from the smoke he'd inhaled. He wiped sweat and soot off his face and neck with his hand. "I knocked the damned idiot unconscious when I found him getting ready to torch the stable."

Beyond shocked, she shook her head and stared down at the sleeping man. She didn't particularly like Kyle, but he'd always done his work. "Why would he want to burn my barn?"

Dylan coughed again, bending over his knees.

She rushed to his side and put her arm around him. "Dylan, are you okay?"

He nodded and coughed again. After he straightened up, he pulled her into his arms. "I'm fine. Peaches, Kyle poisoned your calves and horses. I think he shot at me, too. I just didn't have proof."

She pulled away, shaking her head, not wanting to believe it. "Why..." But she knew, even before he told her.

"Leon," he said between gritted teeth. "He's been paying him to make trouble and to spy on us."

A siren split the night. Within minutes, the early arrivals of the volunteer fire department were on the scene. One of the firefighters ran over to Kyle.

Dylan growled, "He's fine." When the same EMT wanted to treat his burn and put an oxygen mask on him, he brushed him off. "Hell, I was blown up once. This is nothing. Go take care of the damned fire."

The county's ancient fire truck bounced over the iron bridge and came to a skidding stop with gravel flying. A sheriff's department Tahoe followed in the fire engine's dusty wake. After sliding to a halt near them, Zack Cartwright jumped out. "Are y'all okay?"

"Yes." Dylan answered before she had a chance.

Zack looked around, taking in the scene. "What happened?"

The fire chief came running over to them. "Is anyone hurt?" he anxiously asked, but he was clearly looking at his son, now sitting up in the grass.

Dylan turned to the older McPherson. "No. But I suggest you stay out of this, Marlin, and worry about getting the fire out before Charli loses more property."

Kyle pointed at Dylan. "Crazy sumbitch tried to kill me." With his other hand, he rubbed his throat where he had the beginnings of a bruise.

Dylan coughed again, but it wasn't as harsh as before. Ignoring Kyle's accusation, he said to the officials, "I found this yahoo dousing the stables with gasoline after I saw him leave the back of the barn—where the fire started."

Kyle's eyes widened. "Dad, I can explain."

Marlin McPherson's shoulders drooped and he bowed his head as he closed his eyes. "I'm sure you can. You always have a story, Kyle. I'm done saving you. I've been doing it since you were fourteen, but I'm not doing it anymore. You're a disgrace to our family. Your older sister's a teacher. The other risks her life in the war. Your brother's a Texas Ranger. But you..."

He shook his head and his face pinched as if in pain when he turned to the sheriff. "He's all yours, Zack. If he set this fire, throw the book at him. I'll call in the state to make sure no one can claim I doctored the evidence." Chief McPherson nodded toward Charli and swallowed hard, regret visible in the man's eyes. In the light of the harsh red glow, the old firefighter walked away, his shoulders stooped, head hanging.

Zack's question to Kyle pulled her focus back on the arsonist. "Why would you set Miss Monroe's barn on fire, Kyle?"

He jutted his scruffy chin and stared up at the sheriff. "I ain't sayin' nothin' without a lawyer. I know that much."

Cartwright grinned, but his blue eyes flashed dangerously. The sheriff grabbed Kyle by his upper arm, yanking him to his feet. "Fine. Let's get back to town so you can call your lawyer. Wouldn't want you to incriminate yourself." Zack pulled a pair of handcuffs off his service belt. Once Kyle was duly handcuffed and Mirandized, Zack took a two-way radio from the truck and called for a deputy.

Dylan hadn't taken his hand from her waist, giving her comfort and strength in the touch. He was still shirtless, and she was concerned about the burn across his back. While he spoke to Zack about coming to the station in the morning, she looked out on the terrible scene beyond the pickups and the fire trucks filling the driveway. She wrapped her arms around herself and swallowed against the painful lump in her throat.

The barn was a complete loss.

Dylan could have died in the inferno.

Leon had done this. He'd hoped to prove his point.

Zack's next statement had her looking back at the sheriff. "I probably shouldn't tell you this now, but by morning your fire won't be the only news buzzing."

"What is it?" Dylan asked peevishly.

Zack rubbed his stubbly jaw. "Ella Larson was shot dead tonight."

"What?" Dylan's voice raised an octave.

She rasped, "Oh, God! Where's Annie?"

"Julie Larson's caring for her. But she's the prime suspect."

"No." She shook her head and pulled her arms tighter around her. "She wouldn't ever kill her mother."

Dylan wrapped her up from behind, offering his strength, and said to Zack, "You don't believe that, do you?"

Zack shook his head.

Thank God. Her eyes stung, but the reason wasn't the smoky air. She fought the tears. If she started crying, she'd never stop. "Wh--Who would want Ella dead?"

Zack met Dylan's gaze and held it.

She looked from one man to the other, then turned on Dylan. "You know something."

He swallowed and nodded. After pulling her away from the sheriff and Kyle, he said in a low voice, "Ella approached Zack with a confession."

"A confession?"

"She told Zack my grandfather's will is a forgery."

She stared at him. After she closed her mouth and blinked her eyes a few times, she remembered her conversation with Ella from a few days ago. "Annie." Gasping on the rancid air, she shook her head to clear it again then looked at Dylan. "Annie's Leon's daughter."

"Yeah."

After a second pump truck had arrived from a neighboring county, the fire was finally coming under control. With her head on his shoulder, she looked over at the remains of the barn and trembled. In her ear, Dylan whispered, "It's gonna be okay, Peaches."

She clung to him. "I did this to Ella."

He looked down into her face. "No, Charli..."

"I told Ella to tell Annie the truth. That's why she's rebelling so much. Annie thinks her father doesn't love her, but he'd found out Annie wasn't his child. I explained to Ella that Annie had to know the truth to begin her healing." She sobbed and tears gushed. "Ella confessed to save her daughter."

When the black Porsche rolled to a stop behind Zack's SUV, she sniffed back her tears and moved out of Dylan's arms. She clenched her fists to her sides. Her heart raced.

How dare he *show up here?*

The old Charli had been a pawn for men like Leon Ferguson, but she wasn't the same woman any longer.

She knew what true love was, and she wasn't giving it up.

Leon got out of the car at the same time the other sheriff's department Tahoe stopped in the drive. As soon as Leon noticed Zack guiding a handcuffed Kyle toward the approaching deputy, he stopped.

Dylan stepped in front of her and squared his shoulders, his hands fisted by his soot-blackened jeans. "Don't even think about coming any closer, you son-of-a-bitch."

Leon glanced at the sheriff. For the first time since she'd made the man's acquaintance, Leon appeared anxious. He shifted his feet and tucked his hands into the pockets of his jeans. He looked back at Dylan. "I came by to see if Charli was safe. I saw the glow from Oak Springs."

Sara Walter Ellwood

Dylan snorted. "More likely you came by to make sure your *tool* did the job right. Tell me, *Uncle*, were you hoping to have us burned to death in our bed, or were you hoping it would just be me?"

"Dylan." Zack turned toward him. "Don't say or do anything you'll regret later."

Leon smiled stiffly. "Dylan, you really are delusional. I was concerned Charli and you were hurt. I see you aren't, and if you don't need anything, I'll be leaving." Leon sidestepped so he could see her. "I'll be seeing you, Charli."

She took a determined step toward Leon. "You have nothing I need or want, Mr. Ferguson." Her voice shook, anger and hatred ringing through every word. "I would suggest you get the hell off my land before I make things mighty difficult for you."

Leon looked as if he'd been sucker punched.

Dylan slid his arm around her quaking shoulders and held her close to his side.

Leon recovered quickly and glowered at her. "When are you going to tell him the bastard you're carrying is mine?"

Dylan stiffened next to her, but didn't move away. His voice blew past her like a cold arctic wind. "Then I suppose I'll be raising your child as my own, won't I? Because I'll never let you get this ranch--or Charli."

Leon clamped down on his teeth so hard his jaw muscles jerked.

Zack finished with giving the deputy a report, then turned to Leon. "Mr. Ferguson, I suggest you do as the lady says. I'll be by Oak Springs later this morning. I have several questions to ask you about your whereabouts last night around ten PM. So, don't leave the county."

Leon didn't look scared, but he didn't respond to Zack either. He turned on his boot heel, got back into his flashy car and raced out of the drive, kicking up a dust cloud behind him.

Dylan turned her away from the noisy scene. "Let's go make sure the horses are okay and then go in."

Chapter 21

Later in their bedroom, Dylan took Charli into his arms and hung on. They both smelled of smoke, and she was concerned about his injury. He kissed her forehead, her eyes and finally her mouth in a tender, loving way that healed her.

When he pulled away, he gazed into her eyes. "Let's take a shower and get some sleep. The rest of the day's going to be as hellish as first part, if I'm any kind of prophet."

She nodded and took a deep breath. "Dylan, I swear on everything holy I never slept with Leon."

He pressed his lips to hers to still them. "I know."

She pulled back. "We can have a test done..."

He smiled and shook his head. "I trust you, Charli. I'll admit I didn't at first, but I know now the baby's mine."

She sagged against him, and he held her. After a while, they walked into the bathroom, where she insisted on cleaning the burn on his back and checking his legs for more. He flashed a wicked grin when he dropped his tattered jeans. He stood before her naked. She bent to examine the raw spots on his legs, instructed him to sit on the stool by the vanity, and winced at the red splotch on his back.

"This burn isn't bad, but you should have it looked at by a doctor. You could still get an infection." She gently touched a cool, clean washcloth to the red puckered skin.

"It'll be all right." With his chin tucked to his chest, Dylan sounded muffled. "I've been through a lot worse. Once we're done showering, you can slather some burn cream on it and put on a bandage."

While she rinsed the cloth, he stood, took the washcloth from her and laid it on the counter. Slowly, he began undressing her, removing her tank top and then her shorts. She hadn't bothered with panties or a bra. As he lightly rested his hand on her bare belly, she closed her eyes.

When she opened them, the love in his eyes brought a flood of jumbled emotions, and the dam broke, long-held truth flowed freely. "I was a cocaine addict and a prostitute. I worked as a stripper and went by the stage name of Bambi Deere in a Las Vegas dive called Cat Call. Ricardo Rodriguez wasn't my legal husband, although I didn't learn that until-- until later. He was my pimp and the leader of the gang I belonged to."

"Charli," he whispered next to her ear. "I don't care."

She ignored him and went on as if he hadn't spoken. "He's now in prison because I--I turned state's evidence on him. He owned the Cat Call, but his main income came from drug dealing and prostitution. I served a--a year in prison for--for..."

His face hadn't changed in expression. How could he not be surprised or repulsed?

He feathered the fingers of his free hand over her cheek.

She trembled at the gentleness of his touch.

"Charli, I don't care what's in your past."

"I helped Ricardo murder six men because he threatened to stop supplying me with cocaine if I didn't spy on his rival gang leader. I was only convicted of helping with one of the murders. But if I hadn't led him to Tyrone's hideout, those other five men wouldn't be dead." The words hurt as she pushed them out. "I should have served more time. I was sentenced to five years, but paroled after a year. I didn't know Ricardo was going to kill them. He didn't tell me what he planned to do, but I should have known. I should have known...I should have..." She collapsed, but he caught her before she slipped to the floor.

Dylan held her as she sobbed with both shame and relief. He hadn't walked away from her. At last, the sobs stopped and she hiccoughed. He pulled back to look down into her face and brushed away her tears with the pads of his thumbs.

He gently pushed her chin up with the side of his calloused index finger, forcing her to look at him. "You thought I'd walk away because of your past?"

She nodded, drained. "I--I didn't think you could ever love me. No man ever truly loved me before. Not Danny when I gave him my virginity. He promised he could take away my pain. But all he wanted was for me to steal from my grandfather. D.J. didn't love me when he took me to Las Vegas. Ricardo and Leon told me they loved me only to get what they wanted."

She hiccoughed again and shuddered at how close she'd come to losing him. "Leon threatened me. He wanted the ranch, but he also wanted me to agree to marry him. He said he'd fix any paternity test I took to make him out to be the father of our baby. I told him I'd tell you about my past and about his threats. But then he threatened to have you killed and make it look like I did it."

She sniffed back a sob, and he held her tightly against him. "I love you so much, Dylan. How could you love someone like me? And yet, you show me every day you do."

His warmth seeped into her, warming places she hadn't even realized were frozen. After kissing her temple, he smiled and it was like rays of the sun after a long violent storm. He gave as much as he took.

"I love you, Peaches. I don't care what was in your past. I figured out a long time ago you were probably a stripper--best case scenario, a prostitute--worst case scenario--when I found out you were a runaway and lived in Las Vegas. I even figured this Ricardo yahoo was probably your pimp. Dear God." His voice grew gruffer as he spoke. "You were so young. It tears me up inside to think about what you've lived through."

He kissed her softly on the lips. "I understand why we're so drawn to each other. I once told you we had probably more in common than either of us could imagine. I was right. How could I hold your misguided involvement in the murder of that drug dealer against you, when I ordered my men into a situation where I wasn't sure about the dangers?"

He rubbed her back, and she clung to him. "We have a future together."

She blinked as tears flooded her eyes.

With his thumbs, he wiped away the moisture on her cheeks again. "I love you with all my heart and soul."

He kissed her again, the tender kiss deepening when he licked her upper lip. She touched her tongue to his, and he moaned. He plunged into her mouth, filling her with his sweet forgiveness.

When they broke apart, he leaned his forehead on hers. "Now, let's get that shower and some sleep before I fall over from exhaustion." He grinned wickedly, and pressed his hardening erection into her low belly. "Or I decide I'm not tired after all."

Despite the fatigue creeping up on her, she leaned against him, threaded her fingers into his dark hair and puckered her lips into a pout. He awarded her with a groan, and backed her up toward the shower stall. Once inside, the warm water washed away much more than the grime from the fire.

He claimed her mouth and kissed her thoroughly. She broke away to catch her breath, skimmed her lips against his beard-roughened chin to his throat and pressed her mouth to his strong, steady pulse.

Dylan moved his hands from her hair and down her back, over her ass. Moaning, she let her head fall back when he reached between her legs. His mouth caught one of her nipples and suckled while gentle fingers stroked her to a feverish height, but before she climaxed, he backed off and cupped her behind with his hands. When he pulled her up onto her tiptoes, she wrapped her arms around his neck. He backed her against the wall and shifted his weight slightly onto his left leg.

No words passed between them, but they didn't need words to hear what was in each other's hearts. She lifted her legs to wrap them around his waist. He gave her a soft, peace-filled smile as he lowered her onto his erection, filling her with serenity. When he was buried deep inside her, he whispered against her lips, "I'm nothing without you, Charli. But *with* you, I'm whole."

She cried his name when he withdrew and thrust into her again. The orgasm shattered her and built her back up again, transforming her.

And when he growled her name as he found his own release, they had become something more, something beautiful.

* * * *

The ringing phone on the bedside table jarred him awake. Dylan groaned and lifted his head. The time on the alarm clock read 9:45 AM. Bright mid-morning sun filtered around the closed curtains. When Charli shifted beside him, he smiled. She lay against his side with her arm draped over his back.

The phone rang again. He picked it up. "Yeah?"

"Dylan, it's Zack."

Instantly alert, he sat on the edge of the bed. Charli kneeled behind him and rested her hands on his bare shoulders. He mouthed "Zack" over his shoulder. She nodded, but didn't move away. Into the phone, he asked, "What's going on?"

Zack let out a long breath. "Ferguson fled the area. Half the law in Texas is looking for him, but he hasn't turned up at either his business or penthouse. I've called Mrs. Ferguson, but his mother hasn't seen him either. And neither has his lover Elizabeth Sinclair."

He considered the news for a moment. "Ferguson isn't in Dallas. He keeps a plane and a helicopter at the local airstrip. Did you check them out?"

"The plane's gone. If he lands anywhere in the U.S., I'll have him, but my guess is he's fled the country." Zack huffed. "On a brighter note, Kyle decided he'd rather sing than shoulder all the blame, especially when I started suggesting he killed Ella. He's made a full confession. I've called in the D.A. and told him about Ella's confession."

He closed his eyes to absorb all the information, but opened them when Zack continued.

"He believes there's enough to go after Leon for the forgery and for killing Ella. The Texas Rangers are building a case against him for a whole laundry list of crimes, including murder."

Dylan took one of Charli's hands from his shoulder and held it against his chest.

"Ask him about Annie," she chimed in from his side.

He nodded and held the phone so she could hear the answer. "Have you talked to the girl--Annie?"

"She's taking this hard. Jeremy Greenberg refused to have anything to do with her. According to Julie, Jeremy told Annie he isn't her father. He always had a mean streak."

He looked at Charli.

She took the phone. "Zack, do you think I could see her?"

"You'll have to contact Julie," Zack said.

She handed him the receiver again. "Thanks for letting us know, Zack."

"You bet. Until we catch Ferguson, you watch your back, Captain."

"Affirmative."

"Make sure Tracy knows what's up, too. The crazy bastard might try to come after her or her boy to get to you."

"I'll talk to her. Catch him, Zack."

"Roger." Zack hung up.

"God, Dylan." Charli got out of bed and headed for the closet. "I need to see Annie."

"Yes, you probably understand her better than anyone." He rummaged in the dresser drawer for a t-shirt.

"What can you do about the will?" she asked when she returned from getting her clothes for the day.

"I don't know." With a shirt in hand, he turned and leaned against the dresser. "My father is going to get back to me when he finds out what we can do. I'm hoping we can contest it, but things would be so much easier if we could find the original."

She puckered her brow. "Wouldn't he have destroyed the will?"

He pulled on a pair of jeans. "Maybe. But knowing Leon the way I do, I think he kept it."

Sara Walter Ellwood

"Why? Seems awfully risky. He's a businessman, and from what I've heard, a damned shrewd one. Unless he'd keep it for some sick reason, I don't see it."

"Which is precisely why he'd keep it. It's a trophy in his sick mind. He's always despised my relationship with Granddad. He and Leon never got along, despite Granddad's best attempts at trying to be a good father to him. That's why it was such a shock when Leon inherited the ranch and all his money."

* * * *

"Annie," Julie Larson said after leading Charli into the small living room of her apartment above the Longhorn. "Miz Monroe came to see you."

The girl, stoop-shouldered and sitting across an overstuffed chair, grunted and continued to change channels with the remote.

Julie turned red-rimmed eyes on Charli, and she could almost *feel* the hopeful pleading pouring from the other woman.

She sat on the edge of the couch that, if the blanket and pillow were indicators, Annie had used as a bed the night before.

Julie put her hands into the back pockets of her jeans and turned away.

"I'm sorry, Annie." She rested a hand on Annie's arm. "I'm here if you need to talk about what's going on." When no response except more vicious channel changing came from the girl, she took a deep breath.

"You know when I was your age, my momma died, too. I hated a lot of people after that day. My grandfather, my father, the driver of the truck who'd hit her, the bank where she worked. The list goes on. But mostly I hated myself."

Annie looked at her.

"I even thought if I hadn't been born, Momma wouldn't have moved away from the ranch. She wouldn't have been working at a bank in Tulsa. I blamed myself for everything, including her bad choices--which included her sleeping with my father to begin with."

Annie still didn't speak, but sniffed and looked away again.

"But I didn't make those choices, my mother did. In the end, I just had to make sure I didn't make even worse ones, but I didn't realize that until I'd already made them. My hate and anger led me down a road I never want anyone else to follow. Think about coming to the ranch, Annie."

"Aunt Julie told me Leon Ferguson is my father. Why would he kill her?" Annie choked on a sob and peered at her with pleading big brown eyes. "Why?"

She knelt beside the chair and took the girl's free hand. The other held the TV remote in a death grip. "I don't know, Annie, but I'm here to help you figure out how to get through this. I'm not like most therapists you'll probably talk to. I've been there, but more importantly, I'm your friend."

"Will you still let me train your horses?"

She fought the sting of the tears for as long as she could, but it was a losing battle. "You bet."

* * * *

"I was beginning to think you stood me up, hotshot," Dylan said in way of greeting when Zack showed up in the hallway of the meeting room of the country club on Friday afternoon. In spite of the chaos in which the county found itself, the annual charity ball was still going on, which meant he was still slated to talk to the planning committee.

He paced the floor and was sweaty under his pressed white shirt and bolo tie. He still had no idea what he'd say to the group of women gathered to listen to him, but he'd let Zack go first, since his aunt and mother ran this shindig, and wing it from there.

Zack flashed him a smug grin. "Don't get your panties all tangled in a wad. I told you I'd be here. But I *am* trying to hunt down a wanted man. Plus there was a cattle rustling last night."

He let Zack's smart-assed greeting slide. "The bad guys figure y'all are distracted, I guess. Any leads into where Leon might be hiding?"

Zack shook his head. "No. The FBI is now involved, but it's like Ferguson disappeared. His mother swears she knows nothing."

"You don't believe her?" he asked in response to something in Zack's tone.

"I believe her claim of not knowing where he is, but I do think Mrs. Ferguson knows more than she's letting on."

"Maybe she knew about the will forgery. You remember from your Tracy days, Maddie and my mother got along like two wild cats stuck in a burlap sack, don't you? Maddie hated my mother because she felt Mom was Granddad's favorite. Leon's mother would do anything to protect him."

"Maybe. But if she did know about the forgery, she's an accessory to the crime and will go down with her son." Zack looked around the hallway. "How's Charli?"

"She's holding up. Talked Ella's girl into coming out to the ranch and helping with the horses. I think Charli would like for Annie to move in with us. Sam and Julie don't have room for her."

"Not a half-bad idea. Neither Sam nor Julie is parenting material. Sam can barely take care of the kids he has, and Julie is too wild. Charli will be great with Annie."

"Yeah. She knows exactly what she's going through."

"Is Charli at the ranch?"

"No, she and Tracy went to the mall to buy a dress. We're going to the ball tomorrow night. I don't know how much fun we'll have, but we decided to go for it."

Zack groaned. "Don't remind me about the ball."

"Will you be working and had a hot date planned?"

Zack laughed and shook his head. "Hell, I wish I was working. I'll be at the party, but I don't have a date. I can't date anyone."

"Why not?" He frowned. "*You* surely haven't given up women, have you?"

The sheriff narrowed his eyes on him. "I have a six-year-old daughter who still asks me every night when her momma will come home from heaven. I can't confuse her by bringing another woman home. Besides, I'm too busy with work and the ranch." Zack slapped his hat on his thigh and looked away from him. "But God, sometimes I wish I could find a good woman. Amanda needs a mother. She's six going on sixteen."

Winnie Cartwright opened the door of the meeting room and smiled broadly at them. She ushered them into the conference room. "We're happy you could take time to come and talk to us today, gentlemen."

Zack charmed his aunt with a big grin. "Not a problem, ma'am." He glanced at Dylan. "I'm glad we're here, too."

Dylan needed to do this. Talking about what had happened was a way to heal, but so was accepting not everything had been bad. He wasn't speaking about his last mission. He'd tell the ladies about the missions that had defined him, made him want to go back again and again, and given him a feeling of accomplishment.

He wasn't surprised when he saw Brenda sitting beside her mother. As Zack greeted several of the other women, Dylan approached his ex-wife and her mother. "Good day, Mrs. Grady," he said to his former mother-in-law.

Linda Grady scowled at him. "We don't want any trouble here, Dylan. I didn't want Brenda to come, but Winnie insisted she had to be here."

He grinned. "I put Winnie up to it. So, don't worry, I'm not here to cause trouble. Brenda, I'd like to talk to you before we start."

Brenda glanced at her mother and nodded. After she and Dylan were outside the room, she spun to face him. "What do you want?"

He took a deep breath. "I'm sorry."

"What?"

Looking down into her narrowed brown eyes, he gently said, "I'm sorry I never was the husband you wanted me to be. I guess by now you've heard Charli Monroe and I are living together."

"Yes, I've heard."

"I'm in love with her, and I realized you and I were never meant to be. I hope you're as happy with Nicholas as I am with Charli. Goodbye, Brenda."

He walked back inside the conference room, leaving Brenda gaping after him.

While Zack told his own story, Dylan gathered his thoughts.

He needed to accept the past, and put it behind him. With Charli, he was a new man, a better man.

Zack finished his story about his time in the Marines and the attack at the checkpoint that nearly killed him.

With each beat of his heart, Dylan was reborn. Like he'd shed a cocoon. When Zack stepped away to give him the podium, Dylan grinned and spread his wings.

He was free.

Chapter 22

Every eye in the place turned toward Charli as she entered the ballroom on Dylan's arm. She fidgeted and murmured, "Maybe, I should've gotten a longer dress." Or one that wasn't backless, or showed so much cleavage.

Dylan tightened his arm around her waist and leaned over to whisper by her ear, "Stop. Since when did you start feeling uncomfortable in your own skin? You are easily the most beautiful woman in the whole damned place."

"I think you're biased. But that wasn't what I meant."

"Charli, no one here knows your past, and even if they did, I wouldn't care. And you shouldn't either. You are a better person than most of the people in this room."

She relaxed a little.

Tracy huffed as she came up beside her brother and looked over the crowd. "Why did I let you talk me into coming to this thing? I feel stupid."

He lifted his free hand and rubbed his index finger and thumb together. "Here, let me play you a sad song on my little violin."

Tracy rolled her eyes. "You are so juvenile sometimes."

"Go mingle. You might just be surprised who you'll find."

"Yeah, with my luck I'll find Mr. Right, and I'm dressed in a God-awful hot pink bridesmaid dress. I wore this thing to the wedding of a couple who aren't even together anymore. How romantic is that?"

Charli couldn't hide her smile. "You could've bought a dress yesterday, or I offered you one of my dresses. You would've looked great in the little blue slip dress."

"Sure, that would've worked. I'm four inches taller than you and am stick-figure skinny. The strip of silk you call a dress looks great on you, you look great in anything." There was only a hint of envy in her friend's voice, but it wasn't malicious. If anything, it was sisterly. "On me it would have been worse than this rag."

She picked up the full satin skirt of the floor length dress and let it fall in disgust. Turning her indignation on Dylan, she gestured at his Texas tuxedo. "You guys have it so easy. Hell, you wear the same getup to the grocery store."

"Oh, for Christ sakes, Tracy. Go!"

Before she got lost in the crowd, Tracy glanced over her shoulder and stuck her tongue out at him.

"Oh, yeah, sis, that's real mature."

Once they moved toward the bar in the corner, Charli asked, "What do you have up your sleeve?"

"Playing matchmaker." He turned to the bartender, requested two glasses of ginger ale and paid for them. He handed her one of the tall plastic cups. "I only know of one other person here, who doesn't have a date and isn't either too old or too young."

"Zack Cartwright."

"Bingo. I owe my sister. And in many ways, I owe Zack."

She raised a questioning brow.

He sipped the soda and shrugged. "If Tracy hadn't called you about your newspaper ad, I wouldn't've applied for the job." Dylan placed a soft kiss on her temple and grinned lopsidedly. "And as they say--the rest is history.

"And Zack?"

After Dylan sat beside her at an empty table, he said, "He helped me remember my time in the Army wasn't all bad."

A few moments later, he led her onto the dance floor. She hadn't danced in years.

The band, led by Zack's younger brother Logan, broke into an old Alabama love song. She stumbled over the stiletto heels of her strappy sandals, but Dylan supported her and surprised her at his skill as he led into a two-step. Relaxing in his arms, she got caught up in their love feeling so right, just as the lyrics suggested.

His warm breath fanned over the side of her face. "I think I've finally found a country song I like. It's definitely giving me some ideas."

She pulled away and looked up into his desire-darkened eyes, and got some interesting ideas herself.

The song ended and the band shattered the mood by breaking into Charlie Daniels's *The Devil Went Down to Georgia.*

They moved off the dance floor as the dancers lined up for a line-dance. She looked around for Tracy and found her over by the edge of the room talking with Zack, who said something and Tracy laughed. Oh, yeah, they had plenty of sparks to start a fire if given enough kindling.

Before they got back to their table, she excused herself to go to the ladies' room.

She left the bathroom at the end of a long dimly lit corridor. The muted revelry of the party seemed so far way, as a dream on the peripheral of her conscience. On the opposite side of the hall was a darkened coatroom. A glass door barred an exit at the end of the hallway.

Curiously, she peered through the glass into the darkness. A halo of dim light from the streetlight disappeared in the shadows of the thick woods bordering the employee parking lot. The full moon glimmered off the calm water of Gambler's Lake.

A shuffling sound came from behind her.

What was that? She turned around and shivered. From the doorway of the coatroom, Leon stepped out of the darkness hatless and with a lock of hair hanging over his forehead. He hadn't shaved for a few days, and his beard had come in dark and thick. The insane gleam in his brown eyes shook her to her core. Knowing someone would hear her, she opened her mouth to scream. He pulled a handgun with a silencer on the end from behind him.

"Hello, Charli." He pointed the gun at her with the ease of someone used to handling firearms. "I wouldn't do anything stupid if I were you."

Swallowing the scream, she held out her hands in front of her and pressed herself into the corner. "Why are you here?"

His sickly smile never reached his arctic eyes. "I came back to get the two things I can take away from Dylan." Leon paused, and her heart sank into the depths of her boiling stomach. "You and your bastard."

"You're crazy. I'll never go with you."

Definitely the wrong thing to say to a madman. He lost the smile and bore down on her, grabbed her by the hair and yanked her around so her back came up against his chest, hard. She cried out, but choked down the yelp when he shoved the gun next to her temple. *Oh, God, he's going to shoot me.*

"Either alive or dead, it doesn't matter to me how I take those things away."

"Please," she pleaded between sobs, trying to fend off the nausea twisting her belly. "Don't hurt me."

She shuddered as his hot breath fanned over her bare shoulder. "As long as you do as I tell you, I won't."

Giving a jerky nod, she swallowed the bile in her throat. "I'll cooperate."

"I always knew you were a smart girl."

Determined to buy as much time as possible, she asked, "Why do you hate Dylan so much?"

His chuckle grated on her nerves like sandpaper over delicate silk, snagging, ripping. "Because my father preferred him over me."

"You mean because Jason Ferguson willed Oak Springs to him."

Leon tugged on her hair hard enough to bring tears of pain to her eyes. The gun nozzle dug into her temple as he growled next to her ear, "That's part of it. We're leaving. Open the door."

* * * *

While Dylan waited for Charli, Tracy and Zack came to the table. Zack sat next to him and Tracy settled next to Zack.

"Where's Charli?" Tracy asked and sipped from a glass of Zinfandel.

He wondered the same thing himself and glanced at his watch. "She went to the ladies' room, but it was a while ago."

A teenage boy, dressed in the white kitchen help uniform, ran into the middle of the ballroom. Over the band's loud rendition of Little Texas's *God Blessed Texas* and the chatter of over two hundred people, he yelled, "Is the sheriff here?"

"Over here." Zack stood and waited for the kid to run over to the table. "What's going on?"

"I was coming from the kitchen when I heard a noise down the hallway to the bathrooms." The boy gestured wildly with his hands as he spoke in a breathless rush. "When I looked, I saw a man grab a lady back there. It looked like he had a gun and was fixin' to go out the back door."

Dylan was out of his seat, ready to bolt.

"Let's go," Zack said. As they ran through the crowd, he pulled out his cellphone and pushed a key. "Dawn. Leon Ferguson was possibly spotted at the Country Club, armed and considered dangerous. He may have Charli Monroe. Call in the Rangers and the highway patrol to block every road out of the county. Send backup. I'm in pursuit"

At the doorway out into the lobby, Dylan stopped and took a breath. He had to get a game plan. Zack paused and glanced at him.

"If the bastard harms a single hair on her head, I'm killing him, Zack."

"That's why I'm making you a temporary deputy. More paperwork is involved if you kill him, but I can possibly keep your ass out of prison."

He nodded his appreciation.

Zack looked around. "Here's the plan. You're good with the sneaking up on the enemy. So, you follow. Think, Dylan. Don't let the emotion get ahead of reason."

"Got it."

He pulled a Glock from a shoulder holster under his vest. "I'll circle around the back of the building in the cover of the trees."

Dylan nodded again and headed through the door. Zack almost barreled into him when he turned abruptly. "Zack, there's something you should know. Charli's pregnant."

"We'll get to her, Dylan." Zack patted him on the shoulder; the action was strangely comforting. "Now, let's go, Captain."

Zack sprinted for the outer exit. Adrenaline made Dylan drunk as he turned and rushed down the hallway leading to the bathrooms and the employee exit. His heart kicked into his throat like a caged mustang as his mind galloped in a hundred maddening directions. By the time he reached the door, he corralled the stray thoughts and tried to tame his wild heart.

Taking a breath, he was startled to smell the faint scent of peaches. Charli had been here only minutes ago. He slowly opened the door to slip out into the darkness, his instinct, honed by years of training, taking over.

He saw movement between the parked cars and pressed himself into the shadow of the wall. Behind Charli, Leon pushed her toward the trees next to the parking lot with a pistol held to the back of her head.

Crouching, Dylan rushed across the open driving lane and hid by a pickup.

Leon pushed Charli behind a car.

"Where are you taking me?" Charli's voice rung with fear.

"Someplace far away. Hope you like the tropics, Bambi."

With his heart beating painfully in his chest, he sprinted on silent feet toward the woman he loved and the lunatic threatening to take her away. He stepped on a wayward twig, the unwelcome snap warning Leon of his presence. Cursing his luck, he awaited the consequence of his misstep.

Leon dragged Charli around by the hair. For one terrifying moment, he thought Leon would shoot her.

"Let her go." Dylan fisted his hands by his side. If he'd been able to get a little closer, he could've overpowered Leon from behind. But with a gun on Charli, he didn't dare move.

"Dylan!" Charli screamed.

"If it's not GI Joe. Some hero. You're nothing but a fuck-up. You aren't getting what you want this time."

"What's your plan, Ferguson? Kidnapping Charli?" He didn't give a rat's ass what was going on in Ferguson's crazy head, but the longer he kept him talking, the better chance he had of getting Charli away from him. As he held his hands out from his sides, he took a tentative step toward Leon, coming out from behind a car. "This is between you and me. Leave Charli out of it."

Leon turned the gun on him.

Dylan let out the breath he'd been holding.

Charli screamed his name again.

"You're right." Leon sneered. "This is between you and me. But I think I'll keep the little whore anyway. Ever since you moved back here, you've weaseled your way into getting what should've been mine."

"Where's the will, Leon?"

Ferguson chortled humorlessly. "Wouldn't you like to know?"

So, he hadn't destroyed it.

"Other than Oak Springs, what else have I supposedly taken?" He caught a flash of Zack's white shirt as he weaved his way through the woods behind Leon. Dylan glanced at Charli, trying to reassure her with his eyes. Leon held her against him by her hair. Her arms were wrapped tightly around her middle, and she looked as if she'd puke any minute.

"You don't know?"

"Why don't you tell me?"

"My own father threw you in my face! He wished I'd turned out like you."

He kept his surprise out of his expression and voice. Sure, he'd spent a few lazy summers when he was a teenager with Jock, wallowing in their common dislike of Madeline Ferguson, but he didn't understand Leon's assertion. "Why would Jock Blackwell care about me?"

Ferguson's eyes widened and he jerked his head to the side. "So, you figured it out. Or did the son-of-a-bitch tell you when you and he were all buddy-buddy, how he got my mother pregnant? He married her only to dump her for Colleen Stryker before I was even born. Then happily signed the damned adoption papers to give me to that pompous asshole Jason Ferguson."

What the hell did Leon mean by him and Jock being buddies? Jock had tolerated him catching snakes out of the lake to torment Maddie, and told him how proud he was of him for joining the Army. Jock had done a tour in Vietnam. He sympathized with him when Jason Ferguson left Oak Springs to Leon. Colleen was the mother of Jock's eldest illegitimate son. The fact Maddie Ferguson had legally wed Jock came as a shock. But why would Jock sign his son away?

No wonder the oil wells were capped, whether Maddie's father, Jason Ferguson or Jock Blackwell had ordered it. The significance of the action wasn't lost on him.

Leon snarled, "He denied me for years, saying I was really Jason's bastard."

"Was your plan to reopen the oil wells?" He risked a glance behind Leon and Charli. In the combination of moonlight and streetlight, he saw Zack hunker down behind a car with his Glock gripped in a two-handed aim over the hood. He knew Zack couldn't risk taking a shot. If Leon moved or if his aim was off, Charli could be hit, or even Dylan. He had to make Leon angry enough to come after him. "Is that why Jock destroyed his will? He didn't want you getting any richer off the oil under his land."

He was close enough to watch anger contort Leon's features, his eyes burning with a crazy fire. "He intended to split the place up between his bastards. Told me I was never the son he wanted. None of us were, but he felt I deserved less than them. They at least carried his name. I swore I'd contest his will. After all, I'm his only legitimate son."

Light from overhead glittered on the sweat beading on his forehead. "He told me he never wanted me to get my hands on his land." He shifted his feet and snorted. "The Fergusons weren't getting richer from the oil reserve under his land."

"So, Jock destroyed the will." He risked another glance at Zack.

"The fucking prick cheated me out of what should have been mine! That's why I killed him."

Jock had been deemed delusional years before his death. Some folks in town claimed he had bipolar disorder and refused to take his medication as he got older. No one was surprised or questioned his death as being anything but accidental. Jock had supposedly died after falling from a horse. A head injury. But now, as Leon became increasingly irrational, a new possibility played out on the stage of his mind.

Jock and Leon had gone riding together, but only Leon returned to the stable. Then another more frightening scenario sprang up in his thoughts. "Did you kill my grandfather, Leon, after you forged his will?"

Leon laughed bitterly. "No, I didn't have to. He died on his own."

* * * *

Charli remembered Leon's threats from the night he'd called. How could she not remember his admission of murdering Jock Blackwell? She knew in her heart Leon would kill Dylan and steal her away. Nausea threatened to spill the bile bubbling in her stomach, and her mind raced with her possible fate.

Leon would have money stashed away just in case his crimes ever caught up with him. He'd take her to South America and change his name. After he'd used her until he tired of her, he'd kill her, too, and steal her baby to raise as his own--if he didn't kill him or her, too.

In spite of his agitation, Leon aimed the gun with a deadly still hand. His ragged breaths stirred the hair by her ear. Heat and perspiration penetrated through his shirt where she pressed against him, moistening the skin of her bare back. From the sour smell, he hadn't showered in a day or two. Her stomach churned at the thought of how close he held her.

Dylan met her gaze as Leon spoke. She couldn't allow him to hurt Dylan. She had spent years being used by men like Leon. Dylan would never hurt her or take from her. She'd offered him the partnership in the ranch with the hope that by giving him what he'd always wanted, he'd never leave her.

She didn't have to buy Dylan; he loved her and she loved him. She wasn't going to stand by, waiting for him to be killed.

"But I would have killed him," Leon added, breaking into her thoughts.

"Like you killed Ella, the mother of your daughter?"

"Ella was no better than this whore." Leon jerked her hair. "She deserved to die." When his finger twitched on the trigger, she had to act. "And so do you."

She lifted her right leg and brought the long, spiked heel of her sandal down onto the top of his foot with as much force as she could muster.

Leon howled in pain and tossed her to the pavement. A gun exploded, and less than a heartbeat later, another went off, but closer and muffled.

While she searched for Dylan in the dimness, she screamed his name. Was he hit, bleeding, dying?

Leon pitched forward, grabbed his right shoulder, and fell to the ground. The gun flew from his hand.

"Charli!" Dylan fell to her side when she tried to scramble to her feet. "Are you okay?"

She reached for him. He pulled her close, holding her as tightly as she did him. Sobbing and shaking, she stammered, "I--I was so scared. I was afraid he'd kill you and take me away."

"Shhh," he murmured next to her ear. "You're not going anywhere without me."

Sirens sounded in the distance. She started when someone knelt beside her. "I always knew high heels should be considered dangerous weapons."

When she recognized Zack Cartwright's easy Texas drawl, she sagged again in Dylan's arms.

Sara Walter Ellwood

Zack laid his hand on her shoulder. "I'm glad you did what you did, Charli. I was afraid I'd hit you or Dylan if I tried to take a shot. Are you okay?"

She nodded, but couldn't bring herself to pull her face from Dylan's shoulder. Breathing him in, she found strength and reassurance in his clean, breezy scent.

Before she or Dylan could ask, the sheriff said, "Ferguson's not going anywhere."

Dylan turned his head from out of the crook of her neck. "Is he dead?"

"No, I didn't aim to kill. I want him to spend the rest of his life behind bars. Of course, this is Texas. If the other murder charges stick, Ferguson might not be behind bars for long, if you know what I mean."

Dylan nodded, and she got it, too. Unless he got a lenient judge or his wealth and former power influenced a jury, he'd likely get the death penalty.

"Who else did he kill?" Dylan asked.

She lifted her head. "He admitted he killed Jock Blackwell."

Zack nodded. "Apparently, Jock isn't the first relative he's helped into the grave to get what he wanted."

"His grandfather," Dylan said.

"Yep. The Rangers also reopened the investigation on the supposed suicide of the forger who'd signed the will as your grandfather. Leon's own mother suspected him for years of killing her father, but was too afraid of him to come forward until earlier today. Ferguson wanted to reopen the oil well on Oak Springs, but his mother's father forbade it."

"So, he killed him." Dylan puckered his brow. He stood, bringing her with him. "Why didn't Leon open it after he killed him?"

"Because he couldn't. Turns out Maddie's father ordered those oil wells closed when Jock divorced her. Jock's father, Jason Ferguson and Maddie's father were all business partners. When Jock was discharged from the Army, he came home and took over his father's business. The only reason they married was that her father threatened to back out of the deal when Jock got Maddie pregnant. Leon couldn't reopen the well on Oak Springs without Jock's approval to reopen the two on Blackwell Ranch. The crazy old coot wouldn't agree to it and became determined to keep the oil right where it is."

"Why didn't you tell me this before?"

Zack shrugged. "I didn't get the chance. I just found out myself today."

Within moments, the parking lot was ablaze with flashing emergency lights from more than a dozen police cars and two ambulances. Guests from the ball and Country Club staff crowded near the building, as one of the most respected men in the county, maybe in all of Texas, was taken away on a gurney with a police escort.

Tracy rushed over to Dylan and Charli and hugged them. Afterward, Dylan immediately pulled Charli back to his side where she clung to him.

"Let's go home." Dylan turned her away from the ruckus.

Epilogue

One month later

Charli carried two mugs of coffee out onto the front porch.

Dylan lazily pushed the porch swing back and forth with the heel of his worn boot. He reached for the cup of coffee she offered him. "Annie all settled in?"

She sat beside him on the swing. "Yes, she's asleep already. I promised her earlier she and I would go shopping for school clothes tomorrow. I thought we'd go down to Waco."

He chuckled and wrapped his arm around her shoulders, prompting her to look at him.

"What?"

"Nothing. It just amazes me how much the girl has turned around."

She sipped her coffee. "Annie's doing okay, but she has a long way to go. I'm just glad Sam and Julie allowed us to have guardianship of her. And I was able to convince my old therapist to see her by teleconference at the doctor's office."

"If you ask me, I think you're the biggest help for her."

"We can relate to each other."

Night had finally chased away the heat of the summer day. Frogs and crickets filled the darkness with music, while the climbing jasmine and summer roses scented the air with sweet perfume.

After a few moments of enjoying the peacefulness, she said, "Annie asked about Leon. She'd like to meet him."

"You don't think that's a good idea, do you?"

"I don't know. I can understand her need. My biggest regret is never knowing my father."

"Yes, but your father wasn't a crazy murderer. He was a simple cowboy."

"True. I'll have to ask her psychiatrist what she thinks."

He sipped his coffee. "You do have a brother you've never met."

She smiled at him. "I'm thinking about contacting him. I'm not sure I'm ready for the tabloid attention, but I really do want to meet Nate."

He set his mug on a table beside hers. "Speaking of family. Mom and Dad liked what you've done to the house. They really like you. I told you they would."

His parents, sister and nephew had all gone back over to Oak Springs after they'd had supper. Robert and Eileen Quinn had come to Texas two weeks ago for the reading of Jason Ferguson's real will, which, as he had suspected, had been in Leon's possession. The authorities found it in the safe at his Dallas office two days after they'd taken him into custody.

"I like them, too. Tracy got her personality from your mom." She grinned and kissed his nose. "And you look like your dad. No wonder he was able to steal the heart of a born and bred daughter of Texas, even though he's a Yankee."

His low chuckle rippled through her like a summer breeze. "Has he stolen the heart of my Oklahoma cowgirl?"

She shook her head. "He can be very rigid, I guess, but he seems like a fair man. I'll miss them when they leave tomorrow."

When he nuzzled her neck, she squirmed at the tingles his lips caused. "They'll be back."

"Oh, when?" She pulled away and looked at him.

"Dad decided to retire from the government for good this time. I think he and Mom are going to move in with Tracy over on Oak Springs."

"I'll like them living so close." She still had to get to know Dylan's parents, but she could see them becoming close over time. "So, Tracy is officially moving into the house?"

"I'm sure as hell not moving over there."

"That would give the Grapevine some new grapes. Our taking Annie in, her paternity, and my past are becoming boring."

"Wouldn't want the Grapevine to run out of grapes." He reached under the cushion of the swing. "That would just be a damned crying shame."

Her breath caught when she saw the small white box he'd retrieved.

He snapped open the lid to reveal a diamond ring nestled in white satin.

Her hands went over her mouth, muffling her "Oh my God!"

His eyes were as luminous as a cloudless summer sky when she met them. Dylan removed the ring, took her left hand from where she held it over her mouth, and slid it onto her finger. "I love you, Charli, and I can't imagine my life without you. You once offered me a partnership without the complications of marriage. How about we complicate things?" He kissed the back of her trembling left hand. "Will you marry me?"

Her heart swelled, and happy tears welled up in her eyes. She moved her right hand to her throat. She swallowed and somehow pushed words past her wildly beating heart. "Yes. I love you so much, Dylan."

"I know, Peaches." He wrapped his arms around her, pulled her close and kissed her thoroughly.

"So, what are we going to call our ranch?"

She furrowed her brow. "The ranch already has a name."

The ceremonious job of installing the new sign over the driveway entrance had been one of the last things Tom and Jesse did before becoming fulltime ranch hands for Butterfly Ranch.

He kissed her nose. "I don't mean Butterfly, and I don't want to rename Oak Springs. It goes back for generations, but we should combine the businesses, incorporate, under one name."

They had signed papers yesterday making them business partners, combining the two ranches, and they'd agreed to keep the oil wells capped. They were ranchers, nothing else. She nodded in understanding, thought for a moment. "How about Butterfly Springs Cattle Company?"

"I like it." He turned her in his lap so she could rest her back against his chest and her head on his shoulder.

Moonlight shimmered over the skeletal frame of their new barn, and she sighed in total contentment. "I finally became a butterfly."

"I think we both did." She looked up at him, but before she could reply, he rubbed a hand over the slight curve of her belly. Not only had they signed papers making them business partners, they discovered they were having twins--a boy and a girl, if the ultrasound could be trusted. "I can't wait until the babies are born. We'll have to start thinking about names for these little guys."

"I was thinking of maybe naming our son after our grandfathers--Jason Henry. Henry was Hank's real name."

"I'm surprised you'd pick something so mundane." She narrowed her eyes on him, and he grinned at her. "Let's name our daughter after your momma."

"LeAnn Eileen--for your momma, too."

"Mom'll be thrilled."

She laughed and kissed his lips, slow and deep with lots of tongue. "It's settled. Now, let's celebrate our engagement."

"Celebrate?" Dylan feigned confusion.

"Oh, yeah," she purred and stood. Taking his hand, she gave him the little pout he loved.

He let her pull him to his feet. "So, does this celebration involve us getting naked?"

"Definitely." She let go of his hand and stepped away, placing one booted foot directly behind the other, undulating her jeans-covered hips in the seductive roll that drove him crazy. She reached for the top snap of her Western shirt, then the second, the third. "C'mon, cowboy."

He followed her toward the front door and grinned devilishly. "You don't have to tell me twice. I learned how to follow orders a long time ago."

Meet the Author

Although Sara Walter Ellwood has long ago left the farm for the glamour of the big town, she draws on her experiences growing up on a small hobby farm in West Central Pennsylvania to write her stories. She's been married to her college sweetheart for nearly 20 years, and they have two teenagers and one very spoiled rescue cat named Penny. She longs to visit the places she writes about and jokes she's a cowgirl at heart stuck in Pennsylvania suburbia.

She also writes paranormal romantic suspense under the pen name of Cera duBois